MOON HANDBOOKS®

CANADIAN ROCKIES

FOURTH EDITION

ANDREW HEMPSTEAD

© ANDREW HEMPSTEAD

AVALON TRAVEL

CANADIAN ROCKIES

CONTENTS

Discover the Canadian Rockies

Explore the Canadian Rockies

Know the Canadian Rockies

MAPS

MAP SYMBOLS

	Divided Highway
	Primary Road
	Secondary Road
	Unpaved Road
	Railroad
	Trail
	TransCanada Highway
	Provincial/State Highway
	U.S. Highway
◉	Provincial Capital
○	City/Town
✈	Airport
Ⓜ	Must-See Attraction
★	Point of Interest
•	Accommodation
▶	Restaurant/Bar
◀	Mountain
)(	Mountain Pass
	Glacier
⛷	Campground
✦	Ski Area
⛳	Park
⛳	Golf Course
■	Other Location

© AVALON TRAVEL PUBLISHING, INC.

Golden

Yoho National Park

Lake Louise

Banff

Kootenay National Park

Radium Hot Springs

Mt Assiniboine PP

Height of the Rockies PP

Whiteswan Lake Provincial Park

Top of the World Provincial Park

Canmore

Peter Lougheed Provincial Park

Elk Lakes PP

Bragg Creek

Kananaskis Country

ALBERTA

BRITISH COLUMBIA

Akamina-Kishinena PP

Waterton Lakes National Park

Waterton Townsite

Glacier National Park

CANADA
UNITED STATES

IDAHO

MONTANA

25 mi

25 km

Discover the Canadian Rockies

If we can't export the scenery, we'll import the tourists.

William C. Van Horne, president of the
Canadian Pacific Railway, circa 1885

Snowcapped peaks by the hundreds, glaciers and icefields, multihued lakes, rushing rivers, alpine meadows, and an abundance of wildlife make the Canadian Rockies a travel destination that is rivaled by few places in the world. Although Mother Nature dealt a winning hand to the Canadian Rockies, early governments had the foresight to protect most of the land for all time in a string of contiguous parks—each with its own unique character but combining to create one massive swath of wilderness blessed with dramatic beauty.

A northern extension of the Rocky Mountain chain running through the western United States, the region covered by this book extends north from the U.S. border for around 800 kilometers (500 miles). The spine of the Canadian Rockies is the Continental Divide, which runs the length of the range and separates the province of British Columbia in the west from Alberta in the east. Banff and Jasper National Parks, on the east side of the Continental Divide in the province of Alberta, are the best known of the parks. Originally conceived as tourist resorts, the bustling towns of Banff and Jasper serve millions of visitors annually and boast championship golf courses, world-class resorts, hundreds of restaurants, and international shopping. Two more national parks, Kootenay and Yoho, lie west of Banff and Jasper, across the Continental Divide in the province of British Columbia. This side of the Canadian Rockies is much less crowded, but the scenery is no less impressive, especially the area around Lake O'Hara and Emerald Lake. Together, these four national parks make up a complex geological and natural area that has been declared a World Heritage Site by the United Nations Educational, Scientific, and Cultural Organization (UNESCO).

On the British Columbia side of the divide, Mount Assiniboine Provincial Park is favored by backcountry hikers, while at the northern reach of Jasper National Park lies Mount Robson Provincial Park, which surrounds and is named for the highest peak of the Canadian Rockies. In southern Alberta, Waterton Lakes National Park is a hidden gem that lacks the crowds of its northern counterparts, and Kananaskis Country is a preserve developed as a four-season, multiuse recreation area. Beyond the better-known parks are numerous other wilderness areas that may take a little more effort to reach, but the rewards are many—none more apparent than the opportunity to bask in complete solitude.

Most visitors arrive by road, flying in to the Canadian cities of Calgary or Vancouver or arriving along highways that approach from all directions. The region itself is laced with a modern highway system. Roads parallel the Canadian Rockies to both the east and west, with four routes climbing up and over the Continental Divide to provide links between the provinces and access to high alpine elevations. The most spectacular drive in all of the Canadian Rockies is the Icefields Parkway, which runs through an inspirational mountain environment surrounded by glaciated peaks and alpine lakes.

The national parks of the Canadian Rockies are filled with tourism infrastructure—world-class resorts, golf courses, convention centers, multistory car parks, and more—which, on the surface, seems to work against the national park's mandate. But the situation is unique, since the parks have grown from what was originally a moneymaking exercise. For many visitors, the opportunity to vacation in a wilderness setting without sacrificing the amenities of a resort destination is unequaled. Nowhere is this more apparent than in the town of Banff (population 7,700), the largest urban center in any national park in the world.

For those who want to get closer to nature, total wilderness is just steps away from the bustle of Banff, Canmore, and the other towns of the Canadian Rockies. The ideal way to immerse yourself completely in a mountain experience is to rise early and spend your time away from the towns—visiting the region's natural highlights, many of which are road-accessible, others requiring a hike to reach. Ideally, you would then retire to your cabin accommodation or campsite and spend the evening around a roaring fire planning your next day's adventures.

Planning a trip can be overwhelming, but don't let it be. The first thing you should do is forget about any preconceived notions you have about travel to Canada—or more precisely the Canadian Rockies—and instead focus on the experience. Of course you'll want to glimpse the famous lakes, wander through the hallways of the grand mountain resorts, and maybe even try white-water rafting, but try to plan your trip around simply being in the mountains. Think less about specific "sights" and open yourself to discovery.

Start by trying to identify the type of activities you're interested in, which parks you just can't miss, and how much money you want to spend. Once you have put together an outline of your trip, book lodging—as far in advance as possible, especially if you want to include the famous mountain resorts in your itinerary.

Even though the Canadian Rockies region is mostly wilderness, it has a number of midsize towns linked by well-traveled highways. Driving your own vehicle (or a rental car) is a practical way to travel, and it'll give you the flexibility to stay at lodgings out of the main tourist towns. A different approach is to let someone else do the driving. Reaching the Canadian Rockies from the gateway cities of Vancouver and Calgary is easy, and once you've arrived you can join a tour or concentrate on hiking trails that originate near the towns. In Banff, for example, you can choose between a week's worth of hikes that start in town, rent a bike to explore farther afield, and enjoy a white-water rafting trip before moving on to Lake Louise on a scheduled bus service. If you're on a ski vacation, a vehicle isn't necessary because regular shuttles link accommodations to the ski areas.

WHEN TO GO

While the Canadian Rockies can be visited year-round, there are two influxes of visitors—one in the warmer months and the other in winter. Summer in the mountains revolves around outdoor activities such as hiking, biking, canoeing, fishing, and just about anything you can do outdoors. In winter, the focus is on skiing and snowboarding.

Summer (late June–mid-September) is definitely high season, especially the school holiday period of July through August. Simply said, the weather is unbeatable. The season is dominated by long, warm—and sometimes hot—days, everything is open, and there's plenty to do and see. Crowded parks, prices as high as the mountains, and difficulty securing reservations are the downside of summer travel. Obviously these factors aren't a consideration if money is no object or if you plan on disappearing into the backcountry for a week.

Late spring and early fall are excellent times to visit the Canadian Rockies for two reasons: you'll avoid the crowds and you'll save money. Spring (mid-April–late June) is notable for long days of sunlight (in late June it stays light until after 10 P.M.) and a sense of optimism for the upcoming warm months. Golf courses begin opening in early May, it's warm enough to camp out come late May, and the famous lakes become ice-free in June. Fall (mid-September–November) can be delightful, especially September, with lingering warm temperatures and a noticeable decrease in crowds immediately after the long weekend (at the beginning of the month). While fall colors in general lack the intensity of those in the eastern provinces and New England, larch turn a brilliant yellow throughout high alpine areas in late September.

Local ski resorts beginning opening for the winter season (December–mid-April) in late November. The best snow conditions are January–February, although for enthusiasts looking for a combination of good snow and warmer weather, March is an excellent time of year to visit. Winter officially ends before mid-April, but some ski resorts stay open well into May, and it's not until this time of year that the ground begins to warm.

WHAT TO TAKE

Start by packing everything you think you'll need. Then put half of it back in your closet. The airlines have generous baggage limits and you can always upgrade to a larger rental car, but that's not the point—you just never need as much as you think you do.

When planning your trip to the Canadian Rockies, prepare for the outdoors. At the top of your must-bring list should be walking or hiking boots. If you buy a pair especially for the trip, make sure you wear them once or twice before leaving home—just to make sure they are comfortable. In summer, temperatures rarely drop below freezing, so you don't need a down jacket or winter boots. But you should be geared up for a variety of weather conditions, especially at the change of seasons. Do this by preparing to dress in layers, including at least one pair of fleece pants and a heavy long-sleeved top. Bring sunglasses and wide-brimmed hat to provide protection from the strong sunlight. Gloves and a wool hat are a good idea if you're camping. For dining out, casual dress is accepted at all but the most upscale restaurants, where a tie and jacket are required. Finally, bug spray is a summer necessity, but you can pick up the brands that are most effective once you arrive.

Wintertime in the Canadian Rockies brings very different advice. Thanks to modern technology, you can purchase clothing that allows you to be warm and comfortable no matter how cold the temperature gets. Again, dress in layers, starting with long thermal underwear. The best type of outer layer is breathable, wind-resistant pants and a jacket. Warm boots with new liners, lined mittens, and a wool hat are a must. If you're traveling from warmer climes, purchase all the winter necessities in the gateway cities of Calgary or Vancouver. You can also buy clothing in Banff, Canmore, and Jasper, but it's generally more expensive.

Electrical appliances from the United States work in Canada, but those from other parts of the world require a current converter (transformer) to bring the voltage down. Many travel-size shavers, hair dryers, and irons have built-in converters.

Choosing a suitcase or backpack is also important. Think about the type of traveling you'll be doing before making a final decision. A midsize suitcase with wheels is best for carting through airports and lugging around hotels. Fold-over bags are good for keeping formal clothing wrinkle-free, but unless you're in town on business or attending a snazzy function, you probably won't require much in the way of dressy clothing. Besides, this type of suitcase is a bother to pack and unpack.

Airlines allow at least one piece of carry-on luggage per person, which must be small enough to fit in the overhead compartments. (Most luggage stores have guidelines to help you choose the right size). You should pack your carry-on with valuables, medications, smaller breakable items, a sweater, bottled water, reading materials, and vital documents (driver's license, credit card, passport, a printout of your reservations, etc.). Even if you're traveling by bus, train, or your own vehicle, it's a good idea to keep all these things in an easy-to-reach carry-on style bag. The most convenient carry-on bags are small backpacks, which can double as daypacks for sightseeing or hiking.

BANFF NATIONAL PARK

Banff. The crown jewel in Canada's national park system and home to the world's most photographed lakes. But what is this park that was originally established as a tourist attraction really like? Lake Louise, Moraine Lake, and the Icefields Parkway are just some of the park's awe-inspiring highlights, while the town of Banff is the commercial hub. Visiting each of these spots is definitely part of the Banff experience, but the park extends well beyond the reach of the regular tour bus crowd. Biking along the shoreline of Lake Minnewanka, exploring Larch Valley when fall colors are at their height, canoeing across Bow Lake, and hiking in to back-country Skoki Lodge may not be as well known, but each activity allows a glimpse of the park you won't see in the tourist brochures. The grandeur of accommodations such as the Fairmont Banff Springs and Fairmont Chateau Lake Louise never fails to impress. Or go low budget in one of the hostels or spend the night under the stars in one of the many campgrounds.

CANMORE

Canmore is the largest population center in the Canadian Rockies, but don't let that put you off including it in your itinerary. In a little over three decades, it has transformed itself from a coal-mining town without a coal mine to a hotbed of recreational pursuits with an Aspen-esque property market. The town's three golf courses, including SilverTip, rated the hardest course in mainland North America, draw rave reviews. The surrounding mountains are legendary among the climbing fraternity. Hiking trails lead to crystal-clear lakes and mountain peaks. But Canmore should factor into your vacation plans for more practical purposes, such as the range of excellent restaurants and a choice of well-priced family-friendly accommodations.

KANANASKIS COUNTRY

Pronounced exactly as it reads, this recreational playground lies adjacent to Banff National Park and is handy for Calgarians who flock west to revel in a diverse range of activities or simply to do nothing at all. This area was set aside by the oil-rich Albertan government as a four-season recreational playground. If you're looking for wildlife, you'll find it here. Along with scenery that rivals the national parks, the facilities are top-notch—wonderful golfing, world-class skiing, 1,300 kilometers (800 miles) of hiking trails, paved biking trails, 30 lakes stocked with fish, accommodations that even George W. Bush approved of when he stopped by in 2002, and over 2,000 campsites in 31 campgrounds. The catch? There's not one—even entry is free.

KOOTENAY NATIONAL PARK

Kootenay may not have the famous resort towns of Banff and Jasper, but what it has it does well: vast areas of wilderness, abundant wildlife, and a network of hiking trails that are suited to all levels of fitness. Shaped like a lightning bolt, the park is bisected by Highway 93, which provides access to natural attractions like Marble Canyon and the Paint Pots, as well as phenomena such as Radium Hot Springs, which have been tweaked for human enjoyment. Most visitors stick to the shorter hiking trails, leaving the backcountry the haunt of experienced backpackers who revel in solitude. Visitors looking for creature comforts can travel beyond the park to the towns of Radium Hot Springs and Invermere, or stay with a mountain theme and soak up the luxuries of Panorama Mountain Village.

YOHO NATIONAL PARK

Thousands of people pass through Yoho, one of the jewels of Canada's national park system, daily, most traveling along the TransCanada Highway on their way to somewhere else. If only they knew what they were missing. Instead of rushing through, detour to Emerald Lake or up the Yoho Valley. Lake O'Hara is not accessible by public road, but this is a good thing. It makes one of the most scenic regions in all of the Canadian Rockies even more special. The nearby town of Golden isn't within the park, but it hangs its hat on being a recreational paradise for outdoor enthusiasts. Even if you're not into mountain biking or white-water rafting, it's worth a visit to town simply to ride the gondola at Kicking Horse Mountain Resort.

JASPER NATIONAL PARK

Beyond a simple sign at Sunwapta Pass that lets you know you've left Banff National Park and entered Jasper is a natural attraction that will leave you breathless—Columbia Icefield, the largest and most accessible glacier field in the Canadian Rockies. Those not content with just looking can jump aboard a big-wheeled Ice Explorer and get up close and personal with the ancient ice flow. Continuing north, the Icefields Parkway eventually reaches the town of Jasper, a smaller, quieter version of Banff that offers a good range of accommodations and other services. Take a walk down Maligne Canyon, a boat tour on Maligne Lake, and hike the trails below Mt. Edith Cavell and you'll be following in the footsteps of millions before you. Walk the hallowed fairways of Jasper Park Lodge Golf Course and you'll have a different story to tell back at the country club. The many summer-only bungalow camps scattered around town are an authentic way to enjoy an overnight stay.

ALBERTA

BRITISH COLUMBIA

CANADA

USA

WATERTON LAKES NATIONAL PARK

The old cliché that good things come in small packages couldn't be a truer description of Waterton Lakes National Park, separated only by an international border from Glacier National Park in Montana. It's the southernmost of the national parks covered in this guidebook and also takes the longest to reach from the gateway cities. But visitors are rewarded in many ways. The scenery is dramatic, ranging from prairie to glaciated peaks and from bird-rich wetlands to high alpine lakes. If you're looking for wildlife, Waterton Lakes will exceed your expectations. Mule deer and bighorn sheep are common within the townsite and both black and grizzly bears are often sighted along park highways. The one place you're guaranteed a sighting is the buffalo paddock, which holds a herd of plains bison.

This itinerary combines the best of the best—the best-known natural highlights, the hikes you won't want to miss, and the most scenic drives. Understand that you will not see all of the Canadian Rockies in one week, but you won't miss anything major either.

DAY 1

Fly into Calgary, pick up a rental car and head for the mountains. After settling in to your Banff accommodation, spend the afternoon exploring the town, including a stop at the information center and a walk along the Bow River to the Fairmont Banff Springs.

DAY 2

Head to Lake Minnewanka for the morning's first tour boat departure. After a picnic lunch at Two Jack Lake take the Bow Valley Parkway to the village of Lake Louise.

DAY 3

Rise early to visit Lake Louise before the crowds arrive. Drive to Moraine Lake and hike into Larch Valley. Head to Yoho National Park and spend the afternoon driving through the Yoho Valley and visiting Emerald Lake.

DAY 4

Go white-water rafting down the Kicking Horse River. Head north along the Icefields Parkway, bunking down for the night en route to Jasper.

DAY 5

Continue to Jasper and take a morning boat tour on Maligne Lake. After lunch, head west to Mount Robson Provincial Park and view the park's namesake peak as the sun sets. Return to Jasper for the night.

© ANDREW HEMPSTEAD

white-water rafting

© ANDREW HEMPSTEAD

Lake Louise

DAY 6

Make as many stops as time allows on the way back down the Icefields Parkway. At **Columbia Icefield,** choose between an Ice Explorer tour and the hike to Wilcox Pass. Continue south to **Canmore.**

DAY 7

This morning is free to explore the town of Canmore and its history, to walk along the riverfront trails, and to catch up on souvenir shopping before returning to Calgary.

One option for a two-week tour of the Canadian Rockies is simply to pad out the preceding itinerary with more hikes and activities. Although that's what many travelers do, two weeks gives you the opportunity to explore beyond the core national parks, as laid out in this itinerary.

DAY 1

Arrive in Banff for a two-night stay. Explore the town and start your mountain journey with an easy walk—maybe along the Bow River or to Vermilion Lakes.

DAY 2

Expand your exploration of the town to include Lake Minnewanka and the Bow Valley Parkway. Depending on your interests, take an afternoon gondola ride up Sulphur Mountain or book a tee time at the hallowed Banff Springs Golf Course.

DAY 3

Spend the day exploring Kananaskis Country. At Canoe Meadows, just off Highway 40, kayakers often put on quite a show in the rapids of the Kananaskis River.

DAY 4

If you leave Kananaskis Village early you should arrive in Waterton Lakes National Park for a late lunch, even with a one-hour stop at Highwood Pass. Choose between a hike to Bertha Lake or afternoon tea at the Prince of Wales Hotel.

DAY 5

Take a border-crossing tour boat to Goat Haunt, Montana. Keen hikers will want to give the boat trip a miss and instead hike to Crypt Lake. Spend another night in Waterton. You may see deer, elk, and bears on an evening drive to Cameron Lake.

DAY 6

Day 6 is the longest day on the road, around six

Peyto Lake

© ANDREW HEMPSTEAD

SilverTip Golf Course in Canmore

hours to Invermere. The trip can be broken up with a chairlift ride at Fernie Alpine Resort and a detour to Whiteswan Lake Provincial Park.

DAY 7

Drive north to Radium Hot Springs and Kootenay National Park. Pick a local hike that suits your level of fitness, then rest your weary bones in the hot springs.

DAY 8

It's a two-hour drive between Radium Hot Springs and Golden, but there's no hurry as the Kicking Horse Mountain Resort gondola doesn't beginning running until 11 A.M. Arrive at your Yoho National Park accommodation early and spend the rest of the day at your leisure.

DAY 9

If you've done your planning thoroughly, you'll be booked on the shuttle bus to Lake O'Hara on the morning of Day 9. Spend the night along the Bow Valley Parkway.

DAY 10

Rise early for the short drive to Moraine Lake. The rest of the day is yours to spend in the village of Lake Louise.

DAY 11

The earlier you hit the road for Jasper the better your chances of spotting wildlife along the Icefields Parkway. Stop at Bow Lake, Peyto Lake, Columbia Icefield, and as many other spots as time allows.

DAY 12

Visit Maligne Canyon and Maligne Lake, then make the Mt. Edith Cavell Road your main detour on the leisurely southbound journey back through Banff National Park to Canmore.

DAY 13

In Canmore, do some shopping, play a round of golf, take a helicopter ride, or ride the trails of the Nordic Centre.

DAY 14

Depart Canmore for Calgary and your flight home.

The focus of your vacation in the Canadian Rockies should be the outdoors, even with children. Mix up the places you think the children should see with places you know they will enjoy. If you're traveling to the Canadian Rockies as a family, renting a vehicle will make your holiday more enjoyable—upgrade to a minivan for everyone's sanity.

DAY 1

Depart Calgary for Kananaskis Country and Sundance Lodge, where your tepee accommodation awaits. Spend the evening fishing at Mount Lorette Ponds, which are stocked with rainbow trout.

DAY 2

Bypass the town of Banff and head straight for Lake Louise. Take the easy lakeside trail or, if you have older children, head for Lake Agnes Teahouse. Spend the night in the village.

DAY 3

Do your best to rouse the brood early for the spectacular drive along the Icefields Parkway to Jasper. The incentive is a ride on an Ice Explorer across the Columbia Icefield. Spend the night at one of the bungalow camps near Jasper, roasting marshmallows around an open fire.

DAY 4

Take a boat tour on Maligne Lake and a walk through Maligne Canyon, then head south to Yoho National Park. Spend the afternoon paddling on Emerald Lake or walking around its perimeter.

DAY 5

Take a gondola ride at Golden and spend time visiting the grizzly bear rehabilitation center. Drive to Radium Hot Springs to take a soak in the mineral pools, play some mini golf, or saddle up for a horseback ride.

© ANDREW HEMPSTEAD

Maligne Lake, Banff National Park

© ANDREW HEMPSTEAD

Radium Hot Springs

DAY 6

Drive to Banff and spend the rest of the day at your leisure. Children can learn about local wildlife at the Banff Park Museum or take a break from nature at the local water-slide complex and in-door bowling lanes. Spend the evening at the *Oh Canada Eh!* dinner theater.

DAY 7

Drive to Calgary. Along the way you'll pass western Canada's largest outdoor amusement park—a fun stop if time allows.

Camping out is a great way to experience the Canadian Rockies, and you'll save some money to boot. This itinerary works for both tent campers and those who have their own or a rented RV (recreation vehicle). It's important to remember that not all campgrounds have powered sites or accept reservations.

DAY 1

Turn down Highway 40 as you travel west from Calgary to Kananaskis Country. Spend the night in Peter Lougheed Provincial Park.

DAY 2

Plan a leisurely hike to Rawson Lake (pack a fishing pole). Head north, traveling via Spray Lake Provincial Park if you're not put off by unpaved road. In Banff, stay on Tunnel Mountain if you want to walk to town, otherwise head to Two Jack Lake campground.

DAY 3

Beat the traffic by rising early for the drive to Lake Louise. Stop at Johnston Canyon for a short walk to a tall waterfall. Snag a spot at the Lake Louise campground before noon, then spend the afternoon visiting local attractions.

DAY 4

Rise before dawn to catch Moraine Lake at its most pristine, then begin the trip to Jasper along the Icefields Parkway. Choose to camp en route or continue to the campgrounds spread along the highway south of the town.

DAY 5

Spend the morning exploring Jasper attractions like Mount Edith Cavell and Maligne Lake, then head back through Lake Louise to Yoho National Park and pitch your tent for the night.

© ANDREW HEMPSTEAD

Mt. Edith Cavell, Jasper National Park

© ANDREW HEMPSTEAD

Yoho National Park

DAY 6

Drive to Golden and enjoy lunch at the top of Kicking Horse Mountain Resort. Drive south to **Radium Hot Springs.** Stay at one of the commercial campgrounds near town or continue on into **Kootenay National Park** and set up camp there.

DAY 7

Before returning to Calgary, make a stop at the **Paint Pots,** one of Kootenay National Park's most unique natural wonders.

If you enjoy winter sports, you'll love traveling to the Canadian Rockies between December and April. Winter travel and the focus of your vacation will be very different than a summer trip. Instead of hiking and canoeing and barbecuing, you'll be skiing and snowshoeing in a magical mountain setting purified by snow, then retreating to relax around a roaring fire each evening. No vehicle is required for this itinerary.

DAY 1
Depart Vancouver on a VIA Rail train bound for Jasper.

DAY 2
Spend the day skiing or boarding at Marmot Basin. If you're not staying at the Jasper Park Lodge, plan on an evening meal at this historic gem.

DAY 3
Join a guided "ice walk" through the frozen waterfalls of Maligne Canyon. Spend the afternoon traveling the Icefields Parkway to Lake Louise aboard the daily shuttle.

DAY 4
Spend the day at Lake Louise, either downhill skiing at the main resort or cross-country skiing to the end of Lake Louise. Either way, plan on an evening skate in front of the famous Chateau Lake Louise.

DAY 5
Spend the day skiing or boarding at Sunshine Village, then continue to the town of Banff for an evening sleigh ride along the Bow River.

cross-country skiing at the Canmore Nordic Centre

chairlifts at Sunshine Village

DAY 6
Spend the morning at Mount Norquay and then return to Banff for a soak at the Upper Hot Springs.

DAY 7
Catch an airporter to Calgary for a flight to Vancouver or your next destination.

Explore the Canadian Rockies

Banff National Park

This 6,641-square-km (2,564-square-mile) national park encompasses some of the world's most magnificent scenery. The snowcapped peaks of the Rocky Mountains form a spectacular backdrop for glacial lakes, fast-flowing rivers, and endless forests. Deer, moose, elk, mountain goats, bighorn sheep, black and grizzly bears, wolves, and cougars inhabit the park's vast wilderness, while the human species is concentrated in the picture-postcard towns of Banff and Lake Louise—two of North America's most famous resorts. Banff is near the park's southeast gate, 128 km (80 miles) west of Calgary. Lake Louise, northwest of Banff along the TransCanada Highway, sits astride its namesake lake, which is regarded as one of the seven natural wonders of

Must-Sees

Look for **M** to find the sights and activities you
can't miss and **N** for the best dining and lodging.

M Whyte Museum of the Canadian Rockies: If
you visit only one museum in Banff, make it this
one for a snapshot of the park's human history
(page 35).

M Fairmont Banff Springs: You don't need to
book a room here to enjoy the many wonders of
one of the world's great mountain resorts—join a
guided tour, enjoy a meal, or simply wander
through the grandiose public areas (page 39).

M Bow Valley Parkway: This scenic drive between Banff and Lake Louise provides views of
abundant wildlife and many worthwhile stops
(page 43).

M Bourgeau Lake: A steep trail leads to this
lake's rocky shores, populated by colonies of pikas
(page 49).

Bow Lake

M Lake Louise: Famous Lake Louise has hyp-
notized visitors with her beauty for over 100
years. Visitors can rent canoes from the boathouse
(page 78).

M Moraine Lake: If anywhere in the Canadian
Rockies qualified as a Double Must-See, it would be
this deep-blue body of water surrounded by
glaciated peaks (page 78).

M Lake Agnes Trail: You won't completely escape the crowds by hiking this trail from Lake
Louise, but you will leave most of them behind
(page 83).

M Larch Valley: This trek is a good introduction
to hiking in the Canadian Rockies, especially in
fall when the larch trees have turned a brilliant
gold (page 84).

M Bow Lake: Although you can soak up this
lake's beauty from the Icefields Parkway, walk along
its northern shoreline early in the morning to make
the most of this scenic gem (page 93).

M Peyto Lake: Another one of Banff's famous
lakes. The main difference is the perspective from
which it is viewed—a lookout high above its shoreline (page 93).

© ANDREW HEMPSTEAD

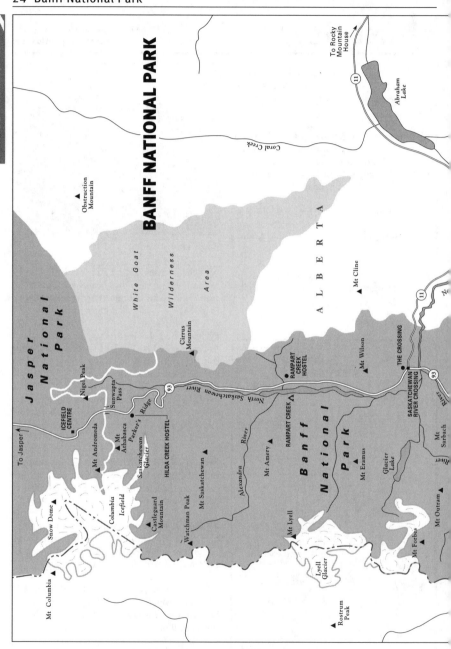

BANFF NATIONAL PARK

To Rocky
Mountain
House

11

Abraham
Lake

Coral Creek

Obstruction
Mountain

White Goat

Wilderness

Area

A L B E R T A

Mt Cline

Jasper

National

Park

Cirrus
Mountain

Mt Wilson

THE CROSSING

11

N₀

Nigel Peak

Sunwapta
Pass

93

North Saskatchewan River

RAMPART
CREEK
HOSTEL

SASKATCHEWAN
RIVER CROSSING

93

ICEFIELD
CENTRE

Mt
Athabasca

Parker's Ridge

Saskatchewan
Glacier

HILDA CREEK HOSTEL

RAMPART CREEK

Banff

National

Park

River

To Jasper

Mt Andromeda

Mt Saskatchewan

Alexandra

Mt Amery

Glacier
Lake

Mt
Sarbach

Watchman Peak

River

Snow Dome

Columbia
Icefield

Castleguard
Mountain

Mt Eranus

Mt Lyell

Mt Outram

Mt Columbia

Lyell
Glacier

Mt Forbes

Rostrum
Peak

© AVALON TRAVEL PUBLISHING, INC.

BANFF NATIONAL PARK
(continued)

10 mi

10 km

Wapiti
Mtn

Red Deer River

Barrier
Mtn

Panther River

Bare Range

Ghost River
Wilderness Area

Mt
Oliver

Panther
Mtn

Vermilion

Range

Palliser Range

Mt
Aylmer

Douglas
Lake

Cascade River

ALBERTA

SKI BANFF @
NORQUAY

Mt
St Bride

Sawback Range

Johnson Creek

Skoki
Lakes

BOW VALLEY
PARKWAY

To Jasper

CASTLE MOUNTAIN
CHALETS

CASTLE MOUNTAIN

CASTLE MOUNTAIN
WILDERNESS
HOSTEL

JOHNSTON
CANYON

1A

LAKE
LOUISE

LAKE LOUISE

BAKER CREEK
CHALETS

PROTECTION
MOUNTAIN

Castle
Mtn

Mt Norquay

ICEFIELDS PARKWAY

93

LAKE LOUISE

1A

93

SUNSHINE
MEADOWS

GONDOLA

To Golden

Kicking Horse
Pass

LAKE AGNES TRAIL

LAKE LOUISE

Mt Temple

Boom
Lake

Storm
Mtn

BOURGEAU LAKE

Redearth Creek

Yoho

National

Park

LARCH VALLEY

MORAINE LAKE

Vermilion
Pass

93

Stanley
Peak

Isabelle
Peak

Shadow
Lake

Kootenay

National

Park

To Radium
Hot Springs

© AVALON TRAVEL PUBLISHING, INC.

the world. The lake is rivaled for sheer beauty only by Moraine Lake, just down the road. Just north of Lake Louise, the Icefields Parkway begins its spectacular course alongside the Continental Divide to Jasper National Park.

One of Banff's greatest drawing cards is the accessibility of its natural wonders. Most highlights are close to the road system. But adventurous visitors can follow an excellent system of hiking trails to alpine lakes, along glacial valleys, and to spectacular viewpoints where crowds are scarce and human impact has been minimal. Summer in the park is busy. In fact, the park receives nearly half of its four million annual visitors in just two months—July and August. The rest of the year crowds outside the town of Banff are negligible. In winter, three world-class winter resorts—Ski Banff @ Norquay, Sunshine Village, and Lake Louise (Canada's second-largest winter resort)—crank up their lifts. Being low season, hotel rates are reasonable. If you tire of downhill skiing and snowboarding, you can try cross-country skiing, ice-skating, or snowshoeing; take a sleigh ride; soak in a hot spring; or go heli-skiing nearby.

The park is open year-round, although occasional road closures occur on mountain passes along the park's western boundary in winter, due to avalanche-control work and snowstorms.

PLANNING YOUR TIME

If you are planning to visit the Canadian Rockies, it is almost inevitable that your itinerary will include Banff National Park, both for its many and varied outdoor attractions and for its central location. The park can be anything you want it to be, depending on the time of year you visit and what your interests are. Hiking is the park's biggest attraction, and many visitors plan their itinerary around walking. I'd suggest mixing it up—choosing from the hikes I've recommended later in this chapter and combining them with visits to the major natural attractions like Lake Minnewanka, Lake Louise, and Moraine Lake as well as canoeing, fishing, and maybe a round of golf. You can book one accommodation for your entire stay or spend an equal number of nights in

Banff and Lake Louise. If you have a family or like the convenience of staying put for your entire vacation, it is practical to book a room in either Banff or Lake Louise and use it as base—spending your days in the park but also venturing farther afield, with, for example, one day scheduled for Yoho National Park and another for a Canmore/Kananaskis combo.

Unless you're a diehard skier or snowboarder, summer is definitely the best time of year to visit. The months of July and August are the busiest, with crowds decreasing exponentially in the weeks before and after these two months. June and September are wonderful times to visit the park. Aside from the crowd factor, in June, wildflowers start blooming and wildlife is abundant. September sees temperatures ripe for hiking, and the turning colors are at their peak. In either month, discounted accommodations are a welcome bonus. In May and the stretch October through November, the park is at its quietest. Temperatures in any of these three months are generally too cool for hiking (although welcome warm spells are common). The park's three alpine resorts begin opening in December and remain in operation until April or May. While skiing and boarding are the big wintertime draw, plan on expanding your experience by joining a sleigh ride, trying snowshoeing, or heading out ice-fishing.

THE LAND

The park lies within the main and front ranges of the Rocky Mountains, a mountain range that extends the length of the North American continent. Although the mountains are composed of bedrock laid down up to one billion years ago, it wasn't until 100 million years ago that forces below the earth's surface transformed the lowland plain of what is now western Canada into the varied, mountainous topography we see today.

The front ranges lie to the east, bordering the foothills. These geographically complex mountains are made up of younger bedrock that has been folded, faulted, and uplifted. The main ranges are older and higher, with the bedrock

© ANDREW HEMPSTEAD

Castle Mountain is one of the park's most distinctive peaks, easily recognized while driving north from the town of Banff.

lying mainly horizontal and not as severely disturbed as the front ranges. Here the pressures have been most powerful; these mountains are characterized by castlelike buttresses and pinnacles, and warped waves of stratified rock. Most glaciers are found among these lofty peaks. The spine of the main range is the **Continental Divide.** In Canadian latitudes to the east of the divide, all waters flow to the Atlantic Ocean; those to the west flow into the Pacific.

Since rising above the surrounding plains these mountains have been eroding. At least four times in the last million years sheets of ice have covered much of the land. Advancing and retreating back and forth like steel wool across the landscape, they rounded off lower peaks and carved formerly V-shaped valleys into broad U-shaped ones (**Bow Valley** is the most distinctive). Meanwhile, glacial meltwater continued carving ever-deeper channels into the valleys, and rivers changed course many times.

This long history of powerful and even violent natural events over the eons has left behind the dramatic landscape visitors marvel over today. Now forming the exposed sides of many a mountain peak, layers of drastically altered sediment are visible from miles away, especially when accentuated by a particular angle of sunlight or a light fall of snow. *Cirques,* gouged into the mountains by glacial action, fill with glacial meltwater each spring, creating trademark translucent green lakes that will take your breath away. The wide, sweeping U-shaped valleys scoured out by glaciers past now create magnificent panoramas that will draw you to pull off the road and gasp in awe; open views are easy to come by here, thanks to a climate that keeps the tree line low.

FLORA

Nearly 700 species of plants have been recorded in the park. Each species falls into one of three distinct vegetation zones, based primarily on altitude. Lowest is the montane zone, which covers the valley floor. Above it, the subalpine zone comprises most of the forested area. Highest of all

Banff National Park

PARK ENTRY

Permits are required for entry into Banff National Park. A **National Parks Day Pass** is adult $7, senior $6, child $3.50 to a maximum of $14 per vehicle ($12 for seniors). It is interchangeable between parks and is valid until 4 P.M. the day following its purchase.

An annual **National Parks of Canada Pass**, good for entry into national parks across Canada, is adult $45, senior $38 to a maximum of $89 per vehicle. History buffs may find a **Heritage Package** worth the money. For adult $59, senior $49 to a maximum of $119 per vehicle it allows unlimited entry to national parks and national historic sites (two of which are in Banff National Park) for a full year from purchase. All passes can be bought at the eastern park gate on the Trans-Canada Highway, the park information centers in Banff or Lake Louise, and at campground kiosks. For more information, check online at the Parks Canada website (www.pc.gc.ca).

is the alpine zone, where climate is severe and vegetation cover is limited.

Montane-zone vegetation is usually found at elevations below 1,350 meters (4,430 feet) but can grow at higher elevations on sun-drenched, south-facing slopes. Because fires frequently affect this zone, **lodgepole pine** is the dominant species; its tightly sealed cones only open with the heat of a forest fire, thereby regenerating the species quickly after a blaze. **Douglas fir** is the zone's climax species and is found in open stands, such as on Tunnel Mountain. **Aspen** is common in older burn areas, while **limber pine** thrives on rocky outcrops.

Dense forests of **white spruce** and **Engelmann spruce** typify the subalpine zone. White spruce dominates up to 2,100 meters (6,890 feet); above 2,100 meters (6,890 feet) to 2,400 meters (7,870 feet), Engelmann spruce is dominant. In areas affected by fire, such as west of Castle Junction, lodgepole pine occurs in dense stands. **Subalpine fir** grows above 2,200 meters (7,550 feet) and is often stunted by the high winds experienced at such lofty elevations.

The transition from subalpine to alpine is gradual and usually occurs around 2,300 meters (7,560 feet). The alpine has a severe climate, with temperatures averaging below zero. Low temperatures, strong winds, and a very short summer force alpine plants to adapt by growing low to the ground with long roots. Mosses, mountain avens, saxifrage, and an alpine dandelion all thrive in this environment. The best place to view the brightly colored carpet of **alpine flowers** is at Sunshine Meadows or Parker's Ridge.

FAUNA

Viewing the park's abundant and varied wildlife is one of the most popular visitor activities in Banff. In summer, with the onslaught of the tourist hordes, many of the larger mammals move away from the heavily traveled areas. It then becomes a case of knowing when and where to look for them. Spring and fall are the best times of year for wildlife viewing; the crowds are thinner than in summer, and big-game animals are more likely to be seen at lower elevations. Winter also has its advantages. Although **bears** are hibernating, a large herd of **elk** winters on the outskirts of the town of Banff, **coyotes** are often seen roaming around town, **bighorn sheep** have descended from the heights, and wolf packs can be seen along the Bow Valley Corridor.

Small Mammals

One of the first mammals you're likely to come in contact with is the **Columbian ground squirrel**, seen throughout the park's lower elevations. The **golden-mantled ground squirrel**, similar in size but with a striped back, is common at higher elevations or around rocky outcrops. The one collecting Engelmann spruce cones is the **red squirrel**. The **least chipmunk** is striped, but smaller than the golden-mantled squirrel. It lives in dry, rocky areas throughout the park.

Short-tailed weasels are common, but **long-tailed weasels** are rare. Look for both in higher subalpine forests. **Pikas** (commonly called rock rabbits) and **hoary marmots** (well known for their shrill whistles) live among rock slides near high-country lakes: look for them around Moraine Lake and along Bow Summit Loop. **Porcupines** are widespread and are most active at night.

Vermilion Lakes is an excellent place to view the **beaver** at work; the best time is dawn or dusk. **Muskrats** and **mink** are common in all wetlands within the park.

Hoofed Residents

The most common and widespread of the park's hoofed residents are **elk**, which number around 2,800. Starting in 2000, a concerted effort was made to keep them out of Banff's downtown core, but they are still congregating around the outskirts of the town, including up near the Tunnel Mountain campgrounds. They can also be seen along the Bow Valley Parkway. **Moose** were once common around Vermilion Lakes, but competition from an artificially expanded elk population caused their numbers to decline, and now only around 100 live in the park. Look for them at Waterfowl Lakes and along the Icefields Parkway near Rampart Creek.

Mule deer, named for their large ears, are most common in the southern part of the park. Watch for them along the Mount Norquay Road and Bow Valley Parkway. **White-tailed deer** are much less common but are seen occasionally at Saskatchewan River Crossing. A small herd of around 20 **woodland caribou** remains in the Dolomite Pass area and Upper Pipestone Valley and is rarely seen.

It is estimated that the park is home to around 900 **mountain goats.** These nimble-footed creatures occupy all mountain peaks, living almost the entire year in the higher subalpine and alpine regions. The most accessible place to view these high-altitude hermits is along Parker's Ridge in the far northwestern corner of the park. The park's **bighorn sheep** have for the most part lost their fear of humans and often congregate at certain spots to lick salt from the road. Your best chance of seeing one of the park's 2,000–2,300 bighorn is at the south end of the Bow Valley Parkway, between switchbacks on Mount Norquay Road, and just beyond Lake Minnewanka along the loop road.

Predators

Coyotes are widespread along the entire Bow River watershed. They are attracted to Vermilion Lakes by an abundance of small game, and many have permanent dens there. **Wolves** had been driven close to extinction by the early 1950s, but today at least four wolf packs have been reported in the park. One pack winters close to town and is occasionally seen on Vermilion Lakes during that period. The **lynx** population fluctuates greatly; look for them in the backcountry during winter. **Cougars** are shy and number less than 20 in the park. They are occasionally seen along the front ranges behind Cascade Mountain.

Bears

The exhilaration of seeing one of these magnificent creatures in its natural habitat is unforgettable. From the road you're most likely to see **black bears,** which actually range in color from jet black to cinnamon brown and number around 50. Try the Bow Valley Parkway at dawn or late in the afternoon. Farther north they are occasionally seen near the road as it passes Cirrus Mountain. Banff's 60-odd **grizzly bears** spend most of the year in remote valleys, often on south-facing slopes away from the Bow Valley Corridor. During late spring they are occasionally seen in residential areas, along the Lake Minnewanka loop road, on the golf course, and in the area of Bow Pass.

The chance of encountering a bear face-to-face in the backcountry is remote. To lessen chances even further, you should take some simple precautions: Never hike alone or at dusk. Make lots of noise when passing through heavy vegetation. Keep a clean camp. Read the pamphlets available at all park visitor centers. At the Banff Visitor Centre (224 Banff Ave.) daily trail reports list all recent bear sightings. Report any bears you see to the Warden's Office (403/762-4506).

Reptiles and Amphibians

The **wandering garter snake** is rare and found only near the Cave and Basin, where warm water from the mineral spring flows down a shaded

THE ELK OF BANFF NATIONAL PARK

Few visitors leave Banff without having seen elk—a large member of the deer family easily distinguished by its white rump. Though the animals have been reported passing through the park for a century, they've never been indigenous. In 1917, 57 elk were moved to Banff from Yellowstone National Park. Two years later 20 more were transplanted and the new herd multiplied rapidly. At that time, coyotes, cougars, and wolves were being slaughtered under a predator-control program, leaving the elk unfettered by nature's population-control mechanisms. The elk proliferated and soon became a problem as they took to wintering in the range of bighorn sheep, deer, moose, and beaver. Between 1941 and 1969, controlled slaughters of elk were conducted in an attempt to reduce the population.

Today, with wolf packs returning to the park, the elk population has stabilized at about 2,800. In summer, look for them in open meadows along the Bow Valley Parkway, along the road to Two Jack Lake, or at Vermilion Lakes.

Each fall, traditionally, hundreds of elk moved into the town itself, but starting in 2000 Parks Canada has been making a concerted effort to keep them away from areas such as the golf course and recreation grounds. The main reason for this is that fall is rutting season, and the libidinal bull elk become dangerous as they gather their harems.

© ANDREW HEMPSTEAD

Elk are common visitors to the local golf course.

You may still see the odd elk feeding in downtown Central Park or walking proudly down Banff Avenue, but it's more likely you'll spot one on the outskirts of town.

---

slope into Vermilion Lakes. Amphibians found in the park include the widespread **western toad;** the **wood frog,** commonly found along the Bow River; the rare **spotted frog;** and the **long-toed salamander,** which spawns in shallow ponds and spends summer under logs or rocks in the vicinity of its spawning grounds.

Birds

Although more than 240 species of birds have been recorded in the park, most are shy and live in heavily wooded areas. One species that definitely isn't shy is the fearless **gray jay,** which haunts all campgrounds and picnic areas. Similar in color, but larger, is the **Clark's nutcracker,** which lives in higher, subalpine forests. Another common bird is the black and white **magpie. Ravens** are frequently encountered, especially around campgrounds.

Several species of **woodpecker** live in subalpine forests. Several species of grouse are also in residence. Most common is the **downy ruffed grouse** seen in montane forest. The **blue grouse** and **spruce grouse** are seen at higher elevations, as is the **white-tailed ptarmigan,** which lives above the tree line. (Watch for them in Sunshine Meadows or on the Bow Summit Loop.) A colony of **black swifts** in Johnston Canyon is one of only two in the Canadian Rockies.

Good spots to view **dippers** and migrating

waterfowl are Hector Lake, Vermilion Lakes, and the wetland area near Muleshoe Picnic Area. A bird blind has been set up below the Cave and Basin but is only worth visiting at dawn and dusk when the hordes of human visitors aren't around. Part of the nearby marsh stays ice free during winter, attracting **killdeer** and other birds.

Although raptors are not common in the park, **bald eagles** and **golden eagles** are present part of the year, and Alberta's provincial bird, the **great horned owl,** lives in the park year-round.

HISTORY

Although the valleys of the Canadian Rockies became ice free nearly 8,000 years ago and native people periodically have hunted in the area since that time, the story of Banff National Park really began with the arrival of the railroad to the area.

The Coming of the Railway

In 1871, Canadian prime minister John A. Mac-Donald promised to build a rail line linking British Columbia to the rest of the country as a condition of the new province joining the confederation. It wasn't until early 1883 that the line reached Calgary, pushing through to **Laggan,** now known as Lake Louise, that fall. The rail line was one of the largest and costliest engineering jobs ever undertaken in Canada.

Discovery of the Cave and Basin

On November 8, 1883, three young railway workers—Franklin McCabe and William and Thomas McCardell—went prospecting for gold on their day off. After crossing the Bow River by raft, they came across a warm stream and traced it to its source at a small log-choked basin of warm water that had a distinct smell of sulphur. Nearby they detected the source of the foul smell coming from a hole in the ground. Nervously, one of the three men lowered himself into the hole and came across a subterranean pool of aqua-green warm water. The three men had found not gold, but something just as precious—a hot mineral spring that in time would attract wealthy customers from around the world. Word of the discovery soon got out, and the gov-

ernment encouraged visitors to the Cave and Basin as an ongoing source of revenue to support the new railway.

A 2,500-hectare (6,177-acre) reserve was established around the springs on November 25, 1885, and two years later the reserve was expanded and renamed **Rocky Mountains Park.** It was primarily a business enterprise centered around the unique springs and catering to wealthy patrons of the railway. At the turn of the 20th century, Canada had an abundance of wilderness; it certainly didn't need a park to preserve it. The only goal of Rocky Mountains Park was to generate income for the government and the Canadian Pacific Railway (CPR).

A Town Grows

After the discovery of the Cave and Basin across the Bow River from the railway station (then known as Siding 29), many commercial facilities sprang up along what is now Banff Avenue. The general manager of the CPR (later to become its vice president), William Cornelius Van Horne, was instrumental in creating a hotel business along the rail line. His most recognized achievement was the Banff Springs Hotel, which opened in 1888. It was the world's largest hotel at the time. Enterprising locals soon realized the area's potential and began opening restaurants, offering guided hunting and boating trips, and developing manicured gardens. Banff soon became Canada's best-known tourist resort, attracting visitors from around the world. It was named after Banffshire, the Scottish birthplace of George Stephen, the CPR's first president.

In 1902, the park boundary was again expanded to include 11,440 square km (4,417 square miles) of the Canadian Rockies. This dramatic expansion meant that the park became not just a tourist resort but also home to existing coal-mining and logging operations and hydroelectric dams. Government officials saw no conflict of interest, actually stating that the coal mine and township at Bankhead added to the park's many attractions. Many of the forests were logged, providing wood for construction, while other areas were burned to allow clear sightings for surveyors' instruments.

WILD BILL PEYTO

These words from a friend sum up Bill Peyto—one of Banff's earliest characters and one of the Canadian Rockies' greatest guides: ". . . rarely speaking—his forte was doing things, not talking about them." In 1886, at the tender age of 18, Ebenezer William Peyto left England for Canada. After traveling extensively he settled in Banff and was hired as an apprentice guide for legendary outfitter Tom Wilson. Wearing a tilted sombrero, fringed buckskin coat, cartridge belt, hunting knife, and six-shooter, he looked more like a gunslinger than a mountain man.

As his reputation as a competent guide grew, so did the stories. While guiding clients on one occasion, he led them to his cabin. Before entering, Peyto threw stones in the front door until a loud snap was heard. It was a bear trap that he'd set up to catch a certain trapper who'd been stealing his food. One of the guests commented that if caught, the trapper would surely have died. "You're damned right he would have," Bill replied. "Then I'd have known for sure it was him."

In 1900, Peyto left Banff to fight in the Boer War and was promoted to corporal for bravery. This title was revoked before it became official after the army officials learned he'd "borrowed" an officer's jacket and several bottles of booze for the celebration. Returning to a hero's welcome in Banff, Peyto established an outfitting business and continued prospecting for copper in Simpson Pass. Although his outfitting business thrived, the death of his wife left him despondent. He built a house on Banff Avenue; its name, "Ain't it Hell," summed up his view of life.

In his later years, he became a warden in the Healy Creek–Sunshine district, where his exploits during the 1920s added to his already legendary name. After 20 years of service he retired, and in 1943, at the age of 75, he passed away. One of the park's most beautiful lakes is named after him, as are a glacier and a popular Banff watering hole (Wild Bill's—a designation he would have appreciated). His face also adorns the large signs welcoming visitors to Banff.

After a restriction on automobiles in the park was lifted in 1916, Canada's best-known tourist resort also became its busiest. More and more commercial facilities sprang up, offering luxury and opulence amid the wilderness of the Canadian Rockies. Calgarians built summer cottages, and the town began advertising itself as a year-round destination. As attitudes began to change, the government set up a Dominion Parks Branch, whose first commissioner, J. B. Hawkins, believed that land set aside for parks should be used for recreation and education. Gradually, resource industries were phased out. Hawkins's work culminated in the National Parks Act of 1930, which in turn led Rocky Mountains Park to be renamed Banff National Park. The park's present boundaries, encompassing 6,641 square km (2,564 square miles), were established in 1964.

Icefields Parkway

Natives and early explorers found the swampy nature of the Bow Valley north of Lake Louise difficult for foot and horse travel. When heading north,

they used instead the Pipestone River Valley to the east. Banff guide Bill Peyto led American explorer Walter Wilcox up the Bow Valley in 1896, to the high peaks along the Continental Divide northeast of Lake Louise. The first complete journey along this route was made by Jim Brewster in 1904. Soon after, A. P. Coleman made the arduous journey, becoming a strong supporter for the route aptly known as The Wonder Trail. During the Great Depression of the 1930s, as part of a relief-work project, construction began on what was to become the Icefields Parkway. The road was completed in 1939, and the first car traveled the route in 1940. In tribute to the excellence of the road's early construction, the original roadbed, when upgraded to its present standard in 1961, was followed nearly the entire way.

Town of Banff

For most of its existence, the town of Banff was run as a service center for park visitors by the Canadian Parks Service in Ottawa, a government department with plenty of economic resources but little idea about how to handle the day-to-day running of a midsized town. Any inconvenience this arrangement caused park residents was offset by cheap rent and subsidized services. In June 1988, Banff's residents voted to sever this tie, and on January 1, 1990, Banff officially became an incorporated town, no different than any other in Alberta (except that Parks Canada controls environmental protection within the town of Banff).

Town of Banff

Many visitors planning a trip to the national park don't realize that the town of Banff is a bustling commercial center. The town's location is magnificent. It is spread out along the Bow River, extending to the lower slopes of Sulphur Mountain to the south and Tunnel Mountain to the east. In one direction is the towering face of Mount Rundle, and in the other, framed by the buildings along Banff Avenue, is Cascade Mountain. Hotels and motels line the north end of Banff Avenue, while a profusion of shops, boutiques, cafés, and restaurants hugs the south end. Also at the south end, just over the Bow River, is the Park Administration Building. Here the road forks—to the right is the historic Cave and Basin Hot Springs, to the left the Fairmont Banff Springs and Banff Gondola. Some people are happy walking along the crowded streets or shopping in a truly unique setting; those more interested in some peace and quiet can easily slip into pristine wilderness just a five-minute walk from town.

SIGHTS WITHIN WALKING DISTANCE OF TOWN

Banff Park Museum

Although displays of stuffed animals are not usually associated with national parks, the Banff Park Museum (93 Banff Ave., 403/762-1558; mid-May–late Sept. daily 10 A.M.–6 P.M., the rest of the year daily 1–5 P.M.; adult $4, senior $3.50, child $3) provides an insight into the park's early history. Visitors during the Victorian era were eager to see the park's animals without actually having to venture into the bush. A lack of roads and scarcity of large game resulting from hunting meant that the best places to see animals, stuffed or otherwise, were the game

paddock, the zoo, and this museum, which was built in 1903. In its early years, the Banff Zoo and Aviary occupied the grounds behind the museum. The zoo kept more than 60 species of animals, including a polar bear. The museum itself was built before the park had electricity, hence the railroad pagoda design using skylights on all levels.

As times changed, the museum was considered outdated; plans for its demolition were put forward in the 1950s. Fortunately, the museum was spared and later restored for the park's 100th anniversary in 1985. While the exhibits still provide visitors with an insight into the intricate workings of various park ecosystems, they are also an interesting link to the park's past. Staff lead a guided tour through the facility Monday–Friday at 3 P.M. and Saturday–Sunday at 2:30 P.M. The museum also has a Discovery Room, where touching the displays is encouraged, and a reading room is stocked with books on the park.

◪ Whyte Museum of the Canadian Rockies

The Whyte Foundation was established in the mid-1950s by local artists Peter and Catherine Whyte to help preserve artistic and historical material relating to the Canadian Rockies. Their museum (111 Bear St., 403/762-2291; daily 10 A.M.–5 P.M.; adult $8, senior and child $4.50) opened in 1968 and has continued to grow ever since. It now houses the world's largest collection of Canadian Rockies literature and art. Included in the archives are more than 4,000 volumes, oral tapes of early pioneers and outfitters, antique postcards, old cameras, manuscripts, and a large photography collection. The highlight is the photography of Byron Harmon, whose black-and-white studies of mountain

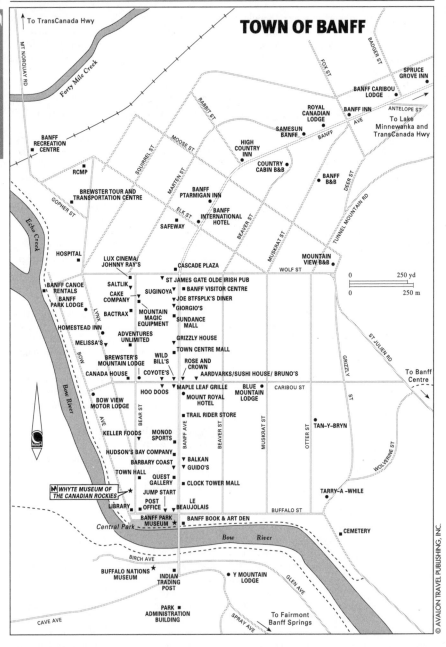

TOWN OF BANFF

To TransCanada Hwy

MT NORQUAY RD

Forty Mile Creek

BADGER ST

FOX ST

SPRUCE GROVE INN

BANFF CARIBOU LODGE

BANFF INN

ANTELOPE ST

ROYAL CANADIAN LODGE

RABBIT ST

BANFF AVE

To Lake Minnewanka and TransCanada Hwy

SAMESUN BANFF

BANFF RECREATION CENTRE

MOOSE ST

HIGH COUNTRY INN

COUNTRY CABIN B&B

DEER ST

BANFF B&B

RCMP

SQUIRREL ST

MARTEN ST

BREWSTER TOUR AND TRANSPORTATION CENTRE

BANFF PTARMIGAN INN

GOPHER ST

ELK ST

BANFF INTERNATIONAL HOTEL

BEAVER ST

MUSKRAT ST

TUNNEL MOUNTAIN RD

SAFEWAY

HOSPITAL

MOUNTAIN VIEW B&B

Echo Creek

LUX CINEMA/ JOHNNY RAY'S

CASCADE PLAZA

WOLF ST

0   250 yd

0   250 m

BANFF CANOE RENTALS

SALTLIK

CAKE COMPANY

LYNX

ST JAMES GATE OLDE IRISH PUB

SUGINOYA

BANFF VISITOR CENTRE

JOE BTFSPLK'S DINER

BANFF PARK LODGE

BACTRAX

MOUNTAIN MAGIC EQUIPMENT

GIORGIO'S

SUNDANCE MALL

ST JULIEN RD

HOMESTEAD INN

ADVENTURES UNLIMITED

GRIZZLY HOUSE

To Banff Centre

MELISSA'S

BOW

TOWN CENTRE MALL

GRIZZLY ST

BREWSTER'S MOUNTAIN LODGE

WILD BILL'S

ROSE AND CROWN

CANADA HOUSE

COYOTE'S

AARDVARKS/SUSHI HOUSE/ BRUNO'S

Bow River

HOO DOOS

BEAR ST

MAPLE LEAF GRILLE

BLUE MOUNTAIN LODGE

CARIBOU ST

BOW VIEW MOTOR LODGE

MOUNT ROYAL HOTEL

BANFF AVE

BEAVER ST

MUSKRAT ST

OTTER ST

TAN-Y-BRYN

AVE

TRAIL RIDER STORE

KELLER FOODS

MONOD SPORTS

WOLVERINE ST

HUDSON'S BAY COMPANY

BARBARY COAST

BALKAN

GUIDO'S

TOWN HALL

QUEST GALLERY

CLOCK TOWER MALL

JUMP START

TARRY-A-WHILE

WHYTE MUSEUM OF THE CANADIAN ROCKIES

LIBRARY

POST OFFICE

LE BEAUJOLAIS

BUFFALO ST

BANFF PARK MUSEUM

BANFF BOOK & ART DEN

Central Park

CEMETERY

Bow   River

BIRCH AVE

BUFFALO NATIONS MUSEUM

INDIAN TRADING POST

Y MOUNTAIN LODGE

GLEN AVE

CAVE AVE

PARK ADMINISTRATION BUILDING

SPRAY AVE

To Fairmont Banff Springs

VICINITY
OF
BANFF

Banff National Park

geography have shown people around the world the beauty of the Canadian Rockies. The downstairs gallery features changing art exhibitions. The museum also houses the library and archives of the Alpine Club of Canada. On the grounds are several heritage homes formerly occupied by local pioneers. Don't miss this one.

The Whyte Museum hosts interesting walking tours through summer. The most popular of these is the Historic Banff Walk, which departs from the museum daily at 11 A.M. and 3 P.M., taking around 90 minutes.

Cascade Gardens and Canada Place

Across the river from downtown, Cascade Gardens offers a commanding view along Banff Avenue and of Cascade Mountain. The gardens are immaculately manicured, making for enjoyable strolling on a sunny day. The stone edifice in the center of the garden is the **Park Administration Building,** which dates to 1936. It replaced a private spa and hospital operated by one of the park's earliest entrepreneurs, Dr. R. G. Brett. Known as Brett's Sanatorium, the original 1886 structure was built to accommodate guests drawn to Banff by the claimed healing qualities of the hot springs' water. In addition to providing a park headquarters, it is home to Canada Place (mid-May–Aug. daily 10 A.M.–6 P.M., Sept.–mid-Oct. daily noon–5 P.M., mid-Oct.–mid-May Wed.–Sun. 1–4 P.M.; free), which is filled with hands-on exhibits that focus on the country's heritage and how this history was shaped by the vastness of the land.

Buffalo Nations Museum

Looking like a stockade, this museum (1 Birch Ave., 403/762-2388; summer daily 10 A.M.–6 P.M., the rest of the year 1–5 P.M.; adult $8, senior $6, child $2.50) overlooks the Bow River across from Central Park. It is dedicated to the heritage of the natives who once inhabited the Canadian Rockies and adjacent prairies. It was named for prominent Banff resident Norman Luxton, who had a close relationship with the natives of the area and was involved in the Banff Indian Days. He operated a trading post on the site for many years before opening the museum in 1952 with the help of the Glenbow-Alberta Institute. The museum contains memorabilia from Luxton's 60-year relationship with the Stoney, as well as an elaborately decorated tepee, hunting equipment, a few stuffed animals, a realistic diorama of a buffalo jump, peace pipes, and traditional clothing. The Indian Trading Post is now one of Banff's better gift shops and is definitely worth a browse.

Cave and Basin National Historic Site

At the end of Cave Avenue, this historic site (403/762-1566; summer daily 9 A.M.–6 P.M., the rest of the year Mon.–Fri. 11 A.M.–4 P.M., Sat.–Sun. 9:30 A.M.–5 P.M.; adult $4, senior $3.50, child $3) is the birthplace of Banff National Park and of the Canadian National Parks system. Here in 1883, three men employed by the CPR stumbled on the hot springs now known as the Cave and Basin and were soon lounging in the hot water—a real luxury in the

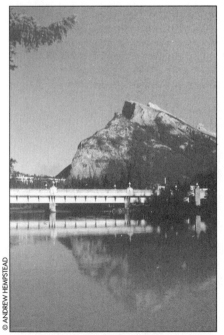

© ANDREW HEMPSTEAD

The Bow River flows through the heart of Banff.

Wild West. They built a fence around the springs, constructed a crude cabin, and began the long process of establishing a claim to the site. But the government beat them to it, settling their claims for a few thousand dollars and acquiring the hot springs.

Bathhouses were installed in 1887, and bathers paid 10 cents for a swim. The pools were eventually lined with concrete, and additions were built onto the original structures. Ironically, the soothing minerals in the water that had attracted millions of people to bathe here eventually caused the pools' demise. The minerals, combined with chlorine, produced sediments that ate away at the concrete structure until the pools were deemed unsafe. After closing in 1975, the pools were restored to their original look at a cost of $12 million. They reopened in 1985 only to close again in 1993 for the same reasons, coupled with flagging popularity.

Although the pools are now closed for swimming, the center is still one of Banff's most popular attractions. Interpretive displays describe the hows and whys of the springs. A narrow tunnel winds into the dimly lit cave, and short trails lead from the center to the cave entrance and through a unique environment created by the hot water from the springs. Interpretive tours run four times daily in summer.

Upper Hot Springs

These springs (Mountain Ave., 403/762-1515; summer daily 9 A.M.–11 P.M., the rest of the year 10 A.M.–10 P.M.), toward the Banff Gondola, were first developed in 1901. The present building was completed in 1935, with extensive renovations made in 1996. Water flows out of the bedrock at 47°C (116.6°F) and is cooled to 40°C (104°F) in the main pool. Once considered for privatization, the springs are still run by Parks Canada and are popular throughout the year. Swimming is $7.50 adults, $6.50 seniors and children; lockers and towel rental extra. Within the complex is **Pleiades Massage & Spa** (403/760-2500), offering a wide range of therapeutic treatments, including massages from $50 for 30 minutes as well as body wraps, aromatherapy, and hydrotherapy.

Banff Gondola

The easiest way to get high above town without breaking a sweat is on this gondola (403/762-2523; summer 7:30 A.M.–9 P.M., shorter hours the rest of the year, closed for two weeks in January; adult $22, child $11), which rises 700 meters (2,300 feet) in eight minutes to the summit of 2,285-meter (7,500-foot) **Sulphur Mountain.** From the observation deck at the upper terminal, the breathtaking view includes the town, Bow Valley, Cascade Mountain, Lake Minnewanka, and the Fairholme Range. Bighorn sheep often hang around the upper terminal. The short **Vista Trail** leads along a ridge to a restored weather observatory. Between 1903 and 1931, long before the gondola was built, Norman Sanson was the meteorological observer who collected data at the station. During this period he made more than 1,000 ascents of Sulphur Mountain, all in the line of duty.

The **Summit Restaurant** (403/762-7486) serves up mediocre food, inexpensive breakfasts, and priceless views. Above this eatery is the **Panorama Room** (403/762-7486; June–mid-Oct.), dishing up more the same, but buffet-style.

From downtown, the gondola is three km (1.9 miles) along Mountain Avenue. May–October **Brewster** (403/762-6767) provides shuttle service to the gondola from downtown hotels ($35 includes gondola ride).

A 5.5-km (3.4-mile) hiking trail to the summit begins from the Upper Hot Springs parking lot. Although it's a long slog, you'll be rewarded with a free gondola ride down—they don't check tickets at the top.

Fairmont Banff Springs

On a terrace above a bend in the Bow River is one of the largest, grandest, and most opulent mountain-resort hotels in the world. What better way to spend a rainy afternoon than to explore this turreted 20th-century castle, seeking out a writing desk overlooking one of the world's most-photographed scenes and penning a long letter to the folks back home?

"The Springs" has grown with the town and is an integral part of local history. William Cornelius Van Horne, vice president of the CPR,

© ANDREW HEMPSTEAD

Fairmont Banff Springs, one of the world's great mountain resorts

decided that the best way of encouraging customers to travel on his newly completed rail line across the Rockies was to build a series of luxurious mountain accommodations. The largest of these was begun in 1886, as close as possible to Banff's newly discovered hot springs. The location chosen had magnificent views and was only a short carriage ride from the train station. Money was no object, and architect Bruce Price began designing a mountain resort the likes of which the world had never seen. At some stage of construction his plans were misinterpreted, and much to Van Horne's shock the building was built back to front. The best guest rooms faced the forested slopes of Sulphur Mountain while the kitchen had panoramic views of the Bow Valley.

On June 1, 1888, it opened, the largest hotel in the world, with 250 rooms beginning at $3.50 per night including meals. Water from the nearby hot springs was piped into the hotel's steam baths. Rumor has it that when the pipes blocked, water from the Bow River was used, secretly supplemented by bags of sulphur-smelling chemicals. Overnight, the quiet community of Banff became a destination resort for wealthy guests from around the world, and the hotel soon became

one of North America's most popular accommodations. Every room was booked every day during the short summer seasons. In 1903, a wing was added, doubling the hotel's capacity. The following year a tower was added to each wing. Guest numbers reached 22,000 in 1911, and construction of a new hotel, designed by Walter Painter, began that year. The original design—an 11-story tower joining two wings in a baronial style—was reminiscent of a Scottish castle mixed with a French country chateau. This concrete-and-rock-faced, green-roofed building stood as it did at its completion in 1928 until 1999, when an ambitious multiyear program of renovations commenced. At first, the most obvious change to those who have visited before will be the new lobby, moved to a more accessible location, but all rooms have also been refurbished, and many of the restaurants changed or upgraded. The Canadian Pacific moniker remained part of the Banff Spring's official name until 2000, when the hotel, and all other Canadian Pacific hotels, became part of the Fairmont Hotels and Resorts chain.

Don't let the hotel's opulence keep you from spending time here. Visit the hotel 11:30 A.M.–

2 P.M. and enjoy a huge buffet lunch combined with a 30-minute **Historic Castle Tour** for $26.95 per person. Call 403/762-2211 for details. Otherwise wander through on your own, admiring the 5,000 pieces of furniture and antiques (most of those in public areas are reproductions), paintings, prints, tapestries, and rugs. Take in the medieval atmosphere of Mount Stephen Hall with its lime flagstone floor, enormous windows, and large oak beams; take advantage of the luxurious spa facility (see *Indoor Recreation*); or relax in one of 12 eateries or four lounges.

The hotel is a 15-minute walk southeast of town, either along Spray Avenue or via the trail along the south bank of the Bow River. **Banff Transit** buses leave Banff Avenue for the Springs twice an hour; $2. Alternatively, horse-drawn buggies take passengers from the Trail Rider Store (132 Banff Ave., 403/762-4551) to the Springs for about $70 for two passengers.

Bow Falls

Small but spectacular Bow Falls is below the Fairmont Banff Springs, only a short walk from downtown. The waterfall is the result of a dramatic change in the course of the Bow River brought about by glaciation. At one time the river flowed north of Tunnel Mountain and out of the mountains via the valley of Lake Minnewanka. As the glaciers retreated, they left terminal moraines, forming natural dams and changing the course of the river. Eventually the backed-up water found an outlet here between Tunnel Mountain and the northwest ridge of Mount Rundle. The falls are most spectacular in late spring when runoff from the winter snows fills every river and stream in the Bow Valley watershed.

To get there from town, cross the bridge at the south end of Banff Avenue, scramble down the grassy embankment to the left, and follow a pleasant trail along the Bow River to a point above the falls. This easy walk is one km (.6 mile); 20 minutes each way. By car, cross the bridge and follow Golf Course signs. From the falls a paved road crosses the Spray River and passes through the golf course.

Banff Centre

On the lower slopes of Tunnel Mountain is Banff Centre, whose surroundings provide inspiration as one of Canada's leading centers for postgraduate students in a variety of disciplines, including Mountain Culture, Arts, and Leadership Development. The Banff Centre opened in the summer of 1933 as a theater school. Since then it has grown to become a prestigious institution attracting artists of many disciplines from throughout Canada. The Centre's **Walter Phillips Gallery** (St. Julien Rd., 403/762-6281; Tues.–Sun. noon–5 P.M.) presents changing exhibits of visual arts from throughout the world.

Activities are held on the grounds of the Banff Centre year-round. Highlights include a summer educational program, concerts, displays, live performances, the Playbill Series, the Banff Arts Festival, and Banff Mountain Festivals, to name a few (see *Festivals and Events*). Call 403/762-6100 for a program, go to the website www.banffcentre.ca, or check the *Crag and Canyon* (published weekly on Wednesday).

SIGHTS AND DRIVES IN THE VICINITY OF TOWN
Vermilion Lakes

This series of shallow lakes forms an expansive montane wetland supporting a variety of mammals and 238 species of birds. Vermilion Lakes Drive, paralleling the TransCanada Highway immediately west of Banff, provides the easiest access to the area. The level of **First Vermilion Lake** was once controlled by a dam. Since its removal, the level of the lake has dropped. This is the beginning of a long process that will eventually see the area evolve into a floodplain forest such as is found along the Fenland Trail. **Second** and **Third Vermilion Lakes** have a higher water level that is controlled naturally by beaver dams. Near First Vermilion Lake is an active osprey nest. The entire area is excellent for wildlife viewing, especially in winter when it provides habitat for elk, coyote, and the occasional wolf.

© ANDREW HEMPSTEAD

Vermilion Lakes and Mount Rundle

Mount Norquay Road

One of the best views of town accessible by vehicle is on this road, which switchbacks steeply to the base of Ski Banff @ Norquay, the local hangout for skiers and boarders. On the way up are several lookouts, including one near the top where bighorn sheep often graze.

To Lake Minnewanka

Lake Minnewanka Road begins where Banff Avenue ends at the northeast end of town. An alternative to driving along Banff Avenue is to take Buffalo Street, opposite the Banff Park Museum, and follow it around Tunnel Mountain, passing the hostel, campground, and several viewpoints of the north face of Mount Rundle, rising vertically from the forested valley. This road eventually rejoins Banff Avenue at the Banff Rocky Mountain Resort.

After passing under the TransCanada Highway **Cascade Falls** is obvious off to the left beyond the airstrip. The base of the falls can be easily reached in five minutes (climbing higher without the proper equipment is dangerous). In winter, these falls freeze and you'll often see ice climbers slowly making their way up the narrow thread of frozen water. Directly opposite is a turn to **Cascade Ponds,** a popular day-use area where local families gather on warmer days to swim, sunbathe, and barbecue.

The next turnout along this road is at **Lower Bankhead.** During the early 1900s, Bankhead was a booming mining town producing 200,000 tons of coal a year. The poor quality of coal and bitter labor disputes led to the mine's closure in 1922. Soon after, all the buildings were moved or demolished. Although for many years the mine had brought prosperity to the park, perceptions changed. The National Parks Act of 1930, which prohibited the establishment of mining claims in national parks, was greeted with little animosity.

From the parking lot at Lower Bankhead, a 1.1-km (.7-mile) interpretive trail leads through the industrial section of the town and past an old mine train. The town's 1,000 residents lived on the other side of the road at what is now known as **Upper Bankhead.** Just before the Upper Bankhead turnoff, the foundation of the Holy Trinity Church can be seen on the side of the hill to the right. Not much remains of Upper Bankhead. It is now a day-use area with picnic tables, kitchen shelters, and firewood. Through the meadow to the west of here are some large slag heaps, concealed mine entrances, and various stone foundations.

Lake Minnewanka

Minnewanka (Lake of the Water Spirit) is the largest body of water in Banff National Park. Mount Inglismaldie (2,964 meters/9,720 feet) and the Fairholme Range form an imposing backdrop. The reservoir was first constructed in 1912, and additional dams were built in 1922 and 1941 to supply hydroelectric power to Banff. Even if you don't feel up to an energetic hike, it's worth parking at the facility area and going for a short walk along the lakeshore. You'll pass a concession selling snacks and drinks, then the tour boat dock, before entering an area of picnic tables and covered cooking shelters—the perfect place for a picnic. Children will love exploring the rocky shoreline and stony beaches in this area, but you should continue farther around the lake, if only to escape the crowds.

Lake Minnewanka Boat Tours (403/762-3473) has a 90-minute cruise to the far reaches of the lake, passing the Devil's Gap formation. It departs from the dock mid-May to the end of September 3–5 times daily (first sailing is 10:30 A.M. and costs adult $32, child $16). Brewster (403/762-6767) offers this cruise combined with a bus tour from Banff for $46 per person. Easy walking trails lead along the western shore. The lake is great for fishing (lake trout to 15 kg/33 lb.) and is the only one in the park where motorboats are allowed. Lake Minnewanka Boat Tours rents aluminum boats with small outboard engines and represents local fishing guides.

From Lake Minnewanka the road continues along the reservoir wall, passing a plaque commemorating the Palliser Expedition, to **Johnson Lake,** which has a lakeside trail, good swimming, and picnic facilities with views across to Mount Rundle. You'll often have to slow down along this stretch of road for bighorn sheep.

BOW VALLEY PARKWAY

Two roads link Banff to Lake Louise. The Trans-Canada Highway is the quicker route, more popular with through traffic. The other is the more scenic 51-km (32-mile) Bow Valley Parkway, which branches off the TransCanada Highway five km (3.1 miles) west of Banff. Cyclists will appreciate this road's two long, divided sections and low speed limit (60 kph/37 mph). Along this route are several impressive viewpoints, interpretive displays, picnic areas, good hiking, great opportunities for viewing wildlife, a hostel, three lodges, campgrounds, and one of the park's best restaurants (see *Accommodations* and *Food*). Between March and late June, the southern end of the parkway (as far north as Johnston Canyon) is closed daily 6 P.M.–9 A.M. for the protection of wildlife.

As you enter the parkway, you pass the quiet, creekside **Fireside** picnic area, where

Upper Johnston Falls

BANFF TO LAKE LOUISE

Banff National Park

LAKE LOUISE

To Yoho National Park
and Icefields Parkway

Lake Louise Village

BOW VALLEY PARKWAY

Luellen Lake

Johnston Creek

Rockbound Lake

Ink Pots

Mt Ishbel

Upper Falls

Johnston Canyon

Lower Falls

JOHNSTON CANYON RESORT

MORAINE LAKE RD

Paradise Valley

BAKER CREEK CHALETS

PROTECTION MOUNTAIN

CASTLE LOOKOUT

Castle Mountain

CASTLE MOUNTAIN

TRANSCANADA HIGHWAY

1A

Bow River

Valley of the Ten Peaks

Larch Valley

Taylor Lake

CASTLE MOUNTAIN CHALETS

93

CASTLE MOUNTAIN WILDERNESS HOSTEL

JOHNSTON CANYON

MORAINE LAKE

Copper Mountain

Pilot Mountain

STORM MOUNTAIN LODGE

BANFF-WINDERMERE HIGHWAY

Redearth Creek

Yoho National Park

ALBERTA
BRITISH COLUMBIA

Kootenay National Park

Vermillion Pass

To Radium Hot Springs

Banff National Park

© AVALON TRAVEL PUBLISHING, INC.

an interpretive display describes how the Bow Valley was formed. At **Backswamp Viewpoint,** you can look upstream to the site of a former dam, now a swampy wetland filled with aquatic vegetation. Farther along the road is another wetland at **Muleshoe.** This wetland consists of oxbow lakes that were formed when the Bow River changed its course and abandoned its meanders for a more direct path. Across the parkway is a one-km (.6-mile) trail that climbs to a viewpoint overlooking the valley. (The slope around this trail is infested with wood ticks during late spring/early summer, so be sure to check yourself carefully after hiking in this area.) To the east, **Hole-in-the-Wall** is visible. This large-mouthed cave was created by the Bow Glacier, which once filled the valley. As the glacier receded, its meltwater dissolved the soft limestone bedrock, creating what is known as a solution cave.

Beyond Muleshoe the road inexplicably divides for a few car lengths. A large white spruce stood on the island until it blew down in 1984. The story goes that while the road was being constructed, a surly foreman was asleep in the shade of the tree, and not daring to rouse him, workers cleared the roadway around him. The road then passes through particularly hilly terrain, part of a massive rockslide that occurred approximately 8,000 years ago.

Continuing down the parkway you'll pass the following sights.

Johnston Canyon

Johnston Creek drops over a series of spectacular waterfalls here, deep within the chasm it has carved into the limestone bedrock. The canyon is not nearly as deep as Maligne Canyon in Jasper National Park—30 meters (100 feet) at its deep-

Lake Minnewanka

TWO JACK LAKESIDE

TWO JACK MAIN

To Canmore and Calgary

Cascade Mountain

Stoney Squaw

Mt Louis

Mt Norquay

Banff

Mt Rundle

Mt Cory

Vermillion Lakes

Sulphur Mtn

Spray River

SEE "VICINITY OF BANFF" MAP

BOW VALLEY PARKWAY

FIRESIDE PICNIC AREA

MULESHOE PICNIC AREA

TRANSCANADA HIGHWAY

SUNSHINE VILLAGE RD

BOURGEAU LAKE

To Sunshine Village

0   3 mi

0   3 km

the notorious Fort Whoop-Up in Lethbridge. During its heady days, five mines were operating, extracting not silver but ore rich in copper and lead. The town had a half-dozen hotels, four or five stores, two real-estate offices, and a station on the transcontinental rail line when its demise began. Two men, named Patton and Pettigrew, salted their mine with gold and silver ore to attract investors. After selling 2,000 shares at $5 each, they vanished, leaving investors with a useless mine. Investment in the town ceased, mines closed, and the people left. Only one man refused to leave. His name was James Smith, but he was known to everyone as Joe. In 1887, when Silver City came under the jurisdiction of the National Parks Service, Joe was allowed to remain. He did so and was friendly to everyone, including Stoney Indians, Father Albert Lacombe (who occasionally stopped by), well-known Banff guide Tom Wilson, and of course to the animals who grazed around his cabin. By 1926, he was unable to trap or hunt due to failing eyesight, and many people tried to persuade him to leave. It wasn't until 1937 that he finally moved to a Calgary retirement home, where he died soon after.

Castle Mountain to Lake Louise

After you leave the former site of Silver City, the aptly named Castle Mountain comes into view. It's one of the park's most recognizable peaks and most interesting geographical features. The mountain consists of very old rock (approximately 500 million years old) sitting atop much younger rock (a mere 200 million years old). This unusual situation occurred as the mountains were forced upward by pressure below the earth's surface, thrusting the older rock up and over the younger rock in places.

The road skirts the base of the mountain, passes Castle Mountain Village (which has gas, food, and accommodations), and climbs a small hill to Storm Mountain Viewpoint, which provides more stunning views and a picnic area. The next commercial facility is **Baker Creek Chalets and Bistro,** an excellent spot for a meal. Then it's on to another viewpoint at Morant's Curve, from where Temple Mountain is visible.

est, compared to 50 meters (165 feet) at Maligne—but the catwalk that leads to the lower falls has been built through the depths of the canyon rather than along its lip, making it seem just as spectacular. The lower falls are one km (.6 mile) from Johnston Canyon Resort, while the equally spectacular upper falls are a further 1.6 km (one mile) upstream. Beyond this point are the **Ink Pots,** mineral springs whose sediments reflect sunlight, producing a brilliant aqua color. While in the canyon, look for nesting great gray owls and black swifts.

Silver City

At the west end of **Moose Meadows,** a small plaque marks the site of Silver City. At its peak this boomtown had a population of 2,000, making it bigger than Calgary at the time. The city was founded by John Healy, who also founded

After passing another picnic area and a chunk of Precambrian shield, the road rejoins the Trans-Canada Highway at Lake Louise.

HIKES THAT START NEAR TOWN

After experiencing the international thrills of Banff Avenue, most people will want to see the *real* park, which is, after all, the reason that millions of visitors flock here, thousands take low-paying jobs just to stay here, and others become so severely addicted that they start families and live happily ever after here.

Although many landmarks can be seen from the roadside, to really experience the park's personality you'll need to go for a hike. One of the best things about Banff's 80-odd hiking trails is the variety. From short interpretive walks originating in town to easy hikes rewarded by spectacular vistas to myriad overnight backcountry

Mount Louis, as seen from a high ridge that is traversed between Cory and Edith Passes

© ANDREW HEMPSTEAD

opportunities, Banff's trails offer something for everyone.

Before attempting any hikes, visit the **Banff Visitor Centre** (224 Banff Ave., 403/762-1550), where staff can advise you on the condition of trails and closures. If you are planning an overnight trip into the backcountry, you *must* pick up a Wilderness Pass from either of the park information centers before heading out; $8 per person per night.

Fenland

- Length: 2 km/1.2 miles (30 minutes) round-trip
- Elevation gain: none
- Rating: easy
- Trailhead: Forty Mile Creek Picnic Area, Mount Norquay Road, 300 meters (.2 mile) north of the rail crossing

If you've just arrived in town, this short interpretive trail provides an excellent introduction to the Bow Valley ecosystem. A brochure, available at the trailhead, explains the various stages in the transition between wetland and floodplain spruce forest, visible as you progress around the loop. This fen environment is prime habitat for many species of birds. The work of beavers can be seen along the trail, and elk are here during winter. This trail is also a popular shortcut for joggers and cyclists heading for Vermilion Lakes.

Tunnel Mountain

- Length: 2.3 km/1.4 miles (30–60 minutes) one-way
- Elevation gain: 300 meters/990 feet
- Rating: easy/moderate
- Trailhead: St. Julien Road, 350 meters (.2 mile) south of Wolf Street

Accessible from town, this short hike is an easy climb to one of the park's lower peaks. It ascends the western flank of Tunnel Mountain through a forest of lodgepole pine, switchbacking past some viewpoints before reaching a ridge just below the summit. Here the trail turns northward, climbing through a forest of Douglas fir to the summit (which is partially treed, preventing 360-degree views).

Bow River/Hoodoos

- Length: 4.8 km/3 miles (60–90 minutes) one-way
- Elevation gain: minimal
- Rating: easy
- Trailhead: Bow River Viewpoint, Tunnel Mountain Drive

From a viewpoint famous for the Fairmont Banff Springs outlook, the trail descends to the Bow River, passing under the sheer east face of Tunnel Mountain. It then follows the river a short distance before climbing into a meadow where deer and elk often graze. From this perspective the north face of Mount Rundle is particularly imposing. As the trail climbs you'll hear the traffic on Tunnel Mountain Road long before you see it. The trail ends at hoodoos, strange limestone-and-gravel columns jutting mysteriously out of the forest. An alternative to returning the same way is to catch the Banff Transit bus from Tunnel Mountain Campgrounds. It leaves every half hour; the trip costs $2.

Sundance Canyon

- Length: 4.4 km/2.7 miles (90 minutes) one-way
- Elevation gain: 100 meters/330 feet
- Rating: easy
- Trailhead: Cave and Basin National Historic Site

Sundance Canyon is a rewarding destination across the river from downtown. Unfortunately, the first three km (1.9 miles) are along a paved road that is closed to traffic (but not bikes) and hard on your soles. Occasional glimpses of the Sawback Range are afforded by breaks in the forest. The road ends at a shaded picnic area from where the 2.4-km (1.5-mile) Sundance Loop begins. Sundance Creek was once a larger river whose upper drainage basin was diverted by glacial action. Its powerful waters have eroded into the soft bedrock, forming a spectacular overhanging canyon whose bed is strewn with large boulders that have tumbled in.

Spray River

- Length: 6 km/3.7 miles (two hours) one-way
- Elevation gain: 70 meters/230 feet
- Rating: easy/moderate
- Trailhead: From the Bow Falls parking lot, cross the Spray River and walk along Golf Course Road to behind the green of the first golf hole on the right-hand side of the road.

This trail follows one of the many fire roads in the park. It is not particularly interesting, but it's accessible from downtown Banff and makes a pleasant way to escape the crowds. From behind the green of the 15th hole on the Stanley Thompson 18, the trail heads uphill into the forest. It follows the Spray River closely—when not in sight the river can always be heard. For those so inclined, a river crossing one km (.6 mile) from the golf course allows for a shorter loop. Continuing south, the trail climbs a bluff for a good view of the Fairmont Banff Springs and Bow Valley. The return journey is straightforward with occasional views, ending at a locked gate behind the Fairmont Banff Springs, a short walk to Bow Falls.

For serious hikers this trail provides access to the park's rugged and remote southern reaches, but there's another interesting option involving this trail for keen day hikers. It involves arranging a lift to the trailhead of the Goat Creek hike in Kananaskis Country (see *Spray Valley Provincial Park* in the *Kananaskis Country* chapter). From this trailhead, it's 19 km/11.8 miles (six hours) one-way back to Banff down the Spray River watershed on a trail that drops 370 meters (1,210 feet) in elevation. The trail is most popular with mountain bikers and cross-country skiers.

Western Slope of Mount Rundle

- Length: 5.4 km/3.3 miles (two hours) one-way
- Elevation gain: 480 meters/1,755 feet
- Rating: moderate
- Trailhead: From the Bow Falls parking lot, cross the Spray River and walk along Golf Course Road to behind the green of the first golf hole on the right-hand side of the road.

At 2,950 meters (9,680 feet), Mount Rundle is one of the park's dominant peaks. Climbing to its summit is possible without ropes, but previous scrambling experience is advised. An alternative is to ascend the mountain's western slope along an easy-to-follow trail that ends just over 1,000 vertical meters (3,280 vertical feet) before the summit. The trail follows the Spray River Trail from Golf Course Road, branching off left after 700 meters (.4 mile). Climbing steadily, it breaks out of the enclosed forest after 2.5 km (1.6 miles). The trail ends in a gully from which the undefined route to the summit begins.

Stoney Squaw

- Length: 2.4-km/1.5-mile loop (one hour round-trip)
- Elevation gain: 180 meters/590 feet
- Rating: easy
- Trailhead: top of Mount Norquay Road, six km (3.7 miles) from town

Looking north along Banff Avenue, Stoney Squaw's 1,884-meter (6,180-foot) summit is dwarfed by Cascade Mountain, directly behind it. To get to the trailhead of a trail that leads to its easily reached summit, follow Mount Norquay Road to a parking lot in front of the resort's day lodge. Immediately to the right of the entrance, a small sign marks the trail. The narrow, slightly overgrown trail passes through a thick forest of lodgepole pine and spruce before breaking out into the open near the summit. The sweeping panorama includes Vermilion Lakes, the Bow Valley, Banff, Spray River Valley, Mount Rundle, Lake Minnewanka, and the imposing face of Cascade Mountain (2,998 meters/9,840 feet). The return trail follows the northwest slope of Stoney Squaw to an old ski run at the opposite end of the parking lot.

Cascade Amphitheatre

- Length: 6.6 km/4.1 miles (2–3 hours) one-way
- Elevation gain: 610 meters/2,000 feet
- Rating: moderate/difficult
- Trailhead: day lodge, top of Mount Norquay Road, six km (3.7 miles) from town

This enormous cirque and the subalpine meadows directly behind Cascade Mountain are one of the most rewarding destinations for hiking in the Banff area. The demanding trail begins by passing the day lodge, then skirting the base of several lifts, and following an old road to the floor of Forty Mile Valley. Keep right at all trail junctions. One km (.6 mile) after crossing Forty Mile Creek, the trail begins switchbacking up the western flank of Cascade Mountain through a forest of lodgepole pine. Along the way are breathtaking views of Mount Louis's sheer east face. After the trail levels off, it enters a magnificent U-shaped valley and the amphitheater begins to define itself. The trail becomes indistinct in the subalpine meadow, which is carpeted in colorful wildflowers during summer. Farther up the valley, vegetation thins out as boulder-strewn talus slopes cover the ground. If you sit still long enough on these rocks, marmots and pikas will slowly appear, emitting shrill whistles before disappearing again.

The most popular route to the summit of 2,998-meter (9,840-foot) Cascade Mountain is along the southern ridge of the amphitheater wall. It is a long scramble up scree slopes and is made more difficult by a false summit; it should be attempted only by experienced scramblers.

C Level Cirque

- Length: 4 km/2.5 miles (90 minutes) one-way
- Elevation gain: 455 meters/1,500 feet
- Rating: moderate
- Trailhead: Upper Bankhead Picnic Area, Lake Minnewanka Road, 3.5 km (2.2 miles) beyond the TransCanada Highway underpass

From a picnic area that sits on the site of an abandoned mining town, the trail climbs steadily through a forest of lodgepole pine, aspen, and spruce to a pile of tailings and broken-down concrete walls. Soon after is a panoramic view of Lake Minnewanka, then the trail reenters the forest before ending in a small cirque with views down the Bow Valley to Canmore and beyond. The cirque is carved into the eastern face of Cascade Mountain, where snow often lingers until July. When the snow melts, the lush soil is covered in a carpet of colorful wildflowers.

Aylmer Lookout

- Length: 12 km/7.5 miles (four hours) one-way
- Elevation gain: 810 meters/2,660 feet
- Rating: moderate/difficult

• Trailhead: Lake Minnewanka, Lake Minnewanka Road, 5.5 km (3.4 miles) beyond the TransCanada Highway underpass

The first eight-km (five-mile) stretch of this trail follows the northern shore of Lake Minnewanka from the day-use area to a junction. The right fork leads to a campground, while the left climbs steeply to the site of an old fire tower on top of an exposed ridge. The deep blue waters of Lake Minnewanka are visible, backed by the imposing peaks of Mount Girouard (2,995 meters/9,830 feet) and Mount Inglismaldie (2,964 meters/9,725 feet). Bighorn sheep often graze in this area. From here a trail forks left and continues climbing to the alpine tundra of Aylmer Pass.

HIKES BETWEEN BANFF AND LAKE LOUISE
Cory Pass
• Length: 5.8 km/3.6 miles (2.5 hours) one-way
• Elevation gain: 920 meters/3,020 feet
• Rating: moderate/difficult
• Trailhead: Fireside Picnic Area, Banff end of the Bow Valley Parkway

This strenuous hike has a rewarding objective—a magnificent view of dog-toothed Mount Louis. The towering slab of limestone rises more than 500 meters (1,640 feet) from the valley below. Just over one km (.6 mile) from the trailhead, the trail divides. The left fork climbs steeply across an open slope on an uneven ridge that it follows before ascending yet another steep slope to Cory Pass—a wild, windy, desolate area surrounded by jagged peaks dominated by Mount Louis. An alternative to returning along the same trail is continuing down into Gargoyle Valley, following the base of Mount Edith before ascending to Edith Pass and returning to the junction one km (.6 mile) from the picnic area. Total distance for this trip is 13 km (eight miles), a long day considering the steep climbs and descents involved.

Bourgeau Lake
• Length: 7.6 km/4.7 miles (2.5 hours) one-way
• Elevation gain: 730 meters/2,400 feet

• Rating: moderate
• Trailhead: signposted parking lot, TransCanada Highway, three km (1.9 miles) west of Sunshine Village Junction

This trail follows Wolverine Creek to a small subalpine lake nestled at the base of an impressive limestone amphitheater. Although the trail is moderately steep, plenty of distractions along the way are worthy of a stop (and rest). Across the Bow Valley, the Sawback Range is easy to distinguish. As the forest of lodgepole pine turns to spruce, the trail passes under the cliffs of Mount Bourgeau and crosses Wolverine Creek (below a spot where it tumbles photogenically over exposed bedrock). After strenuous switchbacks, the trail climbs into the cirque containing Bourgeau Lake. As you continue around the lake's rocky shore, you'll hear the colonies of noisy pikas, even if you don't see them.

Shadow Lake
• Length: 14.3 km/8.9 miles (4.5 hours) one-way
• Elevation gain: 440 meters/1,445 feet
• Rating: moderate
• Trailhead: Redearth Creek Parking Area, TransCanada Highway, 11 km (6.8 miles) west of Sunshine Village Junction

Shadow is one of the many impressive subalpine lakes along the Continental Divide and a popular base for a great variety of day trips. It follows the old Redearth fire road for 11 km (6.8 miles) before forking right and climbing into the forest. The campground is two km (1.2 miles) beyond this junction, and just 500 meters (.3 mile) farther is **Shadow Lake Lodge** (see *Accommodations* for details). The lake is nearly two km (1.2 miles) long, and from its southern shore trails lead to Ball Pass, Gibbon Pass, and Haiduk Lake.

Castle Lookout
• Length: 3.7 km/2.3 miles (90 minutes) one-way
• Elevation gain: 520 meters/1,700 feet
• Rating: moderate
• Trailhead: Bow Valley Parkway, five km (3.1 miles) northwest of Castle Junction

SUNSHINE MEADOWS

Sunshine Meadows, straddling the Continental Divide, is a unique and beautiful region of the Canadian Rockies. It's best known as home to Sunshine Village, a self-contained alpine resort accessible only by gondola from the valley floor. But for a few short months each summer, the area is clear of snow and becomes a wonderland for hiking. Large amounts of precipitation create a lush cover of vegetation—over 300 species of wildflowers alone have been recorded here.

From Sunshine Village, trails radiate across the alpine meadow, which is covered in a colorful carpet of fireweed, glacier lilies, mountain avens, white mountain heather, and forget-me-nots (the meadows are in full bloom late July to mid-August). The most popular destination is **Rock Isle Lake,** an easy 2.5-km (1.6-mile) jaunt from the upper village that crosses the Continental Divide while only gaining 100 meters (330 feet) of elevation. Mt. Assiniboine (3,618 meters/11,870 feet), known as the "Matterhorn of the Rockies," is easily distinguished to the southeast. Various viewpoints punctuate the descent to an observation point overlooking the lake. From here, options include a loop around Larix Lake

and a traverse along Standish Ridge. If the weather is cooperating, it won't matter which direction you head (so long as it's along a formed trail); you'll experience the Canadian Rockies in all their glory.

It's possible to walk the six-km (3.7-mile) restricted-access road up to the meadows, but a more practical alternative is to take the Sunshine Meadows Shuttle along a road closed to public traffic. This service is operated by **White Mountain Adventures** (403/678-4099 or 800/408-0005, www.whitemountainadventures.com). Through a June–September season, buses depart Banff (daily at 9 A.M.; adult $40, child $20 round-trip) and the Sunshine Village parking lot (daily at 9:30 A.M., 10:30 A.M., 11:30 A.M., and 1:30 P.M.; adult $20, child $10 round-trip). For $20 extra, you can explore the meadows with a naturalist, who will lead you through all the highlights. Advance reservations are required for both the bus and guided hike. To get to the base of the gondola from Banff, follow the TransCanada Highway nine km (5.6 miles) west to Sunshine Village Road, which continues a similar distance along Healy Creek to the Sunshine Village parking lot.

© ANDREW HEMPSTEAD

Rock Isle Lake

However you travel through the Bow Valley, you can't help but be impressed by Castle Mountain rising proudly from the forest floor. This trail takes you above the tree line on the mountain's west face to the site of Mount Eisenhower fire lookout, abandoned in the 1970s and burned in the 1980s. From the Bow Valley Parkway, the trail follows a wide pathway for 1.5 km (.9 mile) to an abandoned cabin in a forest of lodgepole pine and spruce. It then becomes narrower and steeper, switchbacking through a meadow before climbing through a narrow band of rock and leveling off near the lookout site. Magnificent panoramas of the Bow Valley spread out before you in both directions. Storm Mountain can be seen directly across the valley.

Rockbound Lake
- Length: 8.4 km/5.2 miles (2.5 hours) one-way
- Elevation gain: 760 meters/2,500 feet
- Rating: moderate/difficult
- Trailhead: Castle Junction, Bow Valley Parkway, 30 km (18.6 miles) west of Banff

This strenuous hike leads to a delightful little body of water tucked behind Castle Mountain. For the first five km (3.1 miles) the trail follows an old fire road along the southern flanks of Castle Mountain. Early in the season or after heavy rain, this section can be boggy. Glimpses of surrounding peaks ease the pain of the steady climb as the trail narrows. After eight km (five miles) you'll come to Tower Lake, backed by grassed slopes, which the trail skirts to the right before climbing a steep slope. From the ridge, Rockbound Lake comes into view, and the reason for its name immediately becomes apparent. A scramble up any of the nearby slopes will reward you with good views.

OTHER RECREATION
Mountain Biking
Whether you have your own bike or you rent one from the many bicycle shops in Banff or Lake Louise, cycling in the park is for everyone. The roads to Lake Minnewanka, Mount Norquay, through the golf course, and along the

Bow Valley Parkway are all popular routes. Several trails radiating from Banff and ending deep in the backcountry have been designated as bicycle trails. These include Sundance (3.7 km/2.3 miles one-way), Rundle Riverside to Canmore (15 km/9.3 miles one-way), and the Spray River Loop (via Goat Creek; 48 km/30 miles round-trip). Farther afield, other trails are at Redearth Creek, Lake Louise, and in the northeastern reaches of the park near Saskatchewan River Crossing. Before heading into the backcountry, pick up the *Trail Mountain Biking Guide* from the Banff or Lake Louise Visitor Centre. Riders are particularly susceptible to sudden bear encounters. Be alert and make loud noises when passing through heavy vegetation.

Bactrax (225 Bear St., 403/762-8177) and **Adventures Unlimited** (207 Caribou St., 403/762-4554) rent front- and full-suspension mountain bikes for $7–12 per hour and $25–48 per day. Rates include a helmet, lock, and biking map. Bactrax also offers mountain-bike tours, including to Vermilion Lakes and along Sundance Canyon. Tours cost $15 per person per hour.

Horseback Riding
Jim and Bill Brewster led Banff's first paying guests into the backcountry on horseback more than 100 years ago. Today visitors are still able to enjoy the park on this traditional form of transportation.

Warner Guiding & Outfitting (www.horseback.com) offers a great variety of trips. Their main office is downtown in the **Trail Rider Store** (132 Banff Ave., 403/762-4551), although trips depart from either **Martin's Stables** (403/762-2832), behind the recreation grounds on Birch Avenue, or **Banff Springs Corral** (403/762-2848), along Spray Avenue. One-hour rides are $30, two hours $54, three hours $73. Other day trips include the three-hour **Mountain Morning Breakfast Ride,** featuring a hearty breakfast along the trail (departs 9 A.M.; $76); **Explorer,** a seven-hour ride up the Spray River Valley (departs 9 A.M.; $140); and the **Evening Steak Fry,** a three-hour ride with a suitably western steak and baked bean dinner along the trail (departs 5 P.M.;

$76). Overnight trips to established backcountry camps and lodges are also available; rates begin at $402 including horse rental, all meals, and two nights' accommodation at Sundance Lodge.

White-Water Rafting and Canoeing

Anyone looking for white-water-rafting action will want to run the **Kicking Horse River,** which flows down the western slopes of the Canadian Rockies into British Columbia. Many operators provide transportation from Banff and Lake Louise (see *Golden* in the *Yoho National Park and Vicinity* chapter).

Rocky Mountain Raft Tours (403/762-3632) offers one-hour ($30) and two-hour ($45) float trips down the Bow River, beginning just below Bow Falls. No rapids are involved, so you'll stay dry.

On a quiet stretch of the Bow River, at the north end of Wolf Street, **Banff Canoe Rentals** (403/762-3632; May–Sept. daily 10 A.M.–7 P.M.) rents canoes for use on the river from where it's an easy paddle upstream to the Vermilion Lakes and Forty Mile Creek; $20 per hour or $50 for a full day of paddling.

Fishing and Boating

The finest fishing in the park is in Lake Minnewanka, where lake trout as large as 15 kg (33 lb.) have been caught. One way to ensure a good catch is through **Lake Minnewanka Boat Tours** (403/762-3473), which offers fishing trips in a heated cabin cruiser; trolling and downrigging are preferred methods of fishing the lake. A half-day's fishing (3.5 hours) is $240 for one or two persons. The company also rents small aluminum fishing boats with outboard motors for $32 for the first hour, then $12 for every extra hour.

The most experienced of local fishing guides is Dan Bell of **Upper Bow Fly Fishing** (403/760-7668, www.upperbowflyfishing.com). Bell has been fishing and guiding in the Banff area for more than 20 years and has represented Canada as a member of the National Fly-Fishing Team on multiple occasions. His purpose-built drift boats are perfect for chasing brown trout along the Bow River downstream from Banff, with regular stops made for fly-casting from the banks. He'll also take interested anglers to high alpine lakes

chasing cutthroat trout. Rates start at $200 per person for a half day on the river and include guiding, gear, and lessons.

Before fishing anywhere in the park you need a national park fishing license ($7 per week, $20 per year), available from the Banff and Lake Louise visitors centers and sport shops throughout the park.

Golfing

One of the world's most scenic golf courses, the **Banff Springs Golf Course,** spreads out along the Bow River between Mount Rundle and Tunnel Mountain. The first course was laid out here in 1911, but in 1928 Stanley Thompson was brought in by the CPR to redesign it into 18 holes and to build what was at the time North America's most expensive course. In 1989 the Tunnel Nine opened (along with a new clubhouse), creating today's 27-hole course.

Between 1997 and 1999 no expense was spared in rebuilding the entire original 18 holes and adding longer tees, while also reverting to Thompson's planned sequence of play, known now as the **Stanley Thompson 18.** The course is typically Thompson, taking advantage of natural contours and featuring elevated tees, wide fairways, treacherous fescue grass rough, and holes aligned to distant mountains. From the back markers it is 7,087 yards and plays to a par of 71. The course is not only breathtakingly beautiful, but it's also challenging for every level of golfer. Pick up a copy of the book *The World's Greatest Golf Holes,* and you'll see a picture of the fourth hole on the Rundle 9. It's a par three, over Devil's Cauldron 70 meters (230 feet) below, to a small green backed by the sheer face of Mount Rundle rising vertically more than 1,000 meters (3,280 feet) above the putting surface. Another unique feature of the course is the abundance of wildlife: there's always the chance of seeing elk feeding on the fairways, or coyotes, deer, or black bears scurrying across.

Greens fees (including cart and driving range privileges) are $195 for the Stanley Thompson 18 ($175 for Canadian residents and Fairmont guests). Rates are discounted to $135 in early June and reduced further through the first and

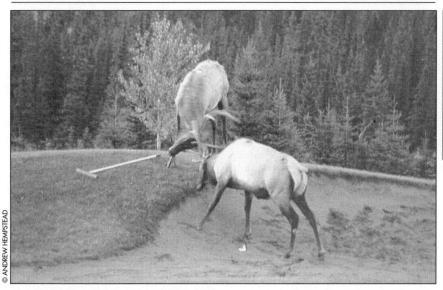

© ANDREW HEMPSTEAD

Please rake the bunkers when you've finished.

last months of operation, May and early October, to $95. The Tunnel 9 offers the same spectacular challenges as Thompson's original layout but lacks the history; nine holes cost $50–65 ($35–55 for Canadian residents and Fairmont guests), depending on the season. Free shuttle buses run from the Fairmont Banff Springs to the clubhouse. (The original 1911 clubhouse still stands, but it has been replaced by a modern, circular building in the heart of the course.) There you'll find club rentals ($40), three putting greens, a driving range, a pro shop, two chipping greens (one hidden up in the trees with surrounding bunkers), and a restaurant. Booking tee times well in advance is essential; call 403/762-6801.

WINTERTIME

From November till May, the entire park transforms itself into a winter playground covered in a blanket of snow. Of Alberta's six world-class winter resorts, three are in Banff National Park. Ski Banff @ Mount Norquay is a small but steep hill overlooking the town of Banff; Sunshine Village perches high in the mountains on the Con-

tinental Divide, catching more than its share of fluffy white powder; and Lake Louise, Canada's second-largest winter resort, spreads over four distinct mountain faces. Apart from an abundance of snow, the resorts have something else in common—spectacular views, which alone are worth the price of a lift ticket.

Other winter activities in the park include cross-country skiing, ice-skating, snowshoeing, dogsledding, and just relaxing. Crowds are nonexistent and hotels reduce rates by up to 70 percent (except Christmas holidays)—reason enough to venture into the mountains. Lift and lodging packages begin at $70 per person.

Ski Banff @ Norquay

Norquay (403/762-4421, www.banffnorquay.com) has two distinct faces—literally and figuratively. There are some great cruising runs and a well-respected ski school, but also the experts-only North American Chair (the one you can see from town), which opens up the famous double-black-diamond Upper Lone Pine run. Snowboarders congregate at a half pipe and terrain park. A magnificent post-and-beam day lodge nestled below the main runs is surrounded on one side by a wide deck that catches the afternoon sun, while holding a cafeteria, restaurant, and bar inside. Lift tickets are adult $52, senior $42, child $20; lift, lesson, and rental packages cost about the same. Hourly passes provide some flexibility (two hours $26, three hours $30, etc). A few runs are lit for night skiing and boarding on Friday evening; $24 adults, $22 seniors, $12 children. A shuttle bus makes pickups from Banff hotels for the short, six-km (3.7-mile) ride up to the resort; $5. The season at Norquay usually runs from early December through early April.

Sunshine Village

Sunshine Village (403/762-6500 or 877/542-2633, www.skibanff.com) has lots going for it—more than six meters (20 feet) of snow annually (no need for snowmaking up here), wide-open bowls, a season stretching for nearly 200 days (mid-Nov.–late May), skiing and boarding in two provinces, and the only slope-side accommodations in the park.

The resort has grown up a lot in the last decade as high-speed quads have replaced old chairlifts and opened up new terrain such as Goat's Eye Mountain, and the original gondola was replaced by what is reputed to be the world's fastest gondola. One of Canada's most infamous runs, Delirium Dive, drops off the northeast-facing slope of Lookout Mountain; to ski or board this up-to-50-degree run, you must be equipped with a transceiver, shovel, probe, and partner, but you'll have bragging rights that night at the bar (especially if you've descended the Bre-X line). Aside from Delirium Dive, the area is best known for its excellent beginner and intermediate terrain, which covers 60 percent of the mountain. The total vertical rise is 1,070 meters (3,510 feet), and the longest run (down to the lower parking lot) is eight km (five miles). Day passes are adult $63, senior $52, child $23, and those younger than 6 ride free. Four days of lift access and three nights' lodging at slopeside Sunshine Inn cost $440 per person in high season—an excellent deal. The inn has a restaurant, lounge, game room, and hot tub. Transportation from Banff, Canmore, or Lake Louise to the resort is $10 round-trip; check the website or inquire at major hotels for the timetable.

Rentals and Sales

Each resort has ski and snowboard rental and sales facilities, but getting your gear down in town is often easier. **Monod Sports** (129 Banff Ave., 403/762-4571) has been synonymous with Banff and the ski industry for more than 50 years, and while the **Rude Boys Snowboard Shop** (downstairs in the Sundance Mall, 215 Banff Ave., 403/762-8480) has only been around since the 1980s, it is *the* snowboarder hangout. Other shops with sales and rentals include **Abominable Ski & Sportswear** (229 Banff Ave., 403/762-2905), **Adventures Unlimited** (207 Caribou St., 403/762-4554), **Mountain Magic Equipment** (224 Bear St., 403/762-2591), **Ski Stop** (203 Bear St., 403/760-1650, as well as in the Fairmont Banff Springs, 403/762-5333), and **Snow Tips** (225 Bear St., 403/762-8177).

© ANDREW HEMPSTEAD

Chairlifts at Sunshine Village rise high above the treeline.

AN ABRIDGED HISTORY OF SKIING IN BANFF NATIONAL PARK

Banff National Park is busiest during summer, but for many visitors from outside North America—especially Europeans and Australians—it is the winter season that they know Banff for. Regardless of its repute, and although winter (Dec.–Apr.) is considered "low season," the park remains busy as ski enthusiasts from around the world gather for world-class skiing and boarding. It hasn't always been this way. As recently as the 1960s, many lodgings—including the famous Fairmont Banff Springs—were open only for the summer season.

With winter tourism nonexistent, the first skiers were Banff locals, who would climb local peaks under their own steam. Due mostly to its handy location close to town, a popular spot was **Mount Norquay,** which was skied as early as the 1920s. In 1948, Canada's first chairlift was installed on the mountain's eastern slopes. In the ensuing years, newer and faster lifts have created a convenient getaway that fulfills the needs of locals and visitors alike, who can buzz up for an afternoon of skiing or boarding on slopes that suit all levels of proficiency.

The first people to ski the **Sunshine Meadows** were two local men, Cliff White and Cyril Paris, who became lost in the spring of 1929 and returned to Banff with stories of deep snow and ideal slopes for skiing. In the following years, a primitive cabin was used as a base for overnight ski trips in the area. In 1938 the Canadian National Ski Championships were held here, and in 1942 a portable lift was constructed. The White family was synonymous with the Sunshine area for many years, running the lodge and ski area while Brewster buses negotiated the steep, narrow road that led to the meadows. In 1980 a gondola was installed to whisk skiers and snowboarders six km (3.7 miles) from the valley floor to the alpine village.

The best known of Banff's three resorts is **Lake Louise,** an hour's drive north of town but still within park boundaries. This part of the park also attracted early interest from local skiers, beginning in 1930 when Cliff White and Cyril Paris built a small ski chalet in the Skoki Valley (now operating as Skoki Lodge). The remoteness of this hut turned out to be impractical, so another was built, closer to the road. In 1954, a crude lift was constructed up Larch Mountain from the chalet. The lift had only just begun operation when a young Englishman, Norman Watson (known as the "Barmy Baronet"), who had inherited a fortune, saw the potential for a world-class alpine resort and made the completion of his dream a lifelong obsession. Over the years more lifts were constructed and two runs—Olympic Men's Downhill and Olympic Ladies' Downhill—were cut in anticipation of a successful bid for the 1968 Winter Olympics (the bid failed).

Basic packages—skis, poles, and boots—are $20–25 per day, while high-performance packages range $30–45. Snowboards and boots rent for $20–40 per day.

Switching Gear (718 10th St., 403/678-1992), down the valley from Banff in nearby Canmore, has an excellent selection of used ski and snowboard equipment, as well as winter clothing at very reasonable prices.

Cross-Country Skiing

No better way of experiencing the park's winter delights exists than skiing through the landscape on cross-country skis. Many summer hiking trails are groomed for winter travel. The most popular areas near town are Johnson Lake, Golf Course Road, Spray River, Sundance Canyon, and upstream from the canoe docks. The booklet *Cross-country Skiing—Nordic Trails in Banff National Park* is available for $1 from the Banff Visitor Centre. Weather forecasts (403/762-2088) are posted at both centers.

Rental packages are available from **Performance Sports** (208 Bear St., 403/762-8222), **Snowtips** (225 Bear St., 403/762-8177), and **Mountain Magic Equipment** (224 Bear St., 403/762-2591). Expect to pay $12–20 per day. **White Mountain Adventures** (403/678-4099) offers lessons for $50 per person, as well as an ice walk through a frozen Johnston Canyon.

Ice-Skating

Skating rinks are located on the **Bow River** just up from Central Park and on the golf course side of the **Fairmont Banff Springs.** The latter rink is lit after dark, and a raging fire is built beside it—the perfect place to enjoy a hot chocolate. Early in the season (check conditions first), skating is possible on **Vermilion Lakes** and **Johnson Lake.** Rent skates from the **Ski Stop** (Fairmont Banff Springs, 403/762-5333) for $5 per hour.

Sleigh Rides

Warner Guiding and Outfitting offers sleigh rides on the frozen Bow River throughout winter. For reservations, call 403/762-4551 or stop by the Trail Rider Store (132 Banff Ave.; $22 per person).

Other Winter Activities

Beyond the skating rink below the Fairmont Banff Springs is an unofficial toboggan run; ask at your hotel for sleds or rent them from **The Ski Stop,** in the Fairmont Banff Springs; $5 per hour.

Go ice-fishing December–April with **Banff Fishing Unlimited** (403/762-4936). Winter fishing is prohibited in Banff National Park, so this company will provide transportation to a heated hut on Spray Lake (Kananaskis Country) along with instruction in jigging for lake trout.

Anyone interested in **ice climbing** must register at the national park desk in the Banff Visitor Centre or call 403/762-1550. The world-famous (if you're an ice climber) Terminator is just outside the park boundary.

If none of these activities appeal to you, head to **Upper Hot Springs** (403/762-1515; daily 10 A.M.–10 P.M.; $7.50) for a relaxing soak.

Camping might not be everyone's idea of a winter holiday, but one section of **Tunnel Mountain Campground** remains open year-round.

INDOOR RECREATION

Fitness and Swimming Facilities

Many of Banff's bigger hotels have fitness rooms, and some have indoor pools. A popular place to swim and work out is in the **Sally Borden Recreation Facility** (Banff Centre, St. Julien Road,

403/762-6450; daily 6:30 A.M.–11 P.M.), which holds a wide range of fitness facilities and a 25-meter-long heated pool. General admission is $9.50, or pay $4 to swim only. **Mountain Magic Equipment,** one block off the main drag (224 Bear St., 403/762-2591), has climbing and bouldering walls (free) with instruction and gear rentals offered for a reasonable price.

Willow Stream

This luxurious spa facility in the Fairmont Banff Springs (403/762-2211; daily 6 A.M.–10 P.M.) is the place to pamper yourself. Opened in 1995 at a cost of $12 million, it sprawls over two levels and 3,000 square meters (.7 acres) of a private corner of the hotel. The epicenter of the facility is a circular mineral pool capped by a high glass-topped ceiling and ringed by floor-to-ceiling windows on one side and on the other by hot tubs fed by cascading waterfalls of varying temperatures. Other features include outdoor salt-water hot tubs, private solariums, steam rooms, luxurious bathrooms, a café featuring light meals, and separate male and female lounges complete with fireplaces and complimentary drinks and snacks. Numerous other services are offered, including facials, body wraps, massage therapy, salon services, and hydrotherapy. Entry to Willow Stream is included in some package rates for guests at the hotel. General admission is $69 per day (book in advance), which includes the use of a locker and spa attire, with almost 100 services available at additional cost (most of these include general admission, so, for example, you can spend the day at Willow Stream and receive a one-hour massage for $139).

Other Indoor Recreation

Fairmont Banff Springs (403/762-2211) has a four-lane, five-pin bowling center; games are $3.75 per person. The **Lux Cinema Centre** (229 Bear St., 403/762-8595) screens new releases for $10 ($7 on Tuesday).

Banff's only water slide is in the **Douglas Fir Resort** (Tunnel Mountain Dr., 403/762-5591; Mon.–Fri. 4–9:30 P.M., Sat.–Sun. 10 A.M.–9:30 P.M.). The two slides are indoors, and the admission price of $7.50 (free for kids younger than age 5) includes use of a hot tub and exercise room.

NIGHTLIFE

Like resort towns around the world, Banff has a deserved reputation as a party town, especially among seasonal workers, the après ski crowd, and young Calgarians. Crowds seem to spread out, with no particular bar being more popular than another or being a place where you can mingle with fellow travelers. Given the location and vacation vibe, drink prices are as high as you may expect, with attitude thrown in for free.

Banff is a nonsmoking town, with a couple of exceptions that are noted below. Also note that the RCMP (police) patrol Banff all night, promptly arresting anyone who even looks like trouble, including anyone drunk or drinking on the streets.

Bars

Wild Bill's (upstairs at 201 Banff Ave., 403/762-0333) is named for Banff guide Bill Peyto and is truly legendary. This frontier-style venue attracts the biggest and best bands of any Banff venue, with bookings that vary from local faves to washed up rockers such as Nazareth; as a general rule, expect alternative music or underground country early in the week and better-known rock or pop Thursday–Sunday. Across the road, the **Maple Leaf Grille** (137 Banff Ave., 403/760-7680) has a stylish space set aside as a bar. The **Barbary Coast** (119 Banff Ave., 403/762-4616) serves up beer and more in a clean, casual atmosphere that is as friendly as it gets in Banff. Across the road from Wild Bill's is the **Rose and Crown** (202 Banff Ave., 403/762-2121), serving British beers and hearty pub fare. It also features a rooftop patio and rock-and-roll bands a few nights a week, but there's not much room for dancing. Also down the main drag is **Tommy's** (120 Banff Ave., 403/762-8888), a perennial favorite for young seasonal workers and those who once were who are now locals.

Away from busy Banff Avenue is **Melissa's** (218 Lynx St., 403/762-5776), which is a long-time favorite drinking hole for locals. It has a

small outdoor patio, a long evening happy hour, a pool table, and multiple TVs. From "Mel's," cut down Bear Street to reach **Saltlik** (221 Bear St., 403/762-2467), best known as an upscale (and upstairs) steakhouse. At street level, an upscale lounge opens to a street-side patio. Around the corner, the **St. James Gate Olde Irish Pub** (207 Wolf St., 403/762-9355) is a large Irish-style bar with a reputation for excellent British-style meals and occasional appearances by Celtic bands. In the vicinity, **Johnny Ray's** (229 Bear St., 403/762-5955) is far enough from Banff Avenue—one block—that most visitors miss it—which in turn makes it popular with older locals ("older" being relative to Banff and meaning over 20).

Hotel Hangouts

Many Banff hotels have lounges open to guests and nonguests alike. They are generally quieter than the bars listed previously and often offer abbreviated menus from adjacent restaurants. For old-world atmosphere, nothing in town comes close to matching the **Sir William Wallace Room,** in the Fairmont Banff Springs (403/762-2211; daily 4 P.M.–midnight). The regal surroundings—and a quirk in the smoking bylaw—make it the perfect place to purchase a premium Cuban cigar to go with your martini. If you want to enjoy a drink in the park's landmark hotel without sucking in secondhand smoke, walk through to the Mezzanine Level **Rundle Lounge** (Fairmont Banff Springs, 403/762-2211; daily noon–1 A.M.), an open space with views extending to the golf course. Below the hotel is the **Waldhaus Pub** (Fairmont Banff Springs, 403/762-2211; daily from 4 P.M.). It has the best deck in town, but it's mainly the haunt of locals coming off the golf course or savvy visitors (such as those who've read this book).

Downtown, the **Mount Royal Hotel** (corner of Banff Ave. and Caribou St., 403/762-3331) has a small lounge off the lobby, while below, accessed from farther up Banff Avenue, is the **Buffalo Paddock** (138 Banff Ave., 403/762-3331), with pool tables. At the opposite end of the style scale is the lounge in the **Voyager Inn** (555 Banff Ave., 403/762-3301), which is worth listing for the fact that it has the cheapest beer in town and drink specials every night (and a liquor store with cheaper prices than downtown). Just past the Voyager Inn is **Bumpers** (603 Banff Ave., 403/762-2622), a steakhouse with a small bar and pool table in a cozy upstairs loft.

Nightclubs

Banff has two nightclubs. Cavernous **Aurora** (downstairs in the Clock Tower Mall at 110 Banff Ave., 403/760-5300) was formerly an infamous gathering place known as Silver City, but renovations in the late 1990s added some class to Banff's clubbing scene. It's respectable early in the evening but becomes one obnoxiously loud, overpriced smoky pickup joint after midnight. The other option is **Hoo Doos** (at 137 Banff Ave. but enter from Caribou St., 403/762-8434), a stylish setup with similar city-like surroundings.

SHOPPING

It may seem a little strange, but city folk from Calgary actually drive into Banff National Park to shop for clothes. This reflects the number of clothing shops in Banff rather than a lack of choice in one of Canada's largest cities.

Canadiana and Clothing

Few companies in the world were as responsible for the development of a country as was the **Hudson's Bay Company** (HBC) in Canada. Founded in 1670, the HBC established trading posts throughout western Canada, many of which attracted settlers, forming the nucleus for towns and cities that survive today, including Alberta's capital, Edmonton. HBC stores continue their traditional role of providing a wide range of goods, in towns big and small across the country. In Banff, the HBC store is at 125 Banff Ave. (403/762-5525).

Another Canadian store, this one famous for its fleeces, sweaters, leather goods, and as supplier to the Canadian Olympic teams, is **Roots** (227 Banff Ave., 403/762-9434). For belts, buckles, and boots, check out the **Trail Rider Store** (132 Banff Ave., 403/762-4551). Pick up your Cana-

© ANDREW HEMPSTEAD

Look for the totem pole in front of the Indian Trading Post.

dian-made Tilley Hat and other Tilley Endurables from **Piccatilley Square,** on the main floor of the Cascade Plaza (317 Banff Ave., 403/762-0302). Check out the **Rude Boys** (215 Banff Ave., 403/762-8480), a snowboard and skate shop downstairs in the Sundance Mall, but don't expect to find anything for your grandparents.

Camping and Outdoor Gear

Inexpensive camping equipment and supplies can be found in **Home Hardware** (221 Bear St., 403/762-2080) and in the low-ceilinged downstairs section of the **Hudson's Bay Company** (125 Banff Ave., 403/762-5525). More specialized needs are catered to at **Mountain Magic Equipment** (224 Bear St., 403/762-2591). The store stocks a large range of top-quality outdoor and survival gear (including climbing equipment) and rents tents ($20 per day), sleeping bags ($12), backpacks ($10), and boots ($10). Mountain Magic Equipment also sells and repairs all types of bikes.

One of the best places to shop for outdoor apparel is locally owned **Monod Sports** (129 Banff Ave., 403/762-4571).

Gifts and Galleries

Banff's numerous galleries display the work of mostly Canadian artists. **Canada House Gallery** (201 Bear St., 403/762-3757) features a wide selection of Canadian landscape and wildlife works and native art. The **Quest Gallery** (105 Banff Ave., 403/762-2722) offers a diverse range of affordable Canadian paintings and crafts as well as more exotic pieces such as mammoth tusks from prehistoric times and Inuit carvings from Nunavut. Across the Bow River from downtown, browse through traditional native arts and crafts at the **Indian Trading Post** (1 Birch Ave., 403/762-2456).

FESTIVALS AND EVENTS

Spring

Most of the major spring events take place at local winter resorts, including a variety of snowboard competitions that make for great spectator viewing. At Lake Louise a half pipe and jump are constructed right in front of the day lodge for this specific purpose. One long-running spring event is the **Slush Cup,** which takes place at Sunshine Village in late May. Events include kamikaze skiers and boarders who attempt to jump an ice-cold pit of water. While winter enthusiasts are at higher elevations, swooshing down the slopes of some of North America's latest-closing resorts, late spring sees the Banff Springs golf course open for the season.

During the second week of June, the **Banff Television Festival** (403/678-1216, www.banfftvfest.com) attracts the world's best television directors, producers, writers, and even actors for meetings, workshops, and awards, with many show screenings open to the public.

Summer

Summer is a time of hiking and camping, so festivals are few and far between. The main event is the **Banff Arts Festival** (403/762-6214 or 800/413-8368, www.banffcentre.ca), a three-

week (mid-July–early Aug.) extravaganza presented by professional artists studying at the Banff Centre. They perform dance, drama, opera, and jazz for the public at locations around town. Look for details in the *Crag and Canyon.*

On July 1, Banff celebrates **Canada Day** with a pancake breakfast, a parade down Banff Avenue, and then an afternoon of fun and frivolity in Central Park that includes events such as a stupid pet tricks competition.

Each summer the national park staff presents an extensive **Park Interpretive Program** at locations in town and throughout the park, including downstairs in the visitors center daily at 8:30 P.M. All programs are free and include guided hikes, nature tours, slide shows, campfire talks, and lectures. For details, consult *The Mountain Guide,* available at the Banff Visitor Centre (403/762-1550), or look for postings on campground bulletin boards.

Fall

Fall is the park's quietest season, but busiest in terms of festivals and events. First of the fall events, on the last Saturday in September, **Melissa's Mini-Marathon** attracts more than 2,000 runners in 3-, 10-, and 22-km races. The **International Banff Springs Wine and Food Festival** is hosted by the Fairmont Banff Springs at the end of October. To encourage tourism during the quietest time of the year, **Winterstart** (Nov.–mid-Dec.) features cheap lodging and a host of fun events. This coincides with the opening of lifts at the park's three winter resorts beginning in mid-November.

One of the year's biggest events is the **Banff Mountain Film Festival,** held on the first weekend of November. Mountain-adventure filmmakers from around the world submit films to be judged by a select committee. Films are then shown throughout the weekend to an enthusiastic crowd of thousands. Exhibits and seminars are also presented, and top climbers and mountaineers from around the world are invited as guest speakers.

Tickets to the Banff Mountain Film Festival go on sale one year in advance and sell out in advance. Tickets for daytime shows start at $40 (for up to 10 films). Night shows are from $30, and all-weekend passes cost around $140 (weekend passes with two nights' accommodations and breakfasts start at a reasonable $250). Films are shown in the two theaters of the Banff Centre. For more information, contact the festival office (403/762-6675); for tickets, call the Banff Centre box office (403/762-6301 or 800/413-8368, www.banffcentre.ca). If you miss the actual festival, it hits the road on the Best of the Festival World Tour. Look for it in your town, or check out the listed website for venues and dates.

Starting in the days leading up to the film festival, then running in conjunction with it, is the **Banff Mountain Book Festival,** which showcases the work of publishers, writers, and photographers whose work revolves around the world's great mountain ranges. Tickets can be bought to individual events ($15–30), or there's a Book Festival Pass and a pass combining both festivals.

Winter

By mid-December lifts at all local winter resorts are open. **Santa Claus** makes an appearance on Banff Avenue at noon on the last Saturday in November; if you miss him there, he usually goes skiing at each of the local resorts on Christmas Day. Events at the resorts continue throughout the long winter season, among them **World Cup Downhill** skiing at Lake Louise in late November. The **Banff/Lake Louise Winter Festival** is a 10-day celebration at the end of January that has been a part of Banff's history since 1917. Look for ice sculpting on the frozen lake in front of the Chateau Lake Louise, the Lake Louise Loppet, barn dancing, and the Town Party.

Accommodations and Camping

Finding a room in Banff National Park in summer is nearly as hard as trying to justify its price. By late afternoon just about every room and campsite in the park will be occupied, and basic hotel rooms begin at around $100. Fortunately, many alternatives are available. Rooms in private homes begin at around $50 s, $60 d. HI–Banff Alpine Centre has dormitory-style accommodations for around $30 per person per night. Bungalows or cabins can be rented, which can be cost-effective for families or small groups. Approximately 2,400 campsites in 13 campgrounds accommodate campers. Wherever you decide to stay, it is vital to book well ahead during summer and the Christmas holidays. The park's off-season is October–May, and hotels offer huge rate reductions during this period. Shop around and you'll find many bargains.

All rates quoted are for a standard room in the high season (June–September).

Reservation Services

Banff Central Reservations (403/277-7669 or 877/542-2633, www.banffreservations.com) is tied in with Sunshine Village but has been providing an excellent booking and reservation service for many years. The local tourism association, the **Banff/Lake Louise Tourism Bureau,** doesn't make bookings, but its website (www.banff lakelouise.com) has detailed listings of all private homes registered to take guests.

IN AND AROUND THE TOWN OF BANFF

Banff has a few accommodations right downtown, but most are strung out along Banff Avenue, an easy walk from the shopping and dining precinct. Nearby Tunnel Mountain is also home to a cluster of accommodations.

Under $50

The only beds in town less than $50 are in dormitories, and therefore, although rates are well less than $50, this is a per-person rate.

HI–Banff Alpine Centre (403/762-4123) is just off Tunnel Mountain Road three km (1.9 miles) from downtown. This large, modern hostel sleeps 216 in small two-, four-, and six-bed dormitory rooms. The large lounge area has a fireplace, and other facilities include a recreation room, public Internet access, bike and ski/snowboard workshop, large kitchen, self-service café/bar, and laundry. In summer, members of Hostelling International pay $29 per person per night (nonmembers $33) for a dorm bed or $83 s or d ($91 for nonmembers) in a private room. The rest of the year, dorm beds are $22 (nonmembers $26) and private rooms $69 s or d (nonmembers $77). During July and August, reserve at least one month in advance to be assured of a bed. The hostel is open all day, but check-in isn't until 3 P.M. To get there from town, ride the Banff Transit bus ($2), which passes the hostel twice an hour during summer. The rest of the year the only transportation is by cab, about $6 from the bus depot. The central reservations line for the Banff Alpine Centre (and all other Hostelling International properties in the Canadian Rockies) is at 403/760-7580 or 866/762-4122, or book online at www.hihostels.ca.

A one-time hospital, the **Y Mountain Lodge** (102 Spray Ave., 403/762-3560 or 800/813-4138, www.ymountainlodge.com) has undergone massive renovations to create an excellent, centrally located choice for budget travelers. Facilities include the casual Sundance Bistro (7 A.M.–9 P.M.), a laundry facility, and the Great Room, a huge living area where the centerpiece is a massive stone fireplace with writing desks and shelves stocked with books scattered throughout. A bed in the dormitory is $31 per person, a private room that shares bathroom facilities is $70 s or d, and an en suite is $90–105 s or d. These rates are reduced outside of summer.

Along the main strip of accommodations and a 10-minute walk to downtown is **Samesun Banff** (449 Banff Ave., 403/762-5521 or 877/562-2783, www.samesun.com). As converted motel rooms, each small dormitory has its own bathroom. Guest amenities include a hot tub, sauna, large communal kitchen, game room with a pool table, TV room, activities desk, bike rentals, courtyard, and laundry. Dorm beds are $31 per person, with a number of private double rooms with kitchenette for $89 s or d.

$50–100

Accommodations in this price range are limited to private rooms at the three backpacker lodges

(above) and at a few bed-and-breakfasts. The best value of these is **Mountain View B&B** (347 Grizzly St., 403/760-9353; May–Sept.; $80 s or d), on a quiet residential street three blocks from the heart of downtown. The two guest rooms are simply furnished, each with a double bed, TV, sink, and bar fridge. They share a bathroom and a common area that includes basic cooking facilities (microwave, toaster, kettle) and opens to a private deck. Off-street parking and a light breakfast round out this excellent choice.

Mrs. Cowan has been offering budget accommodation at the 1926 **Tan-Y-Bryn** (118 Otter St., 403/762-3696) residence for many years. Although furnishings are sparse at best and bathrooms shared, the price is unequaled in town: $50–65 s, $55–75 d includes a light breakfast.

$100–150

Blue Mountain Lodge (137 Muskrat St., 403/762-5134, www.bluemtnlodge.com; $105 s, $119–149 d) is a rambling, older-style lodge with 10 guest rooms, each with a private bath, TV, and telephone. The Trapper's Cabin room is the most expensive, but the gabled ceiling, walls decorated with snowshoes and bearskin, and an electric fireplace create a funky, mountain feel. All guests have use of shared kitchen facilities, a lounge, and Internet access while enjoying an expansive cold buffet breakfast to set you up for a day of hiking.

At the lower end of this price range, **Banff B&B** (440 Muskrat St., 403/762-8806, www.banffbb.com; $125 s or d) is a solid choice for traditional bed-and-breakfast accommodation. The owners have created a home-away-from-home atmosphere in a modern house along a residential street just a short walk from Banff Avenue.

The eight guest rooms at the **Elkhorn Lodge** (124 Spray Ave., 403/762-2299 or 877/818-8488) are nothing special, but travelers on a budget who aren't fans of bed-and-breakfasts will find this older lodge suitable. The four small sleeping rooms are $110 s or d, while larger rooms with fridges are $165. It's halfway up the hill to the Fairmont Banff Springs.

At the far end of the motel strip, the **Banff Voyager Inn** (555 Banff Ave., 403/762-3301 or 800/879-1991, www.banffvoyagerinn.com; $130–170 s or d) sells the least expensive motel rooms in town. The $130 standard rooms face a wall; for $5 extra you can book a superior room, although the word "superior" is used very loosely. The inn also has a year-round outdoor swimming pool, a restaurant, a dimly lit lounge bar, and a liquor store, which you'll want to visit if a late-night party gets going in the room next to yours.

Bumper's Inn is at the far end of the motel strip (603 Banff Ave., 403/762-3386 or 800/661-3518, www.bumpersinn.com). The property is best known for its steakhouse, but behind the restaurant are 39 older-style rooms facing a courtyard for $145 s or d (from $85 in winter).

Two blocks off Banff Avenue, the **Homestead Inn** (217 Lynx St., 403/762-4471 or 800/661-1021, www.homesteadinnbanff.com) is a lot closer to downtown than the other motel properties described in this price range. It's a fairly basic hostelry with a faux Tudor exterior and 27 guest rooms. High-season rates are $140–150 s or d, discounted well below $100 outside of summer.

$150–200

Dating to 1917, **M** **Tarry-A-While** (117 Grizzly St., 403/762-0462, www.tarry.ca) was built for one of the Canadian Rockies' most famous residents, Mary Schäffer, by her outfitter husband Billy Warren. After it escaped demolition in the 1980s, the most recent owners opened the doors to guests, allowing a lucky few to soak up mountain heritage in its most pure form. Guests choose from three rooms, each with its own character. The simply furnished Billy Warren Room is particularly appealing. It features fir-paneled walls, a solid pine bed, and a clawfoot tub in the en suite bathroom. High season (mid-May–mid-Oct.) rates of $150–175 s or d include an expansive breakfast spread and use of two sitting rooms piled high with local literature.

Some of Banff's private residences have cabins for rent. One of the reasons that **M** **Country Cabin Bed & Breakfast** (419 Beaver St., 403/762-3591, www.banffmountaincountry.com

/cabin) is the best of these is the quiet location off busy Banff Avenue but still within easy walking distance of downtown. The log cabin has a separate bedroom, a full bathroom with log and tile features surrounding a jetted tub, and a living area equipped with a fold-out futon and a TV/VCR combo. If you don't feel like dining downtown, you can cook up a storm on the barbecue supplied. Summer rates of $150 s or d, $85 the rest of the year, include a Continental breakfast delivered to your door.

The rooms at the **Banff Inn** (501 Banff Ave., 403/762-8844 or 800/667-1464, www.banffinn.com; $150–170 s or d) are no-frills modern in appearance. Each of the 99 rooms has a log-trimmed balcony, and the facade is Rundlestone (quarried locally and named for Mount Rundle).

The days of Banff motel rooms for less than $100 disappeared in 2001 when bulldozers took to the town's last remaining park-at-your-door motel, the **Spruce Grove Inn** (545 Banff Ave.), now replaced by a modern mountain-style lodge of the same name. Rooms are spacious and a relatively good value at $165 s or d (upgrade to a king bed for $175 s or d). Make reservations and check in at the adjacent Banff Voyager Inn (403/762-3301 or 800/879-1991, www.banff voyagerinn.com).

Toward downtown from the Spruce Grove is the **High Country Inn** (419 Banff Ave., 403/762-2236 or 800/661-1244, www.banffhigh countryinn.com), which has a heated indoor pool, spacious hot tubs, a cedar-lined sauna, and the ever-popular Ticino Swiss/Italian restaurant. All rooms are adequately furnished with comfortable beds and a muted brown color scheme. Standard rooms are $170 s or d, but compared to similarly priced Banff rooms, the High Country's Honeymoon Suite ($240) is an excellent value; it features a king-size bed, fireplace, jetted tub, and a large balcony with views to Cascade Mountain.

Across a quiet road from the river and three blocks from downtown is the old-style **Bow View Motor Lodge** (228 Bow Ave., 403/762-2261 or 800/661-1565, www.bowview.com), which has an outdoor pool, making it a good choice for families. Moderately sized rooms are priced

© ANDREW HEMPSTEAD

The Spruce Grove Inn provides good value among mid-priced lodging.

$160–230 s or d, including some with filtered river views.

The **Rundlestone Lodge** (537 Banff Ave., 403/762-2201 or 800/661-8630, www.rundle stone.com) features mountain-style architecture with an abundance of raw stonework and exposed timber inside and out. At street level is a comfortable sitting area centered on a fireplace, as well as an indoor pool, a lounge-style bar, and a restaurant. Furniture and fittings in the 96 rooms are elegant, and all come with high-speed Internet access. Many rooms have small balconies and gas fireplaces; some are wheelchair accessible. Rooms begin at $190 s or d; suites range $220–310.

$200–250

More than 100 years since Jim and Bill Brewster guided their first guests through the park, their descendants are still actively involved in the tourist industry, operating the central and very stylish **Brewster's Mountain Lodge** (208 Caribou St., 403/762-2900 or 888/762-2900, www.brewsteradventures.com). The building features an eye-catching log exterior with an equally impressive lobby and adjoining lounge in a prime downtown location. The Western theme is continued in the 77 upstairs rooms. Superior rooms feature two queen-size beds or one king-size bed ($220), deluxe rooms offer a private balcony ($240), and loft suites have hot tubs (from $270). All rates include breakfast, and if you don't feel like dining out you can order room service from noon onward. Rates here in the off-season are slashed up to 50 percent.

The 134-room **Banff Ptarmigan Inn** (337 Banff Ave., 403/762-2207 or 800/661-8310, www.bestofbanff.com) is a slick, full-service hotel with tastefully decorated rooms, down comforters on all beds, a restaurant, and a variety of facilities to soothe sore muscles, including a spa, a whirlpool, and a sauna. The 134 rooms start at $230 s or d.

At the downtown end of the motel strip, the **Banff International Hotel** (333 Banff Ave., 403/762-5666 or 800/665-5666, www.banff international.com) looks like any of the other sprawling lumps of commercialism along Banff Avenue, but extensive renovations inside and out in 1999 transformed the rooms into something special. Guests enjoy an abundance of in-room facilities, oak furniture, and marble bathrooms.

Standard rooms are $230 s or d; the much larger corner rooms have mountain views and cost $280.

The following two accommodations are on Tunnel Mountain Road, a 15-minute downhill walk to town. Although falling in the same price range as many of those on Banff Avenue, all units are self-contained, making them good for families, small groups, or those who want to cook their own meals.

Douglas Fir Resort (403/762-5591 or 800/661-9267, www.douglasfir.com) has 133 large condo-style units. Each has a fully equipped kitchen and a lounge with fireplace. Other facilities include a hot tub, an exercise room, squash and tennis courts, a grocery store, and a laundry. Infinitely more important if you have children are the two indoor water slides and heated pool. Rates begin at $210 s or d (children under 14 free), discounted outside of early June to mid-September.

Hidden Ridge Resort (403/762-3544 or 800/661-1372, www.banffhiddenridge.com) sits on a forested hillside away from the main buzz of traffic. Choose from modern condo-style units ($220) or older, much larger wooden chalets that sleep up to six ($240).

$250–300

In the heart of downtown Banff, the venerable **Mount Royal Hotel** (138 Banff Ave., 403/762-3331 or 877/442-2623, www.mountroyal hotel.com) first opened in 1908. Since its purchase by the Brewster Transport Company in 1912, this distinctive red-brick building has seen various expansions and a disastrous fire in 1967, which destroyed the original wing. Today guests are offered 60 tastefully decorated rooms with high-speed Internet access and the use of a large health club with hot tub. Also on the premises are a restaurant and small lounge. Rates are from $250 s or d but are discounted as low as $120 in the shoulder seasons. For a splurge, you won't find better than the Mount Royal suites ($350).

One of Banff's newer hotels is the **Royal Canadian Lodge** (459 Banff Ave., 403/762-3307 or 800/661-1225, www.charltonresorts .com; from $290 s or d), which opened in the

summer of 2000. It features 99 luxuriously appointed rooms, heated underground parking, a lounge and restaurant, a large spa/pool complex, and a landscaped courtyard.

At **Buffalo Mountain Lodge,** a 15-minute walk from town on Tunnel Mountain Road (at Tunnel Mountain Dr., 403/762-2400 or 800/661-1367, www.crmr/bml), you'll notice the impressive timber-frame construction, as well as the hand-hewn construction of the lobby, with its vaulted ceiling and eye-catching fieldstone fireplace. The rooms, chalets, and bungalows all have fireplaces, balconies, large bathrooms, and comfortable beds topped by feather-filled duvets; many have kitchens. And you won't need to go to town to eat—one of Banff's best restaurants, Cilantro Mountain Café, is adjacent to the main lodge. Rack rates start at $300, but book in advance and online to pick up summer rates around $250. (The lodge takes its name from Tunnel Mountain, which early park visitors called Buffalo Mountain, for its shape.)

Over $300

The **Fairmont Banff Springs** (403/762-2211 or 800/257-7544, www.fairmont.com), one of the world's great mountain resort hotels, has undergone massive renovations in the last decade, cementing its position as Banff's premier accommodation. More than $30,000 has been spent installing air-conditioning, updating furnishings, and replacing beds in each of the 770 rooms. Other major changes include moving the lobby to a more accessible side of the hotel and reopening the old lobby as a cavernous lounge area. During the same period, the hotel came under the ownership of Fairmont Hotels and Resorts, losing its century-old tag as a Canadian Pacific hotel and in the process its ties to the historic railway company that constructed the original hotel back in 1888.

Even though the rooms have been modernized, many date to the 1920s, and as is common in older establishments, these accommodations are small. But room size is only a minor consideration when staying in this historic gem. With 12 eateries, four lounges, a luxurious spa facility, a huge indoor pool, elegant public spaces, a 27-

hole golf course, tennis courts, horseback riding, and enough twisting, turning hallways, boardwalks, towers, and shops to warrant a detailed map, you'll not be wanting to spend much time in your room. Unless, of course, you are in the presidential suite, located in the central tower. It has eight rooms, a canopy bed, a hot tub, a baby grand piano, a private pool, and your own private elevator linking each of the three floors.

During summer, rack rates for a regular Fairmont room are $649 s or d, discounted to around $400 the rest of the year. Most summer visitors stay as part of a package—the **Castle Experience** or the **Canadian Rockies Experience.** The Castle Experience is the less expensive of the two and includes golfing and golf lessons, horseback riding, tennis, guided hiking and climbing, mountain-bike rental, canoeing, unlimited entry to Willow Stream spa facilities and one spa treatment, and three meals daily in any of hotel restaurants. This package taken in a Fairmont room costs $1,139 d, but these rooms are fairly small, and for an extra $100 you can stay in a much larger Fairmont Deluxe room. The Canadian Rockies Experience (from $1,279 s or d) includes all that the Castle Experience does, as well as guided fishing, white-water rafting, and all Brewster tours. (You may not want to take full advantage of all the activities offered. But if, for example, you decide to take a golf lesson and follow it up with a round on the hotel's course, go for an afternoon horseback ride, spend an evening at the spa, and dine in the hotel, the actual cost of the room will work out to about $300 for the night.) Outside of summer, check the Fairmont website for package deals that provide deep discounts on the room-only rack rate. Finally, at any time of year, call a day in advance or even stop by the day of—if rooms are available they are sold at up to 50 percent off the rack rate.

On Mountain Avenue, a short walk from the Upper Hot Springs, is **Rimrock Resort Hotel** (403/762-3356 or 888/746-7625, www.rimrockresort.com). The original hotel was constructed in 1903 but was fully rebuilt and opened as a full-service luxury resort in the mid-1990s. Guest amenities include two restaurants, two lounges, a health club, an outdoor patio,

and underground heated parking. Each of 345 well-appointed rooms is decorated with earthy tones offset by brightly colored fabrics. They also feature picture windows, a king-size bed, a comfortable armchair, a writing desk, two phones, a mini-bar, and a hair dryer. This hotel caters to disabled persons as well as any in the park. Since it's set high above the Bow Valley, views for the most part are excellent. Prices range $365–425 depending solely on the views. Regular shuttle buses make the short run to town during summer.

ALONG THE BOW VALLEY PARKWAY AND VICINITY

The Bow Valley Parkway is the original route between Banff and Lake Louise. It is a beautiful drive in all seasons, and along its length are several accommodations, each a viable alternative to staying in Banff.

Under $50

Thirty-two kilometers (20 miles) from Banff along the Bow Valley Parkway, **HI–Castle Mountain Wilderness Hostel** is near several interesting hikes and across the road from a general store with basic supplies. This hostel sleeps 28 and has a kitchen, common room, hot showers, and bike rentals. Members of Hostelling International pay $19, nonmembers $23. Make bookings through the association's reservation line (403/760-7580 or 866/762-4122) or book online (www.hihostels.ca).

$100–150

Johnston Canyon Resort (403/762-2971 or 888/378-1720, www.johnstoncanyon.com; mid-May–early Oct.) is 26 km (16 miles) west of Banff at the beginning of a short trail that leads to the famous canyon. The rustic cabins are older, and some have kitchenettes. On the grounds are tennis courts, a barbecue area, and a general store. Resort dining options are as varied as munching on a burger and fries at the counter of an old-time cafeteria to enjoying oriental-style Chilean sea bass in a dining room that oozes alpine charm. Basic two-person cabins are $129, two-person cabins with a fireplace are $169, and they go up in price all the way to $279 for a Classic cabin complete with cooking facilities and luxurious heritage-style furnishings.

$150–200

M Baker Creek Chalets (403/522-3761, www.bakercreek.com) lies along the Bow Valley Parkway 40 km (25 miles) northwest of Banff and just 10 km (6.2 miles) from Lake Louise. Each of the log chalets (from $225 s or d) has a kitchenette, fireplace, and outside deck (complete with cute woodcarvings of bears climbing over the railings). The Deluxe Trapper's Cabin ($315) is a huge space with a log bed, antler chandelier, wood-burning fireplace, double-jetted tub, and cooking facilities. A lodge wing has eight luxurious suites, each with richly accented log work, a deck, a microwave and fridge, and a deluxe bathroom; $195 s or d, $225 with a double-jetted tub, and $295 with a loft. (Check the website for great off-season deals.) The restaurant here is highly recommended.

Constructed by the Canadian Pacific Railway in 1922, **M Storm Mountain Lodge** (Hwy. 93, 403/762-4155, www.stormmountainlodge.com; early Dec.–mid-Oct.; $169–229 including breakfast) reopened in 2003 after a major restoration project that saw 14 historic cabins returned to their former rustic glory. Each has its original log walls, along with a log bed, covered deck, a wood-burning fireplace, and bathroom with clawfoot tub. They don't have phones or TVs, so there's little to distract you from the past. Outside, the wilderness beckons, with Storm Mountain as a backdrop. The lodge is at Vermilion Pass, a 25-minute drive from Banff or Lake Louise (head west from the Castle Mountain interchange). The lodge restaurant (daily 5–10 P.M.) is one of my favorite places to eat in the park (see *Food*).

Over $200

At Castle Junction, 32 km (20 miles) northwest of Banff, is **Castle Mountain Chalets** (403/762-3868 or 877/762-2281, www.castlemountain .com). Set on 1.5 hectares (four acres), this resort is home to a collection of magnificent log chalets.

Each has high ceilings, beautifully handcrafted log interiors, at least two beds, a stone fireplace, a full kitchen with dishwasher, a bathroom with hot tub, and satellite TV. Rates range $255–335 s or d. At the back of the grounds are several older cabins offered in summer ($180 s or d). Part of the complex is a grocery store, barbecue area, library, and the only gas between Banff and Lake Louise. The nearest restaurants are at Baker Creek Chalets and Johnston Canyon Resort.

Brewster's Shadow Lake Lodge

Brewster's Shadow Lake Lodge (403/762-0116, www.shadowlakelodge.com) is 14 km (8.7 miles) from the nearest road. Access is on foot or, in winter, on skis. The lodge is near picturesque Shadow Lake, and many hiking trails are nearby. Dating to 1928, the oldest structure has been restored as a rustic yet welcoming dining area, with a wood stove in the kitchen. Guests overnight in 12 newer, comfortable cabins. The daily rate, including three meals served buffet-style and afternoon tea, is $180 s, $160 d per person per day. The trailhead is along the Trans-Canada Highway, 19 km (12 miles) from Banff, at the Redearth Creek parking area. The summer season is mid-June to September.

CAMPING

Within Banff National Park, 13 campgrounds hold more than 2,000 sites. Although the town of Banff has five of these facilities with more than 1,500 sites in its immediate vicinity, all fill by early afternoon. The three largest campgrounds are strung out over 1.5 km (.9 mile) along Tunnel Mountain Road, with the nearest sites 2.5 km (1.6 miles) from town. A percentage of sites can be reserved through the **Parks Canada Campground Reservation Service** (877/737-3783, www.pccamping.ca), and it's strongly recommended that you do reserve if you require electrical hookups. Although plenty of sites are available for those without reservations, they fill fast each day (especially in July and August). The official checkout time is 11 A.M., so plan on arriving at your campground of choice earlier in the day than this to ensure getting a site. At more

© ANDREW HEMPSTEAD

Campers at Tunnel Mountain are surrounded by mountain peaks.

popular locations, a lineup forms, waiting for sites to become vacant. This is especially true at the Banff and Lake Louise campgrounds, which offer powered sites. When the main campgrounds fill, those unable to secure a site will be directed to an overflow area along Minnewanka Lake Road. These provide few facilities and no hookups, but cost less. Open fires are permitted in designated areas throughout all campgrounds, but you must purchase a Firewood Permit ($6 per site per night) to burn wood, which is provided at no cost. For general camping information, stop at the Banff Visitor Centre (224 Banff Ave., 403/762-1550) or go the Parks Canada website, www.parkscanada.gc.ca/banff, and follow the camping links.

Near the Town of Banff

Closest to town is **Tunnel Mountain Campground,** which is three campgrounds rolled into one. The location is a lightly treed ridge east of downtown, with views north to Cascade Mountain and south to Mount Rundle. From town, follow Tunnel Mountain Road east, to beyond the Douglas Fir Resort (which is within walk-ing distance for groceries, booze, and laundry). If you're coming in off the TransCanada Highway from the east, bypass town completely by turning left onto Tunnel Mountain Road at the Banff Rocky Mountain Resort. Approaching from this direction, the first campground you pass is the park's largest with 622 well-spaced, relatively private sites ($22 per site), each with a fire ring and picnic table. Other amenities include drinking water, hot showers, and kitchen shelters. This campground has no hookups. It is open mid-May to early September. Less than one km (.6 mile) farther along Tunnel Mountain Road toward town is a signed turnoff ("Hookups") that leads to a registration booth for two more campgrounds. Unless you have a reservation (see above), you'll asked whether you require an electrical hookup ($26 per site) or a site with power, water, and sewer ($30 per site), then sent off into the corresponding campground. The power-only section (closest to town) stays open year-round, the other from mid-May to September. Both have hot showers but little privacy between sites.

Along Lake Minnewanka Road northeast of town are two campgrounds offering fewer services than the others, but with sites that offer more privacy. The pick of the two is **Two Jack Lakeside Campground** (June–mid-Sept.; $22 per site), with 80 sites tucked into trees at the south end of Two Jack Lake, an extension of Lake Minnewanka. Facilities include hot showers, kitchen shelters, drinking water, and flush toilets. It's just over six km (3.7 miles) from the TransCanada Highway underpass. The much larger **Two Jack Main Campground** (mid-June–mid-Sept.; $17 per site) is a short distance farther along the road, with 381 sites spread throughout a shallow valley. It offers the same facilities as Two Jack Lakeside, sans showers. The overflow camping area for these and the three Tunnel Mountain campgrounds is at the beginning of the Lake Minnewanka Road loop, a short walk along Cascade River from a picturesque picnic area.

Bow Valley Parkway

Along Bow Valley Parkway between the town of Banff and Lake Louise are three campgrounds.

Closest to Banff is **Johnston Canyon Campground** (early June–mid-Sept.; $22 per site), between the road and the rail line 26 km (16 miles) west of Banff. It is the largest of the three campgrounds, with 140 sites, and has hot showers but no hookups. Almost directly opposite is Johnston Canyon Resort, with groceries and a restaurant, and the beginning of a trail to the park's best-known waterfalls.

Continuing eight km (five miles) toward Lake Louise, **Castle Mountain Campground** (early June–early September; $17 per site) is also within walking distance of a grocery store (no restaurant), but it has just 44 sites and no showers. Services are limited to flush toilets, drinking water, and kitchen shelters.

Protection Mountain Campground (July–Aug.; $17 per site), a further 14 km (8.7 miles) west and just over 20 km (12.5 miles) from Lake Louise, opens as demand dictates, usually by late June. It offers 89 sites, along with flush toilets, drinking water, and stove-equipped kitchen shelters.

Practicalities

FOOD

Whether you're in search of an inexpensive snack for the family or silver service, you can find it in the town of Banff, which has over 100 restaurants (more per capita than any town or city across Canada). The quality of food varies greatly. Some restaurants revolve solely around the tourist trade while others have reputations that attract diners from Calgary who have been known to stay overnight just to eat at their favorite haunt. While the quality of food is most people's number one priority when dining out, the level of service (or lack of it) also comes into play in Banff, especially if you are paying big bucks for a fine dining meal. Getting it all right—good food, top-notch service, and a memorable ambience—in a tourism-oriented town is rare. Which leads to the restaurants I've recommended below, the best of a very varied bunch.

Groceries

Banff has two major grocery stores. In addition to a wide selection of basic groceries, **Keller Foods** (122 Bear St., 403/762-3663; summer 7 A.M.–10 P.M., shorter hours the rest of the year) has a good deli with pre-made salads and sandwiches, soups to go, and hot chickens. At the other end of downtown is **Safeway** (318 Marten St., 403/762-5329; daily 8 A.M.–11 P.M.).

Budget Stretchers

The best place to begin looking for cheap eats is the Food Court in the lower level of Cascade Plaza (317 Banff Ave.). Here you'll find a juice bar, a small café, and **Banff Edo,** which sells simple Japanese dishes for around $7.50, including a drink. **Cougar Pete's** in the Banff Alpine Centre (Tunnel Mountain Rd., 403/762-4122) features all the usual café-style dishes, such as a pile of nachos for $8; no entrée is more than $12.

A local bylaw prohibiting obtrusive signs and neon lights means that the fast-food chains are easily missed, but that isn't a bad thing; if you must, head to **McDonald's** (116 Banff Ave.) for the most expensive Big Macs this side of Toronto's SkyDome. **Aardvarks** (304 Caribou St., 403/762-5500) is a late-night pizza hangout open until 4 A.M.

Cafés and Coffee Shops

The **Cake Company** (220 Bear St., 403/762-2330) serves great coffee and delicious pastries, muffins, and cakes baked daily on the premises. Another Cake Company outlet is on the lower level of Cascade Plaza; a muffin and coffee is $2.50. **Evelyn's Coffee Bar** (Town Centre Mall, Banff Ave., 403/762-0352) has good coffee and huge sandwiches. The few outside tables—on the busiest stretch of the busiest street in town—are perfect for people watching. **Jump Start** op-

Banff is undeniably busy, but escaping the crowds is possible—head to the deli at Keller's on Bear Street, pick up a pre-made sandwich or freshly prepared salad, then search out an empty picnic table at Two Jack Lake along the Minnewanka Loop road.

© ANDREW HEMPSTEAD

posite Central Park (206 Buffalo St., 403/762-0332) has a wide range of coffee concoctions as well as homemade soups (from $5.50) and sandwiches ($7) that are delicious.

Family-Style Dining

In the Banff Caribou Lodge is **The Keg** (521 Banff Ave., 403/762-4442; daily 7 A.M.–2 A.M.), part of a restaurant chain that began in Vancouver, which is noted for its consistently good steak, seafood, and chicken dishes at reasonable prices. It's also known for upbeat, well-presented servers. All entrées include a 60-item salad bar. Another Keg is downtown (117 Banff Ave., 403/760-3030).

Earl's, upstairs in the heart of the downtown action (229 Banff Ave., 403/762-4414), has more of the same at slightly higher prices. This Alberta-born chain has a reputation for a menu of fusion cuisine that follows food trends, employs bright young servers, and offers a fun atmosphere.

Children will love the food and parents will love the prices at **Old Spaghetti Factory** (upstairs in the Cascade Plaza on Banff Ave., 403/760-2779; daily from 11:30 A.M.). The room is casual-rustic, with a few tables spread along a balcony. Sort through a maze of combinations and specials (kids get their own color-in menu), and the most you'll pay for a meal is $20, which includes soup or salad, a side of bread, dessert, and coffee.

Pronounced "bi-tif-splik's," **Joe Btfsplk's Diner** (221 Banff Ave., 403/762-5529; daily for breakfast, lunch, and dinner) is a faux 1950s-style diner, complete with a jukebox, a counter along the kitchen, and a range of tacky souvenirs. The menu is similarly themed, with daily specials for around $10 at lunch, $15 at dinner, and predictable menu choices that range from Caesar salad to meatloaf.

Steak

Alberta beef is mostly raised on ranchland not far from the park and features prominently on menus throughout town. Finely marbled AAA beef is used in most restaurants and is unequaled in its tender, juicy qualities.

Even though **Bumper's** (603 Banff Ave., 403/762-2622; daily 4:30–10 P.M.) is away from the center of Banff, it's worth leaving the shopping strip and heading out to this popular steakhouse. Large cuts of Alberta beef, an informal atmosphere, efficient service, and great prices keep people coming back. Favorite choices are the slabs of roast prime rib of beef, in four sizes of cuts and cooked to order. Prices range from $18 for the Ladies cut to $29 for the Man Mountain cut, which includes unlimited trips to a small salad bar. Upstairs is the **Loft Lounge**, a good place to wait for a table or relax afterward with an inexpensive drink.

Considered one of Banff's most fashionable restaurants, **⚑ Saltlik** (221 Bear St., 403/762-2467; daily from 11 A.M.) is big and bold and the perfect choice for serious carnivores with cash to spare. The concrete and steel split-level interior is complemented with modish wood furnishings. Facing the street, glass doors fold back to a terrace for warm-weather dining. The specialty is AAA Alberta beef, finished with grain feeding to enhance the flavor, then flash-seared at 650°C (1,200°F) to seal in the juices, and served with a side platter of seasonal vegetables. Entrées are priced comparable to a city steakhouse ($18–35), but the cost creeps up as you add side dishes. If there's anything to fault about the Saltlik, it's the servers, who tend to try too hard.

Casually Canadian

Of the many Banff drinking holes that offer pub-style menus, **Wild Bill's** (201 Banff Ave., 403/762-0333) is a standout. It's named for one of Banff's most famed mountain men, and the decor is suitably Western, with a menu to match. The nachos grande ($9.50) with a side of guacamole ($3) is perfect to share. Later in the day, steaks and spit-roasted chicken are traditional favorites ($15–30). Wild Bill's is open daily from 11 A.M. until well after midnight, but plan on dining before 9 P.M.

A town favorite that has faithfully served locals for many years is **Melissa's** (218 Lynx St., 403/762-5511; daily 7:30 A.M.–10 P.M.), housed in a log building that dates from 1928 (the original Homestead Inn). Lunch and dinner are old-fashioned, casual affairs—choose from a wide variety of generously sized burgers, freshly prepared salads, and mouthwatering Alberta beef.

Bruno's Café & Grill (304 Caribou St., 403/762-8115; open daily 7 A.M.–10 P.M.), named for Bruno Engler, locally renowned photographer, ski instructor, and mountain man, is a cozy little café with a great mountain ambience and comfortable couches.

Classically Canadian

The **Buffalo Mountain Lodge Restaurant** at a lodge of the same name (Tunnel Mountain Road, 403/762-2400; daily 7 A.M.–10 P.M.) offers the perfect setting for a moderate splurge. It features a distinctive interior of hand-hewn cedar beams and Old World elegance—complete with stone fireplace and a chandelier made entirely from elk antlers—along with large windows that frame the surrounding forest. The featured cuisine is referred to as Rocky Mountain, reflecting an abundance of Canadian game and seafood combined with native berries and fruits. The least expensive

Busy Banff Avenue is lined with restaurants.

way to dine on this uniquely Canadian fare is by visiting at lunch and ordering the Rocky Mountain Game Platter, costing $20 for two people. Dinner entrées range $24–33 and include fare like elk sirloin that's given an exotic touch with accompanying quince compote.

The food at **N Storm Mountain Lodge** (Hwy. 93, 403/762-4155; early Dec.–mid-Oct. Fri.–Sun. 5–10 P.M., summer daily 5–10 P.M.) is excellent, but it's the ambience you'll remember long after leaving—an intoxicating blend of historic appeal and rustic mountain charm. The chef uses mostly organic produce with seasonally available game and seafood—bison, venison, wild salmon, and the like—to create tasty and interesting dishes well suited to the I-must-be-in-the-Canadian-wilderness surroundings. Storm Mountain Lodge is a 25-minute drive northwest from Banff; take the TransCanada Highway toward Lake Louise and head west at the Castle Mountain interchange.

Also well worth the drive is **N Baker Creek Bistro** (Baker Creek Chalets, 40 km/24.7 miles northwest of town along the Bow Valley Parkway, 403/522-2182; Sat.–Sun. 7 A.M.–2 P.M., Mon.–Fri. noon–2 P.M. and daily 5–9:30 P.M.). Dining is in a small room that characterizes the term "mountain hideaway," in an adjacent lounge bar, or out on a small deck decorated with pots of colorful flowers. The menu isn't large, but dishes feature lots of Canadian game and produce, with favorites like medallions of venison served with an orange and gin sauce ($29) and roasted duck breast with a cream-based cranberry sauce ($24).

Canadian Contemporary

Occupying the prime position on one of Banff's busiest corners is the **Maple Leaf Grille** (137 Banff Ave., 403/760-7680; daily 11 A.M.–11 P.M.). Take in the dramatic Canadian-themed decor—exposed river stone, polished log work, a two-story interior waterfall, and a moose head. Some tables surround a busy area by the bar and kitchen, so try to talk your way into the upstairs back corner. The cooking uses modern styles with an abundance of Canadian game and produce. The lunch menu has beer-battered halibut and chips, along with lots of lighter salads and

stir-fries ($9–15). Some of Canada's finest ingredients appear on the dinner menu: pan-seared arctic char cooked in an apple and wild sage butter and the apple-crusted pork tenderloin are standouts. Treat yourself to a glass of Canadian ice wine to accompany dessert.

Banff's original bistro-style restaurant, which opened in the early 1990s, is **Coyote's** (206 Caribou St., 403/762-3963; daily 7:30 A.M.–10 P.M.). Meals are prepared in full view of diners, and the menu emphasizes fresh, health-conscious cooking, with just a hint of Southwestern style. To start, it's hard to go past the sweet potato and corn chowder ($6), and then choose from mains as varied as a simple Mediterranean-influenced pasta and a flank steak marinated in Cajun spices and topped with a generous dab of corn and tomato salsa. Entrées range $14–26.

Italian

Banff is blessed with fine Italian restaurants. Casual, no-frills **Guido's** (upstairs at 116 Banff Ave., 403/762-4002; daily from 5:30 P.M.) dishes up generous portions of freshly made pasta, which is cooked to perfection in a variety of classic Italian sauces that appeal to all tastes and diets. Entrées are $11–21, including an inexpensive spaghetti carbonara made with real bacon.

More trendy (reflected in the prices) is **Giorgio's** (219 Banff Ave., 403/762-5114; daily from 4:30 P.M.), which has a stylish decor and a casual Old World atmosphere. Its chefs prepare as many as 400 meals each afternoon, and the lineup for tables through summer is ever present. Pasta dishes begin at $13.

If you are staying up on Tunnel Mountain—or even if you're not—**N Cilantro Mountain Café** (Buffalo Mountain Lodge, 403/760-3008; summer daily 11 A.M.–11 P.M., the rest of the year Wed.–Sun. 5–10 P.M.; closed mid-Sept.–mid-Dec.) is an excellent choice for a casual, well-priced meal. You can choose to dine inside the cozy log cabin that holds the main restaurant and open kitchen, or out on the patio. Starters are dominated by seafood options, but the flatbread, baked to order and delivered with choice of dips ($8), is a good choice to share. The thin-crust, wood-fired pizza for one ($13–16) is the highlight, with a small but varied selection of other mains ($22–26) that change as seasonal produce becomes available. Highly recommended if you want a break from Banff Avenue.

Swiss-Italian

Once one of Banff's busiest restaurants, **M Ticino** (High Country Inn, 415 Banff Ave., 403/762-3848; daily 5–11 P.M.) is a Banff institution that reflects the heritage of park's early mountain guides, with solid timber furnishings, lots of peeled and polished log work, and old wooden skis, huge cowbells, and an alpenhorn decorating the walls. It's named for the southern province of Switzerland, where the cuisine has a distinctive Italian influence. The Swiss chef is best known for a creamy wild mushroom soup, unique to the region; his beef and cheese fondues ($17–25 per person); juicy cuts of Alberta beef; and veal dishes (such as veal scaloppini; $24). Save room for one of Ticino's sinfully rich desserts. Also of note is professional service. Ticino is also open daily from 7 A.M. for a hot and cold buffet breakfast ($12).

Greek

The **Balkan** (120 Banff Ave., 403/762-3454; daily 11 A.M.–11 P.M.) is run by a Greek family, but the menu blends their heritage with the cuisines of Italy, China, and Canada. Select from Greek ribs (pork ribs with a lemon sauce) for $15.95, the Greek chow mein (stir-fried vegetables, fried rice, and your choice of meat) for $11.50, or Greek spaghetti for $9.50. But the most popular dishes are souvlaki ($13.95) and an enormous Greek platter for two ($42).

French

You'll think you've swapped continents when you step into **Le Beaujolais** (212 Buffalo St., at Banff Ave., 403/762-2712; daily from 6 P.M.), a Canadian leader in French cuisine. With crisp white linens, old-style stately decor, and immaculate service, this elegant room has been one of Banff's most popular fine-dining restaurants for 20 years. Its second-floor location ensures great views of Banff, especially from window tables. The dishes feature mainly Canadian produce,

prepared and served with a traditional French flair. Entrées such as braised caribou with blueberries and wild mushrooms begin at $31, but the extent of your final tab depends on whether you choose à la carte items or one of the three- to six-course table d'hôte menus ($55–90)—and also on how much wine you consume. Nationalism shows through in the 10,000-bottle cellar, with lots of reds from the Bordeaux and Burgundy regions of France. Reservations are necessary.

Fondue

Even if you've tried exotic meats, you probably haven't had them in a restaurant like the **M Grizzly House** (207 Banff Ave., 403/762-4055; daily 11:30 A.M.–midnight), which provides Banff's most unusual dining experience. The decor is, to say the least, eclectic (many say eccentric)—think lots of twisted woods, a motorbike hanging from the ceiling, a melted telephone on the wall. Each table has a phone for across-table conversation, or you can call your waiter, the bar, a cab, diners in the private booth, or even those who spend too long in the bathroom. The food is equally unique and the service as professional as anywhere in town. The menu hasn't changed in decades, and this doesn't displease anyone. Most dining revolves around traditional Swiss fondues, but with nontraditional dipping meats such as rattlesnake, alligator, shark, ostrich, scallops, elk, and wild boar. Four-course table d'hôte fondue dinners are $38–56 per person, which includes soup or salad, followed by a cheese fondue, then a choice of one of six meat and seafood fondue (or hot rock) choices, and finally a fruity chocolate fondue. The Grizzly House is also open at lunch, when you can sample Canadian game at reduced prices; an Alberta-farmed buffalo burger is $10, and a smoked duck breast salad is $12.

Japanese

My favorite of the four Japanese restaurants in Banff is **Miki** (Inns of Banff, 600 Banff Avenue, 403/762-4581; daily from 6 P.M.), away from downtown at the far end of the motel strip. Due mostly to its location, getting a table is easy (even one with mountain views). Daily combo specials provide the best value (around $25 for five courses), or choose from the usual array of sushi, prepared in sight of diners.

Back downtown, **Sushi House Banff** (304 Caribou St., 403/762-2971) is a tiny space with a dozen stools set around a moving miniature railway that has diners picking sushi and other delicacies from a train as it circles the chef, loading the carriages as quickly as they empty.

More expensive is **Suginoya** (225 Banff Ave., 403/762-4773; daily 11 A.M.–10:30 P.M.). Choose from the sushi bar, *ozashiki* booths, or regular tables. Traditional *shabu-shabu* and seafood teriyaki are staples. The number of Japanese diners here is indicative of the quality. Expect to pay at least $13 for entrées, $19–25 for one of the combination dinners.

Fairmont Banff Springs

Whether guests or not, most visitors to Banff drop by to see one of the town's biggest tourist attractions, and a meal here might not be as expensive as you think. The hotel itself has more eateries than most small towns—from a deli serving slices of pizza to the finest of fine dining in the Banffshire Club.

If you are in the mood for a snack such as chili and bread or sandwiches to go, head to the Lobby Level and the **Castle Pantry,** which is open 24 hours daily.

Impressive buffets are the main draw at the **Bow Valley Grill,** a pleasantly laid out dining room that seats 275. Each morning from 6:30 A.M. an expansive buffet of hot and cold delicacies, including freshly baked bread and seasonal fruits, is laid out for the masses ($26 per person). Lunch (daily 11:30 A.M.–5:30 P.M.) offers a wide-ranging menu featuring everything from salads to seafood. Through the busiest months of summer, pay for the buffet lunch (11:30 A.M.–2 P.M.; $27) and you'll be invited to a walking tour of the property. In summer, evening diners (6–9 P.M.) order from a menu that appeals to all tastes, while the rest of the year dinner is offered as a buffet, with a different theme each night. The hotel's Sunday brunch, served in the Bow Valley Grill (10:30 A.M.–

2:30 P.M.; $35), is legendary, with chefs working at numerous stations scattered around the dining area and an enormous spread not equaled for variety anywhere in the mountains. Reservations are required for Sunday brunch (as far in advance as possible) and dinner.

Ensconced in an octagonal room of the Manor Wing, **Castello Ristorante** (daily 6–9 P.M.; Jan.–May closed Tues.–Wed.; no jeans) is a seductive dining room with a modern, upscale ambience. The menu is dominated by Italian favorites, with pastas in the $18–26 range and specialties from $22. The **Rundle Lounge** (daily midday–1 A.M.) is a long, narrow piano bar, where most tables offer views down the Bow Valley. The à la carte menu offers no surprises. **Grapes** is an intimate yet casual wine bar noted for its fine cheeses and pâtés. More substantial meals such as fondues are also offered. It's open for lunch and dinner.

The hotel's most acclaimed restaurant is the **Banffshire Club** (Tues.–Sat. 6–10 P.M.), which seats just 76 diners. Like its predecessor, the Rob Roy Room, this fine-dining restaurant is a bastion of elegance, which begins as a harp player serenades you through a gated entrance. Inside, extravagantly rich wood furnishings, perfectly presented table settings, muted lighting, and kilted staff create an atmosphere as far removed from the surrounding wilderness as is imaginable. Most diners choose one of four table d'hôte menus, which range from $100 per person for two courses to $225 for nine courses accompanied by specially selected wines. Reservations and a jacket are required.

Two restaurants lie within the grounds surrounding the hotel, and both are worthy of consideration. Originally the golf course clubhouse, the **Waldhaus Restaurant** (daily 6–10 P.M.) is nestled in a forested area directly below the hotel. The big room is dominated by dark woods and is warmed by a roaring fire. The menu features German specialties, with mains from $17. Below this restaurant is a pub of the same name, with a pub-style dinner menu offered in a casual atmosphere. The **Golf Course Clubhouse** is a seasonal restaurant on the golf course proper that serves light breakfasts, lunch buffets, and more formal dinners. A shuttle bus runs every 30 minutes between the main lobby and the clubhouse.

For all Fairmont Banff Springs dining reservations, call 403/662-6860 or, after 5 P.M., 403/762-2211. During the summer months a desk in the main lobby has all menus posted and takes reservations.

INFORMATION

Many sources of information are available on the park and its commercial facilities. Once you've arrived, the best place to make your first stop is the **Banff Visitor Centre** (224 Banff Ave.; mid-June–Aug. daily 8 A.M.–8 P.M., mid-May–mid-June and Sept. daily 8 A.M.–6 P.M., the rest of the year daily 9 A.M.–5 P.M.). This central complex houses information desks for **Parks Canada** (403/762-1550) and the **Banff/Lake Louise Tourism Bureau** (403/762-0270), as well as a Friends of Banff National Park shop, which stocks a good variety of park-related literature.

National Park Information
On the right-hand side of the **Banff Visitor Centre** is a row of desks staffed by Parks Canada employees. They will answer all of your queries regarding Banff's natural wonders and advise you of trail closures. Anyone planning an overnight backcountry trip should register here and obtain a Wilderness Pass ($8 per person per night). Also here, you can pick up the brochure *Banff and Vicinity Drives and Walks* (a compact guide to things to see and do around Banff), view a free slide show, and watch videos about the park. All questions pertaining to the national park itself can be answered here, or check out the Parks Canada website (www.pc.gc.ca).

The park's **Warden's Office** is in the industrial park (403/762-1470). The **weather office** (403/762-2088) offers updated forecasts. If you want to *see* the weather in Banff, check out the live webcam at www.banffgondola.com. Tune in to 101 on the FM band to listen to Parks Radio.

Tourism Information
In the **Banff Visitor Centre,** across the floor from Parks Canada, is a desk for the Banff/

Lake Louise Tourism Bureau. This organization represents businesses and commercial establishments in the park. Here you can find out about accommodations and restaurants and have any other questions answered. To answer the most frequently asked question, the restrooms are downstairs. For general tourism information, write the Banff/Lake Louise Tourism Bureau (P.O. Box 1298, Banff, AB T1L 1B3, 403/762-8421, www.bannflakelouise.com). A comprehensive commercial site is www.banff.com, with good general information on the park and links to accommodations and commercial operators.

BOOKS AND BOOKSTORES

The Canadian Rockies are one of the most written about, and definitely the most photographed, regions in Canada. As a walk along Banff Avenue will confirm, there is definitely no lack of postcards, calendars, and books about the area. For general reading, the guides and coffee-table books published by **Altitude Publishing** (www.altitudepublishing.com) are the best. Look for **Gem Trek** (www.gemtrek.com) maps at bookstores and gift shops throughout Banff National Park.

Banff Public Library
Banff's library (opposite Central Park at 101 Bear St., 403/762-2661; Mon.–Thurs. 10 A.M.–8 P.M., Fri. 10 A.M.–6 P.M., Sat. 11 A.M.–6 P.M., and Sun. 1–5 P.M.) boasts an extensive collection of nonfiction books, many about the park and its environs, which makes it an excellent rainy-day hangout. It also has a large collection of magazines and newspapers. Internet access is free, but book ahead.

Bookstores
Banff Book & Art Den (94 Banff Ave., 403/762-3919, www.banffbooks.com; summer daily 10 A.M.–9 P.M., the rest of the year until 7 P.M.) is the largest bookstore in the Canadian Rockies, with reading material spread over a split-level hardwood floor. It stocks a large collection of park literature, wilderness guides, coffee-table books, travel guides, and the entire range of Gem

Trek maps. The Book & Art Den has a second store in Fairmont Banff Springs, located beyond the front lobby.

Newspapers

Look for the free *Crag and Canyon* each Wednesday. It's been keeping residents and visitors informed about park issues and town gossip for more than 90 years. The *Rocky Mountain Outlook* is another free weekly newspaper (Thursday) that offers coverage of mountain life and upcoming events. Both are available on stands at businesses throughout the park.

SERVICES

The **post office** (Mon.–Fri. 9 A.M.–5:30 P.M.) is on the corner of Buffalo and Bear Streets opposite Central Park. The general-delivery service here is probably among the busiest in the country, with the thousands of seasonal workers in the area and no home mail-delivery service. A separate desk is set aside for general delivery pick-ups, speeding things up considerably. For all other postal services, try the small and friendly full-service postal outlet in **Cascade Plaza Drug,** in the far corner of the lower level of Cascade Plaza (317 Banff Ave.).

Major banks can be found along Banff Avenue and are generally open 9 A.M.–4 P.M. The **Bank of Montreal** (107 Banff Ave.) allows cash advances with MasterCard, while the **C.I.B.C.** (98 Banff Ave.) accepts Visa. **Freya's Currency Exchange** is in the Clock Tower Mall (108 Banff Ave., 403/762-4652).

The only downtown laundromat is **Cascade Coin Laundry,** on the lower level of the Cascade Plaza (daily 7:30 A.M.–10 P.M. **Chalet Coin Laundry** is on Tunnel Mountain Road at the Douglas Fir Resort, within walking distance of all Tunnel Mountain accommodations (daily 8 A.M.–10 P.M.).

Along Banff Avenue you'll find a handful of one-hour photo places; check around for the cheapest because many have special offers. The most competitive and reliable is the **Film Lab** (202 Banff Ave., 403/762-2126, and up at the Fairmont Banff Springs, 403/762-2011).

Mineral Springs Hospital (301 Lynx St., 403/762-2222) has 24-hour emergency service. **Cascade Plaza Drug,** on the lower level of the Cascade Plaza (317 Banff Ave., 403/762-2245), is open daily until 9 P.M.

Internet Access

Send and receive email and surf the Internet at the following Banff locations:

Banff Public Library: 101 Bear St., 403/762-2661; Mon.–Thurs. 10 A.M.–8 P.M., Fri. 10 A.M.–6 P.M., Sat. 11 A.M.–6 P.M., and Sun. 1–5 P.M.

Cascade Plaza: lower level, 315 Banff Ave.; 403/762-8484; open daily 7:30 A.M.–10 P.M.

Cyberweb Internet Cafe: Sundance Mall, 215 Banff Ave., 403/762-9226; daily 9 A.M.–midnight.

GETTING THERE

From Calgary International Airport

Calgary International Airport, 128 km (80 miles) east, is the closest airport to Banff National Park. **Brewster** (403/762-6767 or 800/661-1152, www.brewster.ca) is one of many companies offering shuttles between the airport and Banff National Park. Its service leaves the airport three times daily, stopping at Banff then continuing to Lake Louise. Calgary to Banff is $45. This shuttle delivers guests to all major Banff hotels as well as the park's main bus terminal, the **Brewster Tour and Transportation Centre,** a five-minute walk from downtown Banff at 100 Gopher Street. The depot has a ticket office, lockers, a café, and a gift shop. It's open daily 7:30 A.M.–10:45 P.M. Other airporter buses are **Banff Airporter** (403/762-3330 or 888/449-2901, www.banffairporter .com) and **Rocky Mountain Sky Shuttle** (403/762-5200 or 403/762-8754, www.rocky mountainskyshuttle.com). The advantage of traveling with these two companies is that they offer door-to-door service for around the same price. Adjacent desks at the airport's Arrivals level take bookings, but reserve a seat by booking over the phone or online in advance. The earliest service back to the airport departs Banff at 5:30 A.M.

Greyhound

Greyhound (403/762-1092 or 800/661-8747, www.greyhound.ca) offers scheduled service from the Calgary bus depot at 877 Greyhound Way SW, five times daily to the Brewster Tour and Transportation Centre at 100 Gopher St. and Samson Mall, Lake Louise. Greyhound buses also leave Vancouver from the depot at 1150 Station St., three times daily for the scenic 14-hour ride to the park.

GETTING AROUND

Most of the sights and many trailheads are within walking distance of town. **Banff Transit** (403/760-8294) operates bus service along two routes through the town of Banff: one from the Fairmont Banff Springs to the RV and trailer parking area at the north end of Banff Avenue, the other from the Fairmont Banff Springs to the Tunnel Mountain Campgrounds. Mid-May to September, buses run twice an hour between 7 A.M. and midnight. From October to December, the two routes are merged as one, with buses running hourly midday to midnight. No local buses run the rest of the year. Travel costs $2 per sector.

Cabs around Banff and Lake Louise are reasonably priced—flag drop is $3, then it's $1.65 per km. From the Banff bus depot to Tunnel Mountain accommodations will run around $7, same to the Fairmont Banff Springs, more after midnight. Companies are **Banff Taxi** (403/762-4444), **Legion Taxi** (403/762-3353), and **Taxi Taxi** (403/762-8000).

The days when a row of horse-drawn buggies eagerly awaited the arrival of wealthy visitors at the CPR Station have long since passed, but the **Trail Rider Store** (132 Banff Ave., 403/762-4551) offers visitors rides around town in a beautifully restored carriage ($11 per person for 15 minutes). Expect to pay $22 per carriage for a short loop along the Bow River.

Car Rental

Plan on renting a vehicle before you reach the park. In addition to high pricing for walk-in customers, the main catch is that no local companies offer unlimited mileage. The most you'll get is a free 150 km, and then expect to pay 25 cents per km. Agencies and their local contact numbers are: **Avis** (403/762-3222), **Budget** (403/762-4565), **Hertz** (403/762-2027), and **National** (403/762-2688). Reservations for vehicles in Banff should be made well in advance, especially in July and August.

Persons with Disabilities

The Banff and Lake Louise Visitor Centres are wheelchair accessible—restrooms, information desks, and theater are all barrier free. Once inside, use the handy Touchsource monitors for a full

---

PARKING PROBLEMS (AND HOW TO AVOID THEM)

The downtown core of Banff is busy year-round, but especially so between late June and early September after 10 A.M. If you're staying in a motel along Banff Avenue or on Tunnel Mountain, don't drive into town—walk or catch a Banff Transit bus (ask at your accommodation for a schedule).

If you do drive into downtown, don't let not finding a parking spot on Banff Avenue ruin your holiday. Head to the parkade at the corner of Bear and Lynx Streets, cross the Bow River and park in recreation grounds, or cruise for a space along Lynx or Beaver Street.

For travelers with RVs or trailers, finding a downtown parking spot can be a challenge. If you're planning on staying at one of the campgrounds on Tunnel Mountain, check in first, then walk or catch the Banff Transit bus (it departs the campground every 30 minutes; $2) to downtown. On the northeast side of town, signposted off Banff Avenue, is an RV parking/trailer drop-off lot. From here Banff Transit buses run every 30 minutes to downtown. If you must bring your rig in town and the few RV-only parking spots at the corner of Lynx and Wolf Streets are taken, there are no options other than the suggestions I give above for regular vehicles.

listing of all barrier-free services within the park. An all-terrain wheelchair is available at the Cave and Basin National Historic Site for use on park trails. To reserve, call 403/762-1566.

Tours

Brewster (403/762-6767 or 877/791-5500, www.brewster.ca) is the dominant tour company in the area. The three-hour Discover Banff bus tour takes in downtown Banff, Tunnel Mountain Drive, the hoodoos, the Cave and Basin, and Banff Gondola (gondola fare not included). This tour runs in summer only and departs from the bus depot daily at 8:30 A.M.; call for hotel pick-up times. Adult fare is $45, children half price. Brewster also runs several other tours. A nine-hour tour to Lake Louise departs select Banff hotels daily; $76. In winter this tour departs Tuesday and Friday mornings, runs five hours, and includes Banff sights; $51. During summer, the company offers tours from Banff to the Banff Gondola ($35; includes gondola ride), Lake Minnewanka ($46; includes two-hour boat cruise), and Columbia Icefield ($98; Ice Explorer extra).

Discover Banff Tours (Sundance Mall, 215 Banff Ave., 403/760-5007 or 877/565-9372, www.banfftours.com) is a smaller company, with smaller buses and more personalized service. Its tour routes are similar to Brewster's: a three-hour Discover Banff tour visits Lake Minnewanka,

THE BREWSTER BOYS

Few guides in Banff were as well known as Jim and Bill Brewster. In 1892, at ages 10 and 12, respectively, they were hired by the Banff Springs Hotel to take guests to local landmarks. As their reputation as guides grew, they built a thriving business. By 1900, they had their own livery and outfitting company, and soon thereafter they expanded operations to Lake Louise. Their other early business interests included a trading post, the original Mt. Royal Hotel, the first ski lodge in the Sunshine Meadows, and the hotel at the Columbia Icefield.

Today, a legacy of the boys' savvy, Brewster, a transportation and tour company, has grown to become an integral part of many tourists' stays. The company operates some of the world's most advanced sightseeing vehicles, including a fleet of Ice Explorers on the Columbia Icefield.

the Cave and Basin, and the hoodoos for $45 adults, $25 children; a full-day trip to the Columbia Icefield is $90 adults, $50 children; and a two-hour Evening Wildlife Safari is $35 adults, $20 children. This company offers a good selection of other tours throughout the year, including a wintertime "Icewalk" in frozen Johnston Canyon ($55).

Lake Louise and Vicinity

Lake Louise is 56 km (35 miles) northwest of Banff along the TransCanada Highway, or a little bit longer if you take the quieter Bow Valley Parkway. The hamlet of Lake Louise, composed of a small mall, hotels, and restaurants, is in the Bow Valley, just west of the TransCanada Highway. The lake itself is 200 vertical meters (660 vertical feet) above the valley floor, along a winding four-km (2.5-mile) road. Across the valley is Canada's second-largest winter resort, also called Lake Louise. It's a world-class facility renowned for diverse terrain, abundant snow, and breathtaking views.

When you see the first flush of morning sun hit Victoria Glacier, and the impossibly steep northern face of Mount Victoria reflected in the sparkling, emerald-green waters of Lake Louise, you'll understand why this lake is regarded as one of the world's seven natural wonders. Overlooking the magnificent scene, Fairmont Chateau Lake Louise is without a doubt one of the world's most photographed hotels. Apart from staring, photographing, and videotaping, the area has plenty to keep you busy. Nearby you'll find some of the park's best hiking, canoeing, and horseback riding. Only a short distance away is Moraine Lake, not as famous as Lake Louise but rivaling it in beauty.

From Lake Louise the TransCanada Highway continues west, exiting the park over Kicking Horse Pass (1,647 meters/5,400 feet) and passing through Yoho National Park to Golden. Highway 93, the famous Icefields Parkway, begins one km (.6 mile) north of the village and heads northwest through the park's northern reaches to Jasper National Park.

Lake Louise

In summer, about 10,000 visitors per day make the journey from the Bow Valley floor up to Lake Louise. By noon the tiered parking lot is often full. An alternative to the road is one of two hiking trails that begin in the village and end at the public parking lot (see *Hiking*). From here several paved trails lead to the lake's eastern shore. From these vantage points the dramatic setting can be fully appreciated. The lake is 2.4 km (1.5 miles) long, 500 meters (1,640 feet) wide, and up to 90 meters (295 feet) deep. Its cold waters reach a maximum temperature of 4°C (39°F) in August.

Fairmont Chateau Lake Louise is a tourist attraction in itself. Built by the CPR to take the pressure off the popular Banff Springs resort, the chateau has seen many changes in the last 100 years, yet it remains one of the world's great mountain resorts. No one minds the hordes of camera-toting tourists who traipse through each day—and there's really no way to avoid them. The immaculately manicured gardens between the chateau and the lake make an interesting foreground for the millions of Lake Louise photographs taken each year. At the lakeshore boathouse, canoes are rented for $40 per hour.

The snow-covered peak at the back of the lake is **Mount Victoria** (3,459 meters/11,350 feet), which sits on the Continental Divide. Amazingly, its base is more than 10 km (6.2 miles) from the eastern end of the lake. Mount Victoria, first climbed in 1897, remains one of the park's most popular peaks for mountaineers. Although the difficult northeast face (facing the chateau) was first successfully ascended in 1922, the most popular and easiest route to the summit is along the southeast ridge, approached from Abbot Pass.

Moraine Lake

Although less than half the size of Lake Louise, Moraine Lake is just as spectacular and worthy of just as much film. It is up a winding road 13 km (eight miles) off Lake Louise Drive. Its rugged setting, nestled in the Valley of the Ten Peaks among the towering mountains of the main ranges, has provided inspiration for millions of people from around the world since Walter Wilcox became the first white man to reach its shore in 1899. Wilcox's subsequent writings—such as "no scene has given me an equal impression of inspiring solitude and rugged grandeur"—

"LAKE OF LITTLE FISHES"

During the summer of 1882, Tom Wilson, an outfitter, was camped near the confluence of the Bow and Pipestone Rivers when he heard the distant rumblings of an avalanche. He questioned Stoney Indian guides and was told the noises originated from the "Lake of Little Fishes." The following day, Wilson, led by a native guide, hiked to the lake to investigate. He became the first white man to lay eyes on what he named Emerald Lake. Two years later, the name was changed to Lake Louise, honoring Princess Louise Caroline Alberta, daughter of Queen Victoria.

A railway station known as Laggan was built where the rail line passed closest to the lake, six kilometers (3.7 miles) away. Until a road was completed in 1926, everyone arrived by train. The station's name was changed to Lake Louise in 1913 to prevent confusion among visitors. In 1890, a modest two-bedroom wooden hotel replaced a crude cabin that had been built on the shore of the lake as word of its beauty spread. After many additions, a disastrous fire, and the addition of a concrete wing in 1925, the chateau of today took shape, minus a convention center that opened in early 2004.

Lake Louise

guaranteed the lake's future popularity. Although Wilcox was a knowledgeable man, he named the lake on the assumption that it was dammed by a glacial moraine deposited by the retreating Wenkchemna Glacier. In fact, the large rock pile that blocks its waters was deposited by major rockfalls from the Tower of Babel to the south. The lake often remains frozen until June, and the access road is closed all winter. A trail leads along the lake's northern shore, and canoes are rented for $25 per hour from the concession below the lodge.

Sightseeing Gondola

During summer the main ski lift at Lake Louise winter resort (403/522-3555) whisks visitors up the face of Mount Whitehorn to Whitehorn Lodge in either open chairs or enclosed gondola cars. The view from the top—

at an altitude of more than two km (1.2 miles) above sea level across the Bow Valley, Lake Louise, and the Continental Divide—is among the most spectacular in the Canadian Rockies. Short trails lead through the forests, across open meadows, and, for the energetic, to the summit of Mount Whitehorn, more than 600 vertical meters (1,970 vertical feet) above. Visitors are free to walk these trails, but it pays to join a guided walk ($3–5) if you'd like to learn about the surrounding environment. After working up an appetite (and working off breakfast), head to the teahouse in the Whitehorn Lodge, try the outdoor barbecue, or, back at the base area, enjoy lunch at the Lodge of the Ten Peaks, the resort's impressive post-and-beam day lodge. The lift operates mid-May to September daily 8:30 A.M.–6 P.M.; adult $21, senior $19, child $10. Dine-and-ride

LAKE LOUISE

To Icefields Parkway and Jasper

Mud Lake

Pipestone River

TRANSCANADA

To Lake Louise gondola and winter resort

Bow River

WHITEHORN RD

LAKE LOUISE INN

STATION RESTAURANT

VILLAGE RD

BOW VALLEY PARKWAY

SENTINEL RD

POST HOTEL
SAMSON MALL

HI-LAKE LOUISE ALPINE CENTRE

MOUNTAINEER LODGE

Tramline Trail

FAIRVIEW RD

1A HWY

(CLOSED TO VEHICLES)

MOON

FAIRMONT CHATEAU LAKE LOUISE

Lake Agnes Trail

DEER LODGE

Louise Creek

TENT CAMPGROUND

Louise Lakeshore

STABLES

PARADISE LODGE AND BUNGALOWS

To Banff

Lake Louise

BOAT HOUSE

LAKE LOUISE DR

Tramline Trail

1A

TRAILER CAMPGROUND

FAIRVIEW LOOKOUT

0   0.3 mi

0   0.3 km

Bow River Loop

Saddleback Trail

MORAINE LAKE RD

© AVALON TRAVEL PUBLISHING, INC.

To Moraine Lake

packages are an excellent deal. Pay an extra $2 per person and have a buffet breakfast (7:30–10:30 A.M.) included with the gondola ride or $6 extra for lunch (11:30 A.M.– 2:30 P.M.). Free shuttles run from Lake Louise accommodations to the day lodge.

HIKING

The variety of hiking opportunities in the vicinity of Lake Louise and Moraine Lake is surely equal to any area on the face of the earth. The region's potential for outdoor recreation was first realized in the late 1800s, and it soon became the center of hiking activity in the Canadian Rockies. This popularity continues today; trails here are among the most heavily used in

the park. Hiking is best early or late in the short summer season. Head out early in the morning to miss the strollers, high heels, dogs, and bearbells that you'll surely encounter during the busiest periods.

The two main trailheads are at Fairmont Chateau Lake Louise and Moraine Lake. Two trails lead from the village to the chateau (a pleasant alternative to driving the steep and busy Lake Louise Drive). Shortest is the 2.7-km/1.7-mile **Louise Creek Trail.** It begins on the downstream side of the point where Lake Louise Drive crosses the Bow River, crosses Louise Creek three times, and ends at the Lake Louise parking lot. The other trail, **Tramline,** is 4.5 km (2.8 miles) longer but not as steep. It begins behind the railway station and follows the route of a narrow-gauge railway that once transported guests from the CPR line to Chateau Lake Louise.

Bow River Loop

• Length: 7 km/4.3 miles (1.5–2 hours)
• Elevation gain: minimal
• Rating: easy
• Trailheads: various points throughout Lake Louise Village, including behind Samson Mall

This loop follows both banks of the Bow River southeast from the railway station. Used by joggers and cyclists to access various points in the village, the trail also links the station to the Lake Louise Alpine Centre, Post Hotel, Samson Mall, both campgrounds, and the Louise Creek and Tramline trails to Lake Louise. Interpretive signs along its length provide information on the Bow River ecosystem.

Louise Lakeshore

• Length: 2 km/1.2 miles (30 minutes) one-way
• Elevation gain: none
• Rating: easy
• Trailhead: Lake Louise, four km (2.5 miles) from TransCanada Highway

Probably the busiest trail in all of the Canadian Rockies, this one follows the north shore of Lake Louise from in front of the chateau to the west end of the lake. Here numerous braided glacial streams empty their silt-filled waters into Lake Louise. Along the trail's length are benches for sitting and pondering what English mountaineer James Outram once described as "a gem of composition and of coloring . . . perhaps unrivalled anywhere."

Plain of the Six Glaciers

• Length: 5.3 km/3.3 miles (90 minutes) one-way
• Elevation gain: 370 meters/1,215 feet
• Rating: easy/moderate
• Trailhead: Lake Louise

Hikers along this trail are rewarded not only with panoramic views of the glaciated peaks of the

looking back at Fairmont Chateau Lake Louise from Louise Lakeshore Trail

main range, but also with a rustic trail's-end tea-house serving homemade goodies baked on a wooden stove. For the first two km (1.2 miles), the trail follows Louise Lakeshore Trail to the western end of the lake. From there it begins a steady climb through a forest of spruce and sub-alpine fir. It enters an open area where an avalanche has come tumbling down (now a col-orful carpet of wildflowers), then passes through a forested area into a vast wasteland of moraines produced by the advance and retreat of Victoria Glacier. Views of surrounding peaks continue to improve until the trail enters a stunted for-est. After switchbacking up through this forest, the trail arrives at the teahouse.

Built by the CPR at the turn of the 20th cen-tury, the teahouse operates the same way now as it did then. Supplies are packed in by horse and all cooking is done in a rustic kitchen. It's open July through early September. After resting, con-tinue one km (.6 mile) to the end of the trail on the narrow top of a lateral moraine. From here the trail's namesakes are visible. From left to right the glaciers are Aberdeen, Upper Lefroy, Lower Lefroy, Upper Victoria, Lower Victoria, and Pope's. Between Mount Lefroy (3,441 me-ters/11,290 feet) and Mount Victoria (3,459 meters/11,350 feet) is Abbot Pass, where it's pos-sible to make out Abbot Hut on the skyline. When constructed in 1922, this stone structure was the highest building in Canada. The pass and hut are named for Phillip Abbot, who died attempting to climb Mount Lefroy in 1896.

⋈ Lake Agnes
• Length: 3.6 km/2.2 miles (90 minutes) one-way
• Elevation gain: 400 meters/1,312 feet
• Rating: moderate
• Trailhead: Lake Louise

This moderately strenuous hike is one of the park's most popular. It begins in front of the chateau, branching right near the beginning of the Louise Lakeshore Trail. For the first 2.5 km (1.6 miles), the trail climbs steeply, switchbacking through a forest of subalpine fir and Engelmann spruce, crossing a horse trail, passing a lookout, and leveling out at tiny Mirror Lake. Here the

old, traditional trail veers right (use it if the ground is wet or snowy), while a more direct route veers left to the Plain of the Six Glaciers. The final elevation gain along both trails is made easier by a flight of steps beside Bridal Veil Falls. The trail ends beside a rustic teahouse overlook-ing Lake Agnes, a subalpine lake nestled in a hanging valley. The teahouse offers homemade soups, healthy sandwiches, and a wide assort-ment of teas.

From the teahouse a one-km (.6-mile) trail leads to Little Beehive and impressive views of the Bow Valley. Another trail leads around the northern shore of Lake Agnes, climbing to Big Beehive (see following hike) or joining to the Plain of the Six Glaciers Trail (see preceding hike), just 3.2 km (two miles) from the chateau and 2.1 km (1.3 miles) from the teahouse at the end of that trail.

Big Beehive
• Length: 5 km/3.1 miles (two hours) one-way
• Elevation gain: 520 meters/1,710 feet
• Rating: moderate
• Trailhead: Lake Louise

The lookout atop the larger of the two "bee-hives" is one of the best places to admire the uniquely colored waters of Lake Louise, more than 500 meters (1,640 feet) directly below. The various trails to the summit have one thing in common—all are steep. But the rewards are worth every drop of sweat along the way. The most popular route follows the Lake Agnes Trail for the first 3.6 km (2.2 miles) to Lake Agnes. From the teahouse, a trail leads to the western end of the lake, then switchbacks steeply up an ex-posed north-facing ridge. At the crest of the ridge, the trail forks. To the right it descends to the Plain of the Six Glaciers Trail; to the left it continues 300 meters (.2 mile) to a log gazebo. This trail is not well defined, but scrambling through the large boulders is easy. Across Lake Louise is Fairview Mountain (2,745 meters/9,000 feet), and behind this peak is the distinctive shape of Mount Temple (3,549 meters/11,645 feet). Views also extend up the lake to Mount Lefroy and northeast to Lake Louise winter resort. Views from the edge of the cliff are spectacular, but be very careful—it's a long, long way down. By returning down the Lake Louise side of the Big Beehive, the loop is 11.5 km (7.1 miles).

Saddleback

- Length: 3.7 km/2.3 miles (90 minutes) one-way
- Elevation gain: 600 meters/1,970 feet
- Rating: moderate
- Trailhead: boathouse, Lake Louise

This trail climbs the lower slopes of Fairview Mountain from beside the boatshed on Lake Louise, ending in an alpine meadow with a view of Mount Temple from across Paradise Valley. Four hundred meters (.2 mile) from the trailhead, the trail forks. Keep left and follow the steep switchbacks through a forest of Englemann spruce and subalpine fir until reaching the flower-filled meadow. The meadow is actually a pass between Fairview Mountain (to the northwest) and Saddle Mountain (to the southeast). Although most hikers are content with the awesome views from the pass and return along the same trail, it is possible to continue to the summit of Fairview (2,745 meters/9,000 feet), a further climb of 400 vertical meters (1,310 vertical feet). The barely discernible, switchbacking trail to the summit begins near a stand of larch trees above the crest of Saddleback. As you would expect, the view from the top is stupendous; Lake Louise is more than one km (.6 mile) directly below. This option is for strong, experienced hikers only. From the Saddleback, the trail descends into Sheol Valley, then into Paradise Valley. The entire loop would be 15 km (9.3 miles).

Paradise Valley

- Length: 18 km/11.2 miles (six hours) round-trip
- Elevation gain: 380 meters/1,250 feet
- Rating: moderate
- Trailhead: Moraine Lake Road, 3.5 km (2.2 miles) from Lake Louise Drive

This aptly named trail makes for a long day hike, but it can be broken up by overnighting at the backcountry campground at the far end of the loop. The trail climbs steadily for the first five km (3.1 miles), crossing Paradise Creek numerous times and passing the junction of a trail that climbs the Sheol Valley to Saddleback (see preceding hike). After five km (3.1 miles) the trail divides again, following either side of the valley to form a 13-km (eight-mile) loop. **Lake Annette** is 700 meters (.4 mile) along the left fork. It's a typical subalpine lake in a unique setting—nestled against the near-vertical 1,200-meter (3,940-foot) north face of snow- and ice-capped **Mount Temple** (3,549 meters/11,645 feet), one of the 10 highest peaks in the Canadian Rockies. This difficult face was successfully climbed in 1966, relatively late for mountaineering firsts. The lake is a worthy destination in itself. Allow yourself four hours round-trip from the trailhead. For those completing the entire loop, continue beyond the lake into an open avalanche area that affords views across Paradise Valley. Look and listen for pikas and marmots among the boulders. The trail then passes through Horseshoe Meadow, crosses Paradise Creek, and heads back down the valley. Keep to the left at all trail crossings and you'll quickly arrive at a series of waterfalls known as the Giant Steps. From the base of these falls, it is eight km (five miles) back to the trailhead.

Larch Valley

- Length: 2.9 km/1.8 miles (60 minutes) one-way
- Elevation gain: 400 meters/1,310 feet
- Rating: moderate
- Trailhead: Moraine Lake, 13 km (eight miles) from Lake Louise Drive

In fall, when the larch trees have turned a magnificent gold and the sun is shining, few spots in the Canadian Rockies can match the beauty of this valley, but don't expect to find much solitude (and don't be too disappointed if the trail is closed in fall—it often is because of wildlife). Although the most popular time for visiting the valley is fall, it is a worthy destination all summer, when the open meadows are filled with colorful wildflowers. The trail begins just past Moraine Lake Lodge and climbs fairly steeply with occasional glimpses of Moraine Lake below. After reaching the junction of the Eiffel Lake Trail, keep right, passing through an open forest of larch and into the meadow beyond. The range of larch is restricted within the park, and this is one of the few areas where they are prolific. Mount Fay (3,235 meters/10,615 feet) is the dominant peak on the skyline, rising above the other mountains that make up the Valley of the Ten Peaks.

Sentinel Pass

- Length: 5.8 km/3.6 miles (2–3 hours) one-way
- Elevation gain: 725 meters/2,380 feet
- Rating: moderate/difficult
- Trailhead: Moraine Lake

Keen hikers should consider continuing through the open meadows of Larch Valley to Sentinel Pass (2,608 meters/8,560 feet), one of the park's highest trail-accessible passes. The length and elevation gain listed are from Moraine Lake. Once in Larch Valley, you're halfway there and have made over half of the elevation gain. Upon reaching Larch Valley, take the formed trail that winds through the open meadow. From the end of the meadow, the trail switchbacks for 1.2 kilometers (.7 mile) up a steep scree slope to the pass, sandwiched between Pinnacle Mountain (3,067 meters/10,060 feet) and Mount Temple (3,549 meters/11,645 feet). From the pass most hikers opt to return along the same trail, although with advanced planning it is possible to continue into Paradise Valley and back to the Moraine Lake access road, a total of 17 km (10.6 miles) one way.

Eiffel Lake

- Length: 5.6 km/3.5 miles (two hours) one-way
- Elevation gain: 400 meters/1,310 feet
- Rating: moderate/difficult
- Trailhead: Moraine Lake

Eiffel Lake is small, and looks even smaller in its rugged and desolate setting, surrounded by the famed Valley of the Ten Peaks. For the first 2.4 km (1.5 miles), follow the Larch Valley Trail (see *Larch Valley* hike), then fork left. Most of the elevation gain has already been made, and the trail remains relatively level before emerging onto an open slope from where each of the 10

peaks can be seen, along with Moraine Lake far below. From left to right the peaks are Fay, Little, Bowlen, Perren, Septa, Allen, Tuzo, Deltaform, Neptuak, and Wenkchemna. The final two peaks are divided by Wenkchemna Pass (2,605 meters/8,550 feet), a further four km (2.5 miles) and 360 vertical meters (1,180 vertical feet) above Eiffel Lake. The lake itself soon comes into view. It lies in a depression formed by a rockslide from Neptuak Mountain. The lake is named for **Eiffel Peak** (3,085 meters/10,120 feet), a rock pinnacle behind it, which with a little imagination could be compared to the Eiffel Tower in Paris.

Consolation Lakes

- Length: 3 km/1.9 miles (one hour) one-way
- Elevation gain: 65 meters/213 feet
- Rating: easy/moderate
- Trailhead: beside the restrooms at Moraine Lake parking lot

This short trail begins with a crossing of Moraine Creek at the outlet of Moraine Lake and ends at a pleasant subalpine lake. The first section of the trail traverses a boulder-strewn rock pile—the result of rock slides on the imposing Tower of Babel (3,100 meters/10,170 feet)—before entering a dense forest of Engelmann spruce and subalpine fir and following Babel Creek to the lower lake. The wide valley affords 360-degree views of the surrounding jagged peaks, including Mount Temple back down the valley and Mounts Bident and Quandra at the far end of the lakes. After eating a picnic lunch (from Laggans, in the Samson Mall) while perched on one of many boulders, you could continue to Upper Consolation Lake by crossing Babel Creek and following a usually wet and muddy trail along the lake's eastern shore.

Skoki Lodge

- Length: 14.4 km/8.9 miles (five hours) one-way
- Elevation gain: 775 meters/2,540 feet
- Rating: moderate/difficult
- Trailhead: end of Fish Creek Road, off Whitehorn Road 1.8 km (1.1 miles) north of Lake Louise interchange

The trail into historic Skoki Lodge is only one of the endless hiking opportunities tucked behind Lake Louise winter resort, across the valley from all hikes detailed previously. The first four km (2.5 miles) of the trail are along a gravel access road leading to Temple Lodge, part of the Lake Louise winter resort. From here, the trail climbs to Boulder Pass, passing a campground and Halfway Hut, above Corral Creek. The pass harbors a large population of pikas and hoary marmots. The trail then follows the north shore of Ptarmigan Lake before climbing again to Deception Pass, named for its false summit. It then descends into Skoki Valley, passing the Skoki Lakes and eventually reaching Skoki Lodge (see *Accommodations and Camping*). Just over one km (.6 mile) beyond the lodge is a campground, an excellent base for exploring the region.

OTHER SUMMER RECREATION

In Lake Louise, "summer fun" means hiking—and lots of it. You may see small fish swimming along the shore of Lake Louise, but the fishing in this lake and all others in the area is poor due to the super-cold glacial water. Talking of cold water, everyone is invited to take a swim in Lake Louise to celebrate the country's national holiday, **Canada Day** (July 1). You don't need to be Canadian to join in—just brave.

Horseback Riding

Through summer, **Brewster Lake Louise Stables** (403/522-3511) offers 90-minute rides to the end of Lake Louise for $65, half-day rides to Lake Agnes Teahouse for $95, and all-day rides up Paradise Valley, including lunch, for $155.

WINTERTIME

Lake Louise is an immense winter playground offering one of the world's premier alpine resorts, unlimited cross-country skiing, ice-skating, sleigh rides, and nearby heli-skiing. Between November and May, accommodation prices are reduced by up to 70 percent (except Christmas holidays). Lift and lodging packages begin at $80 per person, and you'll always be able to get a table at your favorite restaurant.

Lake Louise Resort

Canada's answer to U.S. mega-resorts such as Vail and Killington is Lake Louise (403/522-3555 or 877/253-6888, www.skilouise.com), which opens in November and operates until mid-May. The nation's second-largest winter resort (behind only Whistler/Blackcomb) comprises 1,700 hectares (4,200 acres) of gentle trails, mogul fields, long cruising runs, steep chutes, and vast bowls filled with famous Rocky Mountain powder.

The resort is made up of four distinct faces. The front side has a vertical drop of 1,000 meters (3,280 feet) and is served by eight lifts, including four high-speed quads, and western Canada's only six-passenger chairlift. Resort statistics are impressive: a 990-meter (3,250-foot) vertical rise, 1,700 hectares (4,200 acres) of patrolled terrain, and more than 100 named runs. The four back bowls are each as big as many midsize resorts and are all well above the tree line. Larch and Ptarmigan faces have a variety of terrain, allowing you to follow the sun as it moves across the sky or escape into trees for protection on windy days. Each of the three day lodges has a restaurant and bar. Ski and snowboard rentals, clothing, and souvenirs are available in the Lodge of the Ten Peaks, a magnificent post-and-beam day lodge that overlooks the front face.

Lift tickets are $65 per day adults, $51 seniors, and $19 children younger than 12. Free guided tours of the mountain are available three times daily—inquire at customer service. Free shuttle buses run regularly from Lake Louise accommodations to the hill. From Banff you pay $15 round-trip for transportation to Lake Louise.

Other Winter Activities

The most popular **cross-country skiing** areas are on Lake Louise, along Moraine Lake Road, and in Skoki Valley at the back of the Lake Louise ski area. For details and helpful trail classifications, pick up a copy of *Cross-Country Skiing–Nordic Trails in Banff National Park,* from the Lake Louise Visitor Centre. Before heading out, check the weather forecast at the visitors center or call 403/762-2088. For avalanche reports, call 403/762-1460.

Of all the **skating** rinks in Canada, the one on frozen Lake Louise, in front of the Chateau, is surely the most spectacular. Spotlights allow skating after dark, and on special occasions hot chocolate is served. Skates are available in the chateau at **Monod Sports** (403/522-3837); $12 for two hours.

Brewster Lake Louise Sleigh Rides (403/522-3511) offers rides in traditional horse-drawn sleighs along the shores of Lake Louise beginning from in front of the chateau. Although blankets are supplied, you should still bundle up. The one-hour ride is $20 per person, $14 for children. Reservations are necessary. The rides are scheduled hourly from 11 A.M. on weekends, from 3 P.M. weekdays.

ACCOMMODATIONS AND CAMPING

In summer, accommodations at Lake Louise are even harder to come by than in Banff, so it's essential to make reservations well in advance. Any rooms not taken by early afternoon will be the expensive ones.

Under $50

With beds for $100 less than anyplace else in the village, the **HI–Lake Louise Alpine Centre** (403/522-2200 or 866/762-4122, www.hihostels.ca) is understandably popular. Of log construction, with large windows and high vaulted ceilings, the lodge is a joint venture between the Alpine Club of Canada and the Southern Alberta Hostelling Association. Downstairs is a large reception area and **Bill Peyto's Cafe,** the least expensive place to eat in Lake Louise. Upstairs is a large lounge area and guide's room—a quiet place to plan your next hike or browse through the large collection of mountain literature. Members of Hostelling International pay $34 per person per night (nonmembers $38) for a dorm bed or $99 s or d ($112 for nonmembers) in a private room. Rates are discounted to $27 for a dorm and $78 s or d for a private room ($31

and $86, respectively, for nonmembers) October through May, including throughout the extremely busy winter season. The hostel is open year-round, with check-in after 3 P.M. In summer and on weekends during the winter season, advance bookings (up to six months) are essential. The hostel is on Village Road, less than one km (.6 mile) from Samson Mall.

$150–200

An excellent option for families and those looking for old-fashioned mountain charm is **N Paradise Lodge and Bungalows** (403/522-3595, www.paradiselodge.com; mid-May to mid-Oct.). This family-operated lodge provides excellent value in a wonderfully tranquil setting. Spread out around well-manicured gardens are 21 attractive cabins in four configurations. Each has a rustic, yet warm and inviting interior, with comfortable beds, separate sitting areas, and well-appointed bathrooms. Instead of television, children are kept happy with a playground that includes a sandbox and jungle gym. On Sunday night, a local naturalist presents an outdoor interpretive program for interested guests. The least expensive cabins—complete with a classic cast-iron stove/fireplace combo are $195 s or d, or pay $30 extra for a big deck with soaring valley views. Twenty-four luxury suites, each with a fireplace, TV, one or two bedrooms, and fabulous mountain views, start at $260, or $280 with a kitchen. The Honeymoon Suite, with all of the above as well as a large hot tub, is $300. To get there from the valley floor, follow Lake Louise Drive toward the Fairmont Chateau Lake Louise for three km (1.9 miles); the lake itself is just one km (.6 mile) farther up the hill.

Historic **Deer Lodge** (403/410-7417 or 800/661-1595, www.crmr.com/dl) began life in 1921 as a teahouse, with rooms added in 1925. Facilities include a rooftop hot tub, game room, restaurant, and bar. The least expensive rooms ($175 s or d) are small and don't have phones. Rooms in the $200–250 range are considerably larger, or pay $270 for a heritage-themed Tower Room. Deer Lodge is along Lake Louise Drive, up the hill from the village, and just a five-minute walk from the lake itself.

On the valley floor, **Mountaineer Lodge** (403/522-3844, www.mountaineerlodge.com; May–Oct.) charges from $170 s, $180 d for large, functional guest rooms, many with mountain views. Rates are halved during the first and last months of the operating season.

Aside from the chateau, the **Lake Louise Inn** (210 Village Rd., 403/522-3791 or 800/661-9237, www.lakelouiseinn.com) is the village's largest lodging, with more than 200 units spread throughout five buildings. Beyond the lobby, in the main lodge, is an activities desk, a pizzeria, a restaurant, a bar, a gift shop, and a large indoor pool. Standard rooms are $170 s or d, rising well above $200 for a suite with a fireplace.

Over $200

Originally called Lake Louise Ski Lodge, the **N Post Hotel** (403/522-3989 or 800/661-1586, www.posthotel.com) is one of only a handful of Canadian lodges that have been accepted into the prestigious Relaix & Châteaux organization. Bordered to the east and south by the Pipestone River, it may lack views of Lake Louise, but it is as elegant, in a modern, woodsy way, as the chateau. Each bungalow-style room is furnished with Canadian pine and has a balcony. Many rooms have whirlpools and fireplaces, while some have kitchens. Other facilities include an indoor pool, steam room, and library. The hotel has 17 different room types, with 26 different rates depending on the view. Rates start at $330 s or d per night. Between the main lodge and the Pipestone River are three sought-after cabins, each with a wood-burning fireplace; $270–450 s or d.

At the lake for which it's named, four km (2.5 miles) from the valley floor, is super-luxurious **Moraine Lake Lodge** (403/522-3733 or 800/661-8340, www.morainelake.com; June–Sept.). Designed by renowned architect Arthur Erickson, the lodge is a bastion of understated charm, partially obscured from the masses of day-trippers who visit the lake and yet taking full advantage of its location beside one of the world's most-photographed lakes. The decor reflects the wilderness location, with an abundance of polished log work and solid, practical furnishings in heritage-themed rooms. The rooms have no TVs or phones; in-

Lake Louise's Post Hotel enjoys a centrally located, riverside location.

© ANDREW HEMPSTEAD

stead guests take guided nature walks, have unlimited use of canoes, and are pampered with complimentary afternoon tea and evening liqueurs. Lodge rooms are $465 s or d, King Cabins $530.

The famously fabulous **Fairmont Chateau Lake Louise** (403/522-3511 or 800/257-7544, www.fairmont.com), a historic 500-room hotel on the shore of Lake Louise, has views equal to any mountain resort in the world. But all this historic charm and mountain scenery comes at a price. During the summer season (late June to mid-Oct.), the rack rate for rooms *without* a lake view is $700 s or d, while those with a view are $840. Rooms on the Fairmont Gold Floor come with a private concierge and upgraded everything. As at the company's sister property in Banff, most summer guests book a room as part of a Canadian Rockies Experience package, costing from $600 per person for accommodations, a wide range of activities, and all meals. Official rates drop as low as $200 s, $250 d outside of summer, with accommodation and lift packages often advertised for around $200 d. Children younger than 17 sharing with parents are free, but if you bring a pet it'll be an extra $25.

If you're prepared to lace up your hiking boots for a true mountain experience, consider spending time at **M Skoki Lodge** (403/256-8473 or 800/258-7669 www.skokilodge.com), north of the Lake Louise ski resort and far from the nearest road. Getting there requires an 11-km (6.8-mile) hike or ski, depending on the season. The lodge is an excellent base for exploring nearby valleys and mountains. It dates to 1930, when it operated as a lodge for local Banff skiers, and is now a National Historic Site. Today it comprises a main lodge, three cabins, and a wood-fired sauna. Accommodations are rustic—no electricity, propane heat—but comfortable, with mostly twin beds ($160 per person) in the main lodge and cabins that sleep up to five ($185–200 per person). Rates include three meals daily, including a picnic lunch that guests build from a buffet-style layout before heading out hiking or skiing. The dining room and lounge center on a wood-burning fire, where guests come together each evening to swap tales from the trail. The operating season is mid-June to mid-October and mid-December to mid-April.

Campgrounds

Exit the TransCanada Highway at the Lake Louise interchange, 56 km (35 miles) northwest of Banff, and take the first left beyond Samson Mall and under the railway bridge to reach **Lake Louise Campground,** within easy walking distance of the village. The campground is divided into two sections by the Bow River, but linked by bridge. Individual sites throughout are close together, but some privacy and shade are provided by towering lodgepole pines. Just under 200 serviced (powered) sites are grouped together at the end of the road. In addition to hookups, this section has showers and flush toilets; $26. Across the river are 216 unserviced sites, each with a fire ring and picnic table. Other amenities include kitchen shelters and a modern bathroom complex complete with hot showers. These cost $22 per night. A dump station is near the entrance to the campground ($6 per use). An interpretive program runs throughout summer, nightly at 9 P.M. (except Tuesday) in the outdoor theater. The serviced section of this campground is open year-round, the unserviced section mid-May to September.

From the campground, the Bow River Loop hiking trail leads into the village along either side of the Bow River, crossing at the southern end of the serviced sites and again behind Samson Mall.

FOOD AND DRINK

Other guidebooks encourage readers to "eat at your hotel." Not only is this unhelpful, it's misleading—the village of Lake Louise may exist only to serve travelers, but there are good dining options serving all budgets.

Breakfast

Please don't eat breakfast at the gas station restaurant simply because it is the first place you spot coming off the highway. If you don't feel like a cooked breakfast, start your day off at **M Laggan's Mountain Bakery** (Samson Mall, 403/552-2017; daily 6 A.M.–8 P.M.), *the* place to hang out with a coffee and a freshly baked breakfast croissant, pastry, cake, or muffin. If the tables are full and you manage to somehow reach the cake cabinet, order take-out and enjoy your feast on the grassy bank behind the mall. The chocolate brownie ($1.50) is delicious. Order two slices to save having to line up again.

Across the TransCanada Highway, the **Lodge of the Ten Peaks,** at the base of Lake Louise winter resort (403/522-3555), is open in summer daily 7:30–10:30 A.M. for a large and varied breakfast buffet that costs a super-reasonable $9 per person. An even better deal is to purchase a breakfast/gondola ride combo for $23 (the gondola ride alone is $21). The buffet lunch (11:30 A.M.–2:30 P.M.) is $16, or $27 with the gondola ride. Discounts apply for seniors and children.

If you made the effort to rise early and experienced the early-morning tranquility of Moraine Lake, the perfect place to sit back and watch the tour bus crowds pour in is from the dining room of ▶ **Moraine Lake Lodge** (403/522-3733; June–Sept. daily from 7:30 A.M.). Staying overnight at the lodge may be an extravagant splurge, but breakfast isn't. A simple, well-presented Continental buffet is just $13, while the hot version is a reasonable $16.

Samson Mall and Surrounds

In the center of the action, Samson Mall is a hive of activity each afternoon as campers descend on a single grocery store to stock up on supplies for the evening meal. Prices are high, and by the end of the day stocks are low. The mall is also home to **Laggan's,** a take-out fast-food place, and a liquor store. Upstairs in the mall is the **Lake Louise Village Grill & Bar** (403/522-3879). The tiled entrance looks like a public washroom and the food's ordinary. For a casual meal, much better is **Bill Peyto's Cafe** in the Lake Louise Alpine Centre (Village Rd., 403/522-2200; daily 7 A.M.– 9 P.M.). The food is consistent and well priced. A huge portion of nachos is $7, pasta is $9–12, and stir-fries range $10–14.

Lake Louise Station Restaurant

One hundred years ago visitors departing trains at Laggan Station were keen to get to the Chateau Lake Louise as quickly as possible to begin their adventure. Today, guests from the chateau, other hotels, and even people from as far away as Banff are returning to dine in the restored ▶ **Station Restaurant** (200 Sentinel Rd., 403/522-2600; lunch daily from 11:30 A.M., dinner from 6 P.M.). Although the menu is not extensive, it puts an emphasis on creating imaginative dishes with a combination of Canadian produce and Asian ingredients. Lighter lunches include a Caesar salad topped with roasted garlic dressing—perfect for those planning an afternoon hike. In the evening, expect starters such as red shrimp and scallops with a mild Indonesian orange cream sauce ($10) and entrées like a memorable baked sea bass ($28).

Post Hotel

In 1987, the ▶ **Post Hotel** was expanded to include a luxurious new wing. The original log building was renovated as a rustic, timbered dining room (403/522-3989; daily 11:30 A.M.–2 P.M. and 5–9:30 P.M.) linked to the rest of the hotel by an intimate lounge. Although the dining room isn't cheap, it's a favorite of locals and visitors alike. The chef specializes in European cuisine, preparing several Swiss dishes (such as veal zurichois) to make owner George Schwarz feel less homesick. But he's also renowned for his presentation of Alberta beef, Pacific salmon, and Peking duck. Main meals start at $25. Reservations are essential for dinner.

Fairmont Chateau Lake Louise

Within this famous lakeside hotel is a choice of eateries and an ice-cream shop. For all chateau dining reservations, call 403/522-3511.

The **Poppy Brasserie** has obscured lake views and is the most casual place for a meal. Breakfasts (daily 7–10:30 A.M.) are offered buffet-style ($25 per person), a little expensive for light eaters. Lunch and dinner (daily 11:30 A.M.–8:30 P.M.) are à la carte. The **Walliser Stube** (daily 6–9:30 P.M.) is an elegant two-story wine bar decorated with rich wood paneling and solid oak furniture. It offers a simple menu of German dishes from $18.95 as well as cheese fondue. The **Lakeview Lounge** is along floor-to-ceiling windows with magnificent lake views. Choose this dining area for afternoon tea (daily noon–4 P.M.; reservations required; $27 per person, or $35 with a glass of champagne).

The **Victoria Room** (summer only daily 7 A.M.–9 P.M.) enjoys excellent views across the lake to the mountain for which it's named. This restaurant combines the elegance of a European ballroom with a charming alpine allure. It's open for breakfast, a buffet lunch (Sunday brunch), and evening dining with choices that range from traditional British dishes to innovative Pacific Northwest fare.

The **Fairview Dining Room** (daily 6–9 P.M.) has a lot more than just a fair view. As the chateau's signature dining room, it enjoys the best views and offers the most elegant setting. Appetizers start at $7, while entrées combine Canadian produce with classic European cooking styles (mains $24–37).

Bars and Nightlife

The lounge in the **Post Hotel** (200 Pipestone Dr., 403/522-3989) oozes mountain style and upscale charm. It's cozy, quiet and the perfect place to relax in front of a fire with a cocktail before moving on to the adjacent fine-dining restaurant. Not your scene? Hang out with seasonal workers at the smoky **Lake Louise Grill & Bar** (upstairs in Samson Mall, 403/522-3879) then move across the road with your newfound friends to **Charlie's Pub** (Lake Louise Inn, 403/522-3791) for dancing to recorded music until 2 A.M. Up at the Fairmont Chateau Lake Louise (403/522-3511) is **The Glacier Saloon,** where on most summer nights a DJ plays music ranging from pop to western.

INFORMATION AND SERVICES

Information

The **Lake Louise Visitor Centre** (403/522-3833; mid-June–Aug. daily 8 A.M.–8 P.M., mid-May–mid-June and Sept. daily 8 A.M.–6 P.M., the rest of the year daily 9 A.M.–4 P.M.) is beside Samson Mall on Village Road. This excellent Parks Canada facility has interpretive displays, slide and video displays, and staff on hand to answer questions, recommend hikes suited to your ability, and issue Wilderness Passes to those heading out into the backcountry. Look for the stuffed (literally) female grizzly and read her fascinating, but sad, story.

Bookstores

Woodruff & Blum (Samson Mall, 403/522-3842; daily 9 A.M.–10 P.M.) offers an excellent selection of books on the natural and human history of the park, as well as animal field guides, hiking guides, and general western Canadiana. In the Fairmont Chateau Lake Louise, **Mountain Lights Gift Shop** (403/522-3734) has a similar albeit smaller collection.

Services

A small postal outlet in Samson Mall also serves as a bus depot and car rental agency. Although Lake Louise has no banks, there's a currency exchange in the Fairmont Chateau Lake Louise

and a cash machine in the grocery store. The mall also holds a busy laundromat (summer, daily 8 A.M.–8 P.M., shorter hours the rest of the year). Camping supplies and bike rentals are available from **Wilson Mountain Sports** (403/522-3636; daily 9 A.M.–9 P.M.

Pipestone Photo (403/522-3617; daily 9 A.M.–7 P.M.) has a range of photographic supplies unequaled in all of the Canadian Rockies. It's relatively well priced and has one-hour photo developing.

The closest **hospital** is in Banff (403/762-2222). For the local **RCMP,** call 403/522-3811.

TRANSPORTATION

Getting There

Calgary International Airport is the closest airport to Lake Louise. **Brewster** (403/762-6767 or 800/661-1152, www.brewster.ca), **Banff Airporter** (403/762-3330 or 888/449-2901, www.banffairporter.com), and **Rocky Mountain Sky Shuttle** (403/762-5200 or 762-8754, www.rockymountainskyshuttle.com) offer at least a couple of shuttles per day that continue beyond Banff to Lake Louise from the airport. All charge around the same—$50 each way, with a slight round-trip discount.

Greyhound (403/522-2121) leaves the Calgary bus depot (877 Greyhound Way SW) five times daily for Lake Louise. The fare is less than that charged by Brewster, and the Banff–Lake Louise portion only is around $12. From Vancouver, it's a 13-hour ride to Lake Louise aboard the Greyhound bus.

Getting Around

Samson Mall is the commercial heart of Lake Louise village. If the parking lot out front is full, consider leaving your vehicle across the road behind the Esso gas station, where one area is set aside for large RVs. The campground, alpine center, and hotels are all within easy walking distance of Samson Mall. Fairmont Chateau Lake Louise is a 2.7-km (1.7-mile) walk from the valley floor. The only car-rental agency in the village is **National** (403/522-3870). The agency doesn't have many vehicles;

you'd be better off picking one up at Calgary International Airport. **Lake Louise Taxi & Tours** (Samson Mall, 403/522-2020) charges $2.50 for flag drop, then $1.60 per km. From the mall to Fairmont Chateau Lake Louise runs around $12, to Moraine Lake $25, and to Banff $130. **Wilson Mountain Sports** (Samson Mall, 403/522-3636) has mountain bikes for rent from $15 per hour or $35 per day (includes a helmet, bike lock, and water bottle). Inquire here about canoe rentals for float trips along the Bow River to Banff.

Icefields Parkway–Banff

The 230-km (143-mile) Icefields Parkway, between Lake Louise and Jasper, is one of the most scenic, exciting, and inspiring mountain roads ever built. From Lake Louise it parallels the Continental Divide, following in the shadow of the highest, most rugged mountains in the Canadian Rockies. The first 122 km (76 miles) to Sunwapta Pass (the boundary between Banff and Jasper National Parks) can be driven in two hours, and the entire parkway in four hours. But it's likely you'll want to spend at least a day, probably more, stopping at each of the 13 viewpoints, hiking the trails, watching the abundant wildlife, and just generally enjoying one of the world's most magnificent landscapes. Along the section within Banff National Park are two lodges, three hostels, three campgrounds, and one gas station.

Although the road is steep and winding in places, it has a wide shoulder, making it ideal for an extended bike trip. Allow seven days to pedal north from Banff to Jasper, staying at hostels or camping along the route. This is the preferable direction to travel by bike because the elevation at the town of Jasper is more than 500 meters (1,640 feet) lower than either Banff or Lake Louise.

The parkway remains open year-round, although winter brings with it some special considerations. The road is often closed for short periods for avalanche control—check road conditions in Banff or Lake Louise before setting out. And be sure to fill up with gas; no services are available between November and April.

Lake Louise to Crowfoot Glacier

The Icefields Parkway forks right from the Trans-Canada Highway just north of Lake Louise. The impressive scenery begins immediately. Just three km (1.9 miles) from the junction is **Herbert Lake,** formed during the last ice age, when retreating glaciers deposited a pile of rubble—known as a *moraine*—across a shallow valley and water filled in behind it. The lake is a perfect place for early morning or evening photography, when the Waputik Range and distinctively shaped **Mount Temple** are reflected in its waters.

Traveling north, you'll notice numerous depressions in the steep, shaded slopes of the Waputik Range across the Bow Valley. The cooler climate on these north-facing slopes makes them

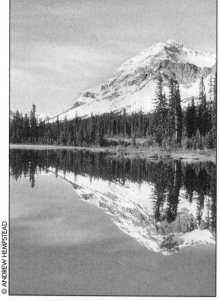

© ANDREW HEMPSTEAD

The Icefields Parkway runs beside this small body of water as it crosses Bow Pass.

prone to glaciation. Cirques were cut by small local glaciers. On the opposite side of the road, **Mount Hector** (3,394 meters/11,130 feet), easily recognized by its layered peak, soon comes into view.

Hector Lake Viewpoint is 16 km (10 miles) from the junction. Although the view is partially obscured by trees, the emerald-green waters nestled below a massive wall of limestone form a breathtaking scene. **Bow Peak,** seen looking northward along the highway, is only 2,868 meters (9,410 feet) high but is completely detached from the Waputik Range, making it a popular destination for climbers. As you leave this viewpoint, look across the northeast end of Hector Lake for glimpses of **Mount Balfour** (3,246 meters/10,650) on the distant skyline.

Crowfoot Glacier

The aptly named Crowfoot Glacier can best be appreciated from a viewpoint 17 km (10.6 miles) north of Hector Lake. The glacier sits on a wide ledge near the top of Crowfoot Mountain, from where its glacial claws cling to the mountain's steep slopes. The retreat of this glacier has been dramatic. Only 50 years ago, two of the claws extended to the base of the lower cliff. Today, they are a shadow of their former selves, barely reaching over the cliff edge.

Bow Lake

The sparkling, translucent waters of Bow Lake are among the most beautiful that can be seen from the Icefields Parkway. The lake was created when moraines deposited by retreating glaciers dammed subsequent meltwater. On still days, the water reflects the snowy peaks, their sheer cliffs, and the scree slopes that run into the lake. You don't need photography experience to take good pictures here! At the southeast end of the lake, a day-use area offers waterfront picnic tables and a trail to a swampy area at the lake's outlet. At the upper end of the lake, you'll find the historic Num-ti-jah Lodge and the trailhead for a walk to Bow Glacier Falls (see *Hiking*).

The road leaves Bow Lake and climbs to **Bow Summit.** As you look back toward the lake, its true color becomes apparent, and the Crowfoot

Glacier reveals its unique shape. At an elevation of 2,069 meters (6,790 feet), this pass is one of the highest points crossed by a public road in Canada. It is also the beginning of the Bow River, the one you camped beside at Lake Louise, photographed flowing through the town of Banff, and fished along downstream of Canmore.

Peyto Lake

From the parking lot at Bow Summit, a short paved trail leads to one of the most breathtaking views you could ever imagine. Far below the viewpoint is Peyto Lake, an impossibly intense green lake whose hues change according to season. Before heavy melting of nearby glaciers begins (in June or early July), the lake is dark blue. As summer progresses, meltwater flows across a delta and into the lake. This water is laden with finely ground particles of rock debris known as rock flour, which remains suspended in the water. It is not the mineral content of the rock flour that is responsible for the lake's unique color, but rather the particles reflecting the blue-green sector of the light spectrum. As the amount of suspended rock flour changes, so does the color of the lake.

The lake is one of many park landmarks named for early outfitter Bill Peyto (see sidebar, *Wild Bill Peyto*). In 1898, Peyto was part of an expedition camped at Bow Lake. Seeking solitude (as he was wont to do), he slipped off during the night to sleep near this lake. Other members of the party coined the name Peyto's Lake, and it stuck.

A farther three km (1.9 miles) along the parkway is a viewpoint from which **Peyto Glacier** is visible at the far end of Peyto Lake Valley. This glacier is part of the extensive **Wapta Icefield,** which straddles the Continental Divide and extends into the northern reaches of **Yoho National Park** in British Columbia.

Beside the Continental Divide

From Bow Summit, the parkway descends to a viewpoint directly across the Mistaya River from **Mount Patterson** (3,197 meters/10,490 feet). Snowbird Glacier clings precariously to the mountain's steep northeast face, and the mountain's

© ANDREW HEMPSTEAD

Peyto Lake

lower, wooded slopes are heavily scarred where rock and ice slides have swept down the mountainside.

As the parkway continues to descend and crosses Silverhorn Creek, the jagged limestone peaks of the Continental Divide can be seen to the west. **Mistaya Lake** is a three-km-long (1.9-mile-long) body of water that sits at the bottom of the valley between the road and the divide, but it can't be seen from the parkway. The best place to view it is from the Howse Peak Viewpoint at Upper Waterfowl Lake. From here the high ridge that forms the Continental Divide is easily distinguishable. Seven peaks can be seen from here, including **Howse Peak** (3,290 meters/10,790 feet). At no point along this ridge does the elevation drop below 2,750 meters (9,000 feet). From Howse Peak, the Continental Divide makes a 90-degree turn to the west. One dominant peak that can be seen from Bow Pass to north of Saskatchewan River Crossing is **Mount Chephren** (3,268 meters/10,720 feet). Its distinctive shape and position away from the

main ridge of the Continental Divide make it easy to distinguish. (Look for it directly north of Howse Peak.)

To Saskatchewan River Crossing

Numerous trails lead around the swampy shores of **Upper** and **Lower Waterfowl Lakes,** providing one of the park's best opportunities to view moose, who feed on the abundant aquatic vegetation that grows in Upper Waterfowl Lake. Rock and other debris that have been carried down nearby valley systems have built up, forming a wide alluvial fan, nearly blocking the Mistaya River and creating Upper Waterfowl Lake.

Continuing north is **Mount Murchison** (3,337 meters/10,950 feet), on the east side of the parkway. Although not one of the park's highest mountains, this gray-and-yellow massif of Cambrian rock comprises 10 individual peaks, covering an area of 3,000 hectares (7,400 acres).

From a parking lot 14 km (8.9 miles) northeast of Waterfowl Lake Campground, a short trail descends into the montane forest to **Mistaya**

Canyon. Here the effects of erosion can be appreciated as the Mistaya River leaves the floor of Mistaya Valley, plunging through a narrow-walled canyon into the North Saskatchewan Valley. The area is scarred with potholes where boulders have been whirled around by the action of fast-flowing water, carving deep depressions into the softer limestone bedrock below.

The **North Saskatchewan River** posed a major problem for early travelers and later for the builders of the Icefields Parkway. This swiftly running river eventually drains into Hudson Bay. In 1989 it was named a Canadian Heritage River. One km (.6 mile) past the bridge you'll come to a panoramic viewpoint of the entire valley. From here the Howse and Mistaya Rivers can be seen converging with the North Saskatchewan at a silt-laden delta. This is also a junction with Highway 11 (also known as David Thompson Highway), which follows the North Saskatchewan River to Rocky Mountain House and Red Deer. From this viewpoint numerous peaks can be seen to the west. Two sharp peaks are distinctive: **Mount Outram** (3,254 meters/10,680 feet) is the closer; the farther is **Mount Forbes** (3,630 meters/11,975 feet), the highest peak in Banff National Park (and the sixth highest in the Canadian Rockies).

To Sunwapta Pass

On the north side of the North Saskatchewan River is the towering hulk of **Mount Wilson** (3,261 meters/10,700 feet), named for Banff outfitter Tom Wilson. The Icefields Parkway passes this massif on its western flanks. A pullout, just past Rampart Creek Campground, offers good views of Mount Amery to the west and Mounts Sarbach, Chephren, and Murchison to the south. Beyond here is the **Weeping Wall,** a long cliff of gray limestone where a series of waterfalls tumbles more than 100 meters (330 feet) down the steep slopes of Cirrus Mountain. In winter this wall of water freezes, becoming a mecca for ice climbers.

After ascending quickly, the road drops again before beginning a long climb to Sunwapta Pass. Halfway up the 360-vertical-meter climb is a viewpoint well worth a stop (cyclists will definitely appreciate a rest). From here views extend down the valley to the slopes of Mount Saskatchewan and, on the other side of the parkway, Cirrus Mountain. Another viewpoint, farther up the road, has the added attraction of a view of Panther Falls across the valley. A cairn at **Sunwapta Pass** (2,023 meters/6,640 feet) marks the boundary between Banff and Jasper National Parks. It also marks the divide between the North Saskatchewan and Sunwapta Rivers, whose waters drain into the Atlantic and Arctic Oceans, respectively.

HIKING
Helen Lake
- Length: 6 km/3.7 miles (2.5 hours) one-way
- Elevation gain: 455 meters/1,500 feet
- Rating: moderate
- Trailhead: across the Icefields Parkway from Crowfoot Glacier Lookout, 33 km (20 miles) northwest from the junction with the Trans-Canada Highway

The trail to Helen Lake is one of the easiest ways to access a true alpine environment from the southern end of the Icefields Parkway. The trail climbs steadily through a forest of Engelmann spruce and subalpine fir for the first 2.5 km (1.6 miles) to an avalanche slope, reaching the tree line and the first good viewpoint after three km (1.9 miles). The view across the valley is spectacular, with Crowfoot Glacier visible to the southwest. As the trail reaches a ridge, it turns and descends into the glacial cirque where Helen Lake lies. Listen and look for hoary marmots around the scree slopes along the lakeshore.

For those with the time and energy, it's possible to continue an additional three km (1.9 miles) to Dolomite Pass; the trail switchbacks steeply up a further 100 vertical meters (330 vertical feet) in less than one km (.6 mile), then descends steeply for a further one km (.6 mile) to Katherine Lake and beyond to the pass.

Bow Glacier Falls
- Length: 3.4 km/2.1 miles (one hour) one-way
- Elevation gain: 130 meters/430 feet

- Rating: easy
- Trailhead: Num-ti-jah Lodge, Bow Lake, 36 km (22.3 miles) northwest from the Trans-Canada Highway

This hike skirts one of the most beautiful lakes in the Canadian Rockies before ending at a narrow but spectacular waterfall. From the parking lot in front of Num-ti-jah Lodge, follow the shore through Willow Flats to a gravel outwash area at the end of the lake. Across the lake are reflected views of Crowfoot Mountain and, farther west, a glimpse of Bow Glacier among the jagged peaks of the Waputik Range. The trail then begins a short but steep climb up the rim of a canyon before leveling out at the edge of a vast moraine of gravel, scree, and boulders. This is the end of the trail, although it's possible to reach the base of Bow Glacier Falls by picking your way through the 800 meters (.5 mile) of rough ground that remains.

Peyto Lake

- Length: 1.4 km/.9 mile (30 minutes) one-way
- Elevation loss: 100 meters/330 feet
- Rating: easy
- Trailhead: unmarked pullout, Icefields Parkway, 2.4 km (1.5 miles) north of Bow Summit

Without doubt the best place to view Peyto Lake is from a popular viewpoint accessible via a short trail from Bow Summit, 41 km (25.5 miles) along the Icefields Parkway from the TransCanada Highway. The easiest way to access the actual shoreline, though, is along this short trail farther along the highway. A pebbled beach, strewn with driftwood, is the perfect setting for picnicking, painting, or just admiring the lake's quieter side. Back at the lake lookout, a rough trail drops nearly 300 meters (980 feet) in 2.4 km (1.5 miles) to the lake.

Chephren Lake

- Length: 4 km/2.5 miles (60–90 minutes) one-way
- Elevation gain: 100 meters/330 feet
- Rating: easy
- Trailhead: Waterfowl Lake Campground, Ice-

© ANDREW HEMPSTEAD

Chephren Lake

fields Parkway, 57 km (35 miles) northwest from the TransCanada Highway

This pale-green body of water (pronounced "Kefren") is hidden from the Icefields Parkway but easily reached. The official trailhead is a bridge across the Mistaya River at the back of Waterfowl Lakes Campground (behind site 86). If you're not registered at the campground, park at the end of the unpaved road running along the front of the campground and walk 300 meters (.2 mile) down the well-worn path to the river crossing. From across the river, the trail dives headlong into a subalpine forest, reaching a crudely signposted junction after 1.6 km (one mile). Take the right fork. This leads 2.4 km to Chephren Lake, descending steeply at the end (this stretch of trail is often muddy). The lake is nestled under the buttresses of Mount Chephren. To the left—farther up the lake—is Howse Peak.

The trail to smaller **Cirque Lake** (4.5 km/2.8 miles from the trailhead) branches left 1.6 km (one mile) along this trail. It is less heavily used, but this lake is popular with anglers for its healthy population of rainbow trout.

Glacier Lake

- Length: 9 km/5.6 miles (2.5–3 hours) one-way
- Elevation gain: 220 meters/770 feet
- Rating: moderate
- Trailhead: an old gravel pit on the west side of the highway, one km (.6 mile) west of Saskatchewan River Crossing

This three-km-long (1.9-mile-long) lake is one of the park's largest lakes not accessible by road. Although not as scenic as the more accessible lakes along the parkway, it's a pleasant destination for a full-day or overnight trip. For the first one km (.6 mile), the trail passes through an open forest of lodgepole pine to a fancy footbridge across the rushing North Saskatchewan River. From there it climbs gradually to a viewpoint overlooking Howse River and the valley beyond, then turns away from the river for a long slog through dense forest to Glacier Lake. A primitive campground lies just over 300 meters (.2 mile) from where the trail emerges at the lake.

Saskatchewan Glacier

- Length: 7.3 km/4.5 miles (two hours) one-way
- Elevation gain: 150 meters/490 feet
- Rating: moderate
- Trailhead: small parking lot, 35 km (22 miles) northwest of the Saskatchewan River Crossing (just before the highway begins its "Big Bend" up to Sunwapta Pass)

The Saskatchewan Glacier, a tongue of ice from the great Columbia Icefield, is visible from various points along the Icefields Parkway. This hike will take you right to the toe of the glacier. After crossing an old concrete bridge, the trail disappears into the forest to the right, joining an overgrown road and continuing up the valley along the south bank of the river. When the toe of the glacier first comes into sight it looks deceptively close, but it's still a long hike away over rough terrain.

Nigel Pass

- Length: 7.4 km/4.6 miles (2.5 hours) one-way
- Elevation gain: 365 meters/1,200 feet
- Rating: moderate
- Trailhead: Icefields Parkway, 2.5 km (1.6 miles) north of the switchback on the "Big Bend"

Park on the east side of the highway and follow the gravel road to a locked gate. Turn right here and cross Nigel Creek on the bridge. The trail is obvious, following open avalanche paths up the east side of the valley. In a stand of Engelmann spruce and subalpine fir two km (1.2 miles) from the trailhead is an old campsite used first by native hunting parties, then by mountaineers exploring the area around the Columbia Icefield. Look for carvings on trees recording these early visitors. From here the trail continues to climb steadily, only increasing in gradient for the last one km (.6 mile) to the pass. The pass (2,195 meters/7,200 feet) marks the boundary between Banff and Jasper National Parks. For the best view, scramble over the rocks to the left. To the north, the view extends down the Brazeau River Valley, surrounded by a mass of peaks. To the west (left) is Nigel Peak (3,211 meters/10,535 feet), and to the southwest are views of Parker's Ridge and the glaciated peaks of Mount Athabasca.

Parker's Ridge

- Length: 2.4 km/1.5 miles (one hour) one-way
- Elevation gain: 210 meters/690 feet
- Rating: easy/moderate
- Trailhead: Icefields Parkway, four km (2.5 miles) south of Sunwapta Pass

From the trailhead on the west side of the highway, this wide path gains elevation quickly through open meadows and scattered stands of subalpine fir. This fragile environment is easily destroyed, so it's important that you stay on the trail. During the short alpine summer, these meadows are carpeted with red heather, white mountain avens, and blue alpine forget-me-nots. From the summit of the ridge, you look down on the two-km-wide (1.2-mile-wide) Saskatchewan Glacier spreading out below. Beyond is Castleguard Mountain, renowned for its extensive cave system.

ACCOMMODATIONS AND CAMPING

Under $50

North of Lake Louise, four and a half hostels are spread along the Icefields Parkway, two in Banff and two in Jasper National Park (the "half" is Hilda Creek Wilderness Hostel, north of Rampart Creek, which has been closed indefinitely after being mostly destroyed by fire in 2002). Facilities at all four are limited, and beds should be reserved as far in advance as possible. For reservations, call 403/760-7580 or 866/762-4122, or book online (www.hihostels.ca). The first, 24 km (15 miles) from Lake Louise, is **HI–Mosquito Creek Wilderness Hostel,** which is near good hiking and offers accommodations for 32 in four cabins. Facilities include a kitchen, wood-heated sauna, and a large common room with fireplace. Rates are $19 per night for members of Hostelling International; nonmembers pay $23. Check-in is 5–10 P.M., and it's open year-round.

HI–Rampart Creek Wilderness Hostel, a further 64 km (40 miles) along the parkway, is nestled below the snowcapped peak of Mount Wilson, with views across the North Saskatchewan River to even higher peaks along the Continental Divide. Like Mosquito Creek, it's near good hiking and has a kitchen and sauna. Its two cabins hold 30 people. Members pay $19 per night, nonmembers $23. It's open nightly mid-May to mid-October and weekends only mid-December to mid-May (closed the rest of the year). Check-in is 5–11 P.M.

$50–150

The Crossing (403/761-7000, www.thecrossingresort.com; mid-March–Nov.) is a large complex 87 km (54 miles) north of Lake Louise and 45 km (28 miles) south of Columbia Icefield. It's also one km (.6 mile) north of Saskatchewan River Crossing, where Highway 11 spurs east along Abraham Lake to Rocky Mountain House and Red Deer. The rooms offer a good combination of size and value but lack the charm of those at Num-ti-jah to the south and the views enjoyed by those at the Columbia Icefield Centre

to the north. Each of 66 units has a phone and television. They are $95 s, $100–110 d, and are heavily discounted outside of June–September. In addition to overnight rooms, The Crossing has the only gas between Lake Louise and Jasper, a self-serve cafeteria, a restaurant, a pub, and a large gift shop.

Over $150

Pioneer guide and outfitter Jimmy Simpson built **Ⓜ Simpson's Num-ti-jah Lodge** (403/522-2167, www.num-ti-jah.com), on the north shore of Bow Lake, 40 km (25 miles) north of Lake Louise, as a base for his outfitting operation in 1920. In those days, the route north from Lake Louise was nothing more than a horse trail. The desire to build a large structure when only short timbers were available led to the unusual octagonal shape of the main lodge. Simpson remained at Bow Lake, a living legend, until his death in 1972 at the age of 95. With a rustic mountain ambience that has changed little since Simpson's passing, an overnight stay at Num-ti-jah is a memorable experience. Just don't expect the conveniences of a regular motel. Under the distinctively red, steeppitched roof of the main lodge are 25 rooms, some that share bathrooms, and there's not a TV or phone in sight. Downstairs, guests soak up the warmth of a roaring log fire while mingling in a comfortable library filled with historic mountain literature. A dining room lined with historic memorabilia is open throughout the day, serving up a breakfast buffet and evening delicacies such as shellfish fettuccini ($20). Rates are $195–220 s or d for a room with shared bath, $230–290 s or d for an en suite. It's open year-round (except November), with rates reduced 40 percent outside of summer.

Campgrounds

Beyond Lake Louise, the first camping along the Icefields Parkway is at **Mosquito Creek Campground** (year-round; $13), 24 km (15 miles) from the TransCanada Highway. Don't be perturbed by the name, though; the bugs here are no worse than anywhere else. The 32 sites are nestled in the forest, with a tumbling creek separating the campground from a hostel. Each site has a picnic table and fire ring, while other amenities include pump water, pit toilets, and a kitchen shelter with an old-fashioned woodstove. If you're camping at Mosquito Creek and want a break from the usual camp fare, consider traveling 17 km/10.6 miles up the highway to the convivial dining room at Num-ti-jah Lodge (403/522-2167) to feast on Canadian-inspired cuisine in a historic dining room.

Waterfowl Lake Campground (late June–mid-Sept.; $17) is 33 km (20 miles) north along the Icefields Parkway from Mosquito Creek. It features 116 sites between Upper and Lower Waterfowl Lakes, with a few sites in view of the lower lake. Facilities include pump water, flush toilets, and kitchen shelters with wood-burning stoves. Rise early to watch the first rays of sun hit Mount Chephren from the shoreline of the lower lake, then plan on hiking the four-km (2.5-mile) trail to Chephren Lake—you'll be first on the trail and back in time for a late breakfast.

Continuing toward Jasper, the Icefields Parkway passes The Crossing, a good place to gas up and buy last-minute groceries before reaching **Rampart Creek Campground** (late June–early Sept.; $13 per site), 31 km (19 miles) beyond Waterfowl Lake and 88 km (55 miles) from Lake Louise. With just 50 sites, this campground fills early. Facilities include kitchen shelters, pit toilets, and pump water.

Canmore

Canmore (pop. 12,000) lies in the wide Bow Valley, 103 km (64 miles) west of Calgary, 28 km (17 miles) southeast of Banff, and on the northern edge of Kananaskis Country. Long perceived as a gateway to the mountain national parks, the town is very much a destination in itself these days. Its ideal mountain location and the freedom it enjoys from the strict development restrictions that apply in the nearby parks have made Canmore the fastest-growing town in Canada, with the population having tripled in the last 20 years.

The surrounding mountains provide Canmore's best recreation opportunities. Hiking is excellent on trails that lace the valley and mountainside slopes, with many high viewpoints

easily reached. Flowing though town, the Bow River offers great fishing, kayaking, and rafting; golfers flock to three scenic courses; and nearby Mount Yamnuska has become the most developed rock-climbing site in the Canadian Rockies. Canmore also hosted the Nordic events of the 1988 Winter Olympic Games and is the home of the Alpine Club of Canada.

PLANNING YOUR TIME

You can include Canmore in your itinerary in a variety of ways. The most obvious one is to make the town a base for your Canadian Rockies vacation. The advantages are less-crowded streets, better-priced accommodations, a choice of

© ANDREW HEMPSTEAD

Must-Sees

an old Canadian Pacific Railway trestle bridge

M Coal-Mining History: Explore Canmore's coal-mining history by walking through the residential area west of downtown. Continue up Canmore Creek, past sealed mine entrances, for the full effect (page 105).

M Grassi Lakes: A short walk is required to reach these two lakes, which are natural highlights of the Canmore region (page 106).

M Chinaman's Peak: Feeling fit? Follow the trail to this summit for valley views that are unsurpassed (page 107).

M *Oh Canada Eh!:* Slightly tacky, but good fun nevertheless, this dinner theater production brings Canada's best-known symbols to life (page 111).

Canmore

CANMORE

SCALE NOT AVAILABLE

© AVALON TRAVEL PUBLISHING, INC.

family-friendly lodgings, and a central location (Banff is a 15-minute drive to the west and Kananaskis Country is a 40-minute drive southeast). Campers should keep in mind that there are much nicer campgrounds elsewhere in the region. If you decide to stay in Banff instead, there's no reason to relocate to Canmore for a night or two—simply visit the town as part of a day trip (or two).

Regardless of whether or not you stay in Canmore, there's plenty to do in the town itself for one day. Plan on two or more if you enjoy being outdoors. A two-day stay might include a morning tee time at **SilverTip Golf Resort** or a horseback ride at **Cross Zee Ranch**. After lunch at **Crazyweed Kitchen** spend the afternoon exploring the Main Street, the museum, and historic buildings west of town. The next morning, lace up your hiking boots for the walk to **Grassi Lakes**. Golfers will probably want to squeeze in another round of golf, this time at **Stewart Creek Golf Course,** but there are plenty of other choices—fishing on Bow River, a rock-climbing lesson, or a helicopter flightseeing trip. Your two evenings could be spent at *Oh Canada Eh!* and the **Sage Bistro.**

THE LAND

Canmore lies in the Bow Valley, flanked by mountains rising up to 1,000 meters (3,280 feet) above the valley floor. To the south and west are the distinctive peaks of the Three Sisters, Mount Lawrence Grassi, impressive Chinaman's Peak, and the southeastern extent of Mount Rundle. Across the valley are the Fairholme Range, Mount Lady Macdonald, and Grotto Mountain. Like the rest of the Canadian Rockies, these mountains began as layers of sedimentary rock laid down on the bed of an ancient sea. The seabed was forced upward over millions of years to create today's lofty peaks, whose sedimentary layers give them a distinct appearance. Through the valley flows the braided Bow River, heading eastward and into the Saskatchewan River system. At the north end of town, the river divides in two, leaving downtown Canmore on a low-lying island

that is protected from annual spring flooding by dikes of large boulders.

Flora and Fauna

Even though much of the valley floor is developed, large tracts of land are protected by Bow Valley Wildland Provincial Park, making the surrounding area a delight for nature lovers. Lowlands on either side of the Bow River are lined with stands of poplar, while the drier mountainsides support extensive stands of **Douglas fir, Engelmann spruce,** and **lodgepole pine.**

The forested valley floor provides habitat for many larger mammals, including around 100 **elk,** most often sighted on the Canmore Golf Course and along the west side of the Bow River. Other larger mammals present include **white-tailed deer, coyotes, black bears,** and **grizzly bears,** all of which are regularly sighted within town limits. **Bighorn sheep** are common on rocky outcrops above Spray Lakes Road. **Cougars** inhabit the surrounding wilderness but are rarely sighted.

Smaller mammals present in Bow River and its adjacent sloughs include a healthy population of **beaver,** as well as **muskrat** and **mink. Red** and **Columbian ground squirrels** and **least chipmunks** inhabit the forests around town, while at higher elevations **golden-mantled ground squirrels** and **pikas** find a home. **Wild rabbits** thrive around the residential streets east of Centennial Park.

Birdlife around Canmore is prolific. **Mallard ducks** are a popular attraction on Policeman's Creek in downtown Canmore. Several active **osprey** nests can be seen along the banks of the Bow River; other permanent residents include **great horned owls, jays,** and **ravens.**

HISTORY

The Hudson's Bay Company explored the Bow Valley corridor and attempted, without success, to establish a fur trade with Stoney natives for most of the 1840s. In 1858, an expedition from the east, led by Captain John Palliser, sent back discouraging reports about the climate and

© ANDREW HEMPSTEAD

Canmore

The North West Mounted Police built this "temporary" post in 1892. It still stands and makes an ideal starting point for exploring the town.

prospects of agriculture in the valley. A few decades later the Canadian Pacific Railway (CPR) chose the Bow Valley Corridor as the route through the mountains, and the first divisional point west of Calgary was established in 1883. It was named Canmore for the 11th-century Scottish king, Malcolm of Canmore.

Coal Mining

The CPR was delighted to discover that the valley was rich with coal, which it could use in the steam engines. Mining on the lower slopes of the Three Sisters and Mount Rundle commenced in 1886, attracting hundreds of miners and their families. Within a few years numerous mines operated around Canmore. In 1899 the CPR moved its divisional point to Laggan (now Lake Louise), but the mines continued to operate, with the most productive mine located on Canmore Creek. Hotels and businesses were established, and a hospital, North West Mounted

Police (NWMP) post, and opera house were built. The Canmore Opera House—reputed to be the only log movie house in the world—still stands and has been relocated to Calgary's Heritage Park.

Many British and European miners were attracted to the area, and the population continued to increase. A small contingent of Chinese miners also lived in Canmore. They didn't stay long, but their memory lives on in the name Chinaman's Peak. A Chinese cook, Ha Ling, was bet $50 that he couldn't climb the peak and return to Canmore in less than six hours. He did, and it's been known as Chinaman's Peak ever since. In 1912, the Canadian Anthracite Coal Company relocated its operation from near present-day Banff to the west side of the Bow River, five km (3.1 miles) from the rail line. **Georgetown,** a bustling little village, sprang up beside the mine. Workers enjoyed electricity and running water in cozy cabins along with their own company store, post office, and a school for the kids. Three short years later, markets dried up and the Anthracite mine closed. Georgetown was abandoned, and the buildings were barged downstream to Canmore.

Recent Times

A little more than 100 years after mining commenced and less than 20 years after the last mine closed, Canmore experienced its second boom—tourism—which today shows no sign of slowing. When the last of Canmore's mines closed in 1979, the population stood at 3,500; today that number has tripled. Half the current residents have lived in town for less than five years. There seems no end to the boom, and the population is estimated to reach 20,000 sometime in the next 20 years. Resort and residential projects costing more than $2 billion have been planned for the next two decades. The largest and most controversial development is **Three Sisters Mountain Village.** When completed, the 840-hectare (2,080-acre) project will include 3,600 residential units, 500 hotel rooms, and three golf courses—all in an environmentally sensitive area along an 11-km (6.8-mile) stretch of the Bow River, between Pigeon Mountain and Chinaman's Peak.

Canmore is a popular spot for moviemakers; big-budget movies filmed in and around town have included *Shanghai Noon, Grizzly Falls, Mystery Alaska, The Edge, Wild America, The Last of the Dogmen, Legends of the Fall, Snow Dogs,* and the 2003 Kevin Costner film *Open Range.*

Sights and Recreation

Canmore sprawls across both sides of the Trans-Canada Highway, with downtown Canmore occupying an island in the middle of the Bow River. Although development sprawls in all directions, large tracts of forest remain intact, including along the river, where paths lead beyond built-up areas and into natural areas. The most expansive of these is 32,600-hectare (80,550-acre) **Bow Valley Wildland Provincial Park,** which has been designated in pockets along the valley floor as well as most of the surrounding mountain slopes along both sides of the valley.

SIGHTS

Through booming times, the original core of Canmore, on the southwestern side of the Trans-Canada Highway, has managed to retain much of its original charm. Many historical buildings line the downtown streets, while other buildings from the coal-mining days are being preserved at their original locations around town. The best way to get downtown from the TransCanada Highway is to take Railway Avenue from Highway 1A and drive down 8th Street, the main drag (parking is easiest one street back along 7th Street, where one parking lot—at 6th Avenue—is designated for RVs).

Downtown

The first building of interest at the east end of the main street is Canmore's original **NWMP post** (609 8th St., 403/678-1955; summer daily 9 A.M.–6 P.M., the rest of year Mon.–Fri. noon–4 P.M.; free), built in 1892. It is one of the few such posts still in its original position, even though at the time of its construction the building was designed as a temporary structure to serve the newly born coal-mining town. The interior is decorated with period furnishings, while out back is a thriving garden filled with the same food crops planted by the post's original inhabitants. The post sits across from Policeman's Creek, a shallow body of water alive with ducks. **Ralph Connor United Church,** a little farther down 8th Street, was built in 1890 and is now a Provincial Historic Site. The church is named for its first reverend, Charles Gordon, who used the pen name Ralph Connor for the 35 books he authored. Canmore Hotel, on the corner of 8th Street and 7th Avenue, was built in 1891 (at a time when three hotels already operated) and is still open for thirsty townsfolk and travelers alike.

Around the corner from the hotel, inside the sparkling new town hall complex is **Canmore Museum and Geoscience Centre** (907 7th Ave., 403/678-2462; Mon.–Fri. 9 A.M.–5 P.M.). This facility highlights the region's rich geological history and its importance to the growth of the town and related industries. Geological formations along three local hikes are described, which, along with a small fossil display, microscopes, and computer resources, make this facility an interesting rainy-day diversion.

Coal-Mining History

Several scenic and historic sights lie across the Bow River from downtown, including the remains of various mining operations. To get there, walk south along 8th Avenue for 500 meters (.3 mile) to the Bow River. With a pedestrian-only bridge and paved paths on both sides of the river leading in either direction, this is a good point to stop and get oriented. A pleasant loop can be made by walking north and crossing the river at the old **CPR trestle bridge,** which once served local mines. Follow the trail back downstream, past the **Mine Shareholders' Cabin,** a log structure built in 1914.

In the same vicinity, a trail leads off from Three Sisters Drive up Canmore Creek, passing the remains of a mine site that was first worked in

DOWNTOWN CANMORE

SCALE NOT AVAILABLE

© AVALON TRAVEL PUBLISHING, INC.

1891. Beyond the visible coal seam and crumbling concrete foundations is a picturesque waterfall tucked below residential development. Backtrack 300 meters (.2 mile) from the end of the trail and climb the wooden steps, crossing Spray Lakes Road to **Quarry Lake.** This small lake lies in an open meadow and is a popular sunbathing and swimming spot.

HIKING

The hiking trails around Canmore are usually passed by in favor of those of its famous neighbors, but some interesting trails do exist. Paved paths around town are suitable for walking, bicycling, and, in winter, skiing. They link Policeman's Creek with the golf course, Nordic center, and Riverview Park on the Bow River.

Grassi Lakes

• Length: 2 km/1.2 miles (40 minutes) one-way
• Elevation gain: 300 meters/980 feet

• Rating: easy/moderate
• Trailhead: Spray Village, beyond the Nordic center, six km (3.7 miles) west of downtown off Spray Lakes Road

This historical trail climbs to two small lakes below Chinaman's Peak. From the parking lot just off Spray Lakes Road, take the left fork 150 meters (.1 mile) along the trail. It climbs steadily to stairs cut into a cliff face before leading up to a bridge over Canmore Creek and to the lakes. Interpretive signs along the trail point out interesting aspects of the Bow Valley and detail the life of Lawrence Grassi, who built the trail in the early 1920s. With Chinaman's Peak as a backdrop, these gin-clear, spring-fed lakes are a particularly rewarding destination. Behind the upper lake, an easy scramble up a scree slope leads to four pictographs (native rock paintings) of human figures. They are on the first large boulder in the gorge. An alternate return route is down a rough access road between the hiking trail and Spray

Lakes Road, passing a broken-down log cabin along the way.

🗻 Chinaman's Peak

- Length: 2.2 km/1.4 miles (90 minutes) one-way
- Elevation gain: 740 meters/2,430 feet
- Rating: moderate/difficult
- Trailhead: Goat Creek parking lot, Spray Lakes Road, nine km (5.6 miles) west of Canmore

Chinaman's Peak is the impressive pinnacle of rock that rises high above Canmore to the southwest. While the sheer eastern face is visible from town, this trail winds up the backside of the mountain and ends with stunning views across the Bow Valley. Leaving your vehicle at the Goat Creek Trailhead, cross the road, then walk up to and over the canal to search out the trail, which begins from behind a small workshed. The trail climbs steadily through subalpine forest of Engelmann spruce before breaking out above the tree line, where views north extend down the glacially carved Goat Creek Valley. The trail then forks; the left fork climbs unforgivingly to Chinaman's Peak, but hikers are rewarded with views no less spectacular by continuing to the right along a lightly marked trail that ends at a saddle. On a clear day, the panorama afforded from this viewpoint is worth every painful step. Take care on the return journey; stay high and to the right and watch for rock cairns and colored flagging to ensure you enter the trees at the right spot.

Cougar Creek

- Length: 9.5 km/6 miles (four hours) one-way
- Elevation gain: 550 meters/1,800 feet
- Rating: moderate
- Trailhead: corner Benchlands Trail and Elk Run Boulevard, east side of TransCanada Highway

This unofficial trail follows a valley carved deeply into the Fairholme Range by Cougar Creek. The length and elevation gain listed are to a high ridge on the boundary of Banff National Park. Few hikers reach this point, with most content to turn around within an hour's travel. The first section of trail runs alongside a manmade channel that acts as a conduit for runoff in years of high snowfall. It's dry most of summer, but extra care should be taken in spring. Cross just before the mouth of the canyon. From this point the rough trail crosses the creekbed 10 times in the first three km (1.9 km) to a major fork. Stay within the left valley, continuing up and around the base of Mount Charles Stewart. From this point, the valley walls close in and it's a steep climb up to the boundary of Banff National Park. On the return journey, continue beyond the parking lot to the Summit Café, where you can relax on the patio with a cool drink.

Mount Lady Macdonald

- Length: 3.5 km/2.1 miles (90 minutes) one-way
- Elevation gain: 850 meters/2,790 feet
- Rating: moderate/difficult
- Trailhead: corner Benchlands Trail and Elk Run Boulevard, east side of TransCanada Highway

Named for the wife of Canada's first prime minister, this peak lies immediately north of Canmore. Follow Cougar Creek to where the canyon begins, and look for a faint trail winding up a grassy bank to the left. Once on the trail, take the steepest option at every fork, then a sharp right 300 meters (.2 mile) after the trail bursts out into a cleared area. This section is steep, climbing through a rock band to the mountain's southern ridge, which you'll follow the rest of the way. The distance and elevation listed are to an unused helipad below the main summit. It's a steep, unrelenting slog, but views across the Bow Valley are stunning. From this point, the true summit is another 275 vertical meters (900 vertical feet) away, along an extremely narrow ridge that drops away precipitously to the east.

Grotto Canyon

- Length: 2 km/1.2 miles (40 minutes) one-way
- Elevation gain: 60 meters/200 feet
- Rating: easy
- Trailhead: Grotto Pond, Highway 1A, 12 km (7.5 miles) east of Canmore

This is one of the most interesting trails around Canmore. From Grotto Pond, this trail first follows a powerline road behind the Baymag plant. Then

ALPINE CLUB OF CANADA

The Alpine Club of Canada (ACC), like similar clubs in the United States and Great Britain, is a nonprofit mountaineering organization whose objectives include encouraging mountaineering through educational programs, exploring and studying alpine and glacial regions, and preserving mountain flora and fauna.

The club was formed in 1906, mainly through the tireless campaign of its first president, Arthur Wheeler. A list of early members reads like a Who's Who of the Canadian Rockies—Bill Peyto, Tom Wilson, Byron Harmon, Mary Schäffer—names familiar to all Canadian mountaineers. Today the club membership includes 3,000 alpinists from throughout Canada.

The original clubhouse was near the Banff Springs Hotel, but in 1980 a new clubhouse was built on benchland at the edge of Canmore to serve as the association's headquarters. The club's ongoing projects include operating the Canadian Alpine Centre (Lake Louise Hostel), maintaining a system of 20 huts throughout the backcountry of the Canadian Rockies, and publishing the annual *Canadian Alpine Journal*—the country's only record of mountaineering accomplishments. A reference library of the club's history is kept at the Whyte Museum of the Canadian Rockies in Banff.

For further information and membership details, contact the Alpine Club of Canada (403/678-3200, www.alpineclubofcanada.ca).

at a signed intersection it takes off through the woods to the mouth of the canyon. No official trail traverses the canyon; hikers simply follow the creekbed through the towering canyon walls. Around 300 meters (.2 mile) into the canyon, look for pictographs to the left. At the two-km (1.2-mile) mark, the canyon makes a sharp left turn at Illusion Rock, where water cascades through a narrow chasm and into the main canyon. Many hikers return from this point, but through the next section of canyon, the valley opens up, passing hoodoos and a cave. It's 6.5 km (four miles) from the trailhead to the end of the valley, with most of the 680 meters (2,230 feet) of elevation gained in the last two km (1.2 miles).

Heart Creek

- Length: 2 km/1.2 miles (40 minutes) one-way
- Elevation gain: 80 meters/260 feet
- Rating: easy
- Trailhead: Lac des Arcs interchange, Trans-Canada Highway, 15 km (9.3 miles) east of Canmore

This well-formed trail is signposted from the Lac des Arcs interchange, 15 km (9.3 miles) east of Canmore along the TransCanada Highway. The trail parallels the highway eastward until reaching a fork. The trail to the right follows Heart Creek for just over one km (.6 mile), crossing the creek

seven times on narrow log bridges. It ends at a cleared area below a spot where Heart Creek is forced through a narrow cleft. Those tempted to continue farther can cross the creek, scramble up a steep, forested ridge, then descend the other side to link up with the creek upstream of the gorge. Cross the creek again for views of another narrow chasm.

Heli-Hiking

Heli-hiking is the summer alternative to heli-skiing—a helicopter does the hard work, and you get to hike in a remote, alpine region that would usually entail a long, steep hike to access. **Alpine Helicopters** (403/678-4802) offers options starting at $260 per person, which includes 15 minutes of flight time and 3–4 hours of hiking. The company is flexible, with ground time and destinations chosen by the clients. Flightseeing (no landing) costs $155 for 25 minutes of airtime. The heliport is along Highway 1A south of downtown. Try to book ahead for these trips; they're very popular with travelers staying in Banff, where there is no flightseeing.

OTHER RECREATION

Canmore Nordic Centre

This sprawling complex on the outskirts of Canmore was built for the 1988 Winter Olympic

Games. The cross-country skiing and biathlon (combined cross-country skiing and rifle shooting) events were held here, and today the center remains a world-class training ground for Canadian athletes in a variety of disciplines. The operation was privatized in 1997 and pronounced a provincial park in 2000. Even in summer, long after the snow has melted, the place is worth a visit. An interpretive trail leads down to and along the west bank of the Bow River to the barely visible remains of Georgetown, a once-bustling coal-mining town. Many other trails lead around the grounds, and it's possible to hike or bike along the Bow River all the way to Banff. **Mountain biking** is extremely popular on 70 km (43.5 miles) of trails. Bike rentals are available at **Trail Sports** (below the day lodge, 403/678-6764; daily 9 A.M.–6 P.M.); $8 per hour and $30 per day for a front-suspension bike, $10 and $40, respectively, for a full suspension bike. In summer, you can also play disc golf (Frisbees are available at Trail Sports). Snowmaking guarantees a ski season running from December through late March, with rentals and instruction available through Trail Sports. The

day lodge (403/678-2400; daily 8 A.M.–4:30 P.M.) has lockers, a lounge area, a café (daily 10 A.M.–4 P.M.), and an information desk.

Fishing

The **Bow River** has good fishing for brown and brook trout, including right downtown between the old railway bridge and Rundle Drive. Follow Highway 1A east from town to access the best river fishing, as well as **Gap Lake** and **Grotto Pond;** the latter is stocked with rainbow trout. The Bow River is renowned for its rainbow trout fishing. This occurs downstream of Canmore toward Calgary and beyond **Ghost Lake,** which holds healthy populations of lake, rainbow, and brown trout.

For all your fishing needs, head to **Wapiti Sports** (1506 Railway Ave., 403/678-5550), which stocks bait and tackle and sells licenses.

Golfing

As with golfing elsewhere in the Canadian Rockies, book all tee times well in advance, but also try to be flexible, because two of Canmore's three courses offer weekday and twilight discounts.

© ANDREW HEMPSTEAD

golfing at SilverTip Resort

The golfing season in Canmore runs from early May to late September.

SilverTip (403/678-1600 or 877/877-5444, www.silvertipresort.com) opened in summer 1998 on a series of wide benches between the valley floor and the lower slopes of Mount Lady Macdonald. It was quickly recognized as one of Canada's finest resort courses, but more tellingly, it boasts a slope rating of 153, the highest of any course in mainland North America. Needless to say, the layout is challenging, with the most distinct feature being an elevation change of 200 meters (660 feet) between the lowest and highest points on the course. Adding to this challenge are narrow, sloping, tree-lined fairways, numerous water hazards, 74 bunkers, and a course length of a frightening 7,300 yards from the back markers. High-season greens fees range from $125 on Monday and Tuesday to $160 on weekends, which includes a mandatory cart (each cart has GPS to help golfers judge distances) and use of the driving range. Twilight fees start at $99.

Stewart Creek Golf Club (403/609-6099 or 877/993-4653, www.stewartcreekgolf.com), another newer layout, lies across the valley in the Three Sisters Mountain Village development. It is shorter than SilverTip but still measures more than 7,000 yards from the back tees. The fairways are relatively wide, but positioning of tee shots is important, and the course is made more interesting by hanging greens, greenside exposed rock, and historic mine shafts. Greens fees are $135, with twilight rates of $85. These rates include use of a power cart and practice facility.

Canmore Golf Course (403/678-4784), built in 1929 as a nine-hole course at the north end of 8th Avenue, has developed into an 18-hole course with a modern clubhouse and a practice facility that includes a driving range. It is an interesting layout, with scenic panoramas and water on some holes. Greens fees are $60 and a cart is $31.

Horseback Riding

Nestled on a wide bench on the northeastern side of town, **Cross Zee Ranch** (403/678-4171) has been guiding visitors through the valley since the 1950s. From expansive stables, rides pass through thickly wooded areas, along colorful meadows, and to high lookouts. Options include Ranger Ridge and Bone Gully (one hour; $28 per person), Sunny Bench (90 minutes; $40), and the Great Aspens ride (two hours; $48).

Climbing

Hundreds of climbing routes have been laid out around Canmore. **Mount Yamnuska,** which rises 900 meters (2,950 feet) above the valley floor east of town along Highway 1A, is the most developed site. Climbers also flock to **Chinaman's Peak, Cougar Creek,** the area behind **Grassi Lakes,** and **Grotto Canyon.** Canmore is home to many qualified mountain guides.

Yamnuska (403/678-4164 or 866/678-4164, www.yamnuska.com) offers basic rock-climbing courses and instruction for all ability levels in ice climbing, mountaineering, and trekking. A good introduction to rock climbing is the weekend-long Basic Rock course, which costs $215. Unique to the company are three-month-long courses that take in all aspects of mountain-oriented skills.

ARTS AND ENTERTAINMENT
Drinking and Dancing

Canmore doesn't have anywhere near the number of bars that nearby Banff is so famous for, but no one ever seems to go thirsty. The **Bolo Ranchhouse** (838 8th St., 403/678-5211) has a beer garden that catches the afternoon sun and is especially busy on weekends. At the other end of the main street is the **Drake Inn** (909 Railway Ave., 403/678-5131), with a small outdoor patio and a nonsmoking section with comfortable lounges. Across the road, at the **Rose and Crown** (749 Railway Ave., 403/678-5168), you'll find a beer garden. All these bars have midweek drink specials, and the latter two have a couple of pool tables.

The **Grizzly Paw Brewing Company** (622 8th St., 403/678-9983) brews its own beer, with six ales produced in-house (look for special winter brews around Christmas). Most are heavy, English-style beers, but the lighter Grumpy Bear Honey Wheat Ale suits most tastes. Away from downtown, **Creekside's Fine Food & Drink** (1005 Cougar Creek Dr., 403/609-2345) provides a relaxed, friendly atmosphere with a wide selection of local and imported beer. Wondering where the cheapest beer in town is? Head to the **Last Call** (637 10th St., 403/678-3934), where you'll find $2 bottled beer on Thursday nights. The rest of the week, it's happy hour 4–8 P.M., daily drink specials, and a bunch of pool-playing locals.

Canmore's only nightclub is **Hooligan's** (Bow Valley Trail, 403/609-2662), and there's live music somewhere in town every weekend. The Drake Inn has a band playing Wednesday–Saturday nights, as does the Rose and Crown, and the Sherwood House has an occasional Sunday afternoon jam session.

Check out the large wine selection at **Alberta Spirits,** in the Canmore Crossing complex on Railway Avenue (403/678-2451).

Oh Canada Eh!

Popularized across the country at Niagara Falls, this musical dinner show (125 Kananaskis Way, off Bow Valley Trail, 403/609-0004 or 800/773-0004) provides a rip-roaring evening of fun and food in a modern building decorated as a cavernous log cabin. It's unashamedly cheesy, but the parade of costumed Canadian characters—such as lumberjacks, natives, Mounties, and even Anne of Green Gables—will keep you laughing as they sing and dance across the floor. The food is surprisingly good, with Canadian favorites such as Alberta beef, salmon, and maple chocolate cake served buffet-style. Performances are nightly through summer at 6:30 P.M., and the all-inclusive cost is adult $55, child $26. **Brewster** (403/762-6767 or 877/791-5500) provides bus transfers from Banff accommodations for $85 per person, inclusive of entry to *Oh Canada Eh!*

FESTIVALS AND EVENTS

Canmore's small-town pride lives on through a busy schedule of festivals and events, which are nearly always accompanied by parades of flag-waving kids, free downtown pancake breakfasts, and an evening shindig somewhere in town.

Winter

Throughout the winter months, locals play **hockey** on ponds and rinks scattered throughout the valley. Things get a little more serious at home games of the **Canmore Eagles** (www.eagles.ab.ca), held at the recreation center along 8th Avenue. Canmore's annual **Winter Carnival** is a two-week celebration including ice-sculpting and kid-and-mutt races. The highlight is the **Sled Dog Classic** held at Canmore Nordic Centre, where up to 100 teams of four, six, eight, and ten dogs are harnessed up and compete in various heats. (Organizers are always looking for volunteers; ask around if you'd like to help.) The festival takes place the last two weeks of January. In early March, the **International Canmore Ice-Climbing Festival** is hosted at venues throughout town, including at a 20-meter-high (66-foot-high) manmade wall of ice beside Bow Valley Trail at 17th Street.

Summer

Canada Day is celebrated with a pancake breakfast, parade, various activities in Centennial Park, and 11 P.M. fireworks. Canmore Nordic Centre hosts a variety of mountain-biking events each summer, highlighted by a stop on the **24 Hours of Adrenalin** tour (www.24hoursofadrenalin.com) in which racers complete as many laps as they can in a 24-hour period, either in teams or as solo riders. For a full listing of mountain-bike races, contact the Nordic center (403/678-2400). On the Heritage Day long weekend, the first weekend of August, Canmore hosts a **Folk Music Festival** (403/678-2524, www.canmorefolkfestival.com), which starts on Sunday and runs through Monday evening. This event, which attracts more than 10,000 fans, features national and international acts performing in Centennial Park, musical workshops, and a free pancake breakfast beside the post office on Heritage Day.

The first Sunday of September is the **Canmore Highland Games** (403/678-9454, www.canmorehighlandgames.ca), a day of dancing, eating, and caber tossing, culminating in a spectacular and noisy parade of pipe bands throughout the grounds of Centennial Park that attracts more than 10,000 spectators. On the Sunday evening, a *ceilidh,* a traditional Scottish celebration involving loud beer-drinking, foot-stomping music, takes place under a massive tent set up in the park for the occasion.

Fall

Fall's major gathering is for the **Festival of the Eagles,** on the third weekend of October and coinciding with the southbound migration of golden eagles. It features talks, slide shows, and field trips.

Accommodations and Camping

Canmore's population boom has been mirrored by the construction of new hotels and motels. Most of the new lodgings are on Bow Valley Trail (Highway 1A), the traditional strip. As with all resort towns in the Canadian Rockies, reservations should be made as far in advance as possible in summer.

More than 40 bed-and-breakfasts operate in Canmore. They are all small, family-run affairs, with only one or two rooms (a local town bylaw limits the number of guest rooms in private homes to just two). During summer, they fill every night. For a full list of B&Bs, check the website of the **Canmore/Bow Valley Bed and Breakfast Association,** www.bbcanmore.com, for one that suits your needs.

As you raise your eyebrows over hotel pricing in Canmore, consider two things: (1) many hotels discount rooms year-round, so use the listed websites to find current deals and packages; and (2) room rates in Canmore are a bargain compared to Banff, just down the road.

Outside the busiest summer period (mid-June to mid-September), room rates are slashed considerably (especially at the more expensive accommodations); with a little bit of searching, expect to find rates that include two lift tickets (at either the Banff or Kananaskis alpine resorts) for the same price as the room-only rate during summer.

IN AND AROUND TOWN

Under $50

HI–Canmore (403/678-3200, www.hihostels.ca) is an excellent hostel-style accommodation at the base of Grotto Mountain. Affiliated with Hostelling International, the lodge is part of headquarters for the Alpine Club of Canada, the coun-

try's national mountaineering organization. In addition to sleeping up to 30 people in seven rooms, it has a kitchen, an excellent library, a laundry room, a bar, a sauna, and a lounge area with a fireplace. Rates are $19 per night for members of Hostelling International or the Alpine Club, while everyone else pays $23. Alpine Club membership is inexpensive and includes a discount at the Lake Louise Alpine Centre. To get there from downtown, follow Bow Valley Trail southeast; it's signposted to the left, 500 meters (.3 mile) after passing under the TransCanada Highway.

$50–100

Aside from one motel, the only accommodations that fall in this price range are bed-and-breakfasts, although rooms less than $100 are limited.

With around $100 budgeted for a room, it's hard to go past **M Riverview and Main,** centrally located half a block beyond the end of the downtown core (918 8th St., 403/678-9777, www.riverviewandmain.com; $85–120 s or d). The rooms are decently sized and brightly decorated, and each has access to a deck. The guest lounge centers on a riverstone, wood-burning fireplace. Rates include a selection of hot and cold breakfast items.

The **Akai Motel** (1717 Mountain Ave., 403/678-4664 or 877/900-2524) is a little old-fashioned, but each room is air-conditioned and has a small kitchenette, TV, and telephone. At $80 s, $90 d, this is Canmore's least expensive motel.

$100–150

Named for one of the valley's original coal-mining communities, the **M Georgetown Inn** (1101

Bow Valley Trail, 403/678-3439 or 800/657-5955, www.georgetowninn.ab.ca) is set up as a country inn of times gone by, complete with a lounge bar and Mélange, a cozy dining room open daily for breakfast and dinner. Each of the 21 rooms has its own individual charm, with a modern twist on decor that features lots of English antiques. The best value are Victoria Rooms, each with a separate sitting area and electric fireplace ($149). Complimentary nonalcoholic drinks and a delicious cooked breakfast are included in rates ranging $129–199 s or d (from $99 in winter).

Opened in 2002, **Windtower Mountain Lodge** (160 Kananaskis Way, 403/609-6600 or 866/609-6600, www.windtowermountainlodge.com) provides hotel and suite accommodations in a much larger condominium development. Complex facilities include a picnic and barbecue area, a fitness center, an outdoor hot tub, a café, and underground parking. Hotel-style rooms range $109–149, depending on size, while

KANANASKIS GUEST RANCH

Built in 1923, the historic Kananaskis Guest Ranch (403/673-3737 or 800/691-5085, www.brewsteradventures.com; June–Sept.), 28 km (17.4 miles) east of Canmore along Highway 1A, has been owned and operated by five generations of the Brewster family, a name synonymous with tourism in the Canadian Rockies. The property is located on a magnificent 800-hectare (2,000-acre) tract of land, alongside the Bow River and below the distinctive peak of Mount Yamnuska.

A traditional Western atmosphere prevails, with the emphasis on horseback riding ($55 for a two-hour ride). Guests also enjoy a well-maintained nine-hole golf course ($28), fishing, rafting, and canoeing. The lodge itself overlooks a small lake. Amenities include an indoor hot tub, a cocktail lounge, a pool table, a dining room, and a lounge. Chalets and cedar-sided cabins are basic but comfortable. Rates are $98–108 per person per day, which includes breakfast and dinner.

suites feature separate bedrooms as well as a full kitchen, private balcony, laundry room, and large well-equipped living area for $179–279 s or d. Either way—and not taking into account perpetually discounted rooms advertised on the website—this is an excellent value, especially for families or small groups.

At the edge of Canmore's downtown core is the **Drake Inn** (909 Railway Ave., 403/678-5131 or 800/461-8730, www.drakeinn.com). It offers bright and cheerfully decorated motel rooms for $99 s, $109 d. Well worth an extra $10 are Creekside Rooms, featuring private balconies overlooking Policeman's Creek. The adjoining bar opens daily at 7 A.M. for the best-value breakfast in town.

Across the creek from the Drake Inn is the **Bow Valley Motel** (610 8th St., 403/678-5085 or 800/665-8189, www.bowvalleymotel.com), offering 25 rooms right on the main shopping strip. The rooms are far from the cutting edge of modern style, but the location and price are right—$100 s or d, $105 with cooking facilities. On-site is an outdoor hot tub and coin-operated laundry facilities.

Not only can you rent one- and two-bedroom units with full kitchens at **Rocky Mountain Ski Lodge** (1711 Bow Valley Trail, 403/678-5445 or 800/665-6111, www.rockymtnskilodge.com), there's plenty of outdoor space for kids to run around, including a playground. Also on the property is a barbecue and picnic area, and a laundry. The self-contained suites, some with loft bedrooms, cost from $160. Standard rooms are $130.

$150–200

The quality of accommodations in this category far exceeds that of similarly priced options elsewhere in the Canadian Rockies. With up to $200 (around US$130) per night to spend on accommodations, I strongly recommend you consider the first two options, each offering a unique mountain ambience impossible to find in a regular motel.

M Lady Macdonald Country Inn (1201 Bow Valley Trail, 403/678-3665 or 800/567-3919, www.ladymacdonald.com; $150–225 s or d)

Creekside Country Inn

exudes a welcoming atmosphere and personalized service not experienced in the larger properties. Its 12 rooms are all individually furnished, with the smallest, the Palliser Room, featuring elegant decor and a magnificent wrought-iron bed. The largest of the rooms is the Three Sisters, which has bright, welcoming pastel-colored decor, a king bed, two-way gas fireplace, hot tub, and uninterrupted views of its namesake. Rates include a hearty hot breakfast in a country-style breakfast room.

M **Creekside Country Inn** (709 Benchlands Trail, 403/609-5522 or 866/609-5522, www .creeksidecountryinn.com) is a modern, mountain-style lodge featuring lots of exposed timber. The 12 rooms are elegant in their simplicity; eight have lofts. Facilities include a lounge with roaring log fire, a small exercise room, a whirlpool, and a steam room. Rates are $159–179 ($79–129 outside of summer), which includes a gourmet Continental breakfast that will set you up for the day.

Along the same strip as Lady Macdonald, the **Days Inn** (815 Bow Valley Trail, 403/609-0075 or 877/609-6266, www.canmoredays inn.com) provides a higher standard of accommodation than is usually associated with this chain. Even standard rooms ($159 s or d) have king-size beds, and each is air-conditioned and well equipped with an array of amenities. If you're a Days Inn aficionado, you'll find the extra space, private balcony, and sleek contemporary styling of the suites worth the higher-than-average cost.

Diagonally opposite the Days Inn is the 30-room **Bear Country Lodge** (1002 Bow Valley Trail, 403/678-1000 or 888/678-1008, www .bearcountrylodge.com). It features eye-catching timber and riverstone styling outside and throughout an impressive lobby, but stops short of continuing to the standard rooms, which are unremarkable ($129 s or d, $149 with a kitchenette). Honey Bear Suites, however, reflect the decor of the public areas, with pine log furnishings, gas fireplaces, and hot tubs ($189 s or d). Rates include a Continental breakfast buffet in a pleasant downstairs dining room. The Bear Country kicks off the trend of more expensive hotels that heavily discount rooms outside of summer, with rates from just $69.

Dominated by exposed log work, the **Westridge Country Inn** (1719 Bow Valley Trail, 403/678-5221 or 800/268-0935, www.westridge countryinn.com) has regularly revamped, air-conditioned rooms, each with a small balcony and fireplace. Summer rates of $159–199 include a light breakfast, while in winter rooms start at $100.

Farther north along the Bow Valley Trail is a Best Western property, the **Pocaterra Inn** (1725 Bow Valley Trail, 403/678-4334 or 888/678-6786, www.pocaterrainn.com). It features a large indoor pool, a fitness room, a sauna, and 83 elegant guest rooms, each with a gas fireplace and microwave. Summer rates for a standard room are $180 s or d. Suites—with king beds, jetted tubs, and fireplaces—provide an excellent value for those looking for accommodations in the $200–250 price range.

With 224 guest rooms, the **Radisson Hotel** (511 Bow Valley Trail, 403/678-3625 or 800/333-3333, www.radisson.ca; $159–209 s or d) is Canmore's largest accommodation. Set around landscaped gardens, this complex also features an excellent restaurant (the Sunday brunch is one of the best in the valley), an indoor pool, a fitness facility, the town's only car-rental agency, and a gift shop. Steeply discounted off-season rates make the Radisson a great deal for non-summer travel.

$200–250

The **M Bear and Bison** (705 Benchlands Trail, 403/678-2058, www.bearandbisoninn.com) is an elegant lodging with nine guest rooms in three different themes. Timber and stone surroundings are complemented by rich heritage tones throughout. Each room has a king-size four-poster bed, a jetted tub, a fireplace, and a private balcony or patio. The lounge has a high vaulted ceiling, a welcoming open fire, and panoramic picture windows. Guests also enjoy an inviting library and a private garden complete with an oversized hot tub. Rates of $275–350 s or d include baked goods on arrival, pre-dinner drinks, and a breakfast you will remember for a

long time. Outside of summer, rates run $160–245.

The **M Paintbox Lodge** (629 10th St., 403/609-0482 or 888/678-6100, www.paint boxlodge.com; $259–409 s or d) has the same upscale charm as the Bear and Bison but enjoys a more central location, just one block from the main street. The lobby itself—exposed hand-hewn timbers, slate tiles, and unique pieces of mountain-themed art—is an eye-catching gem. The upscale mountain decor continues through the eight large guest rooms, each lavishly decorated with muted natural colors and a tasteful selection of heritage artifacts. Rooms also boast beds draped with the finest linens, bathrooms anchored by a deep soaker tub, and high-speed Internet access for those who can't leave their work behind. The more expensive rooms have fireplaces and balconies.

At the base of SilverTip Resort, across the TransCanada Highway from downtown, is **Four Points by Sheraton Canmore** (1 Silvertip Trail, 403/609-4422 or 888/609-4422, www.four pointscanmore.com; from $215 s or d), Canmore's most luxurious chain hotel. It is a full-service property, complete with 99 contemporary guest rooms, 13 suites, in-room high-speed Internet access, a fitness center, a casual Italian restaurant and adjacent bar, a gift store, and a complimentary shuttle to downtown Canmore and Banff.

In Three Sisters Mountain Village, across the Bow River from downtown, is the **Residence Inn by Marriott** (91 Three Sisters Dr., 403/678-3400 or 877/335-8800, www.canmoremarriott .com), Canmore's only all-suite accommodation. Each of 119 units is characterized by bright, contemporary furnishings, a well-equipped kitchen, a separate living area, and a full bathroom. Studio units are $199 s, $209 d; one-bedroom units $229 d; two-bedroom units $269 d. Out front is a small heated pool that is open year-round.

HARVEY HEIGHTS

Lodging in Harvey Heights, eight km (five miles) west of Canmore and less than one km (.6 mile) from the entrance to Banff National Park, may

© ANDREW HEMPSTEAD

A few campsites at Restwell Trailer Park enjoy a creekside setting.

seem a little more pricey than Canmore, but most units are self-contained.

$50–100

The least expensive option at Harvey Heights is a standard motel room at the **Gateway Inn** (403/678-5396 or 877/678-1810, www.gatewayinn.ca), which range $75–89 s or d. Self-contained cabins, each with a kitchenette and adjacent fire pit, are $99–165 s or d, with the more expensive ones having three bedrooms. You'll also find a playground, picnic area, and communal fire pit for evening relaxation.

$100–150

Rundle Ridge Chalets (403/678-5387 or 800/332-1299, www.chalets.ab.ca) is one of the mountains' original bungalow camps, with 37 self-contained log cabins scattered around a pleasant two-hectare (five-acre) property. Summer rates range $109–199. The cabins are winterized, and rates drop as low as $79 midweek in the depths of January.

Next door to Rundle Ridge, **The Stockade** (403/678-5212 or 800/330-3824, www.stockadecabins.com; $155–225 s or d) is smaller but similarly set up. The least expensive option is to stay in one of six bright, cheery log cabins. Seven more modern, kitchen-equipped chalets maintain a distinct mountain atmosphere. All units have wood-burning fireplaces.

$150–200

Banff Boundary Lodge (403/678-9555 or 877/678-9555, www.banffboundarylodge.com) has less outdoor space but is a newer property. The 42 units each have one or two bedrooms, a comfortable lounge area with TV/VCR, and a full kitchen. In summer, units are $210–240 per night, but the rest of the year rates drop as low as $100, an excellent value.

DEADMAN'S FLATS

Deadman's Flats, seven km (4.3 miles) east of Canmore along the TransCanada Highway, is little more than a truck stop, but it has motels, a bed-and-breakfast, and 24-hour dining at a Husky gas station.

$50–100

The best value of the bunch is the **Big Horn Motel** (403/678-2290 or 800/892-9908, www.bighornmotel.com). It offers 27 surprisingly modern, mostly nonsmoking rooms. All have TVs and phones, some have kitchens and balconies, and a couple are wheelchair-accessible. Summer rates start at $79 s, $89 d, while in the off-season you can get a nonsmoking kitchenette for just $50.

$100–150

In an alpine-style, two-story chalet, the **Kiska Inn** (110 1st Ave., 403/678-4041 or 866/678-4041, www.kiska.ab.ca) offers six guest rooms. Each is spacious and features subtly themed rooms (the Canmore Room is particularly appealing). Guest amenities include a shared kitchen, a comfortable lounge room with TV/VCR combo, a backyard barbecue area, and Internet access. Summer rates are a reasonable $115–130 s or d including breakfast.

CAMPGROUNDS

Commercial Campgrounds

The **Restwell Trailer Park** (403/678-5111, www.restwelltrailerpark.com) enjoys a great creekside location off 8th Street in downtown Canmore. It's mostly filled with permanent residents and doesn't try to be anything it's not. Overnight travelers are welcomed, with the best sites situated along a stretch of grass that parallels Policeman's Creek. Unserviced sites are $28, hookups $31–43, self-contained cabins $160 s or d.

Along the Bow Valley Trail toward Banff is the **Rundle Mountain Campground,** opposite the motel of the same name (403/678-2131 or 866/678-2267). Like Restwell, it offers showers, laundry facilities, and hookups, but it's a smaller space with crowded sites. Sites range $24–30.

Other Campgrounds

East of Canmore are three government campgrounds operated by Bow Valley Campgrounds (403/673-2163, www.bowvalleycampgrounds .com). Each has pit toilets, kitchen shelters, and firewood for sale at $6 per bundle. None have hookups. **Bow River Campground** is three km (1.9 miles) east of Canmore at the Three Sisters Parkway overpass; **Three Sisters Campground** is accessed from Deadman's Flats, a further four km (2.5 miles) east, but it has a pleasant treed setting, while **Lac des Arcs Campground** slopes down to the edge of a large lake of the same name seven km (4.3 miles) farther toward Calgary. These campgrounds are open May to mid-September, and all sites are $17. Reservations are taken from April 1.

Practicalities

FOOD

The restaurant scene has come a long way in Canmore in the last few years. While you can still get inexpensive bar meals at the many pubs, other choices run the gamut, from the lively atmosphere of dining in the front yard of a converted residence to an upmarket French restaurant.

Groceries

IGA (daily 7 A.M.–10 P.M.) is a large supermarket on Railway Avenue; especially good are the chicken pot pies, which come heated and ready to eat for $4. It also has an in-house bakery, butcher, and deli, along with a wide selection of fresh seafood. Downtown, **Marra's** (638 8th St.) is a locally owned supermarket open until 8 P.M.

Gourmet Goodies

In front of IGA, **Nutter's** (900 Railway Ave., 403/678-3335) is chock-full of bulk bins—a great place to stock up for hiking trips.

Downtown, **Bella Crusta** (702 6th Ave., 403/609-3366; Mon.–Sat. 10 A.M.–6 P.M.) is the purveyor of the best gourmet pizza in the Bow Valley. Heated slices to go are $5, or pay $12–15 for a family-sized version and heat it yourself, on a barbecue as the friendly staff recommends.

M Crazyweed Kitchen (626 8th St., 403/609-2530; daily 11 A.M.–7 P.M.) dishes up creative culinary fare that gets rave reviews from even cultured Calgarians. Behind the glass counter is a wide choice of freshly made dishes, which may include Thai chicken wraps or curried seafood. Healthy portions are served at tables inside or out, or packed to go.

Away from the downtown core, **JK Bakery** (1514 Railway Ave., 403/678-4232; Mon.–Sat. 7 A.M.–5 P.M.) supplies regular and European-style breads to shops and restaurants throughout the Canadian Rockies. A small café out front serves up soups, sandwiches, and pastries, as well as selling gourmet breads over the counter.

Tucked away in an industrial park beyond the south end of Bow Valley Trail is **Valbella Meats** (104 Elk Run Blvd., 403/678-3637; Mon.–Fri. 8 A.M.–6 P.M., Sat. 9 A.M.–5:30 P.M.). Valbella mainly supplies gourmet meats to Bow Valley restaurants and grocery stores; head there for Canadian specialties such as buffalo, venison, and salmon; fresh cuts of marinated Alberta beef, lamb, chicken, and pork; and cured sausages.

Cafés and Coffee Shops

The **Rocky Mountain Bagel Company** (830 8th St., 403/678-9978; daily 6:30 A.M.–10 P.M.) is a popular early-morning gathering spot. With a central location, it's always busy but manages to maintain an inviting atmosphere. It's the perfect place to start the day with a good strong coffee and fruit-filled muffin.

Down one block, **Beamer's Coffee Bar** (737 7th Ave., 403/609-0111; daily 6:30 A.M.–10 P.M.) is a smaller space with equally good coffee. Out on the Bow Valley Trail (between Dairy Queen and Boston Pizza) is another **Beamer's Coffee Bar** (403/678-3988), this one anchored by a long comfortable couch wrapped around a fireplace— the perfect place to relax with one of Beamer's complimentary daily papers. Across Main Street, the **Coffee Mine** (802 8th St., 403/678-2241; daily from 6:30 A.M.) is a small café with a large local following and a sunny outlook.

Just off Main Street, the **Coffeepot & Curry Stop** (637 10th St., 403/678-2688; Mon.–Fri. 6:45 A.M.–6 P.M., Sat. 10 A.M.–5 P.M.) starts the day by serving up locally roasted coffee then moves on to a lunchtime menu of simple but delicious curries ($7).

The prime location of **Sunfood Cafe** (742 Railway Ave., 403/609-2613; daily 7:30 A.M.– 9 P.M.) won't become apparent until you climb the steps from busy Railway Avenue to the sun-drenched patio and admire the surrounding mountains. I'm a meat lover, but still, I have my favorites at this vegetarian eatery: sugar-free crepes doused with organic maple syrup ($6) for breakfast, tabouli salad with hummus ($8) for lunch, and green Thai coconut curry ($15) in the evening. I then reward myself with Kahlua mocha chocolate cake ($6) for dessert.

Away from downtown, near where Cougar Creek enters Canmore from the Fairholme Range, is the **Summit Café** (1001 Cougar Creek Dr., 403/609-2120; daily 6:30 A.M.–6 P.M.; kitchen closes at 4 P.M.). It features a health-conscious menu including lots of salads, but many people come just to soak up the sun on the outside deck or relax with the daily paper and a cup of coffee.

Downtown Restaurants

Canmore has seen many top-notch restaurants open in the last few years, but the decade-old **Zona's** (710 9th St., 403/609-2000; daily 11 A.M.–2 A.M. but for dinner only outside summer) continues to garner rave reviews. The food is great, but so is the restaurant itself—earthy tones, hardwood floors, rustic furniture, bamboo blinds, and kiln-fired clay crockery create an inviting ambience unequaled in Canmore. The menu takes its roots from around the world, with an emphasis on healthy eating and freshly prepared Canadian produce. Choose from dishes such as Moroccan molasses lamb curry ($15) or a filet of salmon baked and smothered in a maple and whiskey sauce ($19.50). Zona's also serves homemade lemonade and a wide selection of slightly overpriced wines and beers. A large deck provides much-needed extra seating in summer.

In the same vicinity (across 6th Avenue and down the alley) is **Tapas** (633 10th St., 403/609-0583; summer daily 7 A.M.–11:30 P.M., the rest of the year daily 5:30–9:30 P.M.), offering a truly Spanish tapas menu in a jazzed-up heritage home with tables inside, upstairs, and out back. Most dishes fall in the $4–12 range, or order *platos* style and get a thoughtful selection of small dishes for two ($32–40).

Off the top end of Main Street, the **Rocky Mountain Flatbread Co.** (838 10th St., 403/609-5508; daily 5–10 P.M.) is a lovely space of natural tones dominated by a clay wood-fired oven in one corner. The oven is also the main attraction when it comes to the food—gourmet flatbread-style pizzas in the $14–20 range. My advice: start with a bowl of made-from-scratch chicken noodle soup ($6), then move on to the prosciutto, mango, mushroom, and avocado pizza (the $16 size is enough for two people).

Duck down the alleyway 709 8th Street to **Chef's Studio Japan** (403/609-8383; daily 4:30 A.M.–10 P.M.), a Japanese restaurant open daily for lunch and dinner. Seating is at a sushi counter or at regular tables surrounded by original art. The cuisine is not overly inventive, but portions are generous and tempura—always a good litmus test—is light and delicate. Educate yourself in the variety of Japanese cooking styles by ordering one of the hot and cold platters designed for sharing between two.

Bow Valley Trail

I'd recommend dining at **Sage Bistro** (1712 Bow Valley Trail, 403/678-4878; Sun.–Thurs. 8 A.M.–10 P.M., Fri.–Sat. 8 A.M.–11 P.M.) simply because it's one of the few restaurants in Canada that makes shepherd's pie the way it should be—with lamb. But this nuance aside, the innovative Canadian-oriented cuisine and flawless presentation make Sage an excellent choice for dinner. Starters include chicken and asparagus croquettes ($8.75) and Dungeness crab cakes ($12), while mains include familiar favorites with a local twist: grilled bison short ribs ($18) and venison meatloaf ($20). Even if my shepherd's pie recommendation doesn't appeal to you, finish up with maple syrup crème brûlée (trust me, you'll love it). The deck is a wonderful place for breakfast or lunch.

Nearby, in the Best Western Green Gables Inn, is **Chez Francois** (1064 Bow Valley Trail, 403/678-6111; daily from 6:30 A.M.), a stylish French restaurant hidden by a rather nondescript motel facade. At breakfast, there's no need to look further than eggs Benedict—with a choice of Valbella back bacon or smoked salmon—smothered in a perfectly formed hollandaise sauce ($9). Dinner is highlighted by well-priced table d'hôte menus that feature Canadian game and produce, prepared with traditional French flair.

INFORMATION

The best source of pre-trip information (apart from this book, of course) is **Tourism Canmore** (403/678-1295 or 866/226-6673, www.tourism canmore.com). A **Travel Alberta Information Centre,** just off the TransCanada Highway on the west side of town (403/678-5277; May–Sept. 8 A.M.–8 P.M., Oct. 9 A.M.–6 P.M.), provides plenty of information about Canmore and Banff.

The *Rocky Mountain Outlook* and *Canmore Leader* are both filled with local issues and entertainment listings; both are available free on stands throughout the valley.

Quarry Lake, a scenic locale on the western edge of Canmore

Canmore

© ANDREW HEMPSTEAD

Books and Bookstores

Canmore Public Library (700 9th St., 403/678-2468) is open Mon.–Thurs. 11 A.M.–8 P.M., Fri.–Sun. 11 A.M.–5 P.M.

At the top end of the main street, **Café Books** (826 Main St., 403/678-0908, Mon.–Sat. 10 A.M.–6 P.M., Sun. 10 A.M.–5 P.M., later hours in summer) stocks an excellent selection of Canadiana, including hiking guides, coffee table–style pictorials, Rocky Mountain cookbooks, and calendars, as well as nonfiction by local authors. Search out children's books down the back. With a huge collection of used books, **Second Story** (713 8th St., 403/609-2368) hasn't been on the second floor since the weight of the books forced a move downstairs to the basement of the same address. Second Story's selection of nonfiction Canadiana is particularly strong.

SERVICES

The **post office** is on 7th Avenue, beside Rusticana Grocery. **The Lost Sock** laundry (in the small mall on 7th Ave. at 10th St.) is open 24 hours daily and has Internet access. **Canmore Hospital** is along Bow Valley Trail (403/678-5536). For the **RCMP,** call 403/678-5516.

The **Film Lab** (801 8th St., 403/678-6066) provides one-hour photo finishing and basic photography supplies. **Switching Gear** (718 10th St., 403/678-1992) is a consignment store for a wide range of new and used, winter and summer sporting equipment.

Internet Access

In addition to major hotels, send and receive email and surf the Internet at the following Can-more locations: **Beamer's Coffee Bar** (1702 Bow Valley Trail, 403/678-3988; daily 7 A.M.–10 P.M.), **Café Books** (826 8th St., 403/678-0908; Mon.–Sat. 10 A.M.–6 P.M., Sun. 10:30 A.M.–5:30 P.M.), and **Canmore Public Library** (700 9th St., 403/678-2468; Mon.–Thurs. 11 A.M.–8 P.M., Fri.–Sun. 11 A.M.–5 P.M.).

TRANSPORTATION

Getting There

The following companies offer door-to-door service on routes that link Calgary International Airport and Banff: **Banff Airporter** (403/762-3330, www.banffairporter.com) and **Rocky Mountain Sky Shuttle** (403/762-5200, www.rockymountainskyshuttle.com). The cost from Calgary is around $45–50 one-way. Adjacent desks at the airport's Arrivals level take bookings, but reserve a seat by booking over the phone or online in advance.

Greyhound stops behind Rusticana Grocery (801 8th St., 403/678-4465) and offers regular services to Calgary, Banff, and beyond.

Getting Around

The most enjoyable way to get around Canmore is on foot or bike, on the extensive trail network winding throughout the town. **Gear Up** (1302 Bow Valley Trail, 403/678-1636) rents front- and full-suspension mountain bikes, as well as canoes and kayaks. For a cab, call **Apex** (403/609-0030). **Hertz,** based at the Radisson Hotel (511 Bow Valley Trail, 403/678-1630), is Canmore's only rental-car outlet. As with Banff rental companies, free mileage is limited to 150 kilometers per day.

Kananaskis Country

Lying along the east side of the Continental Divide south of Banff National Park and less than one hour's drive from Calgary, this sprawling 4,250-square-km (1,640-square-mile) area of the Canadian Rockies (pronounced can-AN-a-skiss) has been extraordinarily successful in balancing the needs of the 2.4 million outdoor enthusiasts who visit annually while keeping the region in a relatively natural state. Although the area lacks the famous lakes and glaciated peaks of Banff and Jasper National Parks, the landscape rivals those parks in many ways. As well as the areas set aside for recreation, large tracts of land give full protection to wildlife. Throughout Kananaskis Country, wildlife is abundant and opportunities for observation of larger mammals are superb.

Kananaskis Country encompasses seven provincial parks, 1,300 km (800 miles) of hiking trails, a complex network of bike paths, areas for horseback riding (and some for ATVs), a world-class 36-hole golf course, boat and bike rentals, and 30 lakes stocked annually with more than 150,000 fish. The downhill-skiing events of the 1988 Winter Olympic Games were held here at the specially developed Nakiska alpine resort, which is now open to the public. Deeper in the mountains, Fortress Mountain provides more downhill skiing and boarding. Meanwhile, Nordic skiers can glide over hundreds of cross-country skiing trails in the region.

Breaking Kananaskis into Regions

Geographically, Kananaskis Country can be divided into eight areas, each with its own distinct character: Bow Valley Provincial Park,

© ANDREW HEMPSTEAD

Must-Sees

Look for **M** to find the sights and activities you can't miss and **M** for the best dining and lodging.

M Canoe Meadows: This is a groovy little spot to make a stop right beside the highway into Kananaskis Country. Even if kayakers aren't doing their stuff down the manmade rapids, the sparkling waters of the Kananaskis River are worth admiring (page 129).

M Kananaskis Country Golf Course: Non-golfers won't be too impressed, but if you do golf and plan on playing just one round in the Canadian Rockies, book a tee time here (page 132).

M Highwood Pass: In Peter Lougheed Provincial Park, you'll find one of the only places in the Canadian Rockies where you can drive to an area of alpine meadows (page 135).

M Rawson Lake: Hikers visit for a variety of reasons—to go fishing, to admire the wildflowers, or simply to soak up magnificent mountain scenery. Regardless of your own interests, add this destination to your hiking agenda (page 137).

M Bragg Creek: This picturesque hamlet was discovered years ago by Calgarians. Join them browsing the many galleries and taking lunch at an outdoor café (page 145).

KANANASKIS COUNTRY

ALBERTA

Canoe Meadows

Kananaskis Country Golf Course

Bragg Creek

Rawson Lake

Highwood Pass

BRITISH COLUMBIA

0   10 mi
0   10 km

Kananaskis Country Golf Course

© ANDREW HEMPSTEAD

a small park between the TransCanada Highway and Bow River that extends south along either side of the Kananaskis River; Kananaskis Valley, home to a golf course, ski resort, and the accommodations of Kananaskis Village; Peter Lougheed Provincial Park, which rises from fish-filled lakes to the glaciated peaks of the Continental Divide; Spray Valley Provincial Park, named for a massive body of water nestled below the Continental Divide; Sibbald, an integrated recreation area where horseback riding is permitted; Elbow River Valley and adjacent Sheep River Valley, sections of the foothills that rise to Elbow-Sheep Wildland Provincial Park; and in the far south Highwood/Cataract Creek area, where the rugged landscape ranges from forested valleys to snowcapped peaks.

The main highway through Kananaskis Country is **Highway 40,** which branches off the Trans-Canada Highway 76 km (47 miles) west of Calgary. Other points of access are south of Canmore through the Spray Valley; at Bragg Creek on the region's northeast border; west from Millarville, Turner Valley, and Longview in the southeast; or along the Forestry Trunk Road from the south.

PLANNING YOUR TIME

I love planning a camping getaway to Kananaskis Country, especially in summer, when the crowds in Banff can be unbearable—but this is about planning *your* trip. If you're based in Canmore, Banff, or even Calgary, you can easily visit the region in a day, spending your time sightseeing and hiking along Highway 40, then looping back to the TransCanada Highway via Spray Valley Provincial Park. But you should plan to stay longer than a day. If you're camping, you'll be amazed at the number of options (2,300 auto-accessible campsites in 31 campgrounds) and the lack of crowds compared to the national parks. Be warned, though; Calgarians are well aware of this mountain wilderness, and every weekend through summer the region is overrun by urbanites in SUVs and families in minivans. Therefore, plan to arrive during the week and you'll almost always be assured of a spot. For creature comforts, book a two-night stay at one of ho-

tels in **Kananaskis Village** and you'll have time to combine the very best hikes with a round of golf or an extended bike ride.

Information centers are located at each of the main entrances to Kananaskis Country, but the best way to do some pre-trip planning is using the website provided by the Alberta government (click the "Preserving Alberta" link at www.cd.gov.ab.ca). Park headquarters is in Canmore in the Provincial Building (800 Railway Ave., 403/678-5508), although this isn't an official information center. Another good source of information is **Friends of Kananaskis Country** (www.kananaskis.org), a nonprofit organization that promotes educational programs, is involved in a variety of hands-on projects, and promotes Kananaskis Country in partnership with the government.

THE LAND

Kananaskis Country holds two distinct ecosystems: the high peaks of the Continental Divide to the west and the lower, rolling foothills to the east. The glacier-carved **Kananaskis Valley** separates the two. The Elbow and Sheep River Valleys rise in the west to the Front Ranges, which formed around 85 million years ago and have eroded to half their original height. The Main Ranges, which form part of the Continental Divide, are composed of older, erosion-resistant quartzite and limestone, giving them a more jagged appearance.

Flora and Fauna

Kananaskis Country occupies a transition zone between foothills and mountains, and as a result it harbors a wide variety of plant species. In the east, the relatively low-lying Sheep, Elbow, and Sibbald valleys are dominated by stands of **aspen,** interspersed with open meadows. Climbing gradually to the west, you'll pass through the montane zone, with its forests of **Douglas fir, lodgepole pine, white spruce,** and **balsam poplar,** then enter the subalpine zone, where stands of **Engelmann spruce, subalpine fir,** and occasionally **larch** lead up to the tree line. Above the tree line, which here occurs at around 2,300

© AVALON TRAVEL PUBLISHING, INC.

meters (7,550 feet), lie the open meadows of the alpine zone. These meadows lie under a deep cover of snow for most of the year but come alive with color during July when wildflowers bloom. Highwood Pass, along Highway 40, is one of the most accessible areas of alpine terrain in the Canadian Rockies; look for **forget-me-nots, Indian paintbrush,** and **western anemone** along the interpretive trail.

These hills, valleys, and forests are home to an abundance of wildlife, including large populations of **moose, mule deer, white-tailed deer, elk, black bear, bighorn sheep,** and **mountain goat.** Also present, but less likely to be seen, are **wolves, grizzly bears,** and **cougars.**

HISTORY

In 1858, Captain John Palliser bestowed the name Kananaskis on the valley, a pass, and two lakes. Kananaskis was a native who, legend had it, suffered a vicious blow to the head by an enemy but survived. The word itself is thought to mean "the meeting of the water." Aside from Palliser, the region was visited by many names synonymous with exploration of the Canadian Rockies: David Thompson in 1787 and 1800, Peter Fidler in 1792, and James Sinclair leading Scottish settlers to the Oregon Territory in 1841. Throughout these times, and until recent times, the valley remained mostly uninhabited. Logging took place from 1883, mostly in the foothill valleys of the Elbow and Sheep Rivers. Coal was mined at various sites, including Ribbon Creek, by Kananaskis Village, but never on a large scale. To serve these industries, roads were built, including the Forestry Trunk Road (Highway 40), which traverses the entire foothills parallel to the Continental Divide.

1970s to the Present

During Alberta's oil-and-gas boom of the 1970s, oil revenues collected by the provincial government were placed into the Heritage Savings Trust Fund, from where they were channeled into various projects aimed at improving the lifestyle of Albertans. One lasting legacy of the fund is Kananaskis Country, officially designated by premier Peter Lougheed in 1977 as Kananaskis Country Provincial Recreational Area. The mandate was to accommodate a multitude of uses, including primarily recreational pursuits, but Kananaskis Country also holds 21 active oil and gas leases, 14 grazing permits, timber leases, and a hydroelectric station on the Kananaskis River. Since 1977, the provincial government has pumped more than $250 million into Kananaskis Country, with private investors spending a little more than $60 million in that same period. Kananaskis Village was developed in the early 1980s in anticipation of the 1988 Winter Olympic Games.

The first major boundary change since 1977 occurred in early 1996 when Elbow-Sheep Wildland Provincial Park was established; at 76,900 hectares (190,000 acres) it is Alberta's largest provincial park. User demand for more facilities led to the 1999 Kananaskis Country Recreation Policy, but this was roundly rejected by Albertans, and there is currently a development moratorium, which has put on hold grand plans for a ski area, more golf courses, and boat cruises on Spray Lake. The latest area of Kananaskis Country to be declared a provincial park is the Spray Valley, which has created a continuous stretch of protection for the Canadian Rockies from Willmore Wilderness Park in the north to Peter Lougheed Provincial Park in the south.

Bow Valley Provincial Park

This provincial park at the north end of Kananaskis Country straddles the TransCanada Highway just west of the Highway 40 junction and extends south to take in a stretch of the Kananaskis River as far south as, and including, Barrier Lake. Most facilities, including two campgrounds and an information center, lie between the TransCanada Highway and the Bow River, at the confluence of the Kananaskis River. The main access point is Highway 1X, which branches north from the TransCanada Highway 80 km (50 miles) west of Calgary and 26 km (16 miles) east of Canmore.

The park protects a small section of the Bow Valley, which was gouged by glaciers during a succession of ice ages, leaving the typical U-shaped glacial valley surrounded by towering peaks. Three vegetation zones are found within the park, but evergreen and aspen forest predominates. The park was originally within the area protected by Banff National Park, but the boundary was moved westward in 1930 to allow development in the Canmore area. The park of today was originally created in 1959 and expanded in 2000.

To the casual motorist driving along the highway, the park seems fairly unspectacular (and is easily missed), but more than 300 species of plants have been recorded and 60 species of birds are known to nest within its boundaries. The abundance of wildflowers, birds, elk, and smaller mammals can be enjoyed along short interpretive trails.

Popular activities in the park include fishing for brown and brook trout and whitefish in the Bow River, bicycling along the paved trail system, and attending interpretive programs presented by park staff. The main road through the park terminates 12 km (7.5 miles) beyond the information center at a picnic area beside the Bow River.

HIKING

The trails in Bow Valley Provincial Park are short and unassuming. You could hike the entire trail system in a day, but if you choose just one make it the Many Springs Trail.

Montane Trail

- Length: 2.2 km/1.4 miles (30 minutes) round-trip
- Elevation gain: minimal
- Rating: easy
- Trailhead: Visitor Information Centre off Highway 1X

The Montane Trail begins from behind the main information center and, as the name suggests, traverses montane forest of aspen and towering Douglas fir, skirting an open meadow and several eskers (low ridges left behind by retreating glaciers during the last ice age).

Many Springs Trail

- Length: 2.8 km/1.7 miles (40 minutes) round-trip
- Elevation gain: minimal
- Rating: easy
- Trailhead: Elk Flats day-use area

From the trailhead, this well-formed trail makes a loop around a wetland fed by underground springs. The spring water is relatively warm, creating a microclimate that attracts birds and mammals year-round. Look for orchids around damp areas.

Flowing Water Interpretive Trail

- Length: 1.4 km/.9 mile (30 minutes) round-trip
- Elevation gain: minimal
- Rating: easy
- Trailhead: Willow Rock Campground, eastern side of Highway 1X

This trail traverses montane forest along a bench above the Kananaskis River and passes a beaver pond. Interpretive panels along the way explain the importance of water and its relationship to the ecosystem.

Kananaskis Country

BEAT THE CAMPING CROWD

Every weekend throughout summer, thousands of Calgarians flee the city for the mountains. Kananaskis Country—and Peter Lougheed Provincial Park in particular—is the most popular destination. With little more than 500 campsites—most offered on a first-come, first-served basis—the park's six campgrounds fill fast. This isn't usually a problem during the week, but by lunchtime Friday, keen Calgarians are busy setting up camp for the weekend, and by midafternoon all sites will be filled. (Some folks head out on Thursday, stake a spot by paying for three nights' camping, head back to Calgary, then return after work on Fri-

day). The official checkout time is 11 a.m., but plan on arriving earlier than this to secure a site. When every campground is full, a sign at the junction of Highway 40 and Kananaskis Lakes Road directs campers to the Pocaterra day-use area, where overflow camping costs $8. Another option is to continue up and over Highwood Pass to the more remote campgrounds detailed under Highwood/Cataract Creek.

Reservations are taken for some sites at Boulton Creek Campground. Use the website www.kananaskiscamping.com and have your credit card at hand.

PRACTICALITIES

The park holds a number of picnic areas, two excellent campgrounds, and a grocery store (near the entrance to Bow Valley Campground) with bike rentals and firewood sales.

Campgrounds

Facilities at the two campgrounds within the park are as good as any in the Canadian Rockies. Both have showers, flush toilets, firewood for sale ($6 per bundle), and kitchen shelters. Continue beyond the information center to reach **Bow Valley Campground** (May–mid-Oct.), where unserviced sites are $17 and a limited number of sites with power and water are $23. Across Highway 1X, the loop road through **Willow Rock Camp-**

ground (May–late Oct.) passes a few powered sites in an open area ($20) then descends to a smattering of well-spaced unserviced sites ($17), some right near the river. This campground also has a coin laundry. For more information, or for reservations at Bow Valley, contact **Bow Valley Park Campgrounds** (403/673-2163, www.bow valleycampgrounds.com).

Information

The **Visitor Information Centre** (Highway 1X, 403/673-3663; summer Mon.–Fri. 8 A.M.–8 P.M., the rest of the year Mon.–Fri. 8:15 A.M.–4:30 P.M.) offers general information on the park and Kananaskis Country, as well as interpretive displays. The short Montane Trail begins here.

Kananaskis Valley

This is the most developed area of Kananaskis Country, yet summer crowds are minimal compared to Banff. Highway 40 follows the Kananaskis River through the valley between the TransCanada Highway and Peter Lougheed Provincial Park.

SIGHTS

The following sights are along Highway 40 and are detailed from the TransCanada Highway in the north to Peter Lougheed Provincial Park in the south.

M Canoe Meadows

From the TransCanada Highway 76 km (47 miles) west of Calgary, Highway 40 branches south across open rangeland, entering Kananaskis Country beyond the boundary of the Stoney native reserve. The first worthwhile stop along this route is Canoe Meadows, a large day-use area above the sparkling Kananaskis River. Below the picnic area, white-water enthusiasts use a short stretch of river as a slalom course. Manmade obstacles and gates challenge recreational and racing kayakers, while upstream (around the first bend), the manmade Green Tongue creates a steep wave, allowing kayakers to remain in one spot, spinning and twisting while water rushes past them.

Barrier Lake and Vicinity

South from Canoe Meadows, stop at the **Barrier Lake Visitor Information Centre** (403/673-3985; June–mid-Sept. daily 9 A.M.–6 P.M., the rest of the year daily 9 A.M.–4 P.M.). Nestled between Highway 40 and the Kananaskis River, riverside trails lead in both directions, including two km (1.2 miles) downstream to Canoe Meadows. Across the road is Tim Horton's Children's Ranch, set up by a Canadian hockey great to help underprivileged kids enjoy summer camp.

The first main body of water Highway 40 passes is **Barrier Lake,** dominated to the south by the impressive peak of Mount Baldy (2,212 meters/7,257 feet). The lake is manmade but still a

picture of beauty. From a picnic area at its northern end, an official trail leads across the dam, but just as enjoyable is to walk along the southern lakeshore below the highway. Along its length are stretches of sandy beach, small streams, piles of driftwood, and at the end of the lake a massive scree slope that disappears into the lake.

Opposite Barrier Lake is a **University of Calgary** forestry research station, which has been in use since the 1930s. A cabin from this early era still stands, along with a guard's tower put in place during World War II when the facility was used as an internment camp. The cabin is open for inspection in summer Sat.–Sun. 10 A.M.–4 P.M. It's also the starting point for the Forestry Management Interpretive Trail, comprising two interconnected loops that describe the forest and forestry practices.

South to Kananaskis Village and Beyond

After passing a second, lesser-used picnic area at the south end of Barrier Lake, Highway 40 continues south around the base of Mount Baldy and crosses **Wasootch Creek** and another picnic area. The next stop of interest, especially for anglers, is **Mount Lorette Ponds,** a string of five shallow lakes stocked annually with rainbow trout. Originally an oxbow in the Kananaskis River, these lakes were artificially deepened when the construction of Highway 40 cut them off from the main flow of the Kananaskis River. Paved paths lead to and around the ponds, passing quiet picnic spots and wheelchair-accessible fishing platforms.

Kananaskis Village lies just off Highway 40 four km (2.5 miles) south of the ponds. The village was the epicenter of action during the 1988 Winter Olympic Games. Developed specially for the games, the village sits on a high bench below Nakiska—where the downhill events of the games were held—and overlooks a golf course. The village comprises two hotels, restaurants, and other service shops set around a paved courtyard complete with waterfalls and trout-stocked ponds.

© ANDREW HEMPSTEAD

The shallow waters of Mount Lorette Ponds are stocked annually with rainbow trout.

From the village, it's 15 km (9.3 miles) farther south to the border of Peter Lougheed Provincial Park. Just beyond the village is **Wedge Pond.** Originally dug as a gravel pit during golf course construction, it is now filled with water and encircled by a one-km (.6-mile) trail offering fantastic views across the river to towering 2,958-meter (9,700-foot) Mount Kidd.

HIKING

Prairie View

- Length: 6.5 km/4 miles (2–2.5 hours) one-way
- Elevation gain: 420 meters/1,380 feet
- Rating: moderate
- Trailhead: north end of Barrier Lake, Highway 40

This trail provides a variety of options; the most straightforward leads to a high viewpoint atop McConnell Ridge. To get started, cross the Barrier Dam, take the right fork at the first junction, and go left at the second. From this point the trail climbs steadily along an old fire lookout road

to the summit, where views extend south across Barrier Lake to Mount Baldy. The actual site of the fire lookout is one km (.6 mile) farther and 80 vertical meters (260 vertical feet) from the main trail along the ridge. The additional climb to the lookout is well worth the effort; you'll be rewarded with views across Bow Valley to Mount Yamnuska and east across the prairies to Calgary. Back on the main trail, at the 6.5-km (four-mile) mark, you'll come to Jewell Pass, a major trail junction. The options from this point are to descend along Jewell Creek to the shore of Barrier Lake, passing picturesque Jewell Falls (14 km/8.7 miles round-trip from the parking lot; allow four hours), or to continue north into the Quaite Valley and to the Heart Creek trailhead in the Bow Valley (a further eight km/five miles one-way).

Baldy Pass

- Length: 4.5 km/2.8 miles (1.5–2 hours) one-way
- Elevation gain: 520 meters/1,710 feet
- Rating: moderate
- Trailhead: Highway 40, three km (1.9 miles) south of Barrier Lake

This trail traverses Elbow-Sheep Wildland Provincial Park to a 1,990-meter (6,530-foot) divide separating the Kananaskis River and Jumping-pound Creek watersheds. Cross Highway 40 from the unmarked parking lot, entering the woods at the marked trailhead. After 500 meters (.3 mile), at a marked intersection, the trail enters a usually dry watercourse, which it follows the entire way to the pass. Only the last 500 meters (.3 mile) are particularly steep, across an avalanche slope. An even better view than that afforded at the pass can be had by following the northern ridge from the pass. It's a steep scramble, though, gaining as much elevation in one km (.6 mile) as the whole trail gains between the trailhead and pass.

Ribbon Falls

- Length: 9 km/5.6 miles (three hours) one-way
- Elevation gain: 335 meters/1,100 feet
- Rating: moderate
- Trailhead: upper parking lot at Ribbon Creek, off Kananaskis Village access road

Moderate elevation gain and a well-formed trail make this one of the more popular day hikes in the Kananaskis Valley. Following Ribbon Creek through a narrow valley between Mount Kidd and Ribbon Peak, it passes chunks of iron from an old logging camp and the remains of two abandoned log cabins. Beyond the second cabin, the trail enters Dipper Canyon, dotted with pools of water, then climbs across an avalanche slope to a lookout over Ribbon Falls.

Two km (1.2 miles) beyond the falls is Ribbon Lake, but reaching it requires some rock-climbing skills. From the falls, the trail switchbacks up a scree slope to a sheer cliff face. Three lengths of chain and a series of narrow ledges need to be negotiated to reach the clifftop, and then it's a straightforward hike through a subalpine forest to the lake.

Mount Allan (Centennial Ridge)
• Length: 11 km/6.8 miles (4–5 hours) one-way
• Elevation gain: 1,350 meters/4,430 feet
• Rating: difficult
• Trailhead: upper parking lot at Ribbon Creek

This is the highest maintained trail in the Canadian Rockies and one of the few that actually reach a mountaintop. Its final destination is the summit of Mount Allan, on whose slopes the Nakiska ski area lies. From the marked trailhead, it branches to the right, through the Hidden Ski Trail, then left through an open meadow that was the site of the Ribbon Creek Coal Mine. Then the fun starts—the trail gains 610 meters (2,000 feet) of elevation in the next two km (1.2 miles). At the end of this climb the trail arrives atop Centennial Ridge and at the top of the Olympic Platter, starting point for the Men's Downhill at the 1988 Winter Olympic Games. It follows the ridge past a group of intriguing 25-meter-high (82-foot-high) hoodoos known as the Rock Garden, passes a false summit, and then, finally, reaches the top of 2,990-meter (9,810-foot) Mount Allan.

Galatea Creek
• Length: 5.9 km/3.7 miles (two hours) one-way
• Elevation gain: 425 meters/1,390 feet
• Rating: moderate
• Trailhead: Highway 40, 10 km (6.2 miles) south of Mount Kidd RV Park

Galatea Creek flows from high in the Kananaskis Range through a narrow valley bordered to the north by Mount Kidd and to the south by Fortress Ridge. From Highway 40, the trail descends to the Kananaskis River, crossing via a long suspension bridge. Take the left fork once across the river. The trail is easy to follow as it parallels the north bank of Galatea Creek beneath the sheer southern wall of Mount Kidd. It traverses a wide avalanche slope before reaching the final steep ascent to tree-encircled Lillian Lake, which is stocked with rainbow trout. Behind the lake's backcountry campground, a trail continues two km (1.2 miles) to Upper Galatea Lake.

Fortress Lake
• Length: 5 km/3.1 miles (1.5 hours) one-way
• Elevation gain: 280 meters/920 feet
• Rating: easy/moderate
• Trailhead: Fortress Mountain winter resort, 18 km (11 miles) from Fortress Junction

This trail is unmarked but easy enough to follow. From the parking lot at Fortress Mountain—the unofficial trailhead is the cat track—it descends to Aussie Creek. Once across the creek, the trail begins the ascent to the lake, crossing under a T-bar and continuing up to Fortress Ridge. From the upper terminal of Farside chairlift, go left at the fork to reach the lake, a deep blue body of water nestled under the cliff for which the ski area is named. The right fork at the top of the chairlift leads along Fortress Ridge, climbing above the tree line for panoramic views across the Kananaskis Valley. The high point of the ridge is 5.5 km (3.4 miles) from the parking lot, with a more strenuous elevation gain of 530 meters (1,740 feet).

OTHER RECREATION

In Kananaskis Village, **Peregrine Sports** (403/591-7453) rents sporting equipment

Golfing in Kananaskis Country is a spectacular experience.

including mountain bikes (from $8 per hour, $34 per day), fishing rods ($10 per day), canoes ($40 per day), and various downhill and cross-country skiing equipment. Canmore-based **Mirage Adventure Tours** (403/678-4919 or 888/312-7238) runs rafting trips on the Kananaskis River below Barrier Dam for $59 per person.

Kananaskis Country Golf Course

Regularly voted "Best Value in North America" by *Golf Digest,* this 36-hole layout (403/591-7272 or 877/591-2525, www.kananaskisgolf .com) is bisected by the Kananaskis River and surrounded by magnificent mountain peaks. It comprises two 18-hole courses: **Mount Kidd,** featuring undulating terrain and an island green on the 197-yard fourth hole, and **Mount Lorette.** Both courses measure more than 7,000 yards from the back markers. The course opened in 1983 at a cost of almost $1 million per hole. The bunkers alone—filled with pure white silica

from British Columbia—cost $350,000. Renowned golf-course architect Robert Trent Jones, who designed the layout, described the Kananaskis River Valley as "the best spot I have ever seen for a golf course." After marveling at the surrounding mountains, few will disagree with his statement. Just don't let the 142 sand traps, water that comes into play on more than half the holes, or the large rolling greens distract you. Greens fees are $75 (Albertan residents pay $55), and a cart is an additional $15 per person. Golfers enjoy complimentary valet parking and use of the driving range, a restaurant and bar with awesome mountain views, and a well-stocked golf shop.

WINTERTIME

Nakiska

The winter resort of Nakiska (403/591-7777, www.skinakiska.com; for accommodation reservations, call 800/258-7669) was built to host the alpine skiing events of the 1988 Winter Olympic Games. Originally the Olympic events were to be held on existing ski slopes in Banff National Park. Environmentalists succeeded in keeping the games out of the park, but their victory soon turned sour when alternate plans were unveiled to spend $25.3 million creating a new Olympic hill on the slopes of Mount Allan.

The project was controversial right from the start, but environmental politics wasn't the only problem faced here. Anyone familiar with these mountains knows the devastating effect the area's warm, dry chinook winds have on the snow cover—the idea of building a ski hill here seemed ludicrous. The answer was snowmaking. A computerized snowmaking system covering 85 percent of the runs was installed at a cost of $5 million. With 40 km (25 miles) of piping and 343 hydrants, the system is capable of pumping 24 million liters of water a day. So who needs Mother Nature?

In the end, the Olympics came off without a glitch, and Nakiska is now open to the public. Great cruising and fast fall-line skiing on runs cut specially for racing will satisfy the intermediate-to-advanced crowd. The Bronze Chairlift accesses a novice area below the main area. The area has a total of 28 runs and a vertical rise of 735 meters (2,410 feet). Lift tickets are $49 adults, $38 seniors and students, $16 children. Kids ages 5 and younger ski free. Packages are offered in adjacent Kananaskis Village, as well as Canmore, 56 km (35 miles) to the northwest and linked by shuttle Tuesday and Friday through the winter season.

Cross-Country Skiing

The most accessible of Kananaskis Country's 200 km (124 miles) of cross-country trails are in the Ribbon Creek area. Most heavily used are those radiating from Kananaskis Village and those around the base of Nakiska. Most trails are easy to intermediate, including a five-km (3.1-mile) track up Ribbon Creek. Rentals are available in the Village Trading Post in Kananaskis Village.

KANANASKIS VILLAGE

This modern mountain village 90 km (56 miles) from Calgary was built for the 1988 Winter Olympic Games. It was again in the world spotlight when eight of the world's most politically powerful men met here during the G8 Summit in June 2002. In an attempt to prevent anarchy experienced at previous summits, the Canadian government decided on a wilderness destination, the first time the summit had ever taken place outside of a city. The actual summit was accompanied by Canada's largest-ever security operation, leaving world leaders to discuss economic growth, global poverty, sustainable development, and peace and security without interruption. The bulletproof Suburbans and circling fighter planes have long since disappeared, leaving the village to those who want to experience the wilds of Kananaskis Country while still enjoying the comforts of hotels and fine restaurants.

Accommodations

The village is home to two resortlike hotels set around a cobbled courtyard. Outdoor seating

from various eateries spills on to the terrace, and biking and hiking trails radiate out in all directions. All in all, a good place to base yourself for an overnight hotel stay.

Ⓜ Executive Resort at Kananaskis (403/591-7500 or 888/388-3932, www.executive hotels.net) is the smaller and more personal of the two, with guest rooms that combine natural colors with dramatic contemporary styling. Some of the rooms are bedroom lofts with gas fireplaces, kitchenettes, large bathrooms, and sitting rooms ($250 s or d); the others are standard size hotel rooms that begin at $220. Extras include the Mountain Spa facility, a fitness center, an indoor pool, and a restaurant and pub.

The 321-room **Delta Lodge at Kananaskis** (403/591-7711 or 866/432-4322, www.delta hotels.com) is part of an upscale Canadian hotel chain. It offers two distinct types of rooms. In the main lodge are 251 moderately large Delta Rooms, many with mountain views, balconies, and fireplaces. Connected by a covered walkway are 70 Signature Club (a Delta designation) rooms, each boasting elegant Victorian-era charm, a mountain view, a luxurious bathroom complete with bathrobes, extra large beds, and many extras, such as CD players. Guests in this wing also enjoy a private lounge and Continental breakfast. All guests have use of the Summit Spa and Fitness Centre, which comprises a full-facility health club, an indoor swimming pool, whirlpool, steam room, sauna, and a beauty salon with tanning beds. Summer rates for Delta Rooms are $220 s or d, while Signature Club rooms start at $340.

Food

The Delta Lodge (403/591-7711) contains four restaurants and two bars. For a warm, relaxed atmosphere, head to the **Bighorn Lounge** (daily from 11 A.M.), near the arcade's main entrance. It features a bistro-style menu highlighted by a wide variety of appetizers perfect for sharing, such as cheese platters. **Obsessions Deli** serves up light snacks, including healthy sandwiches and rich, handmade truffles. Also in the arcade is the **Fireweed Grill** (daily 6 A.M.–10 P.M.), with a casual Western-style atmosphere, floor-to-ceiling windows, and an adjoining outdoor patio used during summer. Breakfast is served buffet-style daily until 10 A.M. The country-style **Brady's Market** features seasonal produce prepared in traditional European dishes. **Seasons Dining Room** (Tues.–Sat. 6–9:30 P.M.), in the Signature Club wing, is the village's most elegant restaurant. French-Canadian cuisine is served on sterling silver, as a pianist plays in the background; expect to pay $18–30 for an entrée.

Food is also available at **Wildflower Restaurant,** at the adjacent Executive Resort, or at the golf course, where the restaurant offers a casual atmosphere and stunning valley views.

OTHER ACCOMMODATIONS AND INFORMATION

Sundance Lodges

A magnet for families, the privately owned **Sundance Lodges** (403/591-7122, www.sundancelodges.com; mid-May to September) is also a wonderful option for travelers looking to try camping or who want something a little more adventurous than a regular motel room. Campsites cost $19 per night, with rentals including tents, camp stoves, sleeping bags, and utensil kits available for minimal charge. Next up are the tepees ($46–60), 13 of them, each with colorfully painted canvas walls rising from wooden floors. Inside are mattresses, a heater, and a lantern. Finally, you can stay in the Trapper Tent, with similar interior fittings but larger and with a canvas-covered awning over a picnic table. When you tire of hiking and biking on surrounding trails, return to the lodge for fishing in a man-made pond, horseshoes, badminton, and volleyball. Other amenities include a general store, hot showers, a laundry, and Internet access. Sundance sits beside the Kananaskis River, just off Highway 40, 22 km (13.7 miles) south of the TransCanada Highway.

Campgrounds

Mount Kidd RV Park (403/591-7700, www .mountkiddrv.com) is arguably the finest RV park in Canada. It's nestled below the sheer eastern face of Mount Kidd in a forest of spruce and lodgepole pine, along Highway 40 south of Kananaskis Village and the golf course and 26 km (16 miles) from the TransCanada Highway. The campground's showpiece is the Campers Center (yes, the American spelling). Inside is the main registration area and all the usual bathroom facilities as well as whirlpools, saunas, a wading pool, a game room, a lounge, groceries, a concession area, and a laundry room. Outside are two tennis courts, picnic areas by the river, and many paved biking and hiking trails. Most of the 229 campsites are hookups, but the few tenting sites are a good value at $22 per night. Powered sites are $28, with power and water costs $30, and full hookups are $35. The combination of amenities and the mountain location—unequaled anywhere in the Canadian Rockies—makes this an extremely popular campground. Check the website for details of the earliest dates you can book for the various seasons (although the most important point is to book as far in advance as possible).

Those who can survive without such luxuries should continue 6.5 km (four miles) south beyond Mount Kidd RV Park to **Eau Claire Campground** (late June–mid-Sept.; $17), operated by Kananaskis Camping (403/591-7226, www.kananaskiscamping.com). Facilities are limited to 51 sites (those on the outside of the loop afford the most privacy), each with a picnic table and fire pit, along with pump water, pit toilets, and a playground. No reservations are taken, but the website posts up-to-date vacancy numbers. Other options for campers are to continue south along Highway 40 into Peter Lougheed Provincial Park or take Highway 68 east from Barrier Lake to Sibbald Lake.

Information

A short distance along Highway 40 from Highway 1 (but north of Barrier Lake), **Barrier Lake Visitor Information Centre** (403/673-3985; summer daily 9 A.M.–6 P.M., the rest of the year daily 9 A.M.–4 P.M.) is a good place to start your trip into Kananaskis Country. A small information booth operates in Kananaskis Village through the months of summer.

Peter Lougheed Provincial Park

This park is a southern extension of the Kananaskis Valley and protects the upper watershed of the Kananaskis River. It is contained within a high mountain valley and dominated by two magnificent bodies of water: **Upper** and **Lower Kananaskis Lakes.** To the west and south is the Continental Divide and British Columbia, while to the north is Spray Valley Provincial Park and to the east is Elbow-Sheep Wildland Provincial Park. Originally named Kananaskis Provincial Park, it was renamed in 1986 after Peter Lougheed (pronounced LAW-heed). Lougheed was the Albertan premier who, with the help of oil-money–based Heritage Savings Trust Fund, began the development of Kananaskis Country as a multiuse recreation area. The 500-square-km (193-square-mile) wilderness area is the second-largest provincial park in Alberta. Captain John Palliser passed by the Kananaskis Lakes in 1858, summing up the beauty of the lakes by writing "We came upon a magnificent lake, hemmed in by mountains, and studded by numerous islets, very thickly wooded. This lake, about four miles long and one-and-a-half miles wide, receives water from the glacier above, and is a favorite place of resort to the Kootenie Indians."

Highway 40 is the main route through the park. The most important intersection to make note of is five km (3.1 miles) along Highway 40 from the park's north boundary. At this point, Kananaskis Lakes Road branches off to the west, accessing Upper and Lower Kananaskis Lakes. These two lakes are the center of boating and fishing in the park, and opportunities abound for hiking and camping nearby.

Ⓜ Highwood Pass

In the southeastern corner of the park, Highway 40 climbs to Highwood Pass (2,227 meters/7,310 feet), the highest road pass in Canada. On the way up to the pass, a pleasant detour is Valley View Trail, a five-km (3.1 miles) paved road whose route higher up the slopes of the Opal Range allows views across the entire park to the Continental Divide. The pass itself is right at the tree line, making it one of the most accessible alpine areas in all of the Canadian Rockies. Simply step out of your vehicle and follow the interpretive trails through the **Highwood Meadows.** In the vicinity, the **Rock Glacier Trail,** two km (1.2 miles) north of Highwood Pass, leads 150 meters (.1 mile) to a unique formation of moraine rock.

From the pass, Highway 40 descends into the Highwood/Cataract Creek areas of Kananaskis Country (Highwood Junction is 35 km/22 miles from the pass). Highwood Pass is in a critical wildlife habitat and is closed December–June 15.

HIKING

The park offers several interesting interpretive trails and more strenuous hikes. Most trailheads are along Kananaskis Lakes Road, a paved road that leads off Highway 40 to Upper and Lower Kananaskis lakes. Many trails feature interpretive signs; others require an interpretive booklet available from the Visitor Information Centre. **Rockwall Trail,** from the Visitor Information Centre, and **Marl Lake Trail,** from Elkwood Campground, are wheelchair accessible and barrier-free, respectively. These are some of the park's more popular interpretive and day hikes:

Boulton Creek

• Length: 4.9 km/3 miles (90 minutes) round-trip
• Elevation gain: minimal
• Rating: easy
• Trailhead: Boulton Bridge, Kananaskis Lakes Road, 10 km (6.2 miles) from Highway 40

A booklet, available at the trailhead or at the Visitor Information Centre, corresponds with numbered posts along this interpretive trail. The highlighted stops emphasize the valley's human history. After a short climb from a riverside parking lot below the Boulton Creek Trading Post, the trail reaches a cabin built in the 1930s as a

Kananaskis Country

To Spray Lake
and Canmore

Spray Valley
Provincial Park

MOUNT ENGADINE
LODGE

Chester
Lake

Burstall
Lakes

Mud
Lake

Burstall Pass
Trail

Banff
National
Park

Smith-Dorrien
Glacier

Haig
Glacier

Peter   Lougheed

Provincial   Park

Mt Black
Prince

Warspite
Lake

Black Prince
Cirque Trail

Rockwall
Trail

Upper Kananaskis River

Three Isle
Lake

Lower
Kananaskis
Lake

LOWER
LAKE

INTERLAKES

Upper
Kananaskis
Lake

MT SARRAIL

RAWSON LAKE

BRITISH
COLUMBIA

EAU CLAIRE

To Kananaskis Village
and TransCanada Highway

40

FORTRESS
JUNCTION

THE FORTRESS

SMITH-DORRIEN/SPRAY TRAIL

Smith-Dorrien Creek

ALBERTA

PETER LOUGHEED
PROVINCIAL PARK

Kananaskis Trail

Kananaskis River

PARK
ADMINISTRATION
OFFICE

40

Elbow-Sheep

Wildland

Provincial   Park

CANYON

VISITOR INFORMATION
CENTRE

ELKWOOD

WILLIAM WATSON LODGE

Marl Lake
Trail

Marl
Lake

Kananaskis
Lakes Trail

BOULTON CREEK

BOULTON CREEK
TRADING POST

Boulton
Creek Trail

Elbow River

Elbow
Lake

Mt Rae

Ptarmigan
Cirque
Trail

Elk Pass

Boulton Creek

HIGHWOOD
PASS

Pocaterra Creek

40

Kananaskis   Country

Elk   Lakes

Provincial   Park

Upper Elk
Lake

To Highwood
Junction

0   2 mi

0   2 km

© AVALON TRAVEL PUBLISHING, INC.

stopover for forest-ranger patrols. The trail then follows a high ridge and loops back along the other side of the creek to the trailhead.

Rawson Lake

- Length: 3.5 km/2.2 miles (1.5 hours) one-way
- Elevation gain: 305 meters/1,000 feet
- Rating: moderate
- Trailhead: Upper Lake day-use area, Kananaskis Lakes Road, 13 km (eight miles) from Highway 40

This picturesque subalpine lake is one of the most rewarding half-day hiking destinations in Kananaskis Country. It sits in a high cirque and is backed by a towering yet magnificently symmetrical headwall, so it's easy to spend an hour or two soaking up your surroundings once you reach the end of the trail. Snow lies along the trail well into July, and the lake doesn't open for fishing until July 15, but it is nevertheless a popular destination throughout summer.

Make your way to the farthest parking lot at Upper Lake (through the middle of the main parking lot) and begin the trek by taking the Upper Kananaskis Lake Circuit Trail. Sarrail Creek Falls is passed at the one-km (.6-mile) mark, 150 meters (.1 mile) before the Rawson Lake cutoff. Taking the uphill option, you're faced with almost two km (1.2 miles) of switchbacks. The trail then levels out, with boardwalks constructed over boggy sections of trail, suddenly emerging at the lake's outlet. Continue around the southern shore, passed an intriguing elevated outhouse, to small meadows and slopes of scree that disappear into the lake.

Elbow Lake

- Length: 1.3 km/.8 mile (30 minutes) one-way
- Elevation gain: 135 meters/440 feet
- Rating: easy
- Trailhead: Elbow Pass day-use area, Highway 40, 13 km (eight miles) south of Kananaskis Lakes Road

The official trail is a wide road that climbs quickly into the bowl holding shallow Elbow Lake. The

© ANDREW HEMPSTEAD

A hiker enjoys the solitude of Rawson Lake.

lake is a popular spot, especially for summer picnics; campsites are spread around the south shore. An interesting side trip is to Rae Glacier, a small glacier on the north face of Mount Rae. The trail starts on the east shore of the lake, gaining 400 meters (1,310 feet) of elevation in just over two km (1.2 miles).

Elbow Lake is the source of the Elbow River, which flows eastward through Elbow-Sheep Wildland Provincial Park and into the foothills. The short hiking trail from Highway 40 up to the lake is part of a much longer historic route that ran between the two valleys and is still passable for backcountry adventurers.

Ptarmigan Cirque

- Length: 5.6 km/3.5 miles (two hours) round-trip
- Elevation gain: 230 meters/750 feet
- Rating: moderate
- Trailhead: Highwood Pass, Highway 40,

17 km (10.5 miles) south of Kananaskis Lakes Road

The trailhead for this steep interpretive walk is across the road from the parking lot at Highwood Pass. A booklet, available at the trailhead or at the Visitor Information Centre, corresponds with numbered posts along the trail. As you climb into the alpine zone, magnificent panoramas unfold. Along the trail you are likely to see numerous small mammals. Columbian ground squirrels, pikas, least chipmunks, and hoary marmots are all common. At higher elevations the meadows are home to bighorn sheep, mountain goats, and grizzly bears.

Warspite Lake
• Length: 2.1 km/1.3 miles (40 minutes) one-way
• Elevation gain: 100 meters/330 feet
• Rating: easy
• Trailhead: Mount Black Prince day-use area, Smith-Dorrien/Spray Trail, eight km (five miles) from Kananaskis Lakes Road.

This easily reached lake is away from the busiest part of the park, making it an uncrowded yet worthwhile jaunt (also known as the **Black Prince Cirque Trail,** although officially ending well before the actual cirque). Numbered posts along the trail correspond to a booklet available at the trailhead or at the Visitor Information Centre. The trail begins by climbing steadily to an area that was logged in the early 1970s. It then winds up through a forest of Engelmann spruce and subalpine fir, crossing Warspite Creek and emerging at the forest-encircled lake. An unmarked route continues along the north shoreline, then climbs unrelentingly before entering Black Prince Cirque, which was formed by ancient glacial action. Each spring the cirque fills with water, forming small, emerald-green lakes. It's an additional three km (1.9 miles) each way from Warspite Lake to the cirque.

Burstall Pass
• Length: 7.4 km/4.6 miles (2.5 hours) one-way
• Elevation gain: 480 meters/1,575 feet
• Rating: moderate/difficult

• Trailhead: Mud Lake, Smith-Dorrien/Spray Trail, 20 km (12.5 miles) from Kananaskis Lakes Road

From Mud Lake (a popular fishing hole), this trail begins with a three-km (1.9-mile) climb up an old logging road to Burstall Lakes. After traversing some willow flats, it begins climbing again through heavy forest and across avalanche paths to a large cirque. The final ascent to the pass is a real slog, but the view across the Upper Spray Valley (which is in Banff National Park) is worth it. From the pass it is possible to continue to Palliser Pass (two days one-way) and Banff townsite (three days one-way).

OTHER RECREATION

Hiking is the most popular activity in the park but by no means the only one. The **Bike Trail,** a 20-km (12.5-mile) paved trail designed especially for bicycles, begins behind the Visitor Information Centre and follows Lower Kananaskis Lake all the way to the Mount Sarrail Campground. Many other trails are designated for mountain-bike use; inquire at the Visitor Information Centre (403/591-6344). **Boulton Creek Trading Post** (403/591-7678) rents mountain bikes; $8 per hour, $32 per day.

Fishing is fair in Upper and Lower Kananaskis Lakes, where trout and whitefish tease anglers. A nightly interpretive program takes place in campground amphitheaters throughout the park. Look for schedules posted on bulletin boards or check with the Visitor Information Centre.

In winter and spring Highwood Pass is closed to traffic, but Highway 40 entering the park from the north is cleared, and cross-country skiing is excellent.

PRACTICALITIES
William Watson Lodge
This special facility by Lower Kananaskis Lake (P.O. Box 130, Kananaskis Village, AB T0L 2H0, 403/591-7227) is available to disabled persons and Albertan seniors. It provides a wide range of barrier-free facilities, including hiking trails, a

picnic area, and a stocked trout pond. Guests stay in either a campground or one of 22 barrier-free cabins, and they must supply their own bedding and food. The main lodge has a kitchen, lounge, library, laundry room, and a sundeck with gas barbecues. Disabled guests may bring up to three family members or friends. The cost is $5–15 per person per night. Reservations are essential and can be made up to four months in advance by Albertans and up to two months in advance by non-Albertans.

Campgrounds

Within the park are six auto-accessible campgrounds that hold 507 sites. They're linked by bicycle and hiking trails. Firewood is available at each campground for $6 per bundle. All campgrounds in Peter Lougheed Provincial Park are operated by **Kananaskis Camping Inc.** (403/591-7226, www.kananaskiscamping .com), whose website is a wealth of information and includes vacancy reports, updated daily at 10 A.M.

The following campgrounds are listed from north to south along Kananaskis Lakes Road, from Highway 40 to the end of the road.

Canyon Campground (mid-June–early Sept.; $17) comprises two distinct types of camping at the northern end of Lower Kananaskis Lake just over four km (2.5 miles) along Kananaskis Lakes Road from Highway 40. An open meadow provides pull-through sites suited to RVs and trailers (Loop B), while up the hill off to the right, sites are protected by a forest of spruce and fir. Between the two loops is the trailhead for a 1.2-km (.7-mile) hiking path that traverses the Kananaskis Canyon. Another trail leads across Kananaskis Lakes Road to the nearby information center (the trailhead is beside Site 37). Each of 50 sites has a picnic table and fire pit, which along with pit toilets and tap water are the limit of facilities.

Just over one km (.6 mile) south of the information center (and on the same side of the road), **Elkwood Campground** (mid-May–early Sept.; $17) is the largest of the park's campgrounds with 130 sites. It offers showers ($1 for five minutes) along each of four loops, flush toilets, a playground, and an interpretive amphitheater.

Boulton Creek Campground (May–Oct.; $17) has coin-operated showers just beyond the registration gate (complete with rack for those who have a bike), flush toilets, and an interpretive amphitheater. A few of 118 sites have power, and the campground is within walking distance of a restaurant and grocery store. Boulton Creek is the only campground that takes reservations; book through Kananaskis Camping Inc. (403/591-7226, www.kananaskiscamping.com).

Immediately beyond Boulton Creek Campground, turn right to access **Lower Lake Campground** (mid-May–mid-Oct.; $17), with 104 sites spread along three loops. Some sites (along Loop B) come close to the lake but are not within sight. Each private site has a picnic table and fire pit, while campers share pit toilets and two playgrounds. Eight sites are set away from the road—perfect for tent campers who don't mind a short walk. Boulton Creek Trading Post is a short walk up and over Kananaskis Lakes Road from Loop A.

Mount Sarrail Campground (mid-June to the first weekend of Sept.; $15), at the southern end of Upper Kananaskis Lake, 2.5 km (1.6 miles) beyond Lower Lake Campground, is for tenters only. It's described as a walk-in campground, but some sites are right by the main parking lot. It has pit toilets, pump water, and bearproof food caches.

Finally, where Kananaskis Lakes Road branches left to the upper lake and right to the lower lake is an unpaved one-way road through **Interlakes Campground** (mid-May–mid-Oct.; $17), which loops back along the shore of Lower Kananaskis Lake before rejoining Kananaskis Lakes Road. It has 48 sites, many with lake views and some accessible enough to pull through a large RV or trailer. Facilities are basic: pump water, picnic tables, fire pits, and pit toilets, but if you score one of the lakeside sites, you'll be in prime position for a magnificent sunrise.

Boulton Creek Trading Post

Located along Kananaskis Lakes Road, 10 km (6.2 miles) south of Highway 40, this busy hub is the park's only commercial center (mid-May–mid-Oct. 9 A.M.–6 P.M. extended to 10 P.M.

in July and Aug.). It sells groceries, basic camping supplies, fishing tackle and licenses, propane, and firewood. The store also rents bikes. Next door is an unremarkable family-style restaurant serving up pasta, burgers, and the like. A cooked breakfast is $8 (although the restaurant is not open until 9 A.M.). It also has an ice-cream window and serves coffee.

Information

At the excellent **Visitor Information Centre** (four km/2.5 miles along Kananaskis Lakes Road from Hwy. 40, 403/591-6322; summer daily 9 A.M.–7 P.M., the rest of the year Mon.–Fri. 9 A.M.–5 P.M. and Sat.–Sun. 9 A.M.–5 P.M.) ex-

hibits catalog the natural and cultural history of the park through photographs, videos, and hands-on displays, and a great display opened in 2000 telling the story about the bears of Kananaskis Country. The knowledgeable staff hides hordes of literature under the desk, but you have to ask for it. Also ask them to put a movie or slide show on in the theater; most revolve around the park. The movie *Bears and Man* is a classic 1970s flick dealing with public attitude toward bears—one of the first documentaries to do so. A large lounge area that overlooks the valley to the Opal Range is used mainly in winter by cross-country skiers but is always open for trip planning or relaxing.

Spray Valley Provincial Park

The creation of 35,800-hectare (88,460-acre) Spray Valley Provincial Park in 2001 provided the final link in continuous protection between bordering Peter Lougheed Provincial Park in the south and Willmore Wilderness Park beyond the northern reaches of Jasper National Park in the north. To the west lies the remote and rarely traveled south end of Banff National Park, while to the north is the Bow Valley and Canmore. The park's dominant feature is **Spray Lake Reservoir,** a 26-km-long (16-mile-long) body of water that is an integral part of a massive hydroelectric scheme. The Spray Development began in 1948 with construction of a road between Canmore and the Spray River. The next stage was damming the river, creating a reservoir of approximately 2,000 hectares (5,000 acres), then diverting its course through Whiteman's Pass and using the water flow as it drops into the Bow River to generate hydroelectric power. The water drops a total of 300 vertical meters (1,000 vertical feet) and passes through three power plants, which combined generate enough electricity to power a city of 100,000.

Smith-Dorrien/Spray Trail

The Smith-Dorrien/Spray Trail (known as Spray Lakes Road from the Canmore end) is the only road through the park. This 60-km

(37-mile) unpaved (and often dusty) road links Peter Lougheed Provincial Park in the south to Canmore in the north. From the south, the road climbs up the Smith-Dorrien Creek watershed, passing Mud Lake and entering Spray Valley Provincial Park just south of Mount Engadine Lodge. Around three km (1.9 miles) farther north is **Buller Pond** (on the west side of the road), from where the distinctive "Matterhorn" peak of Mount Assiniboine can be seen on a clear day. The road then parallels the eastern shoreline of Spray Lake for more than 20 km (12.5 miles), passing three lakefront picnic areas. The mountains that rise steeply to the east are the same ones visible to the *west* driving along the Kananaskis Valley. They rise to a high point of 3,121 meters (10,240 feet) at **Mount Sparrowhawk** (opposite the picnic area of the same name), which was roundly recommended as having better slopes than the barely adequate Mount Allan for hosting the downhill-skiing events of the 1988 Winter Olympics. In the end, its remote location killed the idea and any development was spared, except for a few lakeside picnic tables across the road. Beyond the north end of Spray Lake, the road passes **Goat Pond** and the Goat Creek trailhead, then descends steeply into the Bow Valley and Canmore.

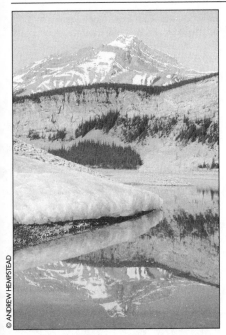

A chunk of ice remains well into summer beside Spray Lake.

The obvious loop—south from the Trans-Canada Highway along Highway 40 to Peter Lougheed Provincial Park, then north through Spray Valley Provincial Park to Canmore and back along the TransCanada Highway to Highway 40—is 150 km (93 miles); allow at least three hours for the entire loop.

HIKING
Watridge Lake
• Length: 3.5 km/2.2 miles (one hour) one-way
• Elevation gain: 50 meters/165 feet
• Rating: easy
• Trailhead: Follow the Smith-Dorrien/Spray Trail 40 km (25 miles) south from Canmore, then head five km (3.1 miles) west to the Mount Shark staging area.

Most of the hiking in Spray Valley Provincial Park requires some route finding; Watridge Lake

is the exception and is open to mountain bikes. The trail begins from behind the information board at the entrance to the main parking lot, skirting a maze of cross-country ski trails and quickly reaching the muddy shoreline of the lake, which is known for excellent cutthroat trout fishing. Dedicated anglers stop here; most other hikers cross the lake's outlet and continue 900 meters/.6 mile (allow 20 minutes one-way) to a delightful spring that bursts from the forested slopes of Mount Shark and flows along a riverbed carpeted in moss.

Jakeroy Glacier
• Length: 4 km/2.5 miles (1.5–2 hours) one-way
• Elevation gain: 600 meters/1,970 feet
• Rating: moderate/difficult
• Trailhead: Spray Lake West Campground

This small, hidden glacier is nestled in the shadow of the Goat Range. Reaching it entails some route finding, but the rewards are ample. To get to the trailhead, follow the campground access road for 1.5 km (.9 mile) beyond the end of the dam wall and park where it crosses a small creek (opposite Site 17). At the No Camping sign on the upstream side of the road, search out the trail that disappears into a forest of lodgepole pine. The trail parallels the creek for much of the way—making a minimal elevation gain through a moss-carpeted valley—until emerging in an open area where the creek flows through a willow-choked meadow. The headwall and hanging valley are now in clear view straight ahead. Continue a little farther, crossing the creek below a waterfall. From this point onward, the trail becomes indistinct, climbing steeply up the scree slope between the cliff face and the tree line. Most of the elevation gain is made in this last one km (.6 mile). The final steep pitch is through a forest of Engelmann spruce and larch into a hanging valley. A moraine running along the left side of the valley affords the best views of the glacier.

Goat Creek
• Length: 19 km/11.8 miles (six hours) one-way
• Elevation loss: 370 meters/1,210 feet
• Rating: easy/moderate

• Trailhead: Smith-Dorrien/Spray Trail, nine km (5.6 miles) west of Canmore

With prearranged transportation, this is an easy trail that gives hikers a real sense of achievement—walking from Kananaskis Country to downtown Banff. Beginning from the north end of the Spray Valley Provincial Park, the trail closely parallels Goat Creek for nine km (5.6 miles) to the confluence of the Spray River, which it then follows all the way to the grounds of the famous Fairmont Banff Springs. This is also a good trail for mountain biking or cross-country skiing. It's downhill all the way.

PRACTICALITIES

The Spray Valley had long been the target of developers, but the creation of a park put an end to proposed heli-skiing and boat tour operations. Existing facilities for visitors include a lodge, a campground, three picnic areas, and a heli-pad used as a staging area for flights into nearby Mount Assiniboine Provincial Park (see the *Other Parks of the Canadian Rockies* chapter).

Mount Engadine Lodge

Although a number of backcountry lodges are scattered through the Canadian Rockies, **Mount Engadine** (403/678-4080, www .mountengadine.com; early June–mid-Oct. and early Feb.–Apr.) is the only one accessible by public road. Technically, this means it's not a true "backcountry" lodge, but it has the feel of one and, besides, most people don't even know it's there as they speed past on unpaved Smith-Dorrien/Spray Trail. It comprises 12 guest rooms in the main lodge and two cabins set on a ridge overlooking an open meadow and small creek. The main lodge has a dining room, a comfortable lounge area, and a beautiful sundeck holding a hot tub. Breakfast is served buffet style, lunch can be taken at the lodge or packed for a picnic, and dinner is served in multiple courses of hearty European specialties. Rates for lodge rooms range from $125 per person for a room with a shared bathroom to $160 for a private bathroom and fireplace. Cabins are $140 per person. All meals are included in these nightly rates. Mount Engadine Lodge is 40 km (25 miles) southwest of Canmore, at the turnoff to the Mount Shark staging area.

Campground

As the name suggests, **Spray Lake West Campground,** the only campground in the park, spreads out along the western shoreline of Spray Lake. Many of the 50-odd sites are private, but facilities are limited to picnic tables, fire pits, and pit toilets. Sites cost $14 per night with firewood an additional $6 per bundle. It's open from when the snow clears (usually late May) to early September.

Sibbald

This small area in the north of Kananaskis Country protects the rolling foothills that descend to the rich grazing land west of Calgary. Access is along partly paved Highway 68, which branches south off the TransCanada Highway 17 km (10.6 miles) west of the Cochrane intersection. Access is also possible from the west, off Highway 40 two km (1.2 miles) south of the Barrier Lake Visitor Information Centre. From the east, Highway 68 climbs through the Jumpingpound Creek watershed to **Jumpingpound Demonstration Forest,** 18 km (11.2 miles) from the highway. The forest is circled by a 10-km (6.2-mile) driving tour, with signs identifying species in surrounding forest. It also passes a portable sawmill, a small picnic area, and a wetland. Meanwhile, Highway 68 continues westward, passing a turnoff to **Sibbald Lake,** the two trails detailed under *Hiking,* a picnic area, and a campground. It then crosses a low divide (look for impressive beaver ponds on the south side of the road) and descends through a narrow valley to Highway 40, the main route through Kananaskis Country. The only other road in Sibbald is the 35-km (22-mile) Powderface Trail, a rough, unsealed road (usually passable by two-wheel drive) that leads south from west of Sibbald Lake to Highway 66 through the Elbow River Valley.

Fishing is a popular activity in Sibbald. Sibbald Lake is stocked with rainbow trout and gets busy. To the west, **Sibbald Meadows Pond** is a quieter body of water, also stocked and surrounded by reeds.

HIKING

Ole Buck Loop
- Length: 4.4 km/2.7 miles (90 minutes) round-trip
- Elevation gain: 170 meters/560 feet
- Rating: easy/moderate
- Trailhead: Sibbald Lake day-use area

This trail makes a loop around the south-facing slopes of Ole Buck Mountain, which rises to the northeast of Sibbald Lake. From the Sibbald Forestry Exhibit, follow a trail between the lake and campground for one km (.6 mile). The Ole Buck Loop Trail branches to the left at this point, crossing Bateman Creek from where the 2.4-km (1.5-mile) loop begins. Views from high points along the trail extend south to Moose Mountain.

Deer Ridge Circuit
- Length: 6 km/3.7 miles (two hours) round-trip
- Elevation gain: 210 meters/690 feet
- Rating: easy/moderate
- Trailhead: Sibbald Lake day-use area

Take the trail south following the access road for 150 meters (.1 mile), then skirt the south shore of Moose Pond to a trail junction. The left fork is the Eagle Hill Trail, while the trail to the right climbs steadily up Deer Ridge. A short spur from the ridge leads to a lookout with views south to Moose Mountain. Returning to the main trail,

© ANDREW HEMPSTEAD

Sibbald Lake

turn left, descending along the north face of the ridge and back to the trailhead.

PRACTICALITIES

Campgrounds

Sibbald Lake Campground (mid-May–mid-Oct.; $17) lies within easy walking distance of Sibbald Lake and is signposted off Highway 68, 24 km (15 miles) west of the TransCanada Highway and 12 km (7.5 miles) east of Highway 40. It contains 134 sites spread along five loops (Loop E comes closest to the lake) winding through a mixed forest of aspen, spruce, and lodgepole pine. Amenities include pit toilets, picnic tables, fire rings, and drinkable well water. Equestrian campers can park and camp at **Dawson Equestrian Campground,** a short distance from Highway 68 along the Powderface Trail. This is a staging area for many horse trails.

Information

The closest information center in Sibbald is **Barrier Lake Visitor Information Centre** (two km/1.2 miles north of the Hwy. 68/Hwy. 40 junction, 403/673-3985; June–mid-Sept. daily 9 A.M.–6 P.M., the rest of the year daily 9 A.M.–4 P.M.).

Elbow River Valley and Vicinity

The Elbow River has its source at Elbow Lake (see *Peter Lougheed Provincial Park*), among the high peaks of Elbow-Sheep Wildland Provincial Park. As it cuts east through the foothills, the Elbow River Valley gradually opens up, exiting Kananaskis Country near the picturesque hamlet of **Bragg Creek** and continuing its eastward flow, draining into the Bow River within Calgary city limits (the "elbow" for which the river was named by David Thompson in 1814 occurs at what is now Glenmore Reservoir, the source of Calgary's drinking water).

The main access is Elbow Falls Road (Highway 66) west from Bragg Creek. It enters Kananaskis Country after eight km (five miles), at the Elbow River Valley Visitor Centre. Close to the eastern boundary lie two good fishing spots: **McLean Pond** and **Allen Bill Pond.** Both are stocked with rainbow trout. Moose Mountain, home to a fire lookout since 1929, can be seen north of the highway. Continuing west there is six-meter-high (20-foot-high) **Elbow Falls,** the highest road-accessible waterfall in Kananaskis Country. Just before the falls an unpaved road leads north to **Ing's Mine,** where a small coal mine operated 1915–1920. Beyond the falls, the road first ascends through an area charred by a 1981 wildfire, and then descends to its end at a camping spot and picnic area, 42 km (26 miles) from Bragg Creek.

HIKING

Sulphur Springs

- Length: 2 km/1.2 miles (40 minutes) one-way
- Elevation gain: 200 meters/656 feet
- Rating: easy/moderate
- Trailhead: Sulphur Springs Creek, Highway 66

Park at Sulphur Springs Creek (just east of Paddy's Flat Campground) and follow the north bank of the small creek upstream, veering left at the cutline to reach the springs. Fed by sulphur-rich water, the springs were diverted through an iron casing in the 1930s.

Paddy's Flat

- Length: 2.2 km/1.2 miles (30 minutes) round-trip
- Elevation gain: minimal
- Rating: easy
- Trailhead: Loop B, Paddy's Flat Campground, 20 km (12.4 miles) west of Bragg Creek

This interpretive trail passes through a forest of lodgepole pine interspersed with white spruce, aspen, and, along a spring-fed creek, poplar before looping back around and following the Elbow River downstream, back to the trailhead. Numbered posts correspond with a brochure available at the beginning of the trail.

Moose Mountain
- Length: 7 km/4.3 miles (2.5–3 hours) one-way
- Elevation gain: 670 meters/2,200 feet
- Rating: moderate/difficult
- Trailhead: seven km (4.3 miles) along an unmarked gravel road that spurs north of Highway 66 700 meters (.4 mile) west of Paddy's Flat Campground

Rising to an elevation of 2,438 meters (8,000 feet), Moose Mountain is the dominant peak in the Elbow River Valley area. Its summit provides 360-degree views over the entire region. From 500 meters (.3 mile) before a gate across the road, the trail follows an old fire-lookout road for four km (2.5 miles), climbing steadily just below the ridgeline. It then descends before climbing again into an open meadow. Here begins the relentless slog to the domelike lower summit, from where it's another 100 vertical meters (330 vertical feet), via switchbacks or a direct climb up a ridge, to the upper summit and fire lookout.

Little Elbow
- Length: 2.5 km/1.6 miles (50 minutes) one-way
- Elevation gain: minimal
- Rating: easy
- Trailhead: Forget-me-not Pond, near the end of Highway 66

This interpretive trail explores a short stretch of the Little Elbow River, just before its confluence with the Elbow River. From Forget-me-not Pond, the trail passes between the road and the river, then it continues upstream, looping past interpretive boards that describe the river and the mammals that live along its length.

PRACTICALITIES
Campgrounds
Five campgrounds, with a combined 551 sites, lie along the Elbow River Valley. The most-developed of the five is **McLean Creek Campground,** 12 km (7.5 miles) west of Bragg Creek and just south of Highway 66, by McLean Creek. At the campground entrance is the Camper Centre with groceries, coin showers, and firewood ($6 per

bundle). As in all campgrounds in Kananaskis Country, each of the 170 sites has a picnic table and fire pit. Unpowered sites are $20 per night, powered sites $23. This is also the only campground along the Elbow Valley that takes reservations; contact **Elbow Valley Campgrounds** (403/949-3132). The other campgrounds and their distances from Bragg Creek are **Gooseberry** (10 km/6.2 miles), **Paddy's Flat** (20 km/12.4 miles), **Beaver Flat** (30 km/18.6 miles), and, at the end of the road, **Little Elbow** (50 km/31 miles). The latter has facilities for campers with horses. Each of these campgrounds has only basic facilities—pit toilets and hand-pumped drinking water—but, still, sites are $17 per night. As at McLean Creek, firewood is available at $6 per bundle. McLean Creek is open year-round, while the other four campgrounds begin opening in mid-May and close between early September and the end of October.

Information
Elbow Valley Visitor Information Centre (403/949-4261; May–Sept. 9 A.M.–5 P.M.) is at the entrance to Kananaskis Country, 10 km (6.2 miles) west of Bragg Creek on Highway 66.

◪ BRAGG CREEK
Bragg Creek is a rural hamlet nestled in the foothills of the Canadian Rockies, 40 km (25 miles) west of Calgary. It lies on the edge of Kananaskis Country, at the entrance to the Elbow River Valley. The town and its quiet, tree-lined streets are a far cry from the hustle and bustle of nearby Canmore and Banff, providing an ideal retreat to kick back and do some golfing, dining, and relaxing in one of the mountains' true gems.

The **Stoney Trail,** an Indian trading route that passed through the area, had been in use for generations when the first white people arrived in the early 1880s. The first settlers were farmers, followed by Calgarians who built weekenders in town. Today many of Bragg Creek's 1,000 residents commute daily to nearby Calgary. The ideal location and quiet lifestyle have attracted artists and artisans—the town claims to

© AVALON TRAVEL PUBLISHING, INC.

Kananaskis Country

maculately manicured golf course with water hazards on 14 of the 18 holes. Greens fees are $59 (discounted to $49 for seniors), which includes use of an excellent practice facility.

Accommodations

Although lacking motels and campgrounds (closest camping is along the Elbow River Valley in Kananaskis Country), Bragg Creek is a popular overnight escape for folks from Calgary. Best of a bunch of bed-and-breakfasts is **Countryside Inn** (call for directions, 403/949-2805), a large country-style house nestled among stands of trees within walking distance of both the river and village. The home has three comfortable guest rooms—one with its own hot tub—a spacious sitting room, a billiards room, and an outdoor hot tub. A hearty breakfast is included in the rates of $100 s, $125 d.

have more painters, potters, sculptors, and weavers than any similarly sized town in Alberta.

Sights and Recreation

Arriving along Highway 22 from either the north or south, you'll be greeted upon arrival in Bragg Creek by a slightly confusing four-way stop intersection with a treed triangle of land in the middle. Take the option along the north (right) side of the distinctive polished log Bragg Creek Trading Post II to access the main shopping center, a western-themed collection of basic town services interspersed with craft shops and cafés. White Avenue, also known as **Heritage Mile** and originally the main commercial strip, has more of the same and leads through an appealing residential area. This road continues southwest to 122-hectare (300-acre) **Bragg Creek Provincial Park,** a day-use area alongside the Elbow River. With a basket of goodies from one of Bragg Creek's many food outlets, leave the main parking lot behind to enjoy a picnic lunch on a riverside picnic table.

Wintergreen Golf & Country Club (403/949-3333), six km (3.7 miles) north of town from the west side of the Elbow River, is an im-

Food

Bragg Creek Shopping Centre holds a wide variety of eateries as well as most services. At the east end, **Pies Plus** (403/949-3450) specializes in meat and fruit pies at reasonable prices, but it doesn't open until 10 A.M. and is closed Monday. Early risers should head to the opposite end of the parking lot to **Bragg Creek Coffee Company** (403/949-3251), which opens weekdays at 6 A.M. and on weekends at 8 A.M. Join locals for an early-morning coffee or head here for the daily $7 soup-and-sandwich lunch special. Back beyond Pies Plus, **M Red Sage Restaurant** (403/949-7243) presents a contemporary ranch-style menu using lots of local game and produce. Choose from a three-bean chili topped with corn-crusted oysters ($13) or stifle those carnivorous cravings with the grilled buffalo ribeye ($22). It's open daily for lunch and dinner, with most lunches under $10.

The **Steak Pit** (43 White Ave., 403/949-3633; daily from 11:30 A.M.) has been a longtime local favorite. The decor is early Canadian, yet realistic and elegant. The dining room, decorated with hand-hewn cedar furniture, is only a small part of the restaurant, which also has a café, lounge, sports bar, and gift shop. Eating here isn't cheap but *is* comparable to Calgary restaurants. The menu sets out to prove great steaks don't necessitate fancy trimmings, and does so with the best cuts of Alberta beef and great spuds.

Sheep River Valley

The Sheep River Valley lies immediately south of the Elbow River Valley, in an area of rolling foothills between open ranchlands to the east and the high peaks bordering **Elbow-Sheep Wildland Provincial Park** to the west. Access is from the town of **Turner Valley** (take Sunset Boulevard west from downtown), along Highway 546. The Kananaskis Country boundary lies 25 km (15.5 miles) west of Turner Valley through rolling ranching land, from which point the highway follows the Sheep River for another 21 km (13 miles) to its confluence with Bluerock Creek.

A short distance west of the entrance to Kananaskis Country is Sandy McNabb Campground and various interpretive trails. Continu-

ing along Highway 546, the road enters **Sheep River Provincial Park.** Originally set aside in 1973 as Sheep River Wildlife Sanctuary, the park protects the winter range of bighorn sheep. The sheep spend summer farther up the valley, and for hundreds of years they have migrated down to the open slopes alongside the Sheep River each fall. Sheep are the most common large mammal in the valley; explorer David Thompson reported that the natives also named the valley for its sheep ("itou-kai-you" in their language). At Bighorn day-use area, a short trail leads to a viewpoint of open meadows that are critical winter habitat for approximately 200 sheep. **Sheep River Falls,** a short distance before the end of the road, is reached by a short walk.

Kananaskis Country

© ANDREW HEMPSTEAD

Sheep River Falls

HIKING

Price's Camp

- Length: 5 km/3.1 miles (1.5 hours) one-way
- Elevation gain: 50 meters/164 feet
- Rating: easy/moderate
- Trailhead: Sandy McNabb day-use area, Highway 546

Although the trail itself is easy, it requires fording the Sheep River, is reached through a maze of cutlines and old logging roads, and can be muddy after rainfall. If all that hasn't put you off, wade across the river upstream of Coal Creek to reach the trailhead. Head west (to the right), following a grassy bench along the river, from which the trail enters a forest of lodgepole pine. When the trail crosses March Creek, head 300 meters (.2 mile) up the north bank of the creek to this abandoned logging camp, a pleasant destination for a picnic lunch.

Foran Grade Ridge

- Length: 2.5 km/1.6 miles (50 minutes) one-way
- Elevation gain: 190 meters/620 feet
- Rating: easy/moderate
- Trailhead: unmarked pullout 1.5 km (.9 mile) west of the winter closure gate at Sandy McNabb day-use area

Climbing steadily from Highway 546, this trail traverses an open field and passes through an aspen forest before reaching the high point of the ridge. From here, views extend up the Sheep River Valley all the way to the Opal Range. The distance given is to this first vantage point. An alternative to returning along the same route is to continue along the ridge for another 2.5 km (1.6 miles), then descend the west side of the ridge to Windy Point Creek, which the trail follows downstream to Highway 40. Either walk back to the trailhead along the highway or cross the road and link up with a trail running through the valley floor for a total trail length of 11 km (6.8 miles).

PRACTICALITIES

Campgrounds

Along Highway 546 are two campgrounds. **Sandy McNabb Campground** (May–mid-Oct.; $17) is the first you'll come to, a short walk from the river right by the entrance to Kananaskis Country. It's named for an Albertan oilman who made an annual pilgrimage to this spot with his family. Each of 98 sites has a picnic table and fire pit (firewood is $6 per bundle). Other facilities are limited to pit toilets and hand-pumped water.

At the end of Highway 546, 21 km (13 miles) farther west, is **Bluerock Campground** (mid-May–mid-Oct.; $17), where some of the 66 sites are set aside for equestrian campers. This campground has similar services to Sandy McNabb.

Both facilities are operated by **High Country Camping** (403/558-2373 or 866/366-2267, www.campingalberta.com). All sites are filled on a first-come, first-served basis.

Highwood/Cataract Creek

The Highwood/Cataract Creek areas stretch from Peter Lougheed Provincial Park to the southern border of Kananaskis Country. This is the least-developed area in Kananaskis Country. The jagged peaks of the Highwood Mountains are its most dominant feature; high alpine meadows among the peaks are home to bighorn sheep, elk, and grizzlies. Lower down, spruce and lodgepole pine forests spread over most of the valley, giving way to grazing lands along the eastern flanks. Higher elevations, including along the Continental Divide, are protected by **Don Getty Wildland Provincial Park.**

The main access from the north is along Highway 40, which drops 600 vertical meters (1,970 feet) in the 35 km (22 miles) between **Highwood Pass** and **Highwood Junction.** From the east, Highway 541 west from Longview joins Highway 40 at Highwood Junction. A lesser-used access is Highway 532, which branches west from Highway 22 about 37 km (23 miles) south of Longview. This unpaved road passes Indian Graves Campground then begins a steep climb to **Plateau Mountain,** high above the tree line and with stunning views back across to the Porcupine Hills. The main summer activities in this area of Kananaskis Country are hiking, horseback riding, climbing, and fishing. Winter use is primarily by snowmobilers.

HIKING

Only a few formal hiking trails are signposted. The rest are traditional routes that aren't well traveled; many require river crossings.

Picklejar Lakes

- Length: 4.2 km/2.6 miles (90 minutes) one-way
- Elevation gain: 470 meters/1,540 feet
- Rating: moderate
- Trailhead: Lantern Creek day-use area (not Picklejar day-use area), three km (1.9 miles)

south of the Mist Creek day-use area, Highway 40

The name of these lakes was coined by early anglers, who claimed fishing them was as "easy as catching fish in a pickle jar." The name stuck, and it's still mostly anglers who are attracted to the four lakes. They lie at the southern end of Elbow-Sheep Wildland Provincial Park. To access the trail, cross the road from Lantern Creek day-use area and walk up the hill 100 meters (330 feet). The trail is unmarked but easy to follow as it passes through a lightly forested area and open meadows to a ridge above Picklejar Creek. Descend and cross the creek, following its north bank up a steep, open slope, or stay high and right across a scree slope to reach the pass at 2,180 meters (7,150 feet). The first lake is 300 meters (.2 mile) beyond the pass. The trail continues past two more lakes before ending at the fourth, which is the largest and has incredibly clear water. A lightly marked trail encircles the fourth lake.

Zephyr Creek

- Length: 4.5 km/2.8 miles (90 minutes) one-way
- Elevation gain: 180 meters/590 feet
- Rating: moderate
- Trailhead: Sentinel day-use area, east of Highwood Junction along Highway 541

The walk itself along Zephyr Creek is easy enough, but the trail commences only after a difficult ford of the Highwood River from Highway 541. From the picnic area, descend and wade across the river to an old logging road. Turn right, then keep left, climbing slowly into the valley through which Zephyr Creek flows. The trail crosses the creek twice before reaching a small cairn marking the entrance into Painted Creek Valley. Where the valley walls close in, 800 meters (.5 mile) from Zephyr Creek, pictographs can be found on the rocky canyon wall, one meter (three feet) up from the ground.

PRACTICALITIES

Campgrounds

All three campgrounds in the Highwood/ Cataract Creek areas are south of Highwood Junction. **Etherington Creek** (May–Nov.; $17) is seven km (4.3 miles) south of the junction, while **Cataract Creek** (mid-May–early Sept.; $17) is five km (3.1 miles) farther south. Both offer primitive facilities, including water, pit toilets, firewood, fire pits, and picnic tables. Continuing south, along Highway 532 up and over Plateau Mountain Ecological Reserve, is 16-site **Indian Graves Campground** (mid-May–mid-Sept.; $15). Reservations are taken for camping at Etherington Creek only; to reserve a site or for general camping information, contact **High Country Camping** (403/558-2373 or 866/366-2267, www.campingalberta.com).

Information and Services

Highwood House (Highwood Junction, May–June Fri.–Sun. 9 A.M.–5 P.M., July–Sept. daily 9 A.M.–8 P.M., and Oct.–Apr. weekends only 9:15 A.M.–5 P.M.) has gas and a grocery store. Also at the junction is **Highwood Ranger Station** (403/558-2151; late June–early Sept. Thurs.–Mon. 10 A.M.–6 P.M.).

Kootenay National Park and Vicinity

Shaped like a lightning bolt, this narrow 140,600-hectare (347,300-acre) park lies on the British Columbia side of the Canadian Rockies. The park's northern section is bordered by Banff National Park and Assiniboine Provincial Park to the east and Yoho National Park to the north. Highway 93, extending for 94 km (58 miles) through the park, provides spectacular mountain vistas. Along the route you'll find many short and easy interpretive hikes, scenic viewpoints, hot springs, picnic areas, and roadside interpretive exhibits. The park isn't particularly noted for its day-hiking opportunities, but backpacker destinations such as Kaufmann Lake and the Rockwall rival almost any other area in the Canadian Rockies. Even if you never leave the highway, the scarred hillsides from wildfires that swept through the park in 2001 and 2003 will be obvious. The fires jumped the highway in places, burnt bridges

Must-Sees

Look for **M** to find the sights and activities you can't miss and **Ⅺ** for the best dining and lodging.

M Paint Pots: These naturally occurring ponds make a colorful stop along Highway 93 (page 156).

M Radium Hot Springs: After a long day hiking, the best recipe for soothing aching muscles is a soak in these mineral waters, located just outside the town of the same name (page 157).

M Stanley Glacier Trail: Although it takes around 90 minutes to reach the end of this trail, the stunning views are worth every step (page 158).

M The Rockwall: This is the domain of serious hikers, but those willing to make the effort are rewarded with one of the most awe-inspiring geological formations in all of the Canadian Rockies (page 159).

M Panorama Mountain Village: This self-contained resort offers something for everyone—golfing, hiking, and biking in summer and world-class skiing and boarding in winter (page 167).

KOOTENAY NATIONAL PARK AND VICINITY

ALBERTA

Paint Pots

Stanley Glacier Trail

The Rockwall

BRITISH COLUMBIA

M Radium Hot Springs

M Panorama Mountain Village

0   10 mi

0   10 km

Kootenay National Park

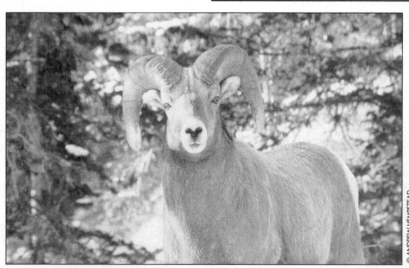

bighorn sheep in Kootenay National Park

© ANDREW HEMPSTEAD

KOOTENAY NATIONAL PARK AND VICINITY

ALBERTA

To Lake Louise

Mt Little

Quadra Mtn

Taylor Lake

Boom Lake

Castle Mtn

CASTLE JUNCTION

1A

Bow

Mt Ishbel

BOW VALLEY PARKWAY

Tokumm Creek

Mt Whymper

Vermillion Pass

Storm Mtn

MARBLE CANYON

VERMILLION PASS BURN

Twin Lakes

Redearth Cr

Pilot Mtn

River

Mt Goodsir

Sharp Mtn

Yoho National Park

Mt Drysdale

PAINT POTS

MARBLE CANYON

Stanley Glacier

STANLEY GLACIER TRAIL

Stanley Peak

Shadow Lake

Banff National Park

Buttress Peak

Mt Mollison

The Rockwall

93

Numa Falls

Isabelle Peak

Scarab Lake

To Banff

Bourgeau Lake

GONDOLA

SUNSHINE VILLAGE

Beaverfoot

River

Kootenay

Vermilion Range

Vermilion

River

Foster Peak

Floe Lake

Verdant

Sunshine Meadows

Quartz Hill

Citadel Peak

BRITISH COLUMBIA

To Golden

Spillimacheen

Mt Verendrye

VERMILION CROSSING

Mt Shanks

Creek

Simpson

River

Surprise

Creek

Mt Wardle

Kootenay National Park

Mount Assiniboine Provincial Park

Columbia

Brisco

95

KOOTENAY CROSSING

Mt Selkirk

Creek

Dasr

Mitchell River

Mt Harkin

Mt Crook

Dog Lake

Mt Docking

Frances Creek

River

MCLEOD MEADOWS

Mt Kindersley

Kootenay

Edgewater

Kindersley Pass

VIEWPOINT

River

Cross

River

Forster Creek

0   5 mi

0   5 km

RADIUM HOT SPRINGS

Sinclair Pass

93

Olive Lake

Radium Hot Springs

93

To Invermere and

95   PANORAMA MOUNTAIN VILLAGE

Kootenay National Park

and information booths, and forced the closure of some trails due to the danger of falling trees; check at local information centers for the latest updates.

Kootenay has the fewest services of the four contiguous mountain national parks. Day-use areas, a gas station and lodge, and three campgrounds are the only roadside services inside the park. The small service town of Radium Hot Springs, at the junction of Highways 93 and 95 near the park's west gate, has a population less than 600 but offers a range of accommodations, cafés and restaurants, gas stations, and grocery stores. Radium and its surroundings are covered in their own section at the end of this chapter. The park is open year-round, although you should check road conditions in winter, when avalanche-control work and snowstorms can close Highway 93 for short periods.

PLANNING YOUR TIME

Just one road passes through Kootenay National Park, and you can travel from one end to the other in under two hours. But plan to spend at least a full day in the park. Traveling from Banff to Invermere, an itinerary may look like this: leave Banff early in the morning and be the first on the trail to **Stanley Glacier.** Make stops at **Marble Canyon** and the **Paint Pots,** then enjoy a late lunch at one of the many riverside picnic areas along the Vermilion River. Spend the afternoon leisurely making your way up and over the park's two highway passes before stopping for a soak at **Radium Hot Springs.**

Because of the limited services, most visitors either camp out or stay in surrounding towns such as Radium Hot Springs or Banff. That said, the three park accommodations I've recommended are all excellent choices for overnight stays.

If your schedule isn't rushed, I recommend spending a couple of days in the town of Radium Hot Springs or Invermere, or in the resort of **Panorama Mountain Village.** The atmosphere is more relaxed than in Banff and prices are cheaper, but more importantly for families on a camping trip, you'll find commercial campgrounds packed with things to do.

THE LAND

Kootenay National Park lies on the western side of the Continental Divide, straddling the Main and Western ranges of the Canadian Rockies. As elsewhere in the Canadian Rockies, the geology of the park is complex. Over the last 70 million years, these mountains have been pushed upward—folded and faulted along the way—by massive forces deep beneath the earth's surface. They've also been subject to erosion that entire time, particularly during the ice ages, when glaciers carved U-shaped valleys and high cirques into the landscape. These features, along with glacial lakes and the remnants of the glaciers themselves, are readily visible in the park today. The park protects the upper headwaters of the **Vermilion** and **Kootenay Rivers,** which drain into the Columbia River south of the park.

Flora

In the lowest areas of the park, in the Kootenay River Valley, **Douglas fir** and **lodgepole pine** find a home. Along the upper stretches of the Vermilion River Valley, where the elevation is higher, **Engelmann spruce** thrive, while immediately above lie forests of **subalpine fir.** The tree line in the park is at around 2,000 meters (6,560 feet) above sea level. This is the alpine, where low-growing species such as **willow** and **heather** predominate. For a short period each summer, these elevations come alive with color as **forget-me-nots, avens,** and **avalanche lilies** flower. Of special interest is the interpretive trail through Vermilion Pass Burn, where fire destroyed 2,400 hectares (5,930 acres) of forest in 1968. Lodgepole pine is the dominant species here. The area affected by the more recent wildfires is an excellent place to see the natural regeneration process at work.

Fauna

Large mammals tend to remain in the Kootenay and Vermilion River Valleys. **White-tailed deer, mule deer, moose, black bears,** and **elk** live year-round at these lower elevations, as do **bighorn sheep,** which can be seen at mineral licks along Highway 93. The most common large mammal present in Kootenay is the **mountain**

goat, but these flighty creatures stay at high elevations, feeding in alpine meadows throughout summer. **Grizzlies** number around 10 within the park; they range throughout the backcountry and occasionally are sighted in spring high on roadside avalanche slopes.

HISTORY

Although their traditional home was along the river valley to the south, the indigenous Kootenay people regularly came to this area to enjoy the hot springs—a meeting place for mountain and Plains bands. Natives called the springs Kootemik (place of hot water). Early European visitors warped Kootemik into Kootenay and applied the name to the local residents. The natives traveled as far east as the Paint Pots area, to collect ocher for ceremonial painting purposes.

In 1905 Randolph Bruce, an Invermere businessman, persuaded the Canadian government and Canadian Pacific Railway (CPR) to build a road linking the Columbia River Valley to the prairie transportation hub of Calgary so that western produce could get out to eastern markets. Construction of the difficult **Banff-Windermere Road** began in 1911. But with three mountain ranges to negotiate and deep, fast-flowing rivers to cross, the money ran out after completion of only 22 km (13.6 miles). To get the highway project going again, the provincial government agreed to hand over an eight-km-wide (five-mile-wide) section of land along both sides of the proposed highway to the federal government. In return, the federal government agreed to finance completion of the highway. Originally called the Highway Park, the land became known as Kootenay National Park in 1920. The highway was finally completed in 1922, and the official ribbon-cutting ceremony was held at Kootenay Crossing in 1923; a plaque marks the spot.

Sights and Recreation

ROAD-ACCESSIBLE SIGHTS

The eastern access to Kootenay National Park is Highway 93 (also known as the Banff-Windermere Highway), which branches west from the TransCanada Highway at **Castle Mountain Junction,** 29 km (18 miles) northwest of Banff and 27 km (16.8 miles) southeast of Lake Louise. From this point, Highway 93 climbs steadily for six km (3.7 miles) to the Continental Divide, crossing it at an elevation of 1,640 meters (5,650 feet). The divide marks the border between Kootenay National Park to the west and Banff National Park to the east.

West from the Continental Divide

Immediately west of the divide is the **Vermilion Pass** Burn. Lightning started the fire that roared through this area in 1968, destroying thousands of hectares of trees. Lodgepole pine, which requires the heat of a fire to release its seeds, was the first plant species to sprout up through the charred ground. More than 30 years later, effects of the devastating fire are still obvious. Along the short **Fireweed Trail** you'll see the growth of a new forest on the floor of the old. **Mount Storm** (3,161 meters/10,370 feet) is the distinctive peak to the east.

PARK ENTRY

Permits are required for entry into Kootenay National Park. A **National Parks Day Pass** is adult $7, senior $6, child $3.50 up to a maximum of $14 per vehicle. It can also be used in Banff National Park and beyond, if that is your direction of travel, and is valid until 4 P.M. the day following its purchase. A **National Parks of Canada Pass,** good for entry into all Canadian national parks for one year from purchase, is adult $45, senior $38 up to a maximum of $89 per vehicle. Both types of pass are available from the western park gate, park information centers, and campground kiosks. For more information, check the Parks Canada website (www.pc.gc.ca).

Kootenay National Park

© ANDREW HEMPSTEAD

Make time to stop for a soak at Radium Hot Springs.

Beyond the Vermilion Pass Burn pullout, the devastation caused by a more recent fire (2003) becomes apparent. Also started by lightning, it began as a number of fires, which came together to cross the highway, burn entire watersheds, and extend high up the surrounding mountains to the extent of the tree line.

Marble Canyon

Be sure to stop and take the enjoyable self-guided trail, one km (.6 mile) each way, which leads along this ice-carved, marble-streaked canyon. The walk takes only about 30 minutes or so, yet as one of several interpretive plaques says, it takes you back more than 500 million years.

From the parking lot, the trail follows a fault in the limestone and marble bedrock through Marble Canyon, which has been eroded to depths of 37 meters (130 feet) by fast-flowing Tokumm Creek. As the canyon narrows, water

roars down through it in a series of falls. The trail ends at a splendid viewpoint where a natural rock arch spans a gorge. Marble Canyon is also the trailhead for the Kaufmann Lake Trail (see *Hiking*).

Paint Pots

A scenic one-km (.6 mile) trail (20 minutes each way) leads over the Vermilion River to this unique natural wonder: three circular ponds stained red, orange, and mustard yellow by oxide-bearing springs. The natives, who believed that animal spirits resided in these springs, collected ocher from around the pools. They mixed it with animal fat or fish oil and then used it in ceremonial body and rock painting. The ocher had a spiritual association and was used in important rituals. Europeans, seeing an opportunity to "add to the growing economy of the nation," mined the ocher in the early 1900s and shipped it to paint manufacturers in Calgary.

Several much longer hiking trails lead off the Paint Pots trail, including one of many routes to the Rockwall (see *Hiking*).

Along the Vermilion River

From the Paint Pots, the highway parallels the glacial-fed Vermilion River for 30 km (19 miles). The first worthwhile stop is **Numa Falls,** where the Vermilion River tumbles over exposed bedrock. Continuing downstream, extensive devastation along the southwestern flanks of Mount Shanks is the result of fire started by lightning strike. The fire destroyed more than 4,000 hectares (9,884 acres) of forest over a two-month period starting in July 2001.

Vermilion Crossing holds the only commercialism in the heart of the park, but compared to neighboring Banff, the development is minuscule. Here you'll find the **Kootenay Park Lodge** complex, which includes historic cabin accommodations, a restaurant, a general store, gas, and an official park information center (open mid-May–mid-Oct.). Across the road from the lodge is a riverside picnic area.

Continuing south, the highway passes two signposted mineral licks (watch for bighorn sheep, mountain goats, and moose), then climbs to a viewpoint for **Hector Gorge.** A pleasant picnic area along this stretch of highway is beside **Wardle Creek.**

Kootenay Valley

As you continue to climb from the Vermilion River and pass small, green Kootenay Pond, your eyes will revel in views of milky green rivers, lush grassy meadows, tree-covered hills, and craggy, snow-capped peaks; keep your eyes peeled for mountain goats. The highway then descends to cross the Kootenay River at **Kootenay Crossing.** This was where the official ribbon-cutting ceremony opening the Banff-Windermere Road took place in 1923. Today you'll find a roadside historical exhibit, hiking trails, and a warden's station. The following stretch of highway passes through an area of high wildlife concentration. Black bears, elk, deer, moose, coyotes, and, in winter, wolves are all regular visitors to cleared areas along the highway.

After passing McLeod Meadows Campground and a riverside picnic area inhabited by a healthy population of chirpy Columbian ground squirrels, Highway 93 climbs to a pullout that affords panoramic views of the entire valley and across to the Mitchell and Vermilion ranges.

West from Sinclair Pass

Beyond the Kootenay Valley viewpoint, Highway 93 tops out at 1,486 meters (4,875 feet) atop **Sinclair Pass.** Just beyond the pass, tiny **Olive Lake** is worth a stop. With outlets that flow in opposite directions and into two different watersheds, the lake is geologically interesting, but for the younger set, spotting brook trout from the viewing platform will prove more attention-grabbing.

From Olive Lake, it's a steep 12-km (7.5-mile) descent along Sinclair Creek to the park's western boundary and the town of Radium Hot Springs. Just after the halfway point is the only road tunnel in the Canadian Rockies. After you emerge from the tunnel, a parking lot on the south side of the road provides the perfect viewing point for sheer red cliffs that form the high point of the Redwall Fault. Through this fracture in the Earth's crust, mineral springs have been bubbling to the surface for thou-

sands of years, staining the surface with red-colored iron oxide.

Radium Hot Springs

This soothing attraction (250/347-9485; summer daily 9 A.M.–11 P.M., the rest of the year daily noon–9 P.M.) lies inside the park but just three km (1.9 miles) northeast of the town of the same name, which is outside the park boundary. It was discovered many centuries ago by the Kootenay people, who, like today's visitors, came to enjoy the odorless mineral water that gushes out of the Redwall Fault at 44°C (111°F). Englishman Roland Stuart purchased the springs for $160 in 1890 and built rough concrete pools to contain the water. Development continued when a visiting millionaire—impressed by the improvement in his paralysis after soaking in the springs—contributed more money to the project. Originally known as Sinclair Hot Springs, after an early settler, the springs' name was changed to Radium in 1915 for the high level of radioactivity in the water. With the declaration of Kootenay National Park in 1922, ownership reverted to the government.

Today the water is diverted from its natural course into the commercial pools, including one that is Canada's largest. Steep cliffs tower directly above the hot pool, whose waters are colored a milky blue by dissolved salts, which include calcium bicarbonate and sulfates of calcium, magnesium, and sodium. The hot pool (39°C, 97°F) is particularly stimulating in winter, when it's edged by snow and covered in steam—your head is almost cold in the chill air, but your submerged body melts into oblivion. Admission is adult $6.50 (or swim all day for $9.75), senior and child $5.50 (day pass $8.75). Towel and locker rentals are available, as are spa services. If you're camping at the park's Redstreak Campground, you can reach the complex on foot.

Sinclair Canyon

From the hot springs, Highway 93 passes through narrow Sinclair Canyon, descending quickly to the town of Radium Hot Springs. The canyon was eroded by the fast-flowing waters of Sinclair Creek, but not enough for a two-lane highway.

Kootenay National Park

But that was nothing a stick of dynamite couldn't fix. In addition to artificially widening the canyon, road builders constructed the highway over the top of the creek where it flows through the narrow gap. Small parking lots above and below the canyon provide an opportunity to pull over and walk through the canyon.

HIKING

Some 200 km (124 miles) of trails lace Kootenay National Park. Hiking opportunities range from short interpretive walks (see *Sights*) to challenging treks through remote backcountry. All trails start from Highway 93 on the valley floor, so you'll be facing a strenuous climb to reach the park's high alpine areas, especially those in the south. For this reason, many hikes require an overnight stay in the backcountry. The following hikes are listed from east to west.

Stanley Glacier
- Length: 4.2 km/2.6 miles (90 minutes) one-way
- Elevation gain: 350 meters/1,150 feet
- Rating: moderate
- Trailhead: Highway 93, seven km (4.4 miles) west of the Continental Divide

Sinclair Canyon

Although this glacier is no more spectacular than those alongside the Icefields Parkway just a few minutes' drive away, the sense of achievement of traveling on foot makes this trail well worth the effort. From Highway 93, the trail crosses the upper reaches of the Vermilion River, then begins a steady climb through an area burned by devastating fires in 1968. After two km (1.3 miles), the trail levels off and begins winding through a massive U-shaped glacial valley, crossing Stanley Creek at the 2.4-km (1.5-mile) mark. In open areas, fireweed, harebells, and yellow columbine carpet the ground. To the west, the sheer face of Mount Stanley rises 500 meters (1,640 feet) above the forest.

The trail officially ends atop the crest of a moraine after 4.2 km (2.6 miles), with distant views to Stanley Glacier. It's possible (and worthwhile) to continue 1.3 km (.8 mile) to the tree-topped plateau visible higher up the valley. After

reaching the top of the first moraine beyond the official trail end, take the left fork, which switchbacks up and over another crest before making a steady ascent through slopes of loose scree to the plateau. Surprisingly, once on the plateau, you'll find a gurgling stream, a healthy population of marmots, and incredible views west to Stanley Glacier and north back down the valley. Be especially careful on the return trip—it's extremely easy to lose your footing on the loose rock.

Kaufmann Lake
- Length: 15 km/9.3 miles (five hours) one-way
- Elevation gain: 570 meters
- Rating: moderate
- Trailhead: Highway 93, Marble Canyon parking lot

This is an overnight backpack trip to a beautiful lake in the extreme north end of the park. The trail follows Tokumm Creek the entire distance, passing through a forest of lodgepole pine before entering an open meadow and crossing many small waterways. Most elevation gain is made in the final two km (1.2 miles), as the trail switchbacks up to the glacial cirque holding Kaufmann Lake. The exquisite lake is surrounded by peaks jutting as high as 3,400 meters (11,150 feet). Two campgrounds lie at the end of the trail.

The Rockwall
- Length: 54 km/33.6 miles (three days) round-trip
- Elevation gain: 760 meters/2,490 feet
- Rating: moderate/difficult
- Trailhead: various points along Highway 93

This is one of the classic hikes in all of the Canadian Rockies. The Rockwall is a 30-km-long (18.6-mile) east-facing escarpment that rises more than 1,000 meters (3,280 feet) from an alpine environment. Four different routes provide access to the spectacular feature; each begins along Highway 93 and traverses a steep valley to the Rockwall's base.

The most popular trail starts at the Paint Pots and follows Helmet Creek 12 km (7.5 miles) to spectacular 365-meter (1,200-foot) Helmet Falls. A further 2.4 km (1.5 miles) takes you to the beginning of the Rockwall trail and a campground, the first of five along the route. The trail then follows the Rockwall in a southeasterly direction for 30 km (18.6 miles), passing magnificent glaciers, waterfalls, and lakes before ending at Floe Lake (see *Floe Lake* hike), 10.4 km (6.5 miles) from the highway.

The Tumbling Creek and Numa Creek drainages provide alternative access routes to the Rockwall and require similar elevation gains. The elevation gain noted here is for the initial climb from the highway; along the route ascents are made to four additional passes, with elevation gains ranging 280–830 meters (920–2,720 feet).

Hikers will need to make arrangements for shuttle transportation between the beginning and end of this route—about 13 km (eight miles) apart—or allow extra time to hike back. As elsewhere in the park, all hikers spending the night in the backcountry must register and pick up a permit ($8 per person per night) at either of the park information centers.

Floe Lake
- Length: 10.4 km/6.5 miles (3.5 hours) one-way
- Elevation gain: 730 meters/2,395 feet
- Rating: moderate/difficult
- Trailhead: Highway 93, eight km (five miles) north of Vermilion Crossing

Of all the lakes in Kootenay National Park, this would have to be the most beautiful. Unfortunately, reaching it requires a strenuous day-trip or an overnight expedition. From Highway 93, the trail crosses the Vermilion River then begins its long ascent of the Floe Creek watershed, passing through a forest of lodgepole pine and making many long switchbacks before leveling off 400 meters (1,310 feet) before the lake. Nestled in a glacial cirque, the gemlike lake's aquamarine waters reflect the Rockwall, a sheer limestone wall rising 1,000 meters (3,280 feet) above the far shore. In fall, stands of stunted larch around the lakeshore turn brilliant colors, adding to the incredible beauty.

Dog Lake
- Length: 2.6 km/1.6 miles (40 minutes) one-way
- Elevation gain: 80 meters (260 feet)
- Rating: easy
- Trailhead: McLeod Meadows Picnic Area, Highway 93

Dog Lake is no Mona Lisa, but it is a popular and easily reached destination, especially for those staying in McLeod Meadows Campground (if you're not camping, park at the picnic area 500 meters/.3 mile to the south). The trail first crosses the wide Kootenay River by footbridge. Then it hops a low ridge over to the shallow lake, which is fringed by marshes at the north end.

Kindersley Summit
- Length: 10 km/6.2 miles (four hours) one-way
- Elevation gain: 1,050 meters/3,445 feet
- Rating: difficult

• Trailhead: Highway 93, two km (1.2 miles) west of Sinclair Pass

The elevation gain on this strenuous day hike will be a deterrent for many, but views from the summit will make up for the pain endured along the way. From Highway 93, the trail climbs through a valley for about three km (1.9 miles), then switchbacks up across several avalanche paths and through more forest before emerging at an alpine meadow on Kindersley Pass. The final two-km (1.2-mile) slog gets you higher, to an elevation of 2,400 meters (7,870 feet) at Kindersley Summit, a saddle between two slightly higher peaks. This is where the scenery makes the journey worthwhile. You'll enjoy views west to the Purcell Mountains, east to the Continental Divide, and, most spectacularly, north over the Kootenay River Valley. An alternate return route to the valley floor follows Sinclair Creek down

from Kindersley Summit. This cuts two km (1.2 miles) off the return distance.

Juniper Trail
• Length: 3.2 km/2 miles (one hour) round-trip
• Elevation gain: 90 meters/295 feet
• Rating: easy
• Trailhead: Highway 93, uphill from the west park gate

Named for the abundance of juniper along one section, this trail traverses a variety of terrain in a relatively short distance. You'll pass Sinclair Creek, an avalanche slope, and a lookout offering views of Windermere Valley and the Purcell Mountains. Beginning on the north side of the road just inside the park boundary, this trail rejoins the highway 1.5 km (.9 mile) farther into the park. There you can retrace your steps back to the start or return along the highway via Sinclair Canyon.

Practicalities

ACCOMMODATIONS

Accommodations within the park are limited, but all of the three recommendations below are good ones. If you feel the need to be in town, see the *Radium Hot Springs* section, which has a dozen or so inexpensive motels.

$50–100
The only lodging in the heart of the park is **Kootenay Park Lodge** (403/762-9196, www .kootenayparklodge.com; mid-May–late Sept.), a cabin complex at Vermilion Crossing, 65 km (40 miles) from Radium Hot Springs. Although no railway passes through the park, the 1923 lodge was one of many built by the Canadian Pacific Railway throughout the Canadian Rockies. It consists of a main lodge with restaurant, 10 cabins, a restaurant, and a gas station/grocery store. The most basic cabins ($90 s or d) each have a bathroom, small fridge, and coffeemaker, with rates rising to $100–130 for a cabin with cooking facilities and a fireplace. Utensil and cooking kits are $10 per day.

$100–150
The well-kept **N Cross River Cabins** (250/ 271-3296 or 877/659-7665; May–Sept.) have a real sense of privacy and of being well away from the well-worn tourist path of Highway 93. And they are—tucked in a riverside setting 15 km (9.3 miles) down Settler's Road, which branches off the highway 114 km (71 miles) from Banff and 32 km (20 miles) from Radium Hot Springs. The eight cabins are equipped with wood-burning fireplaces, log beds draped in down duvets, toilets, and sinks. Showers are located in the main building, along with the main lounge, cooking facilities, a dining area, and a deck. Guests bring their own food and cook in the full kitchen or out on the barbecue. As you can imagine, the atmosphere is convivial, with the cabins attracting outdoorsy types who want to enjoy the Canadian Rockies in their natural state—without room service and fine dining. The cost is $140 s or d, with a two-night minimum stay. Highly recommended.

Over $150

Ⓜ Nipika Mountain Resort (250/342-6516 or 877/647-4525, www.nipika.com) offers the same wilderness experience as the Cross River Cabins and is in the same vicinity—along Settler's Road, which branches off Highway 93 114 km (71 miles) from Banff and 32 km (20 miles) from Radium Hot Springs. Sleeping up to eight people, the cabins are larger than those at Cross River and have full en suite bathrooms and kitchens with wood-burning stoves ($140 s, $200 d). The cabins are modern but were constructed in a very traditional manner—the logs were milled on-site, and construction is dovetail notching. Guests bring their own food and spend their days hiking, fishing, and wildlife watching. In winter, an extensive system of trails is groomed for cross-country skiing.

Campgrounds

The park's largest camping area is **Redstreak Campground** (mid-May–mid-Oct.) on a narrow plateau in the extreme southwest (vehicle access from Highway 93/95 on the south side of Radium Hot Springs township), which holds 242 sites, showers, and kitchen shelters. In summer, free slide shows and talks are presented by park naturalists five nights a week and typically feature topics such as wolves, bears, the park's human history, or the effects of fire. Trails lead from the campground to the hot springs, town, and a couple of lookouts. Unserviced sites are $22, hookups $26–30. Fire permits cost $6 per site per night. A limited number of sites can be reserved through the Parks Canada Campground Reservation Service (877/737-3783, www.pc camping.ca).

The park's two other campgrounds lie to the north of Radium Hot Springs along Highway 93. Both offer fewer facilities (no hookups or showers). The larger of the two is **McLeod Meadows Campground,** beside the Koote-nay River 27 km (16.8 miles) from Radium Hot Springs. Facilities include flush toilets, kitchen shelters, and a fire pit and picnic table at each of the 98 sites. **Marble Canyon,** across the highway from the natural attraction of the same name, offers 61 sites and similar facilities. Both are open mid-May to early September, and all sites cost $17. No reservations are taken in national park campgrounds, but for information, contact the park headquarters at 250/347-9615.

Hikers planning overnight trips in the back-country must register at either of the park information centers and pick up a backcountry camping pass ($8 per person per night).

INFORMATION

Kootenay Park Information Centre (250/347-9615; summer daily 9 A.M.–7 P.M., the rest of the year weekdays only 9 A.M.–5 P.M.) is outside the park in the town of Radium Hot Springs, at the base of the access road to Redstreak Campground. Here you can collect a free map with hiking trail descriptions; find out about trail closures and campsite availability; get the weather forecast; browse through a gift shop; buy park passes and fishing licenses; and register for overnight backcountry trips.

The other source of park information is at **Kootenay Park Lodge,** at Vermilion Crossing (Apr.–May Fri.–Sun. 11 A.M.–6 P.M., June–Sept. daily 10 A.M.–7 P.M., and the early part of Oct. Fri.–Sun. 11 A.M.–6 P.M.). It's worth noting that this is the only privately operated official information center in any Canadian national park—a reflection on the folks running this lodge.

For further park information, contact the park superintendent (P.O. Box 220, Radium Hot Springs, BC V0A 1M0, 250/347-9615) or check the Parks Canada website (www.pc.gc.ca). For park road conditions, call 403/762-1450.

Radium Hot Springs

The small service center of Radium Hot Springs (pop. 900) sits at the southwest entrance to Kootenay National Park, 103 km (64 miles) southwest of Castle Mountain Junction (Banff National Park). Its setting is spectacular; most of the town lies on benchlands above the Columbia River, from which the panoramic views take in the Canadian Rockies to the east and the Purcell Mountains to the west. As well as providing accommodations and other services for park visitors and highway travelers, Radium is a destination in itself for many travelers. The town is just three km (two miles) from the hot springs for which it is named and boasts a wildlife-rich wetland on its back doorstep, two excellent golf courses, and many other recreational opportunities.

SIGHTS AND RECREATION

Columbia River Wetland

Radium sits in the Rocky Mountain Trench, which has been carved over millions of years by the Columbia River. From its headwaters south of Radium, the Columbia flows northward through a 180-km-long (110-mile-long) wetland to Golden, continuing north for a similar distance before reversing course and flowing south into the United States. The wetland nearby Radium holds international significance, not only for its size (26,000 hectares/64,250 acres), but also for the sheer concentration of wildlife it supports. More than 100 species of birds live among the sedges, grasses, dogwoods, and black cottonwoods surrounding the convoluted banks of the Columbia. Of special interest are blue herons in large numbers and ospreys in one of the world's highest concentrations.

The wetland also lies along the Pacific Flyway, so particularly large numbers of ducks, Canada geese, and other migratory birds gather here in spring and autumn. The northbound spring migration is celebrated with the **Wings over the Rockies Bird Festival** (888/933-3311,

www.wingsovertherockies.org), which is held in the first week of May in conjunction with International Migratory Bird Day. The festival features ornithologist speakers, field trips on foot and by boat, workshops, and events tailored especially for children, all of which take place in Radium and throughout the valley. At any time of year, use the festival website to source the valley's best birding spots.

Golfing

The Columbia River Valley supports many golf courses and is marketed around western Canada as a golfing destination. Aside from the excellent resort-style courses and stunning Canadian Rockies scenery, golfers here enjoy the area's mild climate. Warm temperatures allow golfing as early as March and as late as October—a longer season than is typical at other mountain courses.

The 36-hole **Springs at Radium Golf Resort** is a highlight of golfing the Canadian Rockies, comprising two very different courses. One of them, the 6,767-yard, par 72 **Springs Course** (250/347-6200 or 800/667-6444), is generally regarded as one of British Columbia's top 10 resort courses. It lies between the town and steep cliffs that descend to the Columbia River far below. Immaculately groomed fairways following the land's natural contours, near-perfect greens, and more than 70 bunkers filled with imported sand do little to take away from the surrounding mountainscape. Greens fees are $80 for 18 holes (discounted to $54 after 4 P.M.). The resort's second course, the **Resort Course** (250/347-6266 or 800/667-6444), is much shorter (5,306 yards from the tips) but tighter and still challenging. It is nestled in the shadow of the Rockies to the south of Radium, circling the resort's other facilities, which include accommodations, tennis courts, and many other exercise facilities. Greens fees are $49, discounted to $34 after 4 P.M. Both courses have club and cart rentals, with the Springs Course also home to a driving range and teaching academy.

Other Recreation

While golfing is the big draw at Radium, the village is also a base for **Kootenay River Runners** (250/347-9210 or 800/599-4399), who offer white-water rafting trips for adult $64, child $49 for a half-day trip, adult $90, child $74 full-day. This company also offers a more relaxing evening float through the Columbia River Wetland in large and stable voyageur canoes, which depart daily at 5:30 P.M.; the cost is adult $49, child $35. Horse fanciers can rent a ride at **Longhorn Stables** (250/347-9755), one km (.6 mile) north of town.

ACCOMMODATIONS

Radium, with a population of just 900, has more than 30 motels, an indication of its importance as a highway stop for overnight travelers. Those that lie along the access road to Kootenay National Park come alive with color through summer as each tries to outdo the others with floral landscaping. When booking any of these accommodations, ask about free passes to the hot pools.

Under $50

At the top end of the motel strip, closest to the

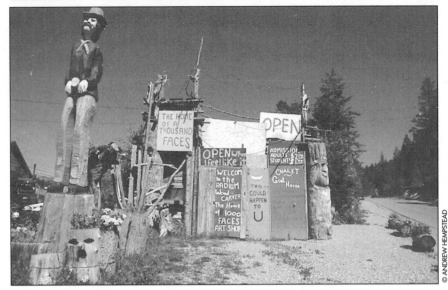

© ANDREW HEMPSTEAD

The closest thing Radium has to a museum is this building, home to a local woodcarver.

national park, N **Misty River Lodge** (5036 Hwy. 93, 250/347-9912, www.radiumhostel .bc.ca) provides an excellent base for travelers on a budget. This converted motel has 11 beds in dormitories ($21 per person) and private rooms that include a $60 room with valley views and a $79 room that combines valley views with a full kitchen. Amenities include a communal kitchen, a lounge, and a big deck with even bigger views to the distant Purcell Mountains. You can also rent bikes and canoes.

$50–100

Kootenay Motel is along Highway 93, up the hill from the junction of Highway 95 (250/347-9490 or 877/908-2020). The rooms are nothing special (but air-conditioned) and rent from $50 s, $58 d, $5 extra for a kitchenette. Also on-site is a barbecue area and pleasant gazebo.

Up the hill a little and across the road is **Black Bear's Inn** (250/347-9565 or 800/688-6138, www.blackbearsinn.com; Apr.–Oct.), with a pleasant outdoor barbecue area; basic sleeping

rooms are $69 s or d, or pay $99 for a room with a private balcony overlooking the valley.

Continuing toward the national park entrance there is the **Gables Motel** (Hwy. 93, 250/347-9866 or 877/387-7007, www.gablesmotel.ca; $69 s or d), where each of the 17 smallish rooms has mountain views and is well-furnished.

Back down toward town is the **Alpen Motel** (250/347-9823 or 888/788-3891, www.alpen motel.com; March–Oct.), which arguably has the best and brightest flowers out front. The air-conditioned rooms are the best along the strip, which is reflected in the price ($99–109 s or d), which includes passes to the hot springs.

Several older motels lie in the quiet residential streets west of Highways 93/95. Least expensive is the **Ritz Motel** (4883 Stanley St., 250/347-9644 or 877/347-9644, www.ritzmotel.com; $60–90 s or d), which is an older motel, but the 13 pine-paneled rooms are large, with separate sleeping areas. Some have kitchens and are air-conditioned. Check-in starts at the earlier-than-usual time of 2 P.M.

Although it undergoes regular revamps, rates at

the **Pinewood Motel** (4870 Stanley St., 250/347-9529 or 888/557-5567, www.pinewood motel.ca) start at a reasonable $70 s or d, or pay $80 for a kitchen-equipped unit with a separate bedroom.

The **Park Inn** (4873 Stanley St., 250/347-9582 or 800/858-1155, www.parkinn.bc.ca) has similar rates to the rest of the bunch, featuring an indoor pool and a covered barbecue area. Standard rooms are $70 s, $75 d, while those with kitchenettes are $80 s, $85 d.

Over $100

Three km (1.9 miles) south of town, **Radium Resort** (250/347-9311 or 800/667-6444, www.radiumresort.com) is surrounded by an 18-hole golf course and holds a wide variety of facilities, including a health club, indoor pool, restaurant, and lounge. Guest rooms overlook the golf course and are linked to the main lodge building by a covered walkway. Regular motel rooms range $160–190 s or d, while kitchen-equipped condos sleeping up to six people start at $240 per night. Check the website or call for specials (rooms are often sold for around $100, even in the middle of summer). Additionally, golf, ski, and spa packages lower rates considerably, especially before and after summer's peak season.

Radium's newest accommodation, the **Prestige Inn** (7493 Main St. W, 250/347-2300 or 877/737-8443, www.prestigeinn.com), sits at the town's main intersection. Facilities include a fitness room, indoor pool, gift shop, spa services, an Italian restaurant, and a lounge bar. Summer rates are $180–230 s or d, but these rates are almost halved in winter.

Campgrounds

Within Kootenay National Park, but accessed from in town off Highways 93/95, is **Redstreak Campground** (see *Campgrounds* in the section on the park). The closest commercial camping is at **Canyon RV Resort,** nestled in its own private valley immediately north of the Highway 93/95 junction (250/347-9564, www.canyonrv.com; Apr.–Oct.; $22–25 per site). Treed sites are spread along a pleasant creek, and all facilities are provided.

Spur Valley Golf Resort, 18 km (11 miles) north of Radium along Highway 95 (250/347-9822, www.spurvalley.com), has 100 sites around a large grassy area. Part of the resort is a full-length nine-hole golf course (across the road) and tennis courts. Sites range $20–24, with firewood an extra $5 per bundle.

Perfectly described by its name, **Dry Gulch Provincial Park** offers 26 sites four km (2.5 miles) south of town. Typical of provincial park camping, each site has a picnic table and fire pit but no hookups. Reservations are not taken; $15 per night.

FOOD

The town of Radium Hot Springs holds several good choices for a food break. For breakfast, head to **Springs Course** restaurant (Stanley St., 250/347-9311; Apr.–Oct. daily 7 A.M.–9 P.M.), at the golf course on the west side of the highway. The view from the deck, overlooking the Columbia River and Purcell Mountains, is nothing short of stunning. The food is good and remarkably inexpensive; in the morning, for example, an omelet with three fillings, hash browns, and toast is just $9. Lunch and dinner are also well priced, with a massive Caesar salad for $7 and main meals $10–18.50, including pastas for $11.

Back in town, **Back Country Jack's** (Main St. W, 250/347-0097; daily 11 A.M.–11 P.M.) is decorated with real antiques and real hard bench seats in private booths. There's a wide variety of platters to share, including Cowboy Caviar (nachos and baked beans) for $7.50 and a surprisingly good barbecued chicken soup ($5). For a main, the half-chicken, half-ribs, and all the extras for two ($24) is a good deal. Across the road, **Horsethief Creek Pub and Eatery** (Main St. E, 250/347-6400) serves up similar fare in more modern surroundings. Both places have a few outdoor tables.

As always, **Husky House Restaurant,** at the corner of Highways 93 and 95 (250/347-9811; daily 7 A.M.–11 P.M.), serves a good, solid menu of typical Canadian fare at reasonable prices. Just around the corner is **Screamer's,** the place to hang out with an ice cream on a hot summer afternoon. The ice cream here has been researched many times, most often when returning from camping trips in the Columbia Valley. Also along this strip is **Mountainside Market,** with an excellent choice of groceries and an in-house deli and butcher.

The restaurant at the **Radium Resort** (three km/1.9 miles south of town, 250/347-9311) caters mostly to golfers throughout the day and resort guests in the evening, but everybody is welcome. Enjoy lunch on the outdoor patio for around $10, or dine on sea bass smothered with a fruit-filled salsa for $24 in the evening. Buffets are offered on Wednesday and Friday nights from 6 P.M. ($22 per person).

INFORMATION

On the east side of the highway, just south of the Highway 93/95 junction, is the **Radium Hot Springs Visitor Info Centre** (250/347-9331 or 800/347-9704, www.rhs.bc.ca). This building is also home to the national park information center. It's open weekdays year-round and in the busier summer months daily 9 A.M.–7 P.M.

NORTH FROM RADIUM ALONG HIGHWAY 95

From Radium, Highway 95 follows the Columbia River north for 105 km (65 miles) to Golden, from where the TransCanada Highway heads east, through Yoho National Park and across the Continental Divide to Banff National Park. Between Radium and Golden are several small, historic towns worthy of a stop. The first is **Edgewater,** where a farmer's market is held each Saturday. Continuing north is **Brisco,** gateway to the mountaineering mecca of **Bugaboo Provincial Park.** Named for a member of the 1859 Palliser expedition, Brisco was founded on the mining industry and later grew as a regional center for surrounding farmland. Brisco General Store is a throwback to those earlier times, selling just about everything. Nearby

Spillimacheen ("white water" to the natives) sits at the confluence of the Spillimacheen River and Bugaboo Creek.

SOUTH ALONG HIGHWAY 93/95

The highway south from Radium takes you 140 km (87 miles) to the city of Cranbrook, which sits on Highway 3, a major transprovincial route across the southern portion of British Columbia. This highway accesses four provincial parks: **Whiteswan, Top of the World, Elk Lakes,** and **Height of the Rockies;** these are covered in the *Other Parks of the Canadian Rockies* chapter.

Invermere

The commercial center of the Columbia River Valley is Invermere (pop. 3,500), on the shoreline of Lake Windermere Lake 15 km (nine miles) south of Radium. The population swells threefold throughout summer as vacation homes in Invermere and surrounding lakeside communities fill with a mostly Albertan influx of visitors who come for the water sports, the swimming, and the holiday atmosphere.

Off the Invermere access road, toward Wilmer, a small plaque marks the site of Kootenae House. Established by David Thompson in 1807, it was the first trading post on the Columbia River. The valley's first permanent settlement, known as Athalmer, was alongside the outlet of Lake Windermere, but continual flooding led to the town's expansion on higher ground. The old townsite is now a popular recreation area, where a pleasant grassy area dotted with picnic tables runs right down to a sandy beach and the warm, shallow waters of the lake. It's on the left as you travel along the Invermere access road. As you approach the town itself, consider a stop at **Windermere Valley Museum** (622 3rd St., 250/342-9769), where the entire history of the valley is contained in seven separate buildings.

Invermere holds motels, eateries, grocery stores, gas stations, a Greyhound bus depot, and a laundry. The motels downtown are a bit overpriced; the best option is **Delphine Lodge** (250/342-6851; $80–100), two km (1.2 miles) north in the small village of Wilmer. Restored to its former glory, this 19th-century hotel has been converted to a boutique bed-and-breakfast. On warm afternoons, you can relax in the beautiful garden, then move inside to the comfy lounge. Rates include a cooked breakfast.

On a Saturday morning in downtown Invermere, you'll find all sorts of goodies at the outdoor **market,** which happens right on the main street. Farther down the hill, the **Quality Bakery** (888/681-9977) lives up to its name with a huge range of ultra-healthy sandwiches and not-so-healthy cakes and pastries. The town's most upscale dining room is **Strand's** (up the hill from the main street at 818 12th St., 250/342-6344; daily 5–9 P.M.). It's contained in a restored 1912 heritage house set on landscaped gardens, with diners seated in small, intimate rooms. The immaculately presented seasonal menu often includes delicacies such as trout, salmon, and venison that are served with a wide selection of vegetables. Dine before 6 P.M. to take advantage of a three-course special for $14.

Along the main drag, on the corner of 5th Street and 7th Avenue, is the **Invermere Visitor Info Centre** (250/342-2844, www.adventure valley.com; July–Aug. daily 9 A.M.–5 P.M.).

Panorama Mountain Village

Recent years have seen a big push at promoting Panorama, in the Purcell Mountains immediately west of Invermere, as a year-round destination by its owners, Intrawest. The resort has a long way to go before becoming the "next Whistler," also owned by Intrawest, but Panorama Mountain Village, comprising a redeveloped base area, a residential subdivision, an open-air gondola to move visitors between the two main villages, a year-round water park,

and a resort-style golf course, is just the first step in future plans. **Greywolf Golf Course** (250/341-4100) is a challenging 7,140 yards from the back tees, with water coming into play on 14 of the 18 holes, including the signature sixth hole, "the Cliffhanger," which requires an accurate tee shot across a narrow canyon to a green backed by towering cliffs. Greens fees are $119, dropping to $75 for twilight rates. Also during the warmer months, there are chairlift rides (noon–5 P.M.), white-water rafting, inflatable-kayak trips down Toby Creek, and horseback riding. In the village itself you'll find tennis, a climbing wall, and a swimming pool.

Skiing first put Panorama on the map, mainly because the resort boasts the third-highest vertical rise of all North American winter resorts (1,200 meters/3,940 feet), behind only Whistler/Blackcomb, also in British Columbia, and Big Sky, Montana. Despite the impressive relief, Panorama offers slopes suitable for all levels of expertise. Lift tickets are adult $59, senior $49, child $27.

The village is also home to **R.K. Heli-Ski** (250/342-3889 or 800/661-6060, www.rkheli ski.com), which operates out of its own "heliplex," complete with a lounge and restaurant. The company is one of the few heli-ski operations that specializes in day trips.

Accommodations in Panorama Mountain Village are all relatively new and can be booked through the resort's main switchboard (250/342-6941 or 800/663-2929, www.panoramaresort .com), as can all summer activities. Outside of the resort's marketing department, summer is still thought of as the off-season, and there are some great summer deals to be had, such as two nights' accommodation and unlimited use of the chairlift for $99 per person.

Kootenay National Park

Yoho National Park and Vicinity

Yoho, a Cree word of amazement, is a fitting name for this 131,300-hectare (324,450-acre) national park in British Columbia on the western slopes of the Canadian Rockies. The TransCanada Highway bisects the park on its run between Lake Louise (Alberta) and Golden (British Columbia). Banff National Park borders Yoho to the east, while Kootenay National Park lies immediately to the south.

Yoho is the smallest of the four contiguous Canadian Rockies national parks, but its wild and rugged landscape holds spectacular waterfalls, extensive icefields, a lake to rival those in Banff, and one of the world's most intriguing fossil beds. In addition, you'll find some of the finest hiking in all of Canada on the park's 300-km (186-mile) trail system.

Within the park are four lodges, four campgrounds, and the small railway town of **Field,** where you'll find basic services. The park is open year-round, although road conditions in winter

Must-Sees

Look for **M** to find the sights and activities you can't miss and **N** for the best dining and lodging.

M Yoho Valley: The valley doesn't become ice-free until June, but when it does, the access road passes natural wonders such as Takakkaw Falls and opens up excellent hikes (page 173).

M Emerald Lake: You can hike, canoe, fish, or simply soak up the mountain scenery (page 173).

M Lake O'Hara: Quite simply, magical. Access is limited by a quota system, so take heed of the reservation information and be prepared for a day of hiking you will always remember (page 174).

M Burgess Shale: The hiking is strenuous along a restricted-access trail, but because this is one of the world's most important paleontological sites, the trek is a once-in-a-lifetime experience (page 176).

M Kicking Horse Mountain Resort: I've ridden each of the four gondolas in the Canadian Rockies, and this one, near Golden, is my favorite for unbeatable top-of-the-world views (page 184).

YOHO NATIONAL PARK AND VICINITY

ALBERTA

BRITISH COLUMBIA

Yoho Valley **M**

Emerald Lake **M**

Kicking Horse Mountain Resort **M**

M Burgess Shale

M

Lake O'Hara

0   10 mi

0   10 km

Emerald Lake

© ANDREW HEMPSTEAD

M Yoho National Park

YOHO NATIONAL PARK AND VICINITY

© AVALON TRAVEL PUBLISHING, INC.

can be treacherous, and occasional closures occur on Kicking Horse Pass. The road out to Takakkaw Falls is closed through winter, and it often doesn't reopen until mid-June.

PLANNING YOUR TIME

Yoho National Park is a gem of a destination, well worth visiting even for just a day. If you do make the park a day trip from Banff, you'll have enough time to drive to **Takakkaw Falls,** hike the loop trail around **Emerald Lake,** and enjoy lunch in between at one of the restaurants I recom-

mend. Organized tours from Banff and Lake Louise follow a similar itinerary—a good option if you don't have a vehicle (children will love being on the bus as it negotiates the road to Takakkaw Falls). The highlight of a visit to Yoho is **Lake O'Hara,** one of the most special places in the Canadian Rockies. Unlike at the region's other famous lakes, you can't simply drive up to O'Hara. Instead, you must make advance reservations for a shuttle bus that trundles up a restricted-access road to the lake.

The summer tourist season in Yoho is shorter than in the other national parks. Emerald Lake

PARK ENTRY

U nless you're traveling straight through and not stopping, a permit is required for entry into Yoho National Park. A **National Parks Day Pass** is adult $7, senior $6, child $3.50 up to a maximum of $14 per vehicle. It can be used in the other national parks and is valid until 4 P.M. the day following its purchase. The **National Parks of Canada Pass,** good for entry into Yoho and all Canada's national parks for one year from purchase, is adult $45, senior $38 to a maximum of $89 per vehicle. Both types of pass are available from the Field Visitor Centre and campground kiosks. For more information on passes, go to the Parks Canada website (www.pc.gc.ca).

doesn't become ice-free until early June, and the road to Takakkaw Falls remains closed until mid-June. While July and August are the prime months to visit, September is also pleasant, both weather- and crowd-wise. Lake O'Hara doesn't become snow-free until early July, but the best time to visit is the last week of September when the forests of larch have turned a brilliant gold color.

The last part of this chapter covers the town of **Golden,** which lies beyond the park's western boundary. Here, the highlight is summer gondola rides at **Kicking Horse Mountain Resort.** The more adventurous can take a white-water rafting trip down the Kicking Horse River or go mountain biking. Including Golden with the highlights of Yoho National Park makes for a very long day trip; an overnight stay either in the park or in Golden will give you two days to enjoy both at a relaxed pace.

THE LAND

The park extends west from the Continental Divide to the western main ranges of the Rocky Mountains. The jagged peaks along this section of the Continental Divide—including famous Mount Victoria, which forms the backdrop for Lake Louise—are some of the park's highest. But the award for Yoho's loftiest summit goes to 3,562-meter (11,686-foot)

Mount Goodsir, west of the Continental Divide in the Ottertail Range.

The park's only watershed is that of the **Kicking Horse River,** which is fed by the Wapta and Waputik icefields. The Kicking Horse, wide and braided for much of its course through the park, flows westward, joining the mighty Columbia River at Golden. The park's many individual geological features of interest—such as Takakkaw and Twin Falls, Natural Bridge, Leanchoil Hoodoos, Emerald Lake, and Lake O'Hara—are covered under *Sights and Recreation.*

Flora

Elevations within the park cover a range of more than 2,500 meters (8,200 feet), making for distinct vegetation changes and more than 600 recorded species of plants. **Douglas fir** is the climax species at lower elevations, but **lodgepole pine** dominates areas affected by fire. **Western red cedar, hemlock,** and the delightful **calypso orchid** can be found in the damp eastern shoreline of Emerald Lake. At higher elevations, where temperatures are lower and precipitation is higher, the familiar subalpine forests of **Engelmann spruce** and **subalpine fir** thrive. The northernmost extent of **larch** exists around Lake O'Hara. Larch is a conifer (evergreen), but its needles turn a stunning orange in fall—a photographer's delight. Above the tree line, where wind and rain have deposited soil, wildflowers such as **heather, Indian paintbrush,** and **arnica** create a carpet of color for a few short weeks midsummer.

Fauna

The animals for which Yoho is best known are fossilized in beds of shale and have been dead for more than 500 million years. But they still create great interest for the role their remains have played in our understanding of life on earth in prehistoric times.

Large mammals are not as common in Yoho as in the other parks of the Canadian Rockies, simply because the terrain is so rugged. Valleys are inhabited by **mule deer, elk, moose, black bears,** and a wide variety of smaller mammals. **Porcupines** are common along Yoho Valley Road. The park has a healthy population of

Yoho National Park

grizzly bears, but sightings are relatively rare because the grizzly tends to remain in remote valleys far from the busy TransCanada Highway corridor. Much of the park is above the tree line; here noisy **marmots** and **pikas** find a home, along with an estimated 400 **mountain goats.** More than 200 bird species have been recorded within the park.

HISTORY

The Kootenay and Shuswap tribes of British Columbia were the first humans to travel through the rugged area that is now the national park. It's believed the men hid their families in the mountains before crossing over to the prairies to hunt buffalo and to trade with other tribes. On their return they set up seasonal camps along the Kicking Horse River to dry the buffalo meat and hides. They used a more northern route than that taken by travelers today, crossing the divide at Howse Pass and descending to the Kootenay Plains beyond the present-day junction of Highways 93 and 11.

The first Europeans to explore the valley of the Kicking Horse River were members of the 1858 Palliser Expedition, which set out to survey the west and report back to the British government on its suitability for settlement. The party approached from the south, climbing the Kootenay and Vermilion watersheds of present-day Kootenay National Park before descending to Wapta Falls. It was here that the unfortunate expedition geologist, Dr. James Hector, inadvertently gave the Kicking Horse River its name. While walking his horse over rough ground, he was kicked unconscious and took two hours to come to, by which time, so

the story goes, other members of his party had begun digging his grave.

Guided by outfitter Tom Wilson, Major A. B. Rogers (for whom Rogers Pass to the west is named) surveyed Kicking Horse Pass in 1881. His favorable report to the Canadian Pacific Railway (CPR) led to this route being chosen for the much-awaited transcontinental railway. The railbed was laid in 1884 and its grade was terribly steep; the first train to attempt the run suffered a brake failure and derailed, killing three workers. In 1909, after dozens more wrecks and derailments, the CPR rerouted the steepest section of the line through the Spiral Tunnels. The highway now follows the original rail grade.

The small township of Field started as a railway maintenance depot at the bottom of treacherous Big Hill. In 1886 the CPR opened Mount Stephen House in Field, both to encourage visitors to this side of the mountains and as a dining stop for customers of the railway. The CPR then built lodges at several natural attractions in the area, including **Emerald Lake Lodge** in 1902, **Lake O'Hara Lodge** in 1913, and **Wapta Lodge Bungalow Camp** in 1921.

As in adjacent Banff, the coming of the railway was a prime catalyst in the formation of Yoho National Park. Upon the opening of the railway line in 1886, 2,600 hectares (6425 acres) of land around the base of Mount Stephen were set aside as Mount Stephen Park Reserve, Canada's second national park. In 1901 the reserve was expanded, and after three further boundary changes, the park of today came into being in 1930. Mining of lead, zinc, and silver continued until 1952, and today remnants of the Monarch and Kicking Horse mines can still be seen on the faces of Mount Stephen and Mount Field, respectively.

Sights and Recreation

ROAD-ACCESSIBLE SIGHTS

As with all other parks of the Canadian Rockies, you don't need to travel deep into the back-country to view the most spectacular features—many are visible from the roadside. The following sights are listed from east to west, starting at the park boundary (the Continental Divide).

Spiral Tunnel Viewpoint

The joy CPR president William Van Horne felt upon completion of his transcontinental rail line in 1886 was tempered by massive problems along a stretch of line west of Kicking Horse Pass. Big Hill was less than five km (3.1 miles) long, but its gradient was so steep that runaway trains, crashes, and other disasters were common. A trail from Kicking Horse Campground takes you past the remains of one of those doomed trains.

Nearly 25 years after the line opened, railway engineers and builders finally solved the problem. By building two spiral tunnels down through two km (1.2 miles) of solid rock to the valley floor, they lessened the grade dramatically and the terrors came to an end. Today the TransCanada Highway follows the original railbed. Along the way is a viewpoint with interpretive displays telling the fascinating story of Big Hill.

◪ Yoho Valley

Fed by the Wapta Icefield in the far north of the park, the **Yoho River** flows through this spectacularly narrow valley, dropping more than 200 meters (660 feet) in the last kilometer (.6 mile) before its confluence with the Kicking Horse River. The road leading up the valley passes the park's main campground, climbs a *very* tight series of switchbacks (watch for buses reversing through the middle section), and emerges at **Upper Spiral Tunnel Viewpoint,** which offers a different perspective on the afore-mentioned tunnel. A further 400 meters (.2 mile) along the road is a pullout for viewing the confluence of the Yoho and Kicking Horse Rivers—a particularly impressive sight as the

former is glacier-fed and therefore silty, while the latter is lake-fed and clear.

Yoho Valley Road ends 14 km (8.7 miles) from the main highway at **Takakkaw Falls,** the most impressive waterfall in the Canadian Rockies. The falls are fed by the Daly and Des Poilus Glaciers of the Waputik Icefield, which straddles the Continental Divide. Meaning "wonderful" in the language of the Cree, Takakkaw tumbles 254 meters (830 feet) over a sheer rock wall at the lip of the Yoho Valley, creating a spray bedecked by rainbows. It can be seen from the parking lot, but it's well worth the easy 10-minute stroll over the Yoho River to appreciate the sight in all its glory.

Natural Bridge

Three km (1.9 miles) west of Field is the turnoff to famous Emerald Lake. On your way out to the lake, you'll first pass another intriguing sight. At Natural Bridge, two km (1.2 miles) down the road, the Kicking Horse River has worn a narrow hole through a limestone wall, creating a bridge. Over time, the bridge will collapse and, well, it won't be such an intriguing sight anymore. A trail leads to several viewpoints—try to avoid the urge to join the idiots clambering over the top of the bridge.

◪ Emerald Lake

Outfitter Tom Wilson stumbled on stunning Emerald Lake while guiding Major A. B. Rogers through the Kicking Horse River Valley in 1881. He was led to the lake by his horse, which had been purchased from natives. He later surmised that the horse had been accustomed to traveling up to the lake, meaning that the horse's former owners must have known about the lake before the white man arrived.

One of the jewels of the Canadian Rockies, the beautiful lake is surrounded by a forest of Engelmann spruce, as well as many peaks more than 3,000 meters (9,840 feet). It is covered in ice most of the year but comes alive with activity for a few short months in summer when hikers, canoeists, and horseback riders take advantage of the magnificent surroundings. **Emerald Lake**

Lodge is the grandest of Yoho's accommodations, offering a restaurant, café, lounge, and recreation facilities for both guests and non-guests (see *Other Recreation* and *Accommodations*).

◪ LAKE O'HARA

Nestled in a high bowl of lush alpine meadows, Lake O'Hara, 11 km (6.8 miles) from the nearest public road, is surrounded by dozens of smaller alpine lakes and framed by spectacular peaks permanently mantled in snow. As if that weren't enough, the entire area is webbed by a network of hiking trails established over the last 90 years by luminaries such as Lawrence Grassi. Trails radiate from the lake in all directions; the longest is just 7.5 km (4.7 miles), making Lake O'Hara an especially fine hub for day hiking. What makes this destination all the more special is that a quota system limits the number of visitors.

Book the Bus

It's possible to walk to Lake O'Hara, but most visitors take the shuttle bus along a road closed to the public. The departure point is a signed parking lot 15 km (9.3 miles) east of Field and three km (1.9 miles) west of the Continental Divide. Buses for day visitors depart between mid-June and early October at 8:30 A.M. and 10:30 A.M., returning at 4:30 P.M. and 6:30 P.M. To book a seat, call the dedicated reservations line (250/343-6433). Reservations are taken up to three months in advance, but as numbers are limited, you will need to call *exactly* three months prior to be assured of a seat; even then, you should call as early in the day as possible. Phone lines are open mid-Mar.–Apr. Mon.–Thurs. 8 A.M.–4 P.M., May Mon.–Fri. 8 A.M.–4 P.M., June–Sept. daily 8 A.M.–4 P.M., and mid-Sept.–early Oct. Mon.–Thurs. 8 A.M.–4 P.M. The reservation fee is $12 per booking, and the bus fare is $15 per person round-trip. The procedure is simple enough, but to be assured a seat, it's important you get it right: for example, to visit on September 30 (when the larch are at their colorful peak), start dialing at 8 A.M. on June 30 (with a credit card ready). Six seats per day are set aside for those who haven't made advance reservations.

© ANDREW HEMPSTEAD

the sweeping view from Opabin Prospect, above Lake O'Hara

They are allotted via the reservation number on a first-come, first-served basis. No-shows are filled on a standby basis by folks waiting around at the parking lot on the day of departure (generally, arrive around 7 A.M., head to the covered shelter, and you'll be the first in line). You have the best chance of snagging a seat on the 8:30 A.M. bus, especially if the weather is bad.

All times—bus departures and reservation center hours—are mountain standard time.

Other Considerations

After the 20-minute bus trip to the lake, day hikers are dropped off at **Le Relais,** a homely log shelter where books and maps are sold, including the recommended Gem Trek Lake *Louise & Yoho* map. Hot drinks and light snacks are served—something to look forward to at the end of the day, as this is also the afternoon meeting place for the return trip (no reservations necessary).

Several overnight options are available at the lake—including a lodge, a campground, and a rustic hut—but each should be booked well in advance (see *Accommodations*).

Lake O'Hara Shoreline
• Length: 2.8 km/1.7 miles (40 minutes) one-way
• Elevation gain: minimal
• Rating: easy
• Trailhead: warden's cabin, across from Le Relais

Most people use sections of this easy loop around Lake O'Hara to access the trails, but it is an enjoyable walk in its own right, especially in the evening. Across from Le Relais, behind the warden's cabin, interpretive boards lay out the various options throughout the valley and explain local history. Heading in a clockwise direction from this point, the trail crosses Cataract Creek, the lake's outlet, then passes along the north shoreline, crossing gullies then reaching Seven Veil Falls at the 1.2-km (.7-mile) mark. Traversing the cool, damp, southern shoreline, the trail passes branches to the Opabin Plateau and a short detour to Mary Lake. Lake O'Hara Lodge is passed at the 2.4-km (1.5-mile) mark, from where it's a short stroll back along the road to Le Relais.

Lake Oesa
• Length: 3 km/1.9 miles (one hour) one-way
• Elevation gain: 240 meters/790 feet
• Rating: easy/moderate
• Trailhead: Shoreline Trail, 800 meters (.5 mile) beyond Cataract Creek

With the Continental Divide peaks of Mount Victoria (3,464 meters/11,365 feet) and Mount Lefroy (3,423 meters/11,230 feet) as a backdrop, this small aqua-colored lake surrounded by talus slopes is one of the area's gems. All the elevation gain is made in the first 2.4 km (1.6 miles), as the trail switchbacks to a ledge overlooking Lake O'Hara. The trail then levels out, passing three small bodies of water before climbing over a low rise and entering the cirque in which Lake Oesa lies.

Opabin Plateau Circuit
• Length: 5.9 km/3.7 miles (two hours) round-trip
• Elevation gain: 250 meters/820 feet
• Rating: easy/moderate
• Trailhead: Shoreline Trail

Separated from Lake Oesa by 2,848-meter (9,344-foot) Mount Yukness, this plateau high above the tree line dotted with small lakes is one of the most picturesque destinations in the Canadian Rockies. The time quoted is an absolute minimum because it's easy to spend an entire day exploring the alpine plateau and scrambling around the surrounding slopes. Two trails lead up to the plateau, which itself is laced with trails. The most direct route is the Opabin Plateau West Circuit, which branches right from the Shoreline Trail 300 meters (.2 mile) beyond Lake O'Hara Lodge. It then passes Mary Lake, climbs steeply, and reaches the plateau in a little less than two km (1.2 miles). Opabin Prospect is an excellent lookout along the edge of the plateau. From this point, take the right forks to continue to the head of the cirque and Opabin Lake. This section of trail passes through a lightly forested area of larch that comes alive with color the second week of September. From Opabin Lake, the East Circuit traverses the lower slopes of Yukness

Mountain, passing Hungabee Lake then descending steeply to Lake O'Hara and ending back along the Shoreline Trail 600 meters (.4 mile) east of Lake O'Hara Lodge.

Lake McArthur

- Length: 3.5 km/2.2 miles (80 minutes) one-way
- Elevation gain: 300 meters (980 feet)
- Rating: easy/moderate
- Trailhead: Le Relais

A personal favorite, this trail leads to the largest and (in my opinion) most stunning body of water in the Lake O'Hara area. Beginning from behind Le Relais, the trail passes through an open meadow and the Elizabeth Parker Hut; stay left to reach Schäffer Lake after 1.6 km (one mile). At a junction beyond that lake, the left fork leads to Lake McArthur and the right fork to McArthur Pass. The lake option climbs steeply for 800 meters (.5 mile), then levels out and traverses a narrow ledge before entering the Lake McArthur Cirque. (Stay high, even if trails descending into the McArthur Valley look like they offer an easier approach). After leveling off, the trail enters the alpine and quickly reaches its maximum elevation and the first views of Lake McArthur. Backed by Mount Biddle and the Biddle Glacier, the deep-blue lake and colorful alpine meadows are an unforgettable panorama.

Odaray Highline

- Length: 2.6 km/1.6 miles (one hour) one-way
- Elevation gain: 280 meters/920 feet
- Rating: easy/moderate
- Trailhead: Le Relais

For a panoramic overview of the Lake O'Hara area with a minimum of energy output, it's hard to beat this trail, which ends atop the Odaray Plateau west of the lake. This trail passes through an important wildlife corridor, and a voluntary program to limit use—and therefore human interference—is in place. Check with park staff for the latest access restrictions. From Le Relais, follow the Lake McArthur Trail to Schäffer Lake as detailed previously, then take the right fork, which climbs gently toward to McArthur Pass.

Just before the pass, take the right fork. From this point, it's a steep one km (.6 mile) up to the lofty perch below Odaray Mountain.

Cathedral Basin

- Length: 7.5 km/4.7 miles (2.5 hours) one-way
- Elevation gain: 300 meters/980 feet
- Rating: moderate
- Trailhead: Lake O'Hara Campground

The trail out to Cathedral Basin is the longest in the Lake O'Hara area, yet it's still an easy day trip for most people. Reach the trailhead from Le Relais by walking the short distance back down the access road or by following Cataract Creek downstream from behind the warden's cabin. From the campground the trail heads northwest, crossing Morning Glory Creek at the 2.4-km (1.5-mile) mark then passing Linda Lake. The final ascent to Cathedral Basin makes a wide loop through an area of ancient rock slides. From this point, the magnificent panorama of the Lake O'Hara area and the backdrop of the Continental Divide are laid out to the southeast.

◪ BURGESS SHALE

High on the rocky slopes above Mount Field is a layer of sedimentary rock known as the Burgess Shale, which contains what are considered to be the world's finest fossils from the Cambrian Period. The site is famous worldwide because it has unraveled the mysteries of a major stage of evolution.

In 1909, Smithsonian Institution paleontologist Charles Walcott was leading a pack train along the west slope of Mount Field, on the opposite side of the valley from the newly completed Spiral Tunnel, when he stumbled across these fossil beds. Encased in the shale, the fossils here are of marine invertebrates about 510 million years old. Generally, fossils are the remains of vertebrates, but at this site some freak event—probably a mudslide—suddenly buried thousands of soft-bodied animals (invertebrates), preserving them by keeping out the oxygen that would have decayed their delicate bodies. Walcott excavated an estimated 65,000 specimens from the site. Today paleontologists continue to uncover perfectly preserved fossils here—albeit in far fewer numbers than in Walcott's day. They've also uncovered additional fossil beds, similar in makeup and age, across the valley, on the north face of Mount Stephen.

Reaching the Two Sites

Protected by UNESCO as a World Heritage Site, the two research areas are open only to those accompanied by a licensed guide. The **Burgess Shale Geoscience Foundation** (250/343-6006 or 800/343-3006, www.burgess-shale.bc.ca; Mon.–Fri. 10 A.M.–3:30 P.M.) guides trips to both sites between July and mid-September. The access to **Walcott's Quarry** is along a strenuous 10-km (6.2-mile) trail that gains 760 meters (2,500 feet) in elevation. Trips leave Friday–Monday at 8 A.M. from the trading post at the Field intersection, returning around 6:30 P.M.; $65 per person. Trips to the more easily reached **Mount Stephen Fossil Beds** depart Saturday and Sunday at 10 A.M., returning at around 4:30 P.M.; $45 per person. The trail to the Mount Stephen beds gains 520 meters (1,710 feet) of elevation in three km (1.9 miles). The trails to both sites are unrelenting in their elevation gain—you must be fit to hike them. Reservations are a must.

EMERALD LAKE HIKES

Emerald Lake Loop

- Length: 5.2 km/3.2 miles (1.5 hours) round-trip
- Elevation gain: minimal
- Rating: easy
- Trailhead: Emerald Lake parking lot, nine km (5.6 miles) from Highway 1

One of the easiest yet most enjoyable walks in Yoho is around the park's most famous lake. The trail encircles the lake and can be hiked in either direction. The best views are from the western shoreline, where a massive avalanche has cleared away the forest of Engelmann spruce. Across the lake from this point, Mount Burgess can be seen rising an impressive 2,599

meters (8,530 feet). Traveling in a clockwise direction, beyond the avalanche slope, the trail to Emerald Basin veers off to the left, and at the 2.2-km (1.4-mile) mark, a small bridge is crossed. Views from this point extend back across the lodge to the Ottertail Range. Beyond the lake's inlet, the vegetation changes dramatically. A lush forest of towering western red cedar creates a canopy, protecting moss-covered fallen trees, thimbleberry, and bunchberry extending to the water's edge. Just over one km (.6 mile) from the bridge, the trail divides: the left fork leads back to the parking lot via a small forest-encircled pond, or continue straight ahead through the grounds of Emerald Lake Lodge. Park staff lead a guided hike around the lake every Saturday morning, departing at 10 A.M. from the parking lot trailhead.

Hamilton Falls

- Length: 800 meters/.5 mile (40 minutes) one-way
- Elevation gain: 60 meters/200 feet
- Rating: easy
- Trailhead: information kiosk, Emerald Lake parking lot

The trail to these falls begins from the Emerald Lake parking lot, down the hill from the bridge to the lodge. It's an easy walk through a forest of Engelmann spruce and subalpine fir to a viewpoint at the base of the falls. A little farther along, the trail begins switchbacking steeply and offers even better views of the cascade.

The trail continues beyond the waterfall to **Hamilton Lake,** which lies in a small glacial cirque a steep 880 vertical meters (2,890 feet) above Emerald Lake. Total distance from Emerald Lake to Hamilton Lake is 5.5 km/3.4 miles (2.5 hours) one-way.

Emerald Basin

- Length: 4.5 km/2.8 miles (1.5–2 hours) one-way
- Elevation gain: 280 meters/920 feet
- Rating: easy/moderate
- Trailhead: Emerald Lake Loop, 1.5 km (.9 mile) from the parking lot

TAKAKKAW FALLS

M uch discussion is made of which is Canada's highest waterfall. Della Falls, on Vancouver Island, also in British Columbia, is 440 meters (1,440 feet) high, but its drop is broken by a ledge. Takakkaw Falls is considerably lower, at 254 meters (830 feet), but the drop is unbroken, which, officially, makes it Canada's highest. There is one thing of which there is no doubt: Takakkaw Falls will leave you breathless, much as it did famous alpinist Sir James Outram and everyone who has viewed the spectacle since.

The torrent, issuing from an icy cavern, rushes tempestuously down a deep, winding chasm till it gains the verge of the unbroken cliff, leaps forth in sudden wildness for a hundred and fifty feet, and then in a stupendous column of pure white sparkling water, broken by giant jets descending rocketlike and wreathed in volumed spray, dashes upon the rocks almost a thousand feet below, and, breaking into a milky series of cascading rushes for five hundred feet more, swirls into the swift current of the Yoho River.

–Sir James Outram,
In the Heart of the Canadian Rockies

© ANDREW HEMPSTEAD

The trail to the delightful Emerald Basin begins from the west shore of Emerald Lake, from where it's a steady three-km (1.9-mile) climb through a subalpine forest to the basin, which, chances are, you'll have to yourself. The most impressive sight awaiting you there is the south wall of the President Range, towering 800 vertical meters (2,625 feet) above.

YOHO VALLEY HIKES

The valley for which the park is named lies north of the TransCanada Highway. As well as the sights discussed previously, it provides many fine opportunities for serious day hikers to get off the beaten track. The following day hikes begin from different trailheads near the end of the road up Yoho Valley. In each case, leave your vehicle in the Takakkaw Falls parking lot.

Twin Falls
• Length: 8 km/5 miles (2.5 hours) one-way
• Elevation gain: 300 meters/980 feet

• Rating: moderate
• Trailhead: Takakkaw Falls parking lot, 14 km (8.7 miles) from Highway 1

This trail takes over where the road through the Yoho Valley ends, continuing in a northerly direction up the Yoho River to Twin Falls, passing many other waterfalls along the way. At spectacular Twin Falls, water from the Wapta Icefield divides in two before plunging off an 80-meter-high (262-foot-high) cliff. Mother Nature may work in amazing ways, but sometimes she needs a helping hand—or so the CPR thought. In the 1920s, the company dynamited one of the channels to make the falls more symmetrical. **Twin Falls Chalet** was built below the falls by the CPR in 1923 and today offers hikers light snacks through the middle of the day.

Iceline
• Length: 6.4 km/4 miles (2.5 hours) one-way
• Elevation gain: 690 meters/2,260 feet

• Rating: moderate/difficult
• Trailhead: Whiskey Jack Hostel

Constructed in 1987, this is one of the most spectacular day hikes in the Canadian Rockies. The length given is from Whiskey Jack Hostel to the highest point along the trail (2,250 meters/7,380 feet). (Day hikers are asked to leave their vehicles across the road from the hostel, in the Takakkaw Falls parking lot.) From the hostel, the trail begins a steep and steady one-km (.6-mile) climb to a point where three options present themselves: the Iceline Trail is to the right, Yoho Pass is straight ahead, and Hidden Lakes is a 300-meter (.2-mile) detour to the left. The Iceline Trail option now enters its highlight—a four-km (2.5-mile) traverse of a moraine below Emerald Glacier. Views across the valley improve as the trail climbs to its 2,220-meter (7,283-foot) crest. Many day hikers return from this point, although officially the trail continues into Little Yoho River Valley. Another option is to continue beyond Celeste Lake and loop back to Takakkaw Falls and the original trailhead, a total distance of 18 km (11.2 miles).

Yoho Pass
• Length: 4.7 km/2.9 miles (two hours) one-way
• Elevation gain: 530 meters/1,740 feet
• Rating: moderate
• Trailhead: Whiskey Jack Hostel

The trail to Yoho Pass, which can be combined with the Iceline Trail, officially begins on the west side of Whiskey Jack Hostel, but hikers are asked to leave their vehicles across the road in the Takakkaw Falls parking lot. It leads 3.7 km (2.3 miles) to picturesque, spruce-encircled Yoho Lake, then continues another easy one km (.6 mile) to the pass. The pass is below the tree line, so views are limited, but from this point it's 5.5 km (3.4 miles) and an elevation loss of 530 meters (1,740 feet) down to Emerald Lake; six km (3.7 miles) and an elevation gain of 300 meters (985 feet) to spectacular Burgess Pass; or 2.4 km (1.5 miles) north, with little elevation gain or loss, to an intersection with the Iceline Trail.

HIKES IN OTHER AREAS OF THE PARK

The hikes detailed as follows are along the Trans-Canada Highway. For the hike to a world-famous paleontological site, see *Burgess Shale.*

Paget Lookout
• Length: 3.5 km/2.2 miles (90 minutes) one-way
• Elevation gain: 520 meters/1,700 feet
• Rating: moderate
• Trailhead: Wapta Lake picnic area five km (3.1 miles) west of the Continental Divide

The trail to this viewpoint is moderately strenuous but worthwhile for the panorama of the Kicking Horse River Valley. The first section of trail traverses a forest of Engelmann spruce. Then the trail breaks out above the tree line just below the lookout, the site of an abandoned fire tower. As an alternative, branch right 1.4 km (.9 mile) along the trail and continue two km (1.2 miles) to **Sherbrooke Lake,** which is fed by the Waputik Icefield.

Hoodoo Trail
• Length: 3 km/1.9 miles (60–90 minutes) one-way
• Elevation gain: 460 meters/1,510 feet
• Rating: moderate
• Trailhead: Hoodoo Creek Campground, 23 km (14.3 miles) southwest of Field

Hoodoos are found in varying forms throughout the Canadian Rockies, but this outcrop, officially known as the Leanchoil Hoodoos, is among the most impressive. Hoodoos are formed by the erosion of relatively soft rock from beneath a cap of harder, more weather-resistant rock. Although these examples require some effort to reach, their intriguing appearance makes the trip worthwhile. The first half of the trail is relatively flat, leaving all the elevation gain to be made in the last, painful 1.5 km (.9 mile).

Wapta Falls
• Length: 2.4 km/1.5 miles (45 minutes) one-way
• Elevation loss: minimal

- Rating: easy
- Trailhead: unmarked parking lot beside Highway 1, 25 km (15.5 miles) west of Field and five km (3.1 miles) east of park boundary

In the park's extreme southwestern corner, this trail follows an old fire road for three km (1.9 miles), then narrows for an easy stroll through thick forest to a viewpoint above these 30-meter high (100-feet-high) falls on the Kicking Horse River. A steep, switch-backing descent leads 500 meters (.3 mile) to a viewpoint at the base of the falls.

OTHER RECREATION
Boating and Fishing
No river or stream is particularly well known for fishing, mainly because most of the water is glacially derived and therefore heavily silt-laden. Species present in the park's lakes and rivers include Dolly Varden and rainbow, lake, and cutthroat trout. A national park **fishing permit** costs $7 for seven days or $20 annually. **Emerald Lake Canoe Rentals,** in a small boatshed on the shore of Emerald Lake (250/343-6000; June–Sept. 9 A.M.–8 P.M.) rents canoes and small boats for $20 per hour, $35 for two hours, or $60 all day. Fishing in Emerald Lake isn't world-class, but there are some trout in the waters, and Emerald Lake Canoe Rentals offers a range of fishing tackle for rent or sale.

Horseback Riding
Emerald Lake Stables, at the lake of the same name (250/344-8982), rents horses through the mid-June to early September season. A one-hour trip along the west shore of Emerald Lake costs $35. Two-hour rides are $70, three-hour rides $100, four-hour rides $130, and all-day rides with lunch go for $175.

Wintertime
The TransCanada Highway through the park is open year-round, but facilities are only open June through mid-September. Some of the trails at higher elevations are impassable until July. Wintertime attracts cross-country skiers who happily slide along the Yoho Valley to frozen Takakkaw Falls or follow the Lake O'Hara trails.

Practicalities

ACCOMMODATIONS
The park provides a variety of options, all well-priced in comparison to Banff. Some travelers make Yoho a base for an entire Canadian Rockies vacation, traveling to Banff (just over an hour's drive east) or Golden (under an hour west) for supplies and civilized diversions.

Under $50
Hostelling International operates **HI–Whiskey Jack Wilderness Hostel** (mid-June–Sept.) in a meadow opposite Takakkaw Falls. Formerly cabins used by the CPR, then staff quarters for a privately run lodge that was destroyed by an avalanche, the hostel provides basic dormitory accommodations for up to 27 guests, who have use of a communal kitchen and showers. Members of Hostelling International pay $19 per night, nonmembers $23. Book a bed through the same reservations center that handles reservations for Banff National Park hostels (403/760-7580 or 866/762-4122, www.hihostels.ca). Check-in is 5–11 P.M.

$100–150
The streets of Field are lined with private homes offering reasonably priced overnight accommodations in rooms of varying privacy and standard. One of the better choices is the **Alpine Guesthouse** (313 2nd Ave., 250/343-6878, www.alpineguesthouse.ca), with a two-bedroom suite—complete with a kitchen, cable TV, outdoor patio, and private entrance for $130 per night. Like everywhere else in Field, it's within walking distance of the general store.

Also in Field is simple yet elegant **Kicking Horse Lodge** (100 Centre St., 250/343-6303 or

Overnighting in a waterfront cabin at Lake O'Hara allows visitors to enjoy the backcountry without sacrificing modern comforts.

800/659-4944, www.kickinghorselodge.net), which offers 14 well-furnished motel-like rooms, a large comfortable lounge, and a restaurant (open in summer only). In July and August, rates are $145–160 s, $160–180 s or d with a kitchenette. The rest of the year, these same rooms are discounted as low as $80—a great alternative to higher-priced Lake Louise for winter visitors.

Over $150

N Emerald Lake Lodge (403/410-7417 or 800/663-6336, www.crmr.com) is a grand, luxury-class accommodation along the southern shore of one of the Canadian Rockies' most magnificent lakes. The original lodge was built in 1902 in the same tradition as the Fairmont Chateau Lake Louise and Fairmont Banff Springs—as a playground for wealthy railway travelers. No original buildings remain (although the original framework is used in the main building); instead guests lap up the luxury of richly decorated duplex-style units and freestanding cabins. Each spacious unit is outfitted in a heritage theme and has a wood-burning fireplace, private balcony, luxurious bathroom, comfortable bed topped by a plush duvet,

and in-room coffee. Other lodge amenities include a hot tub and sauna, swimming pool, restaurant, lounge, and café. Guests can also go horseback riding, or go boating and fishing on Emerald Lake. Rack rates start at $480 s or d, but book online for as low as $330 in summer and as low as $150 in November.

Comprising 29 cabins set around a main lodge alongside the Kicking Horse River, the **Cathedral Mountain Lodge** (250/343-6442, www.cathedralmountain.com; mid-May–Sept.; $365 s or d) complex lies one km (.6 mile) along Yoho Valley Road from the TransCanada Highway. In recent years the original cabins have been replaced by fancy log chalets, with modern amenities and plenty of space to spread out. Each has a log bed, stone fireplace, bathroom with soaker tub, and private deck; A smallish restaurant (daily 7 A.M.–10 P.M.) and grocery store, both open to nonguests, are on the premises.

Spending a night at **Lake O'Hara Lodge** (250/343-6418, www.lakeohara.com) is a special experience, and one that draws familiar faces year after year. On a practical level, it allows hikers not equipped for overnight camping the opportunity to explore one of the finest hiking destinations in all of the Canadian Rockies at their leisure. The 15 cabins, each with a private bathroom, are spread around the lakeshore, while within the main lodge are eight rooms, most of which are twins and share bathrooms. Rates of $420 d for a room in the main lodge (shared bathrooms) and $575–625 d for a lakeside cabin include all meals, taxes, gratuities, and transportation mid-June to September. Located 13 km (eight miles) from Highway 1, the lodge transports guests by shuttle bus from a parking lot three km (1.9 miles) west of the Continental Divide and 15 km (nine miles) east of Field. Between February and April, the eight rooms in the main lodge are available for cross-country skiers for $240 per person, inclusive of meals and ski tours.

Campgrounds

As in other national parks, no reservations are taken for camping in Yoho's vehicle-accessible campgrounds. All sites have a picnic table and fire ring, with a fire permit costing $6 (includes firewood). When all campgrounds are filled, campers will be directed to overflow areas.

The park's main camping area is **Kicking Horse Campground** (mid-May–mid-Oct.; $22 per site), five km (three miles) northeast of Field along the road to Takakkaw Falls. Facilities include coin showers ($1), flush toilets, and kitchen shelters. Back toward the TransCanada Highway, **Monarch Campground** ($14 per site) offers more-limited facilities and less-private sites; **Hoodoo Creek Campground,** along the Trans-Canada Highway 23 km (14 miles) southwest of Field, provides 106 private sites among the trees for $17 per vehicle. Facilities include flush toilets, hot water, kitchen shelters, and an interpretive program.

At the end of the road up the Yoho Valley, **Takakkaw Falls Campground** (July–mid-Sept.; $14) is designed for tent campers only. Park at the end of the road and load up the carts with your gear for a pleasant 400-meter (.2-mile) walk along the valley floor. No showers are provided, and the only facilities are pit toilets and picnic tables.

Just below **Lake O'Hara,** alongside the access road, is a delightful little campground surrounded by some of the region's finest hiking. Each of 30 sites has a tent pad, fire pit, and picnic table, while other facilities include pit toilets, two kitchen shelters with woodstoves, and bearproof food caches. Reservations for sites are made in conjunction with the bus trip along the restricted-access road from Highway 1 to Lake O'Hara; for bus information see *Lake O'Hara* under *Sights and Recreation.* Even though access is aboard a bus, you should treat the trip as one into the backcountry; passengers are limited to one large or two small bags, and no coolers or fold-up chairs are permitted on board the shuttle. Camping is $6 per person per night, the bus costs $15 per person round-trip, and the reservation fee is $12 per booking. Make reservations as far in advance as possible.

FOOD

In downtown Field, ⚇ **Truffle Pigs Café** (318 Stephen St., 250/343-6462) is one of those unexpected finds that makes traveling such a joy. It's at the back of a general store, beyond racks of food basics and rental movies, with seating in a section off to the side or outside on a small patio. The best of the breakfast and lunch dishes are described on a massive blackboard, with freshly baked cookies and locally brewed coffee complementing sandwiches made to order from the glass-fronted deli. In the evening this place really shines, with dishes as adventurous as the Spinach Maple Pecan Salad ($11) and as simple as an Albertan-raised buffalo ribeye steak served with a port-based au jus and a baked potato ($25). It's open in summer daily 7:30 A.M.–10 P.M., the rest of the year it's also open daily, but dinner is only served Friday and Saturday.

Across the road, the **Kicking Horse Lodge** (250/343-6303; daily 8 A.M.–11 A.M., noon–2:30 P.M., and 5–9 P.M.) has a small restaurant that has views over the valley floor. It offers a short but varied dinner menu featuring dishes of wide-ranging appeal (including a delicious herb-crusted pork tenderloin smothered in a mango apple chutney) as well as a daily special and a soup of the day, both of which actually are *special.*

Overlooking an arm of Emerald Lake, **Cilantro on the Lake** (250/343-6321; summer only) is a casual café featuring magnificent views from tables inside an open-fronted, log chalet–style building or out on the lakefront deck. The menu is varied—you can sit and sip a coffee or have a full lunch or dinner. Starters—such as thick and creamy corn and potato chowder—are all less than $10, while mains range $22–33 for an extravagantly rich beef tenderloin served with a lobster and mushroom cream sauce. The café is part of the **Emerald Lake Lodge** resort complex, which also includes a more formal but historically attractive dining room where dinner dishes such as grilled caribou with huckleberry sauce ($32) are served daily from 6 P.M. This restaurant is also open year-round for breakfast and lunch, or choose the more casual lounge bar and sink into one of the comfy couches with an abbreviated but still appealing menu.

The final option for park dining is the restaurant at **Cathedral Mountain Chalets** (250/343-6442; mid-May–Sept. daily 7 A.M.– 10 P.M.), a casual, inexpensive restaurant with a charming mountain ambience. Breakfast comprises a healthy buffet spread of fresh fruit, croissants, and home-baked bread, then it's soup and sandwiches through to the evening, when a basic menu of chicken, beef, and seafood is offered.

TRANSPORTATION

Transportation to and around the park is limited. **Greyhound** (403/762-6767) stops in Field daily on its route between Banff and Golden, from where it continues west to Vancouver. **Brewster** (403/762-6767) offers a 3.5-hour tour of the park, departing Lake Louise daily at 12:30 P.M. (summer only). This tour takes in both the Yoho Valley and Emerald Lake. The cost is adult $53, child $26.50. Brewster's Mountain Lakes and Waterfalls Tour is an extended version of the previous tour, combining the best of Banff National Park with a trip over the divide into Yoho. It departs the Banff depot mid-June to early October daily at 8:10 A.M. through summer. The tour takes nine hours and costs $70 per person.

INFORMATION

The main source of information about the park is the **Field Visitor Centre** on the TransCanada Highway at Field (250/343-6783; summer daily 9 A.M.–7 P.M., the rest of the year daily 9 A.M.– 4 P.M.). Inside you'll find helpful staff, information boards, and interpretive panels. This is also the place to pick up backcountry camping permits, buy topographical maps, and find out schedules for campground interpretive programs. For more information, write Yoho National Park, P.O. Box 99, Field, BC V0A 1G0; or surf the Internet to the Parks Canada website (www.pc .gc.ca). For park road conditions, call 403/762-1450; for avalanche reports, call 403/762-1460.

Golden

From the western boundary of Yoho National Park, the TransCanada Highway meanders down the beautiful Kicking Horse River Valley to the town of Golden (pop. 5,500), at the confluence of the Kicking Horse and Columbia Rivers. As well as being a destination in itself, Golden makes a good central base for exploring the region or as an overnight stop on a tour through the Canadian Rockies that takes in the national parks on the western side of the Continental Divide.

Although Golden is an industrial town through and through—with local mines and huge logging operations that include a lumber mill that opened in 1999—it's also gaining a reputation for local outdoor-recreation opportunities, most notably for its new four-season resort and whitewater rafting down the Kicking Horse River.

SIGHTS AND RECREATION

Take Highway 95 off the TransCanada Highway and you'll find yourself in the old section of town, a world away from the commercial strip along the main highway. There's not really much to see in town, although you may want to check out the small museum on 14th Street. The 8.8-km (5.5-mile) **Rotary Loop** is a paved walking and biking trail that leads across the river from downtown via an impressive timber-frame pedestrian bridge, then upstream across Highway 95 (10th Avenue South) to the campground.

The **Columbia River Wetlands** (see *Radium Hot Springs* in the *Kootenay National Park and Vicinity* chapter) extend as far north as Golden. One easily accessible point of the wetlands is **Reflection Lake,** on the southern outskirts of Golden. Here you'll find a small shelter with a telescope for viewing the abundant birdlife.

Ⓜ Kicking Horse Mountain Resort

What was formerly locally owned Whitetooth Ski Area, spread across the lower slopes of the Purcell Mountains (the runs are easily spotted across the valley as you enter town from the east), is currently undergoing a massive redevelopment program slated for completion in 2007. As well as a new name, Kicking Horse Mountain Resort (250/439-5400 or 866/754-5425, www.kickinghorseresort.com) is basically being rebuilt from scratch, with $75 million invested in new lifts, luxurious ski-in hotels, condominiums, restaurants, and other facilities that will make the resort a year-round destination.

The eight-person detachable Golden Eagle Express gondola transports visitors high into the alpine late June through early September in just 18 minutes. The 360-degree panorama at the summit is equal to any other accessible point in the Canadian Rockies, with the Purcell Mountains immediately to the west and the Columbia Valley laid out below. Graded hiking trails lead from the upper terminal through a fragile, treeless environment, while mountain bikers revel in a challenging descent in excess of 1,000 meters (3,280 feet). The resort has also constructed a sanctuary for orphaned grizzly bears—an interesting diversion for visitors that is included in the price of a gondola ride. A single ride is adult $20, senior $17, child $11. A better deal is the lunchtime combo ticket for adult $29, senior $26, child $13. Mountain bikers pay $20 for a single ride or $32 to ride all day. A rent-and-ride package costs $63 for the full day, including a full-suspension bike. The gondola operates through summer Mon.–Thurs. 11 A.M.–8 P.M., Fri.–Sun. 11 A.M.–10 P.M.

With a vertical rise of 1,260 meters (4,130 feet), 50 percent of terrain designated for experts, lots of dry powder snow, and minimal crowds, Kicking Horse has developed a big reputation since opening for the 2000–2001 winter season. In addition to the 3.5-km-long (2.2-mile-long) gondola, other chairlifts transport skiers and boarders to hidden bowls and, as of the 2002–2003 season, to a high point of 2,450 meters (8,040 feet), giving the resort North America's second-highest vertical rise (1,260 meters/4,135 feet). Lifts operate mid-December to early April and tickets are adult $56, senior and child $24.

GOLDEN

To Blaeberry Mountain
Lodge and Revelstoke

GREYHOUND BUS
DEPOT

LEGENDZ DINER

14TH ST N

Hospital Creek

VISITOR INFO CENTRE (SEASONAL)

PONDEROSA
MOTOR INN

COUNTRY GARDEN
RESTAURANT

GOLDEN DONALD UPPER RD

To Golf Course and
KICKING HORSE
MOUNTAIN RESORT

DYKE RD

FISHER RD

9TH ST N

7TH ST N

10TH AVE N

95

To Yoho
National Park

TRANSCANADA HWY

GOLDEN VIEW RD

Columbia River

FOOT BRIDGE

POST
OFFICE

5TH ST S

GOLDEN BAKERY AND DELI

BACCHUS
BOOKS

Kicking Horse River

7TH ST S

9TH ST S

10TH ST S

6TH AVE S

7TH AVE S

8TH AVE S

KICKING HORSE GRILL

GOLDEN
MUNICIPAL
CAMPGROUND

11TH ST S

12TH ST S

13TH ST S

9TH AVE S

10TH AVE S

13TH AVE S

SPRUCE DR

95

VIEWING
SHELTER

★

Reflection
Lake

MOON

SCALE NOT AVAILABLE

To Cedar House Café
and Radium Hot Springs

Yoho National Park

Take a gondola to the top of Kicking Horse Mountain Resort to enjoy the sublime view.

Facilities in the base lodge include rentals, a cafeteria, and a ski school, while the summit restaurant is also open daily for lunch and Friday and Saturday for dinner. To get to Kicking Horse, follow the signs from Highway 1 into town and take 7th Street North west from 10th Avenue North; it's over the Columbia River and 13 km (eight miles) uphill from this intersection.

White-Water Rafting

Anyone looking for white-water-rafting action will want to run the Kicking Horse River. The rafting season runs late May to mid-September, with river levels at their highest in late June. The Lower Canyon, immediately upstream of Golden, offers the biggest thrills, including a three-km (1.9-mile) stretch of continuous rapids. Upstream of here the river is tamer but still makes for an exciting trip, while even farther upstream, near the western boundary of Yoho National Park, it's more of a float—a good adventure for the more timid visitor. The river is run by several companies, most of which offer the option of half-day ($60–80) or full-day ($100–150) trips. The cost varies with inclusions such as transportation from Banff and lunch.

Alpine Rafting (250/344-6778 or 888/599-5299) offers trips ranging from a family-friendly float to the excitement of descending the Lower Canyon. Transportation from Banff, Lake Louise, and Canmore is an extra charge. Other companies include **Wet 'n' Wild Adventures** (250/344-6546 or 800/668-9119), **Glacier Raft Company** (250/344-6521), **Kootenay River Runners** (250/347-9210 or 800/599-4399), **Canadian Rockies Rafting** (403/678-6535 or 877/226-7625), and **Hydra River Guides** (403/762-4554 or 800/644-8888). From Lake Louise, **Wild Water Adventures** (403/522-2211 or 888/647-6444) leads half-day trips down the river for $64, including a narrated bus trip to their purpose-built Day Base put-in point 27 km (17 miles) east of Golden. Departures are from Lake Louise at 8:30 A.M. and 1:30 P.M. The full-day trip is broken up by a riverside lunch.

Other Summertime Recreation

Golden Golf and Country Club (250/344-2700 or 866/727-7222) is a challenging 18-hole course in a forested section of the valley through town and to the north. This course is generally in excellent condition, with water coming into play on many holes—including the signature 11th and 12th holes along Holt Creek—and numerous streams and lakes to catch wayward shots. Greens fees are $60, or there's a $46 twilight rate.

Check out the website of **Golden Mountain Adventures** (www.adventurerockies.com) for the full range of activities available in the valley. This company can also book packages using local operators and accommodations.

Adventurous souls are drawn to Golden for its thermals, perfect for hang-gliding and paragliding, and to the steep face of Jubilee Mountain, a renowned sport-climbing destination. Cowboys descend on town the first weekend of August for **Golden Rodeo Days.**

ACCOMMODATIONS

You can stay in one of the regular motels lining the highway, but don't. Instead choose one of the unique mountain lodgings that surround the town.

$50–100

Blaeberry Mountain Lodge (250/344-5296, www.blaeberrymountainlodge.bc.ca) is on a 62-hectare (150-acre) property among total wilderness. Rooms are in the main lodge or self-contained cabins, with plenty of activities available to guests. Standard rooms with shared bathroom are $75 s or d, and the large cabins, which feature a separate bedroom and full kitchen, are $145. Breakfast and dinner are offered for $12 and $22, respectively. Blaeberry is nine km (5.6 miles) north of Golden along Highway 1, then seven km (4.3 miles) farther north along Moberly School Road.

If you must stay in a motel, and don't want to spend a fortune, choose the distinctive two-story, lime-green **Ponderosa Motor Inn,** on the Trans-Canada by 12th Ave. (250/344-2205 or 800/881-4233, www.ponderosamotorinn.bc.ca), which has 85 older rooms but offers impressive mountain views, a hot tub, a picnic area and gazebo, and a playground, making it a good value at just $78 s, $88 d ($52 s, $60 d outside of summer).

$100–150

The folks that operate the **Cedar House Café** (735 Hefti Rd., 250/344-4679, www.cedarhousecafe.com) have restored an adjacent cabin, infusing a modern feel without losing any of the property's original charm. Sleeping up to four people, the cabin is spacious and comes with a full kitchen, a wood-burning stove, a laundry, and TV/VCR. It costs just $150 per night.

Over $150

Along Highway 1, a 20-minute drive from Golden back toward Yoho National Park, **Kicking Horse River Chalets** (2924 Kicking Horse Rd., 866/502-5171, www.kickinghorseriverchalets.com) comprises luxurious peeled-log cabins, each with full kitchen and dishwasher, wood-burning fireplace, balcony, and loft. The rate is $240 per night for up to four people.

Campgrounds

Continue south through the old part of town over the Kicking Horse River and take 9th Street

South east at the traffic lights to reach **Golden Municipal Campground** (250/344-5412; mid-May–mid-Oct.). It's a quiet place, strung out along the river and two km (1.2 miles) from downtown along a riverfront walkway. Facilities include picnic shelters, hot coin-operated showers, and 70 sites with fire pits. Adjacent is a recreation center with a swimming pool and fitness facility. Unpowered sites are $16, powered sites $18.

Golfers can stay out at the golf course in a specially developed area for $15 per night.

FOOD

Eagle's Eye Restaurant

At an elevation of 2,347 meters (7,700 feet), the **N Eagle's Eye** is the crowning glory of Kicking Horse Mountain Resort (250/439-5400 or 866/754-5425) and is Canada's highest restaurant. Access is by gondola from the resort's base village, 13 km (eight miles) west of downtown Golden. As you'd expect, the views are stunning and are set off by a stylish timber and stonework interior, including a floor-to-ceiling fireplace and a wide wraparound deck protected from the wind by glass paneling. It's open daily at 11 A.M. for a lunch costing adult $29, senior $26, child $13, which includes the gondola ride. Between 7 and 10 P.M. the setting becomes more romantic and the food more adventurous but remains distinctly Canadian. Dinner mains range $25–40 and include such delights as salmon baked in a saffron-vanilla cream and served with strawberry salsa ($28). All evening diners enjoy a complimentary gondola ride. Reservations required.

Cedar House Café & Restaurant

A five-minute drive south of Golden off Highway 95, the **Cedar House Café** (735 Hefti Rd., 250/344-4679; daily 5–10:30 P.M.) is a good choice for wonderfully flavored food that takes advantage of seasonal Canadian produce. The nightly pasta specials are a good deal, or stick to menu choices such as oyster mushroom enchiladas ($18) and green Thai prawn curry ($16). The dining room is in a log building, but on warmer evenings you'll want to be outside on the deck.

Enjoy the view from Canada's highest restaurant, the aptly named Eagle's Eye.

Downtown

Start your day with the locals at the **Golden Bakery & Deli** (419 9th Ave., 250/344-2928; Mon.–Sat. 6:30 A.M.–6 P.M.), where the coffee is always fresh and the faces friendly. Baked goodies include breads, pastries, cakes, and meat pies, with inexpensive daily specials displayed on a blackboard in a seated section off to the side of the main counter.

Constructed of rough-cut logs complete with bulging burls, the **Kicking Horse Grill** (1105 9th St. S, 250/344-2330; daily from 5:30 P.M.) is one of Golden's finest restaurants. The menu changes with the seasons but always offers distinctly international dishes ranging from paella to sushi. All but the beef dishes are less than $20, with generously portioned starter salads ranging $6.50–8.50.

Out on the Highway

All the usual fast-food places line the TransCanada Highway, as well as **Legendz Diner,** on the west side of the highway (250/344-5059). As the name suggests, it's a 1950s-style diner, complete with attentive staff and filling meals from $9. Across the road, the **Country Garden Restaurant** (1002 TransCanada Hwy., 250/344-5971) is a large, casual family-style restaurant with an excellent range of buffets throughout the day, including dinner for $18.

INFORMATION AND SERVICES

While accommodations, fast-food restaurants, and gas stations line the TransCanada Highway, downtown Golden holds other basic services, including the **post office** (502 9th Ave.). Ninth Avenue also holds outdoor equipment shops and **Baccus Books** (407 9th Ave., 250/344-5600; Mon.–Sat. 10 A.M.–6 P.M.), offering a wide selection of new and used books, with plenty of local reading and detailed maps of the Columbia Valley.

Transportation

Greyhound buses stop four times daily in Golden, utilizing an ATCO trailer tucked away beside the Esso gas station as a depot (250/344-6172). For a cab, call **Mount Seven Taxi** (250/344-5237).

Information

The year-round **Golden Visitor Info Centre** is in the old railway station building (500 10th Ave., 250/344-7125 or 800/622-4653, www.tourismgolden.com; weekdays 8:30 A.M.–4:30 P.M.). Back out on the highway is a seasonal information center (summer daily 9 A.M.–5 P.M.) in a converted gas station beside the Ponderosa Motor Inn. In addition to all the regular brochure racks, it has public Internet access and a handy map of local bike trails.

Yoho National Park

Jasper National Park

*Note: Please see color map of **Jasper National Park** on pages vi-vii.*

Snowcapped peaks, vast icefields, beautiful glacial lakes, soothing hot springs, thundering rivers, and the most extensive backcountry trail system of any Canadian national park make Jasper a stunning counterpart to its sister park, Banff. Lying on the Albertan side of the Canadian Rockies, Jasper protects the entire upper watershed of the Athabasca River, extending to the Columbia Icefield (and Banff National Park) in the south. To the east are the foothills, to the west the Continental Divide (which marks the Alberta–British Columbia border) and Mount Robson Provincial Park. Encompassing 10,900 square km (4,208 square miles), Jasper is a haven for wildlife; much of its wilderness is traveled only by wolves and grizzlies.

The park's most spectacular natural landmarks can be admired from two major roads.

Must-Sees

Look for **M** to find the sights and activities you can't miss and **⅄** for the best dining and lodging.

M Columbia Icefield: Don't miss this glacial area at the southern end of Jasper National Park. Take the Ice Explorer tour to get a close-up view of this natural wonder (page 196).

M Wilcox Pass: Escape the crowds lingering around the Icefield Centre on this hike, where the panorama of the Columbia Icefield is laid out in all its glory (page 200).

M Mount Edith Cavell: Although this peak is visible from various points within the park, no vantage point is as memorable as that from its base, reachable by road from Highway 93A (page 206). For a neck-straining view, take the **Cavell Meadows** Trail (page 211).

M Maligne Canyon: Easy access makes this attraction extremely popular. Visit before 9 A.M. to miss the tour bus crowd (page 207).

Mount Edith Cavell

M Maligne Lake: The most famous body of water in Jasper National Park. And for good reason— it's simply stunning. Take a tour boat to **Spirit Island** (page 208) or hike the **Lake Trail (Mary Schäffer Loop)** along the lake's eastern shore (page 213).

M Astoria River/Tonquin Valley: A trail up the Astoria River leads to the Tonquin Valley, one of the park's most spectacular sights. If you aren't equipped for backcountry camping, consider riding in on horseback and staying at one of two wilderness lodges (page 212).

M Opal Hills: The vast majority of visitors to Maligne Lake area don't travel past the lake's shoreline. Go beyond the ordinary on this trail, which provides stunning views of the whole Maligne Valley from alpine meadows (page 213).

The **Yellowhead Highway** runs east–west from Edmonton to British Columbia through the park. The **Icefields Parkway,** regarded as one of the world's great mountain drives, runs north–south, connecting Jasper to Banff. At the junction of these two highways is the park's main service center—the town of **Jasper.** With half the population of Banff, its setting—at the confluence of the Athabasca and Miette Rivers, surrounded by rugged, snowcapped peaks—is a little less dramatic, though still beautiful. But the town is also less commercialized than Banff and its streets a little quieter—a major plus for those looking to get away from it all.

Many of the park's campgrounds are accessible by road, while others dot the backcountry. Hiking is the number one attraction, but fishing, boating, downhill skiing and snowboarding, golfing, horseback riding, and white-water rafting are also popular. The park is open year-round, although road closures do occur on the Icefields Parkway during winter months due to avalanche-control work and snowstorms.

PLANNING YOUR TIME

It's a cliché, but backcountry enthusiasts could spend a full summer exploring Jasper and still not see everything. If you're planning to visit Jasper, I'm assuming you *do* enjoy the outdoors—hiking, fishing, watching wildlife, and the like—but maybe not with a backpack full of provisions strapped to your back. Keeping this in mind, I'd recommend spending four days in the park. The best choices for accommodations are the summer-only cabin complexes, so book for three nights and spend your days exploring natural attractions such as **Mount Edith Cavell** and **Maligne Lake.** If you're traveling up from Lake Louise, plan on spending the first day along the **Icefields Parkway,** arriving at **Columbia Icefield** before the crowds. If your time in Jasper is limited to two days and one night, you should have enough time to visit each of the natural attractions I mark as must-see sights, walk a couple of the shorter trails, and even squeeze in a rafting trip or golf game.

Jasper is delightful in winter. You can spend your time doing all the same activities as in Banff, but without the pizzazz of Banff Avenue and the crowds of Lake Louise and Sunshine Village ski resorts. Most of the wintertime action revolves around skiing and boarding at **Marmot Basin,** but you can also try cross-country skiing or snowshoeing, walk through an ice canyon, and take a sleigh ride. In the evening, you can kick back in front a roaring fire knowing that you're paying a lot less for lodging than you would be in Banff.

THE LAND

Although the peaks of Jasper National Park are not particularly high, they are among the most spectacular along the range's entire length. About 100 million years ago, layers of sedimentary rock—laid down here up to a billion years ago—were forced upward, folded, and twisted under tremendous pressure into the mountains seen today. The land's contours were further altered during four ice ages that began around one million years ago. The last ice age ended about 10,000 years ago, and the vast glaciers began to retreat. A remnant of this final sheet of ice is the huge Columbia Icefield; covering approximately 325 square km (125 square miles) and up to 400 meters (1,300 feet) deep, it's the most extensive icefield in the Rocky Mountains. As the glaciers retreated, piles of rock melted out and were left behind. Meltwater from the glaciers flowed down the valleys and was dammed up behind the moraines. **Maligne Lake,** like many other lakes in the park, was created by this process. The glacial silt suspended in the lake's waters produces amazing emerald, turquoise, and amethyst colors; early artists who painted these lakes had trouble convincing people that their images were real.

In addition to creating the park's gemlike lakes, the retreating glaciers carved out the valleys that they ever-so-slowly flowed through. The Athabasca River Valley is the park's largest watershed, a typical example of a U-shaped, glacier-carved valley. The Athabasca River flows north through the valley into the Mackenzie

PARK ENTRY

Permits are required for entry into the park. A **National Parks Day Pass** is adult $7, senior $6, child $3.50 up to a maximum of $14 per vehicle ($12 for seniors). It can also be used in neighboring Banff National Park if you're traveling down the Icefields Parkway and is valid until 4 P.M. the day following its purchase. An annual **National Parks of Canada Pass**—good for entry into all of Canada's national parks—is $45 adults and $38 seniors up to a maximum of $89 per vehicle.

Both types of pass can be purchased at the park information center, at the booth along the Icefields Parkway a few kilometers south of the town of Jasper, and at campground kiosks. If you're traveling north along the Icefields Parkway, you'll be required to stop and purchase a park pass just beyond Lake Louise. The Parks Canada website (www.pc.gc.ca) has detailed pass information.

River System and ultimately into the Arctic Ocean. The glacial silt that paints the park's lakes is also carried down streams into the Athabasca, giving the river a pale-green milky look. Another beautiful aspect of the park's scenery is its abundance of waterfalls. They vary from the sparkling tumble of Punchbowl Falls, where Mountain Creek cascades down a limestone cliff into a picturesque pool, to the roar of Athabasca Falls, where the Athabasca River is forced through a narrow gorge.

FLORA

Elevations in the park range from 980 meters (3,215 feet) to more than 3,700 meters (12,140 feet). That makes for a wide range of resident plant life. Only a small part of the park lies in the montane zone. It is characterized by stands of **Douglas fir** (at its northern limit) and **lodgepole pine**, while **balsam poplar, white birch,** and **spruce** also occur. Savanna-like grasslands occur on drier sites in valley bottoms. Well-developed stretches of montane can be found along

the floors of the Athabasca and Miette River Valleys, providing winter habitat for larger mammals such as elk.

The subalpine zone, heavily forested with evergreens, extends from the lower valley slopes up to the tree line at an elevation of around 2,200 meters (7,220 feet). The subalpine occupies 40 percent of the park's area. The dominant species in this zone is lodgepole pine, although **Engelmann spruce, subalpine fir, poplar,** and **aspen** also grow here. The park's extensive stands of lodgepole pine are inhabited by few large mammals because the understory is minimal. Wildflowers are common in this zone and can be found by the roadside, in clearings, or on riverbanks.

Timberline here lies at an elevation of 2,050–2,400 meters (6,275–7,870 feet) above sea level. Above this elevation is the alpine zone, where the climate is severe (the average yearly temperature is below freezing), summer is brief, and only a few stunted trees survive. The zone's plant species grow low to the ground, with extensive root systems to protect them during high winds and through the deep snow cover of winter. During the short summer, these open slopes and meadows are carpeted with a profusion of flowers such as **golden arnicas, bluebells, pale columbines,** and red and yellow **paintbrush**. Higher still are brightly colored **heather, buttercups,** and **alpine forget-me-nots.**

FAUNA

Wildlife is abundant in the park and can be seen throughout the year. During winter many larger mammals move to lower elevations where food is accessible. February and March are particularly good for looking for animal tracks in the snow. By June, most of the snow cover at lower elevations has melted, the crowds haven't arrived, and animals can be seen feeding along the valley floor. In fall, tourists move to warmer climates, the rutting season begins, bears go into hibernation, and a herd of elk moves into downtown Jasper for the winter.

While the park provides ample opportunities for seeing numerous animals in their natural habitat, it also leads to human-animal encounters that are not always positive. For example, less than 10 percent of the park is made up of well-vegetated valleys. These lower areas are essential to the larger mammals for food and shelter but are also the most heavily traveled by visitors. Game trails used for thousands of years are often bisected by roads, and hundreds of animals are killed each year by speeding motorists. Please drive slowly in the park.

Campground Critters

Several species of small mammals thrive around campgrounds, thanks to an abundance of humans who are careless with their food. **Columbian ground squirrels** are bold and will demand scraps of your lunch. **Golden-mantled ground squirrels** and **red squirrels** are also common. The **least chipmunk** (often confused with the golden-mantled ground squirrel thanks to similar stripes) can also be seen in campgrounds; they'll often scamper across your hiking trail then sit boldly on a rock waiting for you to pass.

Aquatic Species

Beavers are common between the town of Jasper and the park's east gate. Dawn and dusk are the best times to watch these intriguing creatures at work. Wabasso Lake, a 2.6-km (1.6-mile) hike from the Icefields Parkway, was created by beavers; their impressive dam has completely blocked the flow of Wabasso Creek. Also common in the park's wetlands are **mink** and **muskrat;** search out these creatures around the lakes on the benchland north of the town of Jasper.

Ungulates

Five species of deer inhabit the park. The large-eared **mule deer** is commonly seen around the edge of the town or grazing along the north end of the Icefields Parkway. **White-tailed deer** can be seen throughout the park. A small herd of **woodland caribou** roams throughout the park; they are most commonly seen during late spring, feeding in river deltas. The town of Jasper is in the home range of about 500 **elk,** which can be seen most of the year around town or along the high-way northeast and south of town. **Moose,** although numbering fewer than 100 in all of Jasper, can occasionally be seen feeding on aquatic plants along the major drainage systems.

In summer, **mountain goats** browse in alpine meadows. A good place for goat watching is Goat Lookout on the Icefields Parkway. Unlike most of the park's large mammals, these sure-footed creatures don't migrate to lower elevations in winter, but stay sheltered on rocky crags where wind and sun keep the vegetation snow-free. Often confused with the goat is the darker **bighorn sheep.** The horns on the males of this species are thick and often curl 360 degrees. Bighorns are common in the east of the park at Disaster Point and will often approach cars. An estimated 2,500 bighorn reside in the park.

Bears

Numbering around 80 within Jasper National Park, **black bears** are widespread and occasionally wander into campgrounds looking for food. They are most commonly seen along the Icefields Parkway in spring, when they first come out of hibernation. **Grizzly bears** are occasionally seen crossing the Icefields Parkway at higher elevations early in summer. For the most part they remain in remote mountain valleys, and if they do see, smell, or hear you, they'll generally move away. Read *Keep the Wild in Wildlife* before setting out into the woods; the pamphlet is available at information centers throughout the park.

Reclusive Residents

Several of the park's resident species keep a low profile, usually out of sight of humans. Populations of the shy and elusive **lynx** fluctuate with that of their primary food source, the snowshoe hare. The largest of the big cats in the park is the **cougar** (also called the mountain lion), a solitary carnivore that inhabits remote valleys. Jasper's **wolves** are one of the park's success stories. After being driven to near extinction, the species has rebounded. Five packs now roam the park, but they keep to the deep wilderness rarely traveled by people. While not common in the park, **coyotes** can be seen in cleared areas alongside the roads, usually at dawn and dusk.

Other Mammals

The **pine marten** is common but shy; look for them in subalpine forests. The **short-tailed weasel**—a relative of the marten—is also common, while the **long-tailed weasel** is rare. At higher elevations look for **pikas** in piles of fallen rock. **Hoary marmots** live near the upper limits of vegetation growth, where their shrill warning whistles carry across the open meadows; The Whistlers area, accessed by tramway, supports a healthy population of these noisy creatures.

Birds

The extensive tree cover in the lower valleys hides many species of birds, making them seem less abundant than they are; 248 species have been recorded. The two you're most likely to see are the **gray jay** and **Clark's nutcracker,** which regularly joins picnickers for lunch. Also common are black-and-white **magpies,** raucous **ravens,** and several species of **ducks,** which can be seen around lakes in the Athabasca River Valley. Harlequin ducks nest in the park during early summer. A stretch of the Maligne River is closed during this season to prevent human interference.

The colony of **black swifts** in Maligne Canyon is one of only two in Alberta. Their poorly developed legs make it difficult for them to take off from their nests in the canyon walls—they literally fall before becoming airborne. High alpine slopes are home to **white-tailed ptarmigan,** a type of grouse that turns white in winter. Also at this elevation are flocks of **rosy finches** that live under overhanging cliffs. In subalpine forests the songs of **thrushes** and the tapping of **woodpeckers** can be heard.

At dusk, **great horned owls** swoop silently through the trees, their eerie call echoing through the forest. **Golden eagles** and **bald eagles** can be seen soaring high above the forests, and 15 pairs of **ospreys** are known to nest in the park, many along the Athabasca River between town and the east park gate.

HISTORY

In the summer of 1810, David Thompson, one of Canada's greatest explorers, became the first white man to enter the Athabasca River Valley. The following winter, when Thompson was mak-

White-tailed ptarmigan inhabit alpine meadows throughout Jasper National Park.

MARY SCHÄFFER

In the early 1900s, exploration of mountain wilderness areas was considered a man's pursuit; however, one spirited and tenacious woman entered that domain and went on to explore areas of the Canadian Rockies that no white man ever had.

Mary Sharples was born in 1861 in Pennsylvania and raised in a strict Quaker family. She was introduced to Dr. Charles Schäffer on a trip to the Rockies, and in 1889 they were married. His interest in botany drew them back to the Rockies, where Charles collected, documented, and photographed specimens until his death in 1903. Mary also became apt at these skills. After hearing Sir James Hector (the geologist on the Palliser Expedition) reciting tales of the mountains, her zest to explore the wilderness returned. In 1908, Mary, guide Billy Warren, and a small party set out for a lake that no white man had ever seen but that the Stoney Indians knew as Chaba Imne (Beaver Lake). After initial difficulties, they succeeded in finding the elusive body of water now known as Maligne Lake. In Mary's words, "There burst upon us . . . the finest view any of us have ever beheld in the Rockies." In 1915 Mary married Billy Warren, continuing to explore the mountains until her death in 1939. Her success as a photographer, artist, and writer were equal to any of her male counterparts, but she is best remembered for her unwavering love of the Canadian Rockies—her "heaven of the hills."

---

ing the first successful crossing of the Continental Divide, some of his party remained in the Athabasca River Valley and constructed a small supply depot east of the present town. The depot grew into a small trading post named Henry House and was used for many years by the North West Company. Other trading posts were built along the Athabasca River, including one that became known as Jasper's House, for the clerk Jasper Hawse. This particular post was first established in 1813, then moved to the outlet of Jasper Lake in 1829.

By 1865, with the fur trade over and the Cariboo goldfields emptying along routes easier than over Yellowhead Pass, the Athabasca River Valley had no permanent residents. One prospector who did return over Yellowhead Pass was Lewis Swift, who in 1892 made his home in the abandoned buildings of Jasper's House, farming a small plot of land beside the Athabasca River. "Old Swift" became known to everyone, providing fresh food and accommodations for travelers and generating many legendary tales, such as the day he held the Grand Trunk Pacific Railway at gunpoint until they agreed to reroute the line away from his property.

In 1907, aware that the coming of the railway would mean an influx of settlers, the federal government set aside 13,000 square km (5,000 square miles) as Jasper Forest Park, buying all the land, save for the parcel owned by Lewis Swift. A handful of homesteaders continued to live in the valley, but the land on which they lived was leased. The threat of oversettlement of the valley had been abated, but as a designated forest park, mining and logging were still allowed.

Mining and a Link to the Outside World

In 1908, Jasper Park Collieries staked claims in the park. By the time the railway came through in 1911, mining activity was centered at Pocahontas (near the park's east gate), where a township was established and thrived. During an extended miners' strike, the men spent their spare time constructing log pools at Miette Hot Springs, which were heavily promoted to early park visitors. The mine closed in 1921 and many families relocated to Jasper, which had grown from a railway camp into a popular tourist destination. By this time the park boundaries had changed dramatically. In 1911, the park had been reduced to two-thirds its original size, then in 1914 enlarged to include Maligne Lake and Columbia Icefield, then enlarged yet again in 1928 to take in Sunwapta Pass. Today's borders were set in 1930, when Jasper was officially designated a national park.

And what of Old Swift? Well, after working as the park's first game warden for four years, he hung onto his land until 1935. The government of the day made various offers, but Swift ended up selling to a wealthy Englishman who operated a dude ranch on the site until finally selling the land to the government in 1962.

Jasper Grows

In 1911, a construction camp was established for the Grand Trunk Pacific Railway near the present site of downtown Jasper. When the northern line was completed, visitors flocked into the remote mountain settlement, and its future was assured. The first accommodation for tourists was 10 tents on the shore of Lac Beauvert that became known as Jasper Park Camp. In 1921, the tents were replaced and the original Jasper Park Lodge was constructed. By the summer of 1928, a road was completed from Edmonton and a golf course was built. As the number of tourists to the park continued to increase, existing facilities were expanded. In 1940 the Icefields Parkway opened, linking Jasper to Banff and making the park more accessible.

Town of Jasper

The modern infrastructure of Jasper began developing in the 1960s, but until 2002 the townsite was run from Ottawa by Parks Canada. Jasper is now officially incorporated as a "town," with locally elected residents serving as mayor and council members. Decisions made by the council must still balance the needs of living in a national park, but also represent locals who call the park home. On the surface, obvious visible changes of this autonomy are a new emergency services building, a new wastewater treatment plant, and improvements to an ever-increasing downtown parking problem. One thing hasn't changed, and that's the basic premise of the town's existence: more than 50 percent of Jasper's 5,200 residents work in the hospitality industry, serving the needs of two million visitors annually.

Icefields Parkway–Jasper

Sunwapta Pass (2,040 meters/6,690 feet), four km (2.5 miles) south of the Columbia Icefield, marks the boundary between Banff and Jasper National Parks.

The following sights along the Icefields Parkway are detailed from south to north, from the Icefield Centre to the town of Jasper, a distance of 105 km (65 miles). The scenery along this stretch of road is no less spectacular than the other half through Banff National Park, and it's easy to spend at least a full day en route.

No gas is available along this stretch of the Icefields Parkway. The nearest gas stations are at Saskatchewan River Crossing (Banff National Park) and in the town of Jasper, 150 km (93 miles) apart, so keep your tank topped up to be safe.

M COLUMBIA ICEFIELD

The largest and most accessible of 17 glacial areas along the Icefields Parkway is 325-square-km (125-square-mile) Columbia Icefield, beside the Icefields Parkway at the south end of the park, 105 km (65 miles) south from Jasper and 132 km (82 miles) north from Lake Louise. It's a remnant of the last major glaciation that covered most of Canada 20,000 years ago, and it has survived because of its elevation at 1,900–2,800 meters (6,230–9,190 feet) above sea level, cold temperatures, and heavy snowfalls. From the main body of the ice cap, which sits astride the Continental Divide, six glaciers creep down three main valleys. Of these, **Athabasca Glacier** is the most accessible and can be seen from the Icefields Parkway; it is one of the world's few glaciers that you can drive right up to. It is an impressive 600 hectares (1,480 acres) in area and up to 100 meters (330 feet) deep. The speed at which glaciers advance and retreat varies with the long-term climate. Athabasca Glacier has retreated to its current position from across the highway, a distance of more than 1.6 km (one mile) in a little more than 100 years. Currently it retreats up to two meters (six feet) per year. The rubble between

COLUMBIA ICEFIELD

the toe of Athabasca Glacier and the highway is a mixture of rock, sand, and gravel known as *till,* deposited by the glacier as it retreats.

The icefield is made more spectacular by the impressive peaks that surround it. **Mount Athabasca** (3,491 meters/11,450 feet) dominates the skyline, and three glaciers cling to its flanks. **Dome Glacier** is also visible from the highway; although part of Columbia Icefield, it is not actually connected. Instead it is made of ice that breaks off the icefield 300 meters (980 feet) above, supplemented by large quantities of snow each winter.

Exploring the Icefield

From the Icefields Parkway, an unpaved road leads down through piles of till left by the re-

treating Athabasca Glacier to a parking area beside Sunwapta Lake. An interesting alternative is to leave your vehicle beside the highway and take the 1.6-km (one-mile) hiking trail through the lunarlike landscape to the parking area. From this point, a short path leads up to the toe of the glacier. (Along the access road, look for the small markers showing how far the toe of the glacier reached in years gone by; the farthest marker is across the highway beside the stairs leading up to the Icefield Centre.)

The icefield can be dangerous for unprepared visitors. Like all glaciers, the broken surface of the Athabasca is especially hazardous because snow bridges can hide its deep crevasses. The crevasses are uncovered as the winter snows

© ANDREW HEMPSTEAD

along the Icefields Parkway

melt. The safest way to experience the glacier firsthand is on specially developed vehicles with balloon tires that can travel over the crevassed surface. The Ice Explorers are operated by **Brewster** (780/852-3332, www.brewster.ca). The 90-minute tour of Athabasca Glacier includes time spent walking on the surface of the glacier. The tour, which begins with a bus ride from the Icefield Centre, costs $30 adults, $15 children, and operates from mid-April to mid-October 9 A.M.–5 P.M. (try to plan your tour for before 10 A.M. or after 3 P.M., after the tour buses have departed for the day). The ticketing office is on the main floor of the Icefield Centre (no reservations are taken), with the surrounding area resembling an airport departure lounge—check the television screens for departure times and ensure you make your way to the correct gate. Early in the season the glacier is still covered in a layer of snow and is therefore not as spectacular as during the summer. If you're in Banff or Jasper without transportation, consider Brewster's day trip to the Columbia Icefield, which lasts 10 hours and costs $98 per person, excluding Ice Explorer (eight hours and $91 from Lake Louise).

Icefield Centre

The magnificent Icefield Centre, which opened in summer 1996, is nestled at the base of Mount Wilcox, overlooking the Athabasca Glacier. Costing more than $16 million, the building is as environmentally friendly as possible: lights work on motion sensors to reduce electricity, some water is reused, suppliers must take their packaging with them after deliveries, and the entire building freezes in winter.

The center is the staging point for Ice Explorer tours, but before heading out onto the icefield, don't miss the **Glacier Gallery** on the lower floor. This large display area details all aspects of the frozen world, including the story of glacier formation and movement. The centerpiece is a scaled-down fiberglass model of the Athabasca Glacier, which is surrounded by hands-on displays and audiovisual presentations.

Back on the main floor of the center you'll find a Parks Canada desk (780/852-6288)—a good source of information for northbound visitors—Ice Explorer ticketing desk, restrooms, and the obligatory gift shop.

Upstairs you'll find the cavernous **Columbia Café,** with snacks and hot drinks to go on the right and an overpriced cafeteria-style restaurant to the left. Both are open daily 9 A.M.–6 P.M. Across the hallway is the **Glacier Dining Room,** open daily 7–10 A.M. for a breakfast buffet, reopening 6–9:30 P.M. for ordinary Chinese-Canadian fare (mains range $17–30). The only redeeming feature of these dining options has nothing to do with the food—the view from both inside and out on the massive deck is stupendous. (For northbound travelers, my advice is to pick up lunch at Laggan's Mountain Bakery in Lake Louise.)

The Icefield Centre also holds a limited number of hotel rooms. Check-in is on the main level, and details can be found in the *Accommodations* section.

The entire Icefield Centre closes down for the winter in mid-October, reopening the following year in mid-April. During summer, the complex (including display area) is open daily 9 A.M.–11 P.M. with reduced hours outside of July and August.

COLUMBIA ICEFIELD TO THE TOWN OF JASPER

Sunwapta Lake, at the toe of the Athabasca Glacier, is the source of the **Sunwapta River,** which the Icefields Parkway follows for 48 km (30 miles) to Sunwapta Falls.

Immediately north of Icefield Centre is an unheralded pullout that few travelers stop at, but that allows for an excellent panorama of the area away from the crowds. Across the glacial-green Sunwapta River is a wasteland of till and a distinctive terminal moraine left behind by the retreating **Dome Glacier.** Between the Dome and Athabasca glaciers is 3,459-meter (11,350-foot) **Snow Dome.**

Eight km (five miles) north from the Icefield Centre, the road descends to a viewpoint for **Stutfield Glacier.** Most of the glacier is hidden from view by a densely wooded ridge, but the valley floor below its toe is littered with till left by the glacier's retreat. The main body of the Columbia Icefield can be seen along the clifftop high above, and south of the glacier you can see Mount Kitchener.

Six km (3.7 miles) farther down the road is **Tangle Ridge,** a grayish-brown wall of limestone over which Beauty Creek cascades. At this point the Icefields Parkway runs alongside the Sunwapta River, following its braided course through the **Endless Range,** the eastern wall of a classic glacier-carved valley.

Sunwapta Falls

A further 41 km (25 miles) along the road a 500-meter (.3-mile) spur at Sunwapta Falls Resort leads to Sunwapta Falls. Here the Sunwapta River changes direction sharply and drops into a deep canyon. The best viewpoint is from the bridge across the river, but it's also worth following the path on the parking lot side of the river downstream along the rim of the canyon. Two km (1.2 miles) farther downstream the river flows into the much-wider Athabasca Valley.

Goat Lookout

After following the Athabasca River for 17 km (11 miles), the road ascends to a lookout with picnic tables offering panoramic river views. Below the lookout is a steep bank of exposed glacially ground material containing natural deposits of salt. The local mountain goats spend most of their time on the steep slopes of Mount Kerkeslin, to the northeast, but occasionally cross the road and can be seen searching for the salt licks along the riverbank, trying to replenish lost nutrients.

Athabasca Falls

Nine kilometers (5.6 miles) beyond Goat Lookout and 32 km (20 miles) south of Jasper, the Icefields Parkway divides when an old stretch of highway (Highway 93A) crosses the Athabasca River and continues along its west side for 25 km (15.5 miles) before rejoining the Parkway seven km (4.3 miles) south of the town. At the southern end of this loop, the Athabasca River is forced through a narrow gorge and over a cliff into a cauldron of roaring water below. As the river slowly erodes the center of the riverbed, the falls will move upstream. Trails lead from a day-use area to various viewpoints above and below the falls. The trail branching under Highway 93A follows an abandoned river channel before emerging at the bottom of the canyon. Facilities at Athabasca Falls include picnic tables and toilets.

Continuing North to Jasper

Take Highway 93A beyond Athabasca Falls to reach Mount Edith Cavell, or continue north along the Icefields Parkway to access the following sights. The first worthwhile stop along this route is **Horseshoe Lake,** reached along a 350-meter (.2-mile) trail from a parking lot three km (1.9 miles) north of Athabasca Falls. The southern end of this delightful little body of water is ringed by a band of cliffs (popular with locals in summer as a cliff-diving spot), but many private (unofficial) picnic spots line its western shoreline.

Two km (1.2 miles) north of the Horseshoe Lake parking lot are a couple of lookouts with spectacular views across the Athabasca River to **Athabasca Pass,** used by David Thompson on his historic expedition across the continent. To the north of the pass lies Mount Edith Cavell. From this lookout it is 26 km (16 miles) to the town of Jasper.

HIKES ALONG ICEFIELDS PARKWAY

For those who aren't comfortable hiking in remote areas, the trails branching off the Icefields Parkway can be somewhat intimidating. If that sounds like you, consider one of the shorter walks not detailed below, such as to Horseshoe Lake (see *Continuing North to Jasper*).

Ⓜ Wilcox Pass

- Length: 4 km/2.5 miles (90 minutes) one-way
- Elevation gain: 340 meters/1,115 feet
- Rating: moderate
- Trailhead: Wilcox Creek Campground, three km (1.9 miles) south of the Icefield Centre

Views of the Columbia Icefield from the Icefields Parkway pale in comparison with those achieved along this trail on the same side of the valley as the Columbia Icefield Centre. This trail was once used by northbound outfitters because,

100 years ago, Athabasca Glacier covered the valley floor and had to be bypassed. Beginning from the north side of Wilcox Creek Campground, the trail climbs through a stunted forest of Engelmann spruce and subalpine fir to a ridge with panoramic views of the valley, Columbia Icefield, and surrounding peaks. Ascending gradually from there, the trail enters a fragile environment of alpine meadows. From the pass, most hikers return along the same trail (the distance quoted), although it is possible to continue north, descending to the Icefields Parkway at Tangle Ridge, 11.5 km (7.1 miles) along the road from the trailhead.

Fortress Lake

- Length: 24 km/15 miles (7–8 hours) one-way
- Elevation gain: minimal
- Rating: moderate
- Trailhead: Sunwapta Falls, 58 km (36 miles) south of the town of Jasper

The trail to this seldom-visited lake straddling the Continental Divide gains little elevation, making it popular with mountain-bike riders experienced in backcountry travel. After crossing the canyon below Sunwapta Falls, the trail meanders along the east bank of the Athabasca River for 15 km (9.3 miles), then crosses it. Beyond the main bridge you'll need to ford the braided Chaba River, then continue southwest along the river flats for six km (3.7 miles) to the east end of Fortress Lake. The lake lies within British Columbia in **Hamber Provincial Park.** Its shores are difficult to traverse because they lack established trails. At the end of the trail, **Fortress Lake Wilderness Retreat** (250/344-2639, www.fortresslake.com) provides cabin accommodations, mostly for anglers who fly in by helicopter from Golden, but hikers are also welcomed.

Geraldine Lakes

- Length: 5 km/3.1 miles (two hours) one-way
- Elevation gain: 410 meters/1,350 feet
- Rating: moderate
- Trailhead: Geraldine Fire Road, off Highway 93A one km (.6 mile) from Athabasca Falls

HIKING IN JASPER NATIONAL PARK

The 1,200 km (745 miles) of hiking trails in Jasper are significantly different from those in the other mountain national parks. The park has an extensive system of interconnecting backcountry trails that, for experienced hikers, can provide a wilderness adventure rivaled by few areas on the face of the earth. For casual day hikers, on the other hand, opportunities are more limited.

Most trails in the immediate vicinity of the town have little elevation gain and lead through montane forest to lakes. The trails around Maligne Lake, at the base of Mount Edith Cavell, and along the Icefields Parkway have more rewarding objectives and are more challenging. These are covered in detail throughout the chapter. The most popular trails for extended backcountry trips are the **Skyline Trail,** between Maligne Lake Road and Maligne Lake (44.5 km/27.6 miles, three days each way); the trails to **Amethyst Lakes** in the Tonquin Valley (19 km/11.8 miles, one day each way) and **Athabasca Pass** (50 km/31 miles, three days each way), which was used by fur traders for 40 years as the main route across the Canadian Rockies; and the **South Boundary Trail,** which traverses a remote section of the front ranges into Banff National Park (160 km/100 miles, 10 days each way).

Before setting off on any hikes, whatever the length, go to the **park information center** in downtown Jasper or the Parks Canada desk in the Icefield Centre along the Icefields Parkway for trail maps, trail conditions, and trail closures.

The first of the four Geraldine Lakes is an easy two-km (1.2-mile) hike from the end of the 5.5-km (3.4-mile) Geraldine Fire Road. The forest-encircled lake reflects the north face of Mount Fryatt (3,361 meters/11,030 feet). The trail continues along the northwest shore, climbs steeply past a scenic 100-meter-high (330-foot-high) waterfall, and traverses some rough terrain where the trail becomes indistinct; follow the cairns. At the end of the valley is another waterfall. The trail climbs east of the waterfall to a ridge above the second of the lakes, five km (3.1 miles) from the trailhead. Although the trail officially ends here, it does continue to a campground at the south end of the lake. Two other lakes, accessible only by bush bashing, are farther up the valley.

Valley of the Five Lakes

- Length: 2.3 km/1.4 miles (40 minutes) one-way
- Elevation gain: 60 meters/200 feet
- Rating: easy
- Trailhead: Icefields Parkway, 10 km (6.2 miles) south of the town of Jasper

These lakes, nestled in an open valley, are small but make a worthwhile destination. From the trailhead, 10 km (6.2 miles) south of town along the Icefields Parkway, the trail passes through a forest of lodgepole pine, crosses a stream, and climbs a ridge from where you'll have a panoramic view of surrounding peaks. As the trail descends to the lakes, turn left at the first intersection to a point between two of the lakes. These lakes are linked to Old Fort Point by a tedious 10-km (6.2-mile) trail through montane forest.

ICEFIELDS PARKWAY ACCOMMODATIONS

The two lodges and two hostels along the parkway proper are covered in this section. The several accommodations along the Icefields Parkway but within close proximity to the town of Jasper are detailed under the *Town of Jasper* section.

Under $50

Reservations for the two hostels can be made by contacting Hostelling International (780/852-3215, www.hihostels.ca). At both facilities, check-in is 5–11 P.M., but the main lodges are open all day.

Beauty Creek Hostel, 17 km (10.5 miles) north of Columbia Icefield and 144 km (90 miles) north from Lake Louise, is nestled in a small stand of Douglas fir between the Icefields

Parkway and the Sunwapta River. Each of its separate male and female cabins sleeps 12 and has a woodstove. A third building holds a well-equipped kitchen and dining area. Members $12, nonmembers $17. Open May–September.

Farther north is **Athabasca Falls Hostel,** 32 km (20 miles) south of the town Jasper and 198 km (123 miles) north from Lake Louise. It is larger than the one at Beauty Creek and has electricity. Athabasca Falls is only a few minutes' walk away. Members of Hostelling International pay $13, nonmembers $18. It's closed on Tuesday night October–April.

$150–200

Historic **Sunwapta Falls Resort** (780/852-4852 or 888/828-5777, www.sunwapta.com; May–mid-Oct.) is 55 km (34 miles) south of the town of Jasper and within walking distance of the picturesque waterfall for which it is named. It features 52 motel-like units, with either two queen beds or one queen bed and a fireplace; some have balconies. Rates are $179–199 s or d, reduced to $100 outside of the busy July to mid-September period. In the main lodge is a lunchtime self-serve restaurant popular with passing travelers. In the evening this same room is transformed into the Endless Chain Restaurant, featuring simply prepared Canadian game and seafood in the $18–26 range and a delectable wild berry crumble for $6.

Columbia Icefield Chalet (780/852-6550 or 877/423-7433, www.brewster.ca; May–Sept.), the top story of Columbia Icefield Centre, lies in a stunning location high above the tree line and overlooking the Columbia Icefield, 105 km (65 miles) south of the town of Jasper and 132 km (82 miles) north of Lake Louise. It features 29 standard rooms, 17 of which have glacier views, and three larger, more luxurious corner rooms. All

units have satellite TV and phones. Rates June to mid-September range $185–205 s or d, while the last week of May and the first few days in October, rates start at $110. (For the view alone, the more expensive rooms are well worth the extra $20.) Because of the remote location, dining options are limited to the in-house café and restaurant. The **Glacier Dining Room** opens daily at 7 A.M. for a breakfast buffet, reopening 6–9:30 P.M. for dinner. On the same level is a cafeteria-style café and a snack bar. All food outlets are designed around the basic needs of passing highway travelers.

CAMPING ALONG THE ICEFIELDS PARKWAY

Aside from Whistlers and Wapiti Campgrounds at the top end of the Icefields Parkway (see *Campgrounds* under *Town of Jasper*), there are five campgrounds along this stretch of highway.

Wilcox Creek and **Columbia Icefield Campgrounds** are within two km (1.2 miles) of each other at the extreme southern end of the park, just over 100 km (62 miles) south of the town of Jasper 105 km (65 miles) and around 125 km (78 miles) north of Lake Louise. Both are primitive facilities with pit toilets, cooking shelters, and fire rings; all sites are $13. Smallish sites at Columbia Icefield Campground are set in a stunted subalpine forest of aspen and spruce, with views extending across to the Athabasca Glacier. Immediately to the south, Wilcox Creek offers larger sites, better suited to RVs and trailers, but with no hookups.

Jonas Creek, Honeymoon Lake, and **Mount Kerkeslin Campgrounds** are all within a 50-km (31-mile) stretch continuing north. All cost $13 per night and have primitive facilities (no hookups or showers).

Town of Jasper

At the top end of the Icefields Parkway, 280 kilometers (174 miles) north of Banff and a 3.5-hour drive west of the provincial capital, Edmonton, the town of Jasper is the service center of the park.

With all the things to do and see in the surrounding wilderness, it's amazing how many people hang out in town. July and August are especially busy; much-needed improvements to the parking situation have had little impact on the traffic—try for a parking spot in the lot along the railway line. The best way to avoid the problem is to avoid town during the middle of the day. The park information center, on Connaught Drive, is the only real reason to be in town. The shaded park in front of the center is a good place for people-watching, but you may get clobbered by a wayward hacky sack. Connaught Drive, the town's main street, parallels the rail line as it curves through town. Also along this road you'll find the bus depot, rail terminal, restaurants, motels, and a parking lot. Behind Connaught Drive is Patricia Street (one-way eastbound), which has more restaurants and services and leads to more hotels and motels on Geikie Street. Behind this main core are rows of neat houses—much less pretentious than those in Banff—and all the facilities of a regular town, including a library, school, post office, museum, swimming pool, and hospital.

SIGHTS IN AND AROUND THE TOWN OF JASPER

Downtown

At the back of town is the excellent **Jasper-Yellowhead Museum and Archives** (400 Pyramid Lake Rd., 780/852-3013; mid-June–Sept. daily 10 A.M.–9 P.M., the rest of the year Thurs.–Sun. 10 A.M.–5 P.M.; adult $4, child $2), as unstuffy as any museum could possibly be and well worth a visit even for nonmuseum types. The main gallery features colorful, modern picture boards with exhibits that take visitors along a timeline of Jasper's human history through the fur trade,

the coming of the railway, and the creation of the park. Documentaries are shown on demand in a small television room. The museum also features extensive archives, including hundreds of historical photos, manuscripts, documents, maps, and videos.

The **Wildlife Museum** (corner of Connaught Dr. and Miette Ave., 780/852-3361; daily 9 A.M.–10 P.M.), in the darkened bowels of the Whistlers Inn, is a throwback to a bygone era, when displays of stuffed animals were considered the best way to extol the wonders of nature. "See animals in their natural setting" cries museum advertising, but the shrubbery looks suspiciously like fake Christmas trees and the bull elk seems to be screaming "Get me out of here!" Yep, they even charge you for it—exchange $3 for a token at the Whistlers' reception desk.

Patricia and Pyramid Lakes

A winding road heads through the hills at the back of town to these two picturesque lakes, formed when glacial moraines dammed shallow valleys. The first, to the left, is Patricia; the second, farther along the road, is Pyramid, backed by **Pyramid Mountain** (2,765 meters/9,072 feet). Both lakes are popular spots for picnicking, fishing, and boating. Boat rentals are available at **Pyramid Lake Boat Rentals,** across the road from the resort of the same name (780/852-4900). Canoes, rowboats, paddleboats, and kayaks are $28 for the first hour and $18 for each additional hour. The resort also rents motorboats for $40 per hour. From the resort, the road continues around the lake to a bridge, which leads to an island popular with picnickers. The road ends at the quieter end of the lake.

Jasper Tramway

This tramway (780/852-3093; adult $21, child $9) climbs more than 1,000 vertical meters (3,280 feet) up the steep north face of **The Whistlers,** named for the hoary marmots that live on the summit. The tramway operates two 30-passenger cars that take seven minutes to reach the upper

VICINITY OF JASPER

To Edmonton and Miette Hot Springs

Pyramid Mountain

SIXTH BRIDGE

MALIGNE CANYON HOSTEL

Pyramid Lake

Jasper National Park

Maligne Canyon

MALIGNE LAKE

PYRAMID LAKE RESORT

Patricia Lake

PATRICIA LAKE BUNGALOWS

PYRAMID RIDING STABLES

Edith Lake

Annette Lake

Riley Lake

Cottonwood Slough

PINE BUNGALOWS

Upper Mina Lake

SEE "TOWN OF JASPER" MAP

SAWRIDGE INN

FAIRMONT JASPER PARK LODGE

Cabin Lake

Jasper

Lac Beauvert

Lower Mina Lake

MOUNT ROBSON INN

OLD FORT POINT

Caledonia Lake

Miette

River

YELLOWHEAD

Jasper National Park

To Prince George, BC

TEKARRA LODGE

ALPINE VILLAGE

93A

JASPER INTERNATIONAL HOSTEL

WHISTLERS

Athabasca

JASPER TRAMWAY

JASPER HOUSE BUNGALOWS

WAPITI

GONDOLA

The Whistlers

Valley of the Five Lakes

BECKER'S CHALETS

FEE STATION

ICEFIELDS

0   1 mi

0   1 km

93A

River

PARKWAY

93

To Banff National Park

MARMOT BASIN

To Wabasso Campground and MOUNT EDITH CAVELL

© AVALON TRAVEL PUBLISHING, INC.

To Pyramid Lake

To Hwy 16

TONQUIN PRIME RIB VILLAGE ▼

TONQUIN INN ●

To Maligne Canyon and Mette Hot Springs

JUNIPER ST

CONNAUGHT DR

16

TOWN OF JASPER

JASPER INN ●

BEAR HILL LODGE ●

Pyramid Benchland Trail

PYRAMID LAKE RD

BONHOMME ST

ASPEN AVE

GEIKIE ST

PATRICIA ST

Athabasca River

YELLOWHEAD HWY

JASPER-YELLOWHEAD MUSEUM ★

ACTIVITY CENTRE ■

JASPER AQUATIC CENTRE ■

To Mina Lakes

CEDAR AVE

PALISADES ▼

▼ ▼ BEAR'S PAW BAKERY

▼ JASPER PIZZA PLACE

ASTORIA HOTEL ●

TOTEM SKI SHOP ■

SOURCE FOR SPORTS ■

JASPER CAMERA & GIFT ■

DENJIRO ▼

PARK INFROMATION CENTRE

ELM AVE

LIBRARY ■

POST OFFICE ■

LA FIESTA ▼

WHISTLERS INN ■

CHABA THEATRE ■

ATHABASCA HOTEL ■

VIA RAIL STATION/BUS DEPOT ■

MALIGNE AVE

HOSPITAL ■

ON-LINE SPORT & TACKLE ■

OUR NATIVE LAND ■

MOUNTAIN FOODS & CAFÉ ▼

CANTONESE RESTAURANT ▼

ANDY'S BISTRO ▼

SOMETHING ELSE RESTAURANT ▼

PATRICIA CENTRE ■

FIDDLE RIVER ▼

MALIGNE TOURS ▼

CONNAUGHT SQUARE ■

MIETTE AVE

FREEWHEEL CYCLE ■

NUTTER'S ▼

SOFT ROCK CAFÉ ■

KONTOS RESTAURANT ▼

JASPER MARKETPLACE ■

PINE AVE

L & W RESTAURANT ▼

VILLA CARUSO ▼

SCALE NOT AVAILABLE

To Icefields Parkway, Banff (Banff National Park) and Prince George, BC

To Old Fort Point

terminal, during which time the conductor gives a lecture about the mountain and its environment. From the upper terminal, a 1.4-km (.9-mile) trail leads to the 2,470-meter (8,104-foot) true summit. The view is breathtaking; to the south is the Columbia Icefield, and on a clear day you can see Mount Robson (3,954 meters/12,970 feet)—the highest peak in the Canadian Rockies—to the northwest. Free two-hour guided hikes leave the upper terminal for the true summit daily at 10 A.M., 11 A.M., 2 P.M., and 3 P.M. You should allow two hours on top and, on a clear summer's day, two more hours in line at the bottom. The tramway is three km (1.9 miles) south of town on Highway 93 (Icefields Parkway) and then a similar distance up Whistlers Road. It operates in summer daily 8:30 A.M.–10 P.M., shorter hours April–June and September to mid-October, closed the rest of the year.

Edith and Annette Lakes

These two lakes along the road to Jasper Park Lodge—across the Athabasca River from town—are perfect for a picnic, swim, or pleasant walk. They are remnants of a much larger lake that once covered the entire valley floor. The lakes are relatively shallow; therefore, the sun warms the water to a bearable temperature for swimming. In fact, they have the warmest waters of any lakes in the park. The 2.5-km (1.6-mile) **Lee Foundation Trail** encircles Lake Annette and is wheelchair accessible. Both lakes have day-use areas with beaches and picnic areas.

Jasper Park Lodge

Accommodations are not usually considered sights, but then this is the Rockies, where grand railway hotels attract as many visitors as the more legitimate natural attractions. Jasper Park Lodge has been the premier accommodation in the park since it opened in 1921. Back then it was a single-story structure, reputed to be the largest log building in the world. It burned to the ground in 1952 but was rebuilt. Additional bungalows were erected along Lac Beauvert, forming a basis for today's lodge. Rows of cabins radiate from the main lodge, which contains restaurants, lounges, and the town's only covered shopping arcade.

Today up to 900 guests can be accommodated in 446 rooms. A large parking area for nonguests is located on Lodge Road, behind the golf clubhouse; you're welcome to walk around the resort, play golf, dine in the restaurants, and, of course, browse through the shopping promenade—even if you're not a registered guest. On the lakeshore in front of the lodge is a boat rental concession; canoes and kayaks can be rented for $20 per 30 minutes. From the main lodge, a hiking trail follows the shoreline of Lac Beauvert through the golf course, linking up with other trails at Old Fort Point. To walk from town will take one hour.

MOUNT EDITH CAVELL

This 3,363-meter (11,033-foot) peak is the most distinctive and impressive in the park. Known to Indians as the "White Ghost" for its snowcapped summit, the mountain was given its official name in honor of a British nurse who was executed

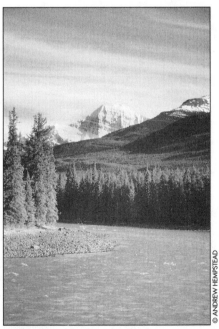

Mount Edith Cavell, seen from across the Athabasca River

© ANDREW HEMPSTEAD

for helping prisoners of war escape German-occupied Belgium during World War I. The peak was first climbed that same year; today the most popular route to the summit is up the east ridge (to the left of the summit). The imposing north face (facing the parking lot) has been climbed but is rated as an extremely difficult climb.

Getting a Closer Look

For those less adventurous, several vantage points, including downtown Jasper and the golf course, provide good views of the peak. But the most impressive place to marvel at the mountain is from directly below the north face. A 14.5-km (nine-mile) road winds up the Astoria River Valley from Highway 93A, ending right below the face. This steep, narrow road has many switchbacks. Trailers must be left in the designated area at the bottom. Highway 93A was the original Icefields Parkway, following the southeast bank of the Athabasca River. The route has now been bypassed by the more direct one on the other side of the river.

From the parking lot at the end of the road, you must strain your neck to take in the magnificent sight of the mountain's 1,500-meter (4,920-foot) north face and **Angel Glacier,** which lies in a saddle on the mountain's lower slopes. On warm days, those who are patient may be lucky enough to witness an avalanche tumbling from the glacier, creating a roar that echoes across the valley. From the parking area, the **Path of the Glacier Trail** (one hour round-trip) traverses barren moraines deposited by the receding Angel Glacier and leads to some great viewpoints. For other hiking opportunities in the vicinity of Mount Edith Cavell, see *Hikes near Mount Edith Cavell.*

MALIGNE LAKE AND VICINITY

Maligne Lake, one of the world's most photographed lakes, lies 48 km (30 miles) southeast of Jasper. It's the source of the **Maligne River,** which flows northward to Medicine Lake and then disappears underground, eventually emerging downstream of Maligne Canyon. The river

was known to the natives as Chaba Imne (River of the Great Beaver), but the name by which we know it today was coined by a missionary. After his horses were swept away by its swift-flowing waters in 1846, he described the river as being *"la traverse maligne."* Driving up the Maligne River Valley to the lake is a 600-million-year-old lesson in geology that can be appreciated by anyone.

Maligne Canyon

As the Maligne River drops into the Athabasca River Valley, its gradient is particularly steep. The fast-flowing water has eroded a deep canyon out of the easily dissolved limestone bedrock. The canyon is up to 50 meters (165 feet) deep, yet so narrow that squirrels often jump across. At the top of the canyon, opposite the teahouse, you'll see large potholes in the riverbed. These potholes are created when rocks and pebbles become trapped in what begins as a shallow depression; under the force of the rushing water, they carve jug-shaped hollows into the soft bedrock.

An interpretive trail winds down from the parking lot, crossing the canyon six times. The most spectacular sections of the canyon can be seen from the first two bridges, at the upper end of the trail. In summer a teahouse operates at the top of the canyon. To avoid the crowds at the upper end of the canyon, an alternative would be to park at Sixth Bridge, near the confluence of the Maligne and Athabasca Rivers, and walk *up* the canyon (see *Hiking in the Maligne Lake Area*). The **Maligne Lake Shuttle** (780/852-3370) stops at the canyon eight times daily along its run between 627 Patricia Street in downtown Jasper and Maligne Lake; fare is $9 one-way from town. In winter, guided tours of the frozen canyon are an experience you'll never forget (see *Wintertime*).

Medicine Lake

From the canyon, Maligne Lake Road climbs to Medicine Lake, which does a disappearing act each year. The water level fluctuates due to a network of underground passages that emerge downstream in Maligne Canyon. At the northwest end of the lake, beyond where the outlet should be, the riverbed is often dry. In fall, when runoff from the

Jasper National Park

© ANDREW HEMPSTEAD

Oft-photographed Spirit Island is the turn-around point for tour boats on Maligne Lake.

mountains is minimal, the water level drops, and by November the lake comprises a few shallow pools. Natives believed that spirits were responsible for the phenomenon, hence the name.

Maligne Lake

At the end of the road, 48 km (30 miles) from town, is Maligne Lake, the largest glacier-fed lake in the Canadian Rockies and second largest in the world. The first paying visitors were brought to the lake in 1929, and it has been a mecca for camera-toting tourists from around the world ever since. Once at the lake, activities are plentiful. But other than taking in the spectacular vistas, the only thing you won't need your wallet for is hiking one of the numerous trails in the area.

The most popular tourist activity at the lake is a 90-minute narrated cruise on a glass-enclosed boat up the lake to oft-photographed **Spirit Island.** Cruises leave in summer, every hour on the hour 10 A.M.–5 P.M., with fewer sailings in May and September; $35 adults, $17.50 children. Many time slots are booked in blocks by tour companies; therefore, reservations are suggested. Rowboats and canoes can be rented at the Boat House, a provincial historic site dating

to 1929, for $15 per hour or $70 per day. Double sea kayaks go for $20 per hour and $85 per day. The lake also has excellent trout fishing (for details, see *Other Recreation*).

All commercial operations to and around the lake are operated by **Maligne Tours** (627 Patricia St., 780/852-3370, www.malignelake.com), based in downtown Jasper. At the lake itself, in addition to the cruises and boat rentals, Maligne Tours operates a souvenir shop and large café with a huge area of tiered outdoor seating overlooking the lake. The **Maligne Lake Shuttle** runs from the Maligne Tours office and from various hotels out to the lake eight times daily through summer (four times daily in spring and fall). The first shuttle leaves for the lake each morning at 8:30 A.M.; $28 round-trip.

EAST ALONG HIGHWAY 16

From Jasper, it's 50 km (31 miles) to the park's eastern boundary along Highway 16, following the Athabasca River the entire way. Beyond the turnoff to Maligne Lake, Highway 16 enters a wide valley flanked to the west by The Palisade and to the east by the Colin Range. The valley is a classic montane environment, with open meadows and forests of Douglas fir and lodgepole pine. After crossing the Athabasca River, 20 km (12 miles) from Jasper, the highway parallels **Jasper Lake,** left as the last ice age ended. Along the lake are several viewpoints and picnic areas. At the lake's northern outlet, a plaque marks the site of **Jasper House** (the actual site is across the river from the highway). The next worthwhile stop is **Disaster Point,** four km (2.5 miles) farther north. This is a great spot for viewing bighorn sheep, which gather at a mineral lick, an area of exposed mineral salts. Disaster Point is on the lower slopes of Roche Miette, a distinctive 2,316-meter-high (7,600-foot-high) peak that juts out into the Athabasca River Valley. Across the highway the braided Athabasca River is flanked by wetlands alive with migrating birds spring and fall.

Miette Hot Springs Road branches south from the highway 43 km (27 miles) east of Jasper. This junction marks the site of **Pocahontas,** a coal mining town in existence between 1910 and 1921. The mine itself was high above the township, with coal transported to the valley floor by cable car. All buildings have long since been removed, but a short interpretive walk leads through the remaining foundations. One km (.6 mile) along Miette Hot Springs Road, a short trail leads to photogenic **Punchbowl Falls.** Here Mountain Creek cascades through a narrow crevice in a cliff to a pool of turbulent water.

Miette Hot Springs

After curving, swerving, rising, and falling many times, Miette Hot Springs Road ends 18 km (11 miles) from Highway 16 at the warmest springs in the Canadian Rockies (780/866-3939; mid-May–mid-Oct. 10:30 A.M.–9 P.M., extended to 8:30 A.M.–10:30 P.M. in summer). In the early 1900s, these springs were one of the park's biggest attractions. In 1910, a packhorse trail was built up the valley and the government constructed a bathhouse. The original hand-hewn log structure was replaced in the 1930s with pools that remained in use until new facilities were built in 1985. Water that flows into the pools is artificially cooled from 54°C (128°F) to a soothing 39°C (100°F). A newer addition to the complex is a

cool plunge pool. Admission is $6.25 for a single swim or $8.75 for the day (senior and child $5.25 and $7.75, respectively).

Many hiking trails begin from the hot springs complex; the shortest is from the picnic area to the source of the springs (allow five minutes each way). The springs is also home to a café, while a restaurant and lodging are adjacent.

HIKES AROUND THE TOWN OF JASPER

Pyramid Benchland

- Length: 7 km/4.3 miles (two hours) round-trip
- Elevation gain: 120 meters/400 feet
- Rating: easy
- Trailhead: Jasper-Yellowhead Museum, Pyramid Lake Road

Numerous official and unofficial hiking trails weave across the benchland immediately west of the town of Jasper. From the far corner of the parking lot beside the museum, a well-marked trail climbs onto the benchland. Keep right, crossing Pyramid Lake Road, and you'll emerge on a bluff overlooking the Athabasca River Valley. Bighorn sheep can often be seen grazing here. If you return to the trailhead from here, you will have hiked seven km (4.3 miles). The trail continues north, disappearing into the montane forest until arriving at Pyramid Lake. Various trails can be taken to return to town; get a map at the park information center before setting out.

Mina Lakes

- Length: 2.5 km/1.5 miles (50 minutes) one-way
- Elevation gain: 70 meters/230 feet
- Rating: easy
- Trailhead: Jasper-Yellowhead Museum, Pyramid Lake Road

Lower and Upper Mina Lakes lie on the benchland described previously. The trailhead is the same as the Pyramid Lake Loop, except instead of keeping right, you'll need to take the first left fork (signposted as Route 8 to Cabin Creek West), which climbs up onto the bench, then crosses a treeless 100-meter-wide (328-foot-wide) corridor, cleared to act as a firebreak for the town. Cabin Lake Road passes along the firebreak, leading west (left) to manmade Cabin Lake and east (right) to Pyramid Lake Road. Continuing straight ahead, the trail climbs gradually through a typical montane forest of lodgepole pine, Douglas fir, and poplar before emerging at Lower Mina Lake. After a further 500 meters (.3 mile) and just beyond the end of Lower Mina Lake, the upper lake and a pebbly stretch of beach are reached. The distance given above is to this point, but with a map in hand, it's possible to continue along the shore of the upper lake; two km (1.2 miles) beyond the end of the lake the trail forks—looping back along Cabin Lake Road via Cabin Lake to the left and to Riley Lake to the right.

Patricia Lake Circle
• Length: 5-km/3.1-mile loop (90 minutes round-trip)
• Elevation gain: minimal
• Rating: easy
• Trailhead: two km (1.2 miles) along Pyramid Lake Road

This trail begins across the road from the riding stables on Pyramid Lake Road. It traverses a mixed forest of aspen and lodgepole pine—prime habitat for larger mammals such as elk, deer, and moose. The second half of the trail skirts Cottonwood Slough, where you'll see several beaver ponds. Unlike the name suggests, this trail doesn't encircle Patricia Lake, but instead just passes along a portion of its southern shoreline.

The Palisade
• Length: 11 km/6.8 miles (four hours) one-way
• Elevation gain: 850 meters/2,790 feet
• Rating: difficult
• Trailhead: the end of Pyramid Lake Road, eight km (five miles) from town

The destination of this strenuous hike is the site of an old fire lookout tower atop a high ridge between the Athabasca River Valley and Pyramid Mountain. From the locked gate at the end of Pyramid Lake Road, the trail crosses Pyramid

Creek after one km (.6 mile), then climbs steadily for the entire distance along a forest-enclosed fire road (take the right fork at the 7.5-km/4.7-mile mark). Once at the end of the trail, it's easy to see why this site was chosen for the lookout; the panorama extends down the valley and across Jasper Lake to Roche Miette (2,316 meters/7,600 feet).

Old Fort Point
• Length: 6.5-km/4-mile loop (two hours round-trip)
• Elevation gain: 60 meters/200 feet
• Rating: easy
• Trailhead: take Highway 93A south from downtown, follow the first left after crossing Highway 16, and park beside the Athabasca River.

Old Fort Point is a distinctive knoll above the Athabasca River, to the east of town. Although it is not likely that a fort was ever located here, the first fur-trading post in the Rockies, Henry House, was just downstream. It's easy to imagine fur traders and early explorers climbing to this summit for 360-degree views of the Athabasca and Miette Rivers. From the parking lot beyond the single-lane vehicle bridge over the Athabasca River, climb the wooden stairs, take the left trail to the top of the knoll, and then continue back to the parking lot along the north flank of the hill.

The Whistlers
• Length: 8 km/5 miles (three hours) one-way
• Elevation gain: 1,220 meters/4,000 feet
• Rating: difficult
• Trailhead: three km (1.9 miles) along Whistlers Road from Highway 93

This steep ascent, the park's most arduous day hike, is unique in that it passes through three distinct vegetation zones in a relatively short distance. (For the less adventurous, Jasper Tramway traverses the same route described here; see *Sights in and Around the Town of Jasper*.) From the trailhead on Whistlers Road, immediately below the hostel, the trail begins climbing and doesn't let up until you merge with the crowds getting off the tramway at the top. The trail begins in a montane forest of aspen and white birch, climbs through a subalpine forest of Engelmann spruce and alpine fir, then emerges onto the open, treeless tundra, which is inhabited by pikas, hoary marmots, and a few hardy plants. Carry water with you because none is available before the upper tramway terminal. If you've taken the tramway, free guided hikes are offered around the summit area.

HIKES NEAR MOUNT EDITH CAVELL

Cavell Road begins from Highway 93A, 13 km (eight miles) south from the town of Jasper, and winds through a subalpine forest, ascending 300 meters (980 feet) in 14.5 km (nine miles). Trailheads are located at the end of the road (Cavell Meadows Trail and a short interpretive trail) and across from the hostel two km (1.2 miles) from the end (Astoria River/Tonquin Valley Trail). A third trailhead is on Marmot Basin Road where it crosses Portal Creek (Maccarib Pass Trail).

Cavell Meadows

- Length: 4 km/2.5 miles (1.5 hours) one-way
- Elevation gain: 380 meters/1,250 feet
- Rating: moderate
- Trailhead: parking lot at the end of Cavell Road, 27.5 km (17 miles) south of town

This trail, beginning from the parking lot beneath Mount Edith Cavell, provides access to an alpine meadow and panoramic views of Angel Glacier. The trail begins by following the paved Path of the Glacier Loop, then branches left, climbing steadily through a subalpine forest of Engelmann spruce and then stunted subalpine fir to emerge facing the northeast face of Mount Edith Cavell and Angel Glacier. The view of the glacier from this point is nothing less than awesome, as the ice spills out of a cirque, clinging to a 300-meter-high (984-foot-high) cliff face. The trail continues to higher viewpoints and an alpine meadow that, by mid-July, is filled with wildflowers.

© ANDREW HEMPSTEAD

Jasper's backcountry holds a healthy population of grizzlies, but they are rarely encountered by hikers.

🏔 Astoria River/Tonquin Valley

- Length: 19 km/11.8 miles (6–7 hours) one-way
- Elevation gain: 450 meters/1,480 feet
- Rating: moderate
- Trailhead: opposite the hostel on Cavell Road

From Cavell Road, this trail descends through a forest on the north side of Mount Edith Cavell for five km (3.1 miles), then crosses the Astoria River and begins a long ascent into spectacular Tonquin Valley. Amethyst Lakes and the 1,000-meter (3,280-foot) cliffs of the Ramparts first come into view after 13 km (eight miles). At the 17-km (10.5-mile) mark the trail divides. To the left it climbs into Eremite Valley, where there is a campground. The right fork continues, following Astoria River to Tonquin Valley, Amethyst Lakes, and a choice of four campgrounds.

Maccarib Pass

- Length: 21 km/13 miles (7–8 hours) one-way
- Elevation gain: 730 meters/2,400 feet
- Rating: moderate/difficult
- Trailhead: 6.5 km (four miles) up Marmot Basin Road

This trail is slightly longer and gains more elevation than the trail along Astoria River but is more spectacular. It strikes out to the southwest, following Portal Creek for a short distance, then passes under Peveril Peak before making a steep approach to Maccarib Pass, 12.5 km (7.8 miles) from the trailhead. The full panorama of the Tonquin Valley can be appreciated as the path gradually descends from the pass. At Amethyst Lakes it links up with the Astoria River Trail, and many options for day hikes head out from campgrounds at the lakes.

HIKES IN THE MALIGNE LAKE AREA

Maligne Lake, 48 km (30 miles) from the town of Jasper, provides more easy hiking with many opportunities to view the lake and explore its environs. To get there, take Highway 16 east for four km (2.5 miles) from town and turn south on Maligne Lake Road. The first three hikes detailed are along the access road to the lake; the others leave from various parking lots at the northwest end of the lake.

Maligne Tours (627 Patricia St., 780/852-3370) organizes hikes led by knowledgeable guides along the Lake Trail (one hour; $10 per person) and into the Bald and Opal Hills (four hours; $40 per person). This same company provides transportation to the lake. The **Maligne Lake Shuttle** runs from downtown and some hotels out to the lake four to six times daily; $14 one-way.

Maligne Canyon

- Length: 3.7 km/2.3 miles (90 minutes) one-way
- Elevation gain: 125 meters/410 feet
- Rating: moderate
- Trailhead: Turn off to Sixth Bridge 2.5 km (1.6 miles) along Maligne Lake Road from Highway 16.

Maligne Canyon is one of the busiest places in the park, yet few visitors hike the entire length of the canyon trail. By beginning from the lower end of the canyon, at the confluence of the Maligne and Athabasca Rivers, you'll avoid starting your hike alongside the masses and you'll get to hike downhill on your return (when you're tired). To access the lower end of the canyon, follow the one-km (.6-mile) spur off Maligne Lake Road to Sixth Bridge. Crowds will be minimal for the first three km (1.9 miles) to Fourth Bridge, where the trail starts climbing. By the time you get to Third Bridge, you start encountering adventurous hikers coming down the canyon, and soon thereafter you'll meet the real crowds—high heels, bear-bells, and all. Upstream of here the canyon is deepest and most spectacular. (See *Maligne Lake and Vicinity* for details of the walk starting from the *top* of Maligne Canyon.)

Watchtower Basin

- Length: 10 km/6.2 miles (3.5 hours) one-way
- Elevation gain: 630 meters/2,070 feet
- Rating: moderate/difficult
- Trailhead: Maligne Lake Road, 24 km (15 miles) from Highway 16

Watchtower is a wide, open basin high above the crowds of Maligne Lake Road. All the elevation gain is made during the first six km (3.7 miles) from Maligne Lake Road, through a dense forest of lodgepole pine and white spruce. As the trail levels off and enters the basin, it continues to follow the west bank of a stream, crossing it at km 10 (mile 6.2) and officially ending at a campground. To the west and south the **Maligne Range** rises to a crest three km (1.9 miles) beyond the campground. From the top of this ridge, at the intersection with the Skyline Trail, it is 17.5 km (11 miles) northwest to Maligne Canyon, or 27 km (17 miles) southeast to Maligne Lake. By camping at Watchtower Campground, day trips can be made to a small lake in the basin or to highlights of the Skyline Trail such as the Snowbowl, Curator Lake, and Shovel Pass.

Jacques Lake

- Length: 12 km/7.5 miles (3–3.5 hours) one-way
- Elevation gain: 100 meters/330 feet
- Rating: moderate
- Trailhead: Beaver Lake Picnic Area, 28 km (17.4 miles) from Highway 16 along Maligne Lake Road

The appeal of this trail, which begins from the southeast end of Medicine Lake, is its lack of elevation gain and the numerous small lakes it skirts as it travels through a narrow valley. On either side, the severely faulted mountains of the Queen Elizabeth Ranges rise steeply above the valley floor, their strata tilted nearly vertical.

Lake Trail (Mary Schäffer Loop)

- Length: 3.2-km/2-mile loop (one hour round-trip)
- Elevation gain: minimal
- Rating: easy
- Trailhead: Boat House, Maligne Lake

This easy, pleasant walk begins from beside the Boat House, following the eastern shore of Maligne Lake through an open area of lakeside picnic tables to a point known as **Schäffer Viewpoint,** named for the first white person to

see the valley. Across the lake are the aptly named Bald Hills, the Maligne Range, and, to the southwest, the distinctive twin peaks of Mount Unwin (3,268 meters/10,720 feet) and Mount Charlton (3,217 meters/10,550 feet). After dragging yourself away from the spectacular panorama, continue along a shallow bay before following the trail into a forest of spruce and subalpine fir, then looping back to the middle parking lot.

Opal Hills

- Length: 8.2-km/5.1-mile loop (three hours round-trip)
- Elevation gain: 455 meters/1,500 feet
- Rating: moderate
- Trailhead: north corner, upper parking lot, Maligne Lake

This trail begins from behind the information board in the corner of the parking lot, climbing steeply for 1.5 km (.9 mile) to a point where it divides. Both options end in the high alpine meadows of the Opal Hills; the trail to the right is shorter and steeper. Once you are in the meadow, the entire Maligne Valley can be seen below.

Bald Hills

- Length: 5.2 km/3.2 miles (two hours) one-way
- Elevation gain: 495 meters/1,620 feet
- Rating: moderate
- Trailhead: picnic area at the end of Maligne Lake Road

This trail follows an old fire road for its entire distance, entering an open meadow near the end. This was once the site of a fire lookout. The 360-degree view takes in the jade-green waters of Maligne Lake, the Queen Elizabeth Ranges, and the twin peaks of Mount Unwin and Mount Charlton. The Bald Hills extend for seven km (4.3 miles), their highest summit not exceeding 2,600 meters (8,530 feet). A herd of caribou summers in the hills.

Moose Lake

- Length: 1.4 km/.9 mile (30 minutes) one-way
- Elevation gain: minimal
- Rating: easy

• Trailhead: picnic area at the end of Maligne Lake Road

This trail begins 200 meters (.1 mile) along the Bald Hills Trail, spurring left along the Maligne Pass Trail (signposted). One km (.6 mile) along this trail, a rough track branches left, leading to Moose Lake—a quiet body of water where moose are sometimes seen. To return, continue along the trail as it descends to the shore of Maligne Lake, a short stroll from the picnic area.

OTHER SUMMER RECREATION

Several booking agents represent the many recreation-tour operators in Jasper. **Jasper Adventure Centre,** in the lobby of the Chaba Theatre (604 Connaught Dr., 780/852-5595 or 800/565-7547, www.jasperadventurecentre.com) takes bookings for all of the following activities, as well as for accommodations and for transportation to various points in the park and beyond. **Maligne Tours** (627 Patricia St., 780/852-3370) operates all activities in the Maligne Lake area, including the famous lake cruise.

Mountain Biking

Bicycling in the park continues to grow in popularity: the ride between Banff and Jasper, along the Icefields Parkway, attracts riders from around the world. In addition to the paved roads, many designated unpaved bicycle trails radiate from the town. One of the most popular is the Athabasca River Trail, which begins at Old Fort Point and follows the river to a point below Maligne Canyon. Cyclists are particularly prone to sudden bear encounters; make noises when passing through heavily wooded areas. The brochure *Mountain Biking Trail Guide* lists designated trails and is available from the information center and all local sport shops. Rental outlets include **On-line Sport & Tackle** (600 Patricia St., 780/852-3630), **Source for Sports** (406 Patricia St., 780/852-3654), **Freewheel Cycle** (618 Patricia St., 780/852-3898), **Vicious Cycle** (630 Connaught Dr., 780/852-1111), and the **Activity Centre** at Jasper Park Lodge (780/852-5708). Expect to pay $6–10 per hour or $26–40 for any 24-hour period.

Horseback Riding

On the benchlands immediately behind the town of Jasper is **Pyramid Riding Stables** (Pyramid Lake Road, 780/852-7433). The stables offer one-, two-, and three-hour guided rides for $30, $51, and $70, respectively. The one-hour trip follows a ridge high above town, providing excellent views of the Athabasca River Valley. **Skyline Trail Rides** (Jasper Park Lodge, 780/852-4215) offers a one-hour guided ride around Lake Annette ($35 per person) and a 4.5-hour ride to Maligne Canyon ($99 per person). Both companies operate between mid-April and October.

Overnight pack trips consist of 4–6 hours of riding per day, with a few nights spent at a remote mountain lodge where you can hike, boat, fish, or ride. Rates start at $180 per person per day for meals, accommodation, and a horse, of course. For details, contact **Skyline Trail Rides** (780/852-4215 or 888/852-7787, www.skyline trail.com) or **Tonquin Valley Adventures** (780/852-1188, www.tonquinadventures.com).

White-Water Rafting

Within the park, the **Athabasca** and **Sunwapta Rivers** are run by a half dozen outfitters, while across the border in British Columbia, the **Fraser River** is another option for a guided rafting trip. On the Athabasca River, the Mile 5 Run is an easy two-hour float that appeals to all ages. Farther upstream, some operators offer a trip that begins from below Athabasca Falls, on a stretch of the river that passes through a narrow canyon; this run takes three hours. The boulder-strewn rapids of the Sunwapta and Fraser Rivers offer more thrills and spills—these trips are for the more adventurous and last 3–4 hours. Most companies offer a choice of rivers and provide transportation to and from downtown hotels. Expect to pay $45–55 for trips on the Athabasca and $70 for the Sunwapta and Fraser. The following companies run at least two of three rivers: **Maligne Rafting Adventures** (780/852-3370), **Raven Adventures** (780/852-4292), **Rocky Mountain River Guides** (780/852-3777), and **White Water Rafting** (780/852-7238 or 800/557-7238). **Jasper Raft Tours** (780/852-

FLOAT BACK IN TIME

If white-water rafting sounds a little too adventurous for your liking, consider an easy float down the Athabasca River in a historic 10-meter (33-foot) **voyageur canoe.** These large, stable craft were developed more than 200 years ago specifically for travel along Canadian waterways. In those days, when the rivers and lakes were used as highways, voyageur canoes were the vessel of choice for everyone from fur traders to noted explorers such as David Thompson and Alexander Mackenzie.

The voyageur canoes used by **Rocky Mountain Voyageurs** (780/852-3343 or 877/852-3343, www.jaspercanoes.com) are an exact replica in size

and shape of the original design, but instead of birchbark, fiberglass and Kevlar are used in their construction, and they are sectional, allowing for easy transportation. Costumed guides—complete with plaid shirts and sashes—point out prominent natural features and relate historic tales as these canoes and up to 12 passengers float gently down the Athabasca River for about one hour from Old Fort Point. No rapids are encountered, and unless it's raining, you won't get wet. The cost is $48 adults, $29 children, which includes round-trip transfers from downtown Jasper. Departure times are daily at 9 A.M. and 2 P.M. between June and early September.

© ANDREW HEMPSTEAD

2665) floats a 16-km (10-mile) stretch of the Athabasca River in large, stable inflatable rafts; $50 adults, $20 children.

Fishing

Fishing in the many alpine lakes—for rainbow, brook, Dolly Varden, cutthroat, and lake trout, as well as pike and whitefish—is excellent. Many outfitters offer guided fishing trips. Whether you fish with a guide or by yourself, you'll need a national park fishing license ($7 per week, $20 per year), available from the park information center or On-line Sport & Tackle (600 Patricia St.). Maligne Lake is the most popular fishing hole; in 1980, a 10-kg (22-pound) rainbow trout was caught in its deep waters.

Stable 5.5-meter (18-foot) Freighter canoes with a small electric motor are the preferred fishing boat on Maligne Lake. They are available at the lakeside **Boat House** (780/852-3370; June–Aug. daily 8:30 A.M.–6:30 P.M.) for $90

per day, with rod and reel rentals extra. Guided fishing trips on the lake are offered from the Boat House by **Maligne Tours** (780/852-3370); half-day $125 per person for two people, full-day $170 per person for two.

Currie's Guiding (780/852-5650) offers trips to Maligne Lake (full-day $190 per person) and to Talbot Lake, a shallow body of water east of town renowned for its pike fishing. Rates include equipment and instruction. **Source for Sports** (406 Patricia St., 780/852-3654) and **On-line Sport & Tackle** (600 Patricia St., 780/852-3630) sell and rent fishing tackle and also have canoe and boat rentals.

Golfing

The world-famous **Jasper Park Lodge Golf Course** (780/852-6090) was designed by renowned golf-course architect Stanley Thompson. The course opened in 1925, after 200 men had spent an entire year clearing trees and laying out the holes to Thompson's design. Renovations were made in 1994, but the course plays as it did when it first opened. It is consistently ranked as one of the top 10 courses in Canada. The 18-hole, 6,670-yard course takes in the contours of the Athabasca River Valley as it hugs the banks of turquoise-colored Lac Beauvert. It is a true test of accuracy, and with holes named The Maze, The Bad Baby, and The Bay, you'll need lots of balls. Greens fees for 18 holes vary with the season: $185 mid-June to September, $130 mid-May to mid-June, and $100 in early May and from October 1 through closing (usually mid-October). These rates are discounted for Canadian residents. An electric cart is $38 per round. Golfing after 5 P.M. is discounted to just over $100—a great deal during the long days of June and July. Other facilities include a driving range, club rentals ($30–48), a restaurant, and a lounge.

Indoor Recreation

The **Jasper Aquatic Centre** (401 Pyramid Lake Rd., 780/852-3663) has an Olympic-size swimming pool; admission $5. The **Jasper Activity Centre,** next door (780/852-3381), has squash courts, indoor and outdoor tennis courts, a climbing wall, a weight room, and an indoor skate park; admission $6.50.

WINTERTIME

Winter is certainly a quiet time in the park, but that doesn't mean there's a lack of things to do. Marmot Basin offers world-class alpine skiing; many snow-covered hiking trails are groomed for cross-country skiing; portions of Lac Beauvert and Pyramid Lake are cleared for ice-skating; horse-drawn sleighs travel around town; and Maligne Canyon is transformed into a magical, frozen world. Hotels reduce rates by 40–70 percent through winter, and many offer lodging and lift tickets for less than $80 per person.

Marmot Basin

The skiing at Marmot Basin (780/852-3816 or 800/363-3078, www.skimarmot.com) is highly underrated. A huge injection of cash in recent years has meant even better facilities are offered, and new lifts have opened up addi-

Marmots inhabit boulder-strewn slopes throughout alpine areas of the Canadian Rockies. The summit of the Whistlers has a particularly high population.

tional terrain. Lifts now take skiers and boarders into Charlie's Basin, a massive powder-filled bowl, and to the summit of Eagle Ridge, which accesses open bowls and lightly treed glades of two other mountain faces. Local Joe Weiss saw the potential for skiing in the basin in the 1920s and began bringing skiers up from the valley. A road was constructed from the highway in the early 1950s, and the first paying skiers were transported up to the slopes in a Sno-Cat. The first lift, a 700-meter (2,300-foot) rope tow, was installed on the Paradise face in 1961, and the area has continued to expand ever since. Marmot Basin now has nine lifts servicing 680 hectares (1,675 acres) of terrain with a vertical rise of 900 meters (2,940 feet). The longest run is 5.6 km (3.5 miles). Marmot doesn't get the crowds of the three resorts in Banff National Park, so lift lines are uncommon. The season runs from early December to late April. Lift tickets are adult $55, senior $40, child $20. (Throughout Jasper in January celebrations, tickets are just $40.) Rentals are available at the resort or in town at **Totem Ski Shop** (408 Connaught Dr., 780/852-3078).

Buses depart three times daily for Marmot Basin from most Jasper hotels; $8 one-way, $14 round-trip. The first departure is 8–8:30 A.M.

Cross-Country Skiing

For many people, traveling Jasper's hiking trails on skis is just as exhilarating as on foot. An extensive network of 300 km (185 miles) of summer hiking trails is designated for skiers, with around 100 km (62 miles) groomed. The four main areas of trails are along Pyramid Lake Road, around Maligne Lake, in the Athabasca Falls area, and at Whistlers Campground. A booklet available at the park information center details each trail and its difficulty. Weather forecasts and avalanche-hazard reports are also posted here.

Rental packages are available from **Source for Sports** (406 Patricia St., 780/852-3654), the rental shop at **Jasper Park Lodge** (780/852-3433), and **Totem Ski Shop** (408 Connaught Dr., 780/852-3078), offering rentals, repairs, and sales.

Maligne Canyon

By late December, the torrent that is the Maligne River has frozen solid. Where it cascades down through Maligne Canyon, the river is temporarily stalled for the winter, creating remarkable formations through the deep limestone canyon. **Maligne Tours** (627 Patricia St., 780/852-3370) offers exciting three-hour guided tours into the depths of the canyon throughout winter, daily at 9 A.M., 1 P.M., and 6 P.M.; $24 adults, $12.50 children.

ARTS AND ENTERTAINMENT

The **Chaba Theatre** (604 Connaught Dr., 780/852-4749) shows first-run movies in its two theaters.

Bars and Nightclubs

The most popular nightspot in town is the **Atha-B,** in the Athabasca Hotel (510 Patricia St., 780/852-3386), where bands play some nights. It gets pretty rowdy with all the seasonal workers, but it's still enjoyable; minimal cover charge. This hotel also has a large lounge and a bar with a pool table and a popular 5–7 P.M. happy hour. **Pete's** (upstairs at 614 Patricia St., 780/852-6262) has a jam on Tuesday night and bands playing Friday–Sunday. The music varies—it could be blues, rock, or Celtic. The **De'd Dog Bar and Grill,** in the Astoria Hotel (404 Connaught Dr., 780/852-3351), is a large, dimly lit sports bar with pool tables and plenty of locals drinking copious amounts of beer, especially during the 5–7 P.M. happy hour. Right downtown, the **Whistle Stop Pub,** in the Whistlers Inn (105 Miette Ave., 780/852-3361), has a great atmosphere with a classic wooden bar and memorabilia everywhere.

Escape the smoky bar scenes at the **Downstream Bar** (620 Connaught Dr., 780/852-9449), a nonsmoking place that opens at 4 P.M. and has live music Friday and Saturday. You don't need to be a guest of Jasper's finest hotel, the Jasper Park Lodge (780/852-3301), to enjoy the ambience of its three lounges: the **Emerald Lounge** has comfortable indoor seating and a long outdoor terrace overlooking Lac Beauvert; **Tent City** is a sports-style bar with a relaxed atmosphere and two pool tables; while **Palisade's** is a winter-only bar attracting the après theater crowd each evening. Most of Jasper's other large hotels, including the Amethyst Lodge, Jasper Inn, and Marmot Lodge, also have cocktail lounges.

Shopping

Jasper certainly doesn't provide the shopping experience found in Banff, but several interesting shops beckon on rainy days. **Our Native Land** (601 Patricia St., 780/852-5592) is a large shop chock-full of authentic arts and crafts produced by artisans from throughout western Canada. Search out everything from moosehide moccasins to masks (check out the musk ox head near the back of the store). It also stocks Inuit soapstone carvings from the Canadian Arctic. **Bearberry** (612 Connaught Dr., 780/852-1112) features a good cross-section of Canadiana. Beyond the information center, **Pine Cones & Pussy Willow** (308 Connaught Dr., 780/852-5310) is a little less tacky than your average souvenir shop, with furry toys and plastic rulers complemented by the works of local artists.

Within 100 meters (330 feet) of the information center is **Source for Sports** (406 Patricia St., 780/852-3654) and the **Totem Ski Shop** (408 Connaught Dr., 780/852-3078), both with a good stock of camping gear and other outdoor equipment. Before getting carried away at these specialty stores, check out **Home Hardware** (625 Patricia St., 780/852-5555) for basic camping supplies.

Festivals and Events

Summer is prime time on the park's events calendar. **Canada Day** (July 1) celebrations begin with a pancake breakfast and progress to a flag-raising ceremony (in front of the information center) and a parade along Connaught Drive. Live entertainment and a fireworks display end the day. The **Jasper Lions Pro Indoor Rodeo,** on the second weekend of August, dates from 1933 and attracts pro cowboys from across Canada. Apart from the traditional rodeo events, the fun includes a mechanical bull, a children's rodeo, a casino, pancake breakfasts, the ever-

popular stick-pony parade, and the crowning of Miss Jasper. Most of the action takes place in the arena at the Jasper Activity Centre, behind town on Pyramid Lake Road (780/852-4622).

On the other side of the calendar, winter is not totally partyless—**Jasper in January** is a two-week celebration that includes fireworks, special evenings at local restaurants, a chili cook-off, discounted lift tickets at Marmot Basin, and all the activities associated with winter.

Park Interpretive Program

Parks Canada offers a wide range of interpretive talks and hikes throughout summer. Each summer night in the **Whistlers Campground Theatre** a different slide show and movie program is shown. The theater is near the shower block. The **Wabasso Campfire Circle** takes place each Saturday night just before dusk; hot tea is supplied while various speakers talk about wildlife in the park.

Many different guided hikes are offered (all free) throughout summer; check bulletin boards at the park information center and campgrounds, or call 780/852-6176.

ACCOMMODATIONS IN AND AROUND TOWN

In summer, motel and hotel rooms here are expensive. Most of the motels and lodges are within walking distance of town and have indoor pools and restaurants. Luckily, alternatives to staying in $200-plus hotel rooms do exist. The best alternatives are the lodges scattered around the edge of town. Open in summer only, each offers a rustic yet distinct style of accommodation in keeping with the theme of staying in a national park. Additionally, many private residences have rooms for rent in summer; three hostels are close to town; and there's always camping in the good ol' outdoors.

Unless otherwise noted, accommodations discussed here are within walking distance of downtown Jasper. Rates quoted are for a standard room in summer. Outside the busy June–September period most lodgings reduce rates drastically (ask also about ski packages during winter).

Under $50

Staying in hostels isn't for everyone, but it's the only type of accommodation in the park that comes close to falling into this price category.

Hostelling International–Canada (www.hi hostels.ca) operates five hostels in Jasper National Park, but none right in downtown Jasper. Reservations are highly recommended at all hostels during July and August. Make these by calling 780/852-3215 or 877/852-0781 or through other major hostels such as those in Lake Louise, Banff, Calgary, or Edmonton.

On the road to the Jasper Tramway, seven km (4.3 miles) south from town off the Icefields Parkway, is **Jasper International Hostel,** which has 84 beds in men's and women's dorms, a large kitchen, a common room, showers, public Internet access, an outdoor barbecue area, and mountain-bike rentals. Members of Hostelling International pay $20, nonmembers $25. In the summer months this hostel fills up every night. The front desk is open daily noon–midnight. Cab fare between downtown Jasper and the hostel is $18.

Maligne Canyon Hostel is on Maligne Lake Road, beside the Maligne River and a short walk from the canyon. Although rustic, it lies in a beautiful setting. The 24 beds are in two cabins; other amenities include electricity, a kitchen, and a dining area. Rates are $13 for members, $18 for nonmembers. Check-in is between 5 P.M. and 11 P.M. The hostel is closed on Wednesday October–April.

M Mount Edith Cavell Hostel (mid-June–Oct.) offers a million-dollar view for the price of a dorm bed. It's 13 km (eight miles) up Cavell Road off Highway 93A, and because of the location there's usually a spare bed. Opposite the hostel are trailheads for hiking in the Tonquin Valley, and it's just a short walk to the base of Mount Edith Cavell. The hostel is rustic but has a kitchen, dining area, and outdoor wood sauna. Members pay $13 per night, nonmembers pay $18. Check-in is 5–11 P.M.

$50–100

If you're simply looking for somewhere to rest your head, consider Jasper's least expensive hotel rooms at the downtown **Athabasca Hotel** (510 Patricia St., 780/852-3386 or 877/542-8422, www.athabascahotel.com). This historic three-story brick building dates to 1928, replacing the original structure of the same name, which was the town's first hotel. The cheapest of its 61 rooms share bathrooms and are above a noisy bar, but the price is right—$75–109 s or d. This hotel also has more expensive rooms, each with a vaguely Victorian decor and private bathrooms ($118–154 s or d).

The cheapest motel-style units at **Patricia Lake Bungalows** (780/852-3560, www.patricia lakebungalows.com), beside the lake of the same name, a five-minute drive north from Jasper along Pyramid Lake Road, fall into this price range (from $85 per night), but it is worth paying extra for a freestanding unit. Comfortable but older cottages with kitchens and TV start at $135 s or d, rising to $170 for those with either

PRIVATE HOME ACCOMMODATIONS

At last count, Jasper had more than 100 residential homes offering accommodations. They often supply nothing more than a room with a bed, but the price is right at $50–100 single or double. Use of a bathroom is usually shared with other guests or the family; few have kitchens and only a few supply light breakfast. In most cases, don't expect too much with the lower-priced choices. The positive side, apart from the price, is that your hosts are usually knowledgeable locals, and downtown is only a short walk away. For a full listing that includes the facilities at each approved property, write **Jasper Home Accommodation Association,** P.O. Box 758, Jasper, AB T0E 1E0, or check out www.stayin jasper.com.

The park information center has a board listing private home accommodations with rooms available for the upcoming night. Most have signs out front, so you could cruise the residential streets (try Connaught, Patricia, and Geikie) looking for a Vacancy sign, but checking at the information center is easier.

"SUMMER ONLY" LODGING

The earliest tourists to Jasper came by train, but as the automobile gained popularity in the 1920s, accommodations were built specifically to cater to visitors who arrived by motor vehicle. Typically, these "bungalow camps" consisted of a cluster of cabins set around a central lodge where meals were served and—with no need for the railway—were spread throughout the park. This type of accommodation remains in various forms today, a popular alternative for those who don't need the luxuries associated with hotels and the services of downtown Jasper. They are generally only open May to early October.

a lake view or fireplace. Suites ($190–250) are a good value in relation to similar-sized rooms elsewhere in town. Other amenities include a barbecue area and an outdoor hot tub.

Typifying a bungalow camp of the 1950s, **Pine Bungalows** (780/852-3491, www.pine bungalows.com; May–mid-Oct.) lies on a secluded section of the Athabasca River opposite the northern entrance to town. Sparse but comfortable motel-style units with kitchenettes are $90 s or d, individual wooden cabins with kitchens and fireplaces begin at $135 (most cabins face the river, but numbers 1 and 3 enjoy the best views). More modern two-bedroom log cabins are $175.

$100–150

No hotels fall into this price range, but the three accommodations detailed as follows all offer excellent value for money.

With a variety of cabin layouts and a central location, **N Bear Hill Lodge** (100 Bonhomme St., 780/852-3209, www.bearhilllodge.com, mid-Apr.–mid-Oct.) makes a great base camp for travelers who want the cabin experience within walking distance of downtown services. The original cabins are basic, but each has a TV, bathroom, gas fireplace, and coffee-making facilities ($145 s or d; $165 with a kitchenette). Chalet Rooms are larger and more modern, and each has a wood-burning fireplace but no

kitchen ($165). Colin Rooms are more spacious still; each has a jetted tub, gas fireplace, and limited cooking facilities ($185). Units are discounted 40 percent during the first and last months of operation. Breakfasts ($8 per person) feature a wide selection of freshly baked items, fruit, and cereals.

One of the least expensive of a string of lodges immediately south of downtown is family-run **Jasper House Bungalows** (four km/2.5 miles south along the Icefields Parkway, 780/852-4535, www.jasperhouse.com; May–mid-Oct.). It comprises 56 cedar log cabins, each with a TV and coffeemaker, ranging $140–195 s or d (those at the upper end of this price range are fully self-contained and overlook the river). Basic motel-style units are $140 s or d, $160 with a kitchenette. Also on site is a old-style rustic restaurant open through the summer season for breakfast and lunch

Farther south along the Icefields Parkway, **N Becker's Chalets** (780/852-3779, www.beckerschalets.com; May–mid-Oct.) is spread along a picturesque bend on the Athabasca River six km (3.7 miles) south of town. This historic lodging took its first guests more than 50 years ago and continues to be a park favorite for many guests who make staying here an annual ritual. Moderately priced chalets, each with kitchenette, gas fireplace, and double bed ($135, or $165 for those on the riverfront), are an excellent deal. Deluxe log duplexes featuring all the modern conveniences, including color TV, range $170–220. Also available are a few one-bed sleeping rooms ($90). Becker's also boasts one of the park's finest restaurants.

$150–200

The lure of **N Tekarra Lodge** (Hwy. 93A, 1.6 km/one mile south from downtown, 780/852-3058 or 888/962-2522, www.tekarralodge.com; May–Sept.) is its historic log cabins and forested setting on a plateau above the confluence of the Miette and Athabasca Rivers. Each cabin has been totally modernized yet retains a cozy charm, with comfortable beds, fully equipped kitchenettes, wood-burning fireplaces, and smallish but adequate bathrooms. High season rates start at $189 with the Athabasca Cabins best suited for small families. An on-site restaurant is open for breakfast (7:30–11 A.M.) and dinner (5–11 P.M.). Other amenities include bike rentals and a laundry room. From the lodge, hiking trails lead along the Athabasca River in both directions as well as over the river to the golf course and Jasper Park Lodge.

A short distance south along Highway 93A from Tekarra Lodge, at the junction of the Icefields Parkway three km (1.9 miles) south of town, is **Alpine Village** (780/852-3285, www.alpinevillagejasper.com; late Apr.–mid-Oct.). This resort is laid out across well-manicured lawns, and all buildings are surrounded by colorful gardens of geraniums and petunias. After a day exploring the park, guests kick back on a row of Adirondack chairs scattered along the Athabasca River, directly opposite the resort. The older sleeping cabins have been renovated ($150 s or d, $170 with a kitchen and fireplace), while the newer deluxe one-bedroom log cabins feature stone fireplaces and modern furnishings ($190). The Deluxe Family Cabins ($310) sleep up to five, with two beds in an upstairs loft, a fireplace, and a full kitchen.

This is the price range that most downtown Jasper hotel rooms fall within. Right downtown is the 35-room **Astoria Hotel** (404 Connaught Dr., 780/852-3351 or 800/661-7343, www.astoriahotel.com), a European-style lodging built in 1924 and kept in the same family since. Rooms are brightly furnished and each has a fridge, TV, and VCR. Standard rooms are $180 s or d, while much larger Superior rooms, complete with full bath, are $200. Outside of summer, these same rooms cost $100 and $125, respectively. Note that there is no elevator in this four-story hotel.

Other hotel choices include the **Tonquin Inn** (100 Juniper St., 780/852-4987 or 800/661-1315, www.tonquininn.com; from $199 s or d), with an indoor pool, an outdoor hot tub, laundry facilities, a steakhouse restaurant, and a sunny lounge bar; and **Maligne Lodge** (780/852-3143 or 800/661-1315, www.malignelodge.com; $189 s or d), also with an indoor pool. These places are worth considering outside of summer, when the cabin ac-

© ANDREW HEMPSTEAD

Alpine Village, one of many accommodations offering peaceful settings away from downtown

commodations are closed and rates are discounted substantially.

$200–250

Near the end of Pyramid Lake Road, north from downtown, it's impossible to miss the sprawling grounds of **Pyramid Lake Resort** (780/852-4900 or 888/962-2522, www.pyramidlakeresort.com), the only lodging away from town (besides Jasper Park Lodge) that is open year-round. Plenty of water-based activities and rentals (across the road), an interpretive program, a fitness center, and a large barbecue area make the resort a good choice for families. Summer-only cabins, with separate bedrooms, full baths, and lake views, range $225–265 s or d. In addition to lake views, motel-style units feature gas fireplaces and kitchenettes for $285 (discounted below $150 in the off-season).

On Connaught Drive southwest of downtown, **Mount Robson Inn** (780/852-3327 or 800/587-3327, www.mountrobsoninn.com; from $210 s or d) has 78 rooms, each air-conditioned and with coffeemakers, alarm clocks, and hair dryers—in other words you could be staying in a generic city hotel. On the plus side, the suites here are a good deal (relative to other Jasper accommodations); each holds two separate bedrooms, a full bathroom with additional outside vanity, and a fireplace for $280–325 per unit.

Jasper Inn (98 Geikie St., 780/852-4461 or 800/661-1933, www.jasperinn.com) is a modern chateau-style lodging of brick and red cedar. Many rooms have private balconies, and more than 100 are self-contained suites with kitchenettes and fireplaces. Other features include a large indoor pool and a sundeck overlooking a Japanese rock garden. Rates start at $220 s or d, with kitchen units starting at $230. The Upper Loft Suites, complete with kitchen, fireplace, and—as the name suggests—a bedroom in the loft, are a much better deal at $235 s or d (from $109 outside of summer).

The **Sawridge Inn** (82 Connaught Dr., 780/852-5111 or 800/661-6427, www.sawridge jasper.com) offers 154 air-conditioned rooms built around a large atrium and indoor pool. Also contained within the atrium is a fine-dining restaurant and lounge. Rooms overlooking the atrium are $229 s or d, outward-facing rooms with big balconies are $259, or pay $289 for an extra-spacious room with a king bed. Rates are reduced up to 60 percent outside of the busiest mid-June to September period.

$250–350

Château Jasper (96 Geikie St., 780/852-5644 or 800/661-1315, www.chateaujasper.com) is one of Jasper's nicest lodgings. Guest rooms are spacious and elegantly finished with maple furnishings and low ceilings that give them a cozy feel. Bathrooms are particularly well equipped, with guests also enjoying the use of plush bathrobes. Summer rates start at $325 s or d, but as you move into these higher priced places, off-season discounts become steeper—in this case, rooms throughout the winter season are just $135 s or d. The restaurant is one of Jasper's best.

Over $350

Ⓜ Jasper Park Lodge (780/852-3301 or 800/ 257-7544, www.fairmont.com) lies along the shore of Lac Beauvert (meaning "beautiful green lake" in French) across the Athabasca River from downtown. This is the park's original resort and its most famous. It has four restaurants, three lounges, horseback riding, tennis courts, a championship golf course, and Jasper's only covered shopping arcade. The main lodge features stone floors, carved wooden pillars, and a high ceiling. The 446 rooms vary in configuration and are spread out over the expansive property. All have coffeemakers, TV, telephones, and Internet access. The least expensive units ($549 s or d) are smallish, hold two twin beds, and offer no views. Also away from the lake, Fairmont Rooms ($549 s or d) are contained in rows of cedar-lined chalets; each has a patio or balcony. Similar in size and layout, but with water views, are Fairmont Deluxe Rooms ($559 s or d). Jasper Premier Rooms ($629 s or d) have a distinct country charm, and each has either a sitting room or patio with lake views. Moving up to the more expensive options, Lakeview Suites ($759 s or d) overlook Lac Beauvert and are backed by the 18th fairway of the golf course. Each features a patio or balcony, fireplace, and two TVs.

Most guests don't pay the summer rack rates quoted here. The cost of lodging is usually included in one of the plethora of packages offered, such as the Grand Canadian Lodge Experience, which includes golf, meals, taxes, and gratuities and brings the cost of a standard room down to well less than $400 per night (click on the "Package Finder" link on the Fairmont website for all the options). Outside of summer, Jasper Park Lodge becomes a real bargain, with rooms with lake views (remember it'll be frozen in winter) for well less than $200.

The various historic cabins provide Jasper Park Lodge's premier accommodations. Starting from $800 per night, they are priced beyond the reach of most travelers but are mentioned here simply because they are among the most exclusive rooms in all of Canada. They have hosted true royalty (Queen Elizabeth) and movie royalty (Marilyn Monroe, during the filming of *River of No Return*). They range from the secluded and cozy Athabasca Cabin to the 1928, five-bedroom Point Cabin overlooking the lake. The largest is

Milligan Manor, an eight-bedroom, 657-square-meter (7,075-square-foot) "cottage" beside the golf clubhouse.

ACCOMMODATIONS EAST OF TOWN

Two accommodations east of the town of Jasper but still within the park boundary are open in summer only.

$50–100

Located at the site of a once-bustling coal mining town, **Pocahontas Bungalows** (780/866-3732 or 888/852-7737; May–Sept.) is at the bottom of the road that leads to Miette Hot Springs, 43 km (27 miles) east of Jasper along Highway 16. Sleeping-room cabins start at $90 s or d, or pay $100 for a kitchen-equipped unit; motel rooms are $125. Best of all are the newer log cabins from where you can watch the brood frolicking in the outdoor pool. Each is equipped with a full kitchen, separate bedroom, TV, and fireplace ($190 s or d). You can dine at the resort restaurant (open for breakfast and dinner) or pick up supplies in Jasper and cook up a storm in the shaded barbecue area.

$100–150

Miette Hot Springs Bungalows (780/866-3750) is within walking distance of the park's only hot springs, 18 km (11 miles) from Highway 16 and 61 km (38 miles) from town. Motel units are $125, while bungalows, each with cooking facilities, start at $145. Guest facilities include a covered barbecue area, restaurant, and laundry room.

HINTON ACCOMMODATIONS

This medium-sized town lies along Highway 16, approximately 19 km (12 miles) east of the park gate and 69 km (43 miles) east of the town of Jasper. Staying here provides an inexpensive alternative to staying in the park. The strip of motels, restaurants, fast-food places, and gas stations along Highway 16 is the place to start looking for a room.

$50–100

The best value is **Pines Motel** (709 Gregg Ave., 780/865-2624, www.pines-motel.com; $69 s, $79–99 d), with 21 regularly revamped rooms adjacent to the local golf course. Each room has a microwave, fridge, and coffeemaker.

The dowdy-looking **Big Horn Motel** (780/865-1555), beside the Husky gas station, has surprisingly good rooms, some larger than others; $70 s, $75 d, kitchenettes an extra $10.

$100–150

Holiday Inn Hinton (780/865-3321 or 800/262-9428, www.holiday-inn.com; from $99 s, $109 d) has everything you'd expect from a Holiday Inn—reliable rooms, a restaurant, a fitness room, and kid-friendly extras like PlayStation.

One of Hinton's newer accommodations is the **Ramada Hinton** (500 Smith St., 780/865-2575 or 888/644-6866, www.ramadahinton.com), which offers 55 fairly spacious, comfortable rooms, each with a microwave, coffeemaker, and well-equipped bathroom. Other hotel features include a fitness room, hot tub, restaurant, lounge, and laundry room. Standard rooms are $119 s or d, two-bedroom loft suites complete with kitchens are $149, while the King Suite comes with a king bed, jetted tub, two gas fireplaces, and a private balcony with mountain views for less than $200 (about the same you'd pay for a basic, boring hotel room in the park).

OTHER LODGING OPTIONS
Tonquin Valley

Jasper's two backcountry lodges are southwest of Jasper in the spectacular Tonquin Valley. Accessible only on foot or horseback or, in winter, by skiing, both lodges are open to hikers (with advance reservations); most guests stay as part of a package that includes horseback riding.

Dating to 1939, **Tonquin Amethyst Lake Lodge** (780/852-1188, www.tonquinadventures.com) was extensively upgraded in the early 1990s. Private cabins have wood-burning heaters, twin log beds with thick blankets, oil lanterns, and a spectacular view. The rate, $145 per person per night, includes accommodations, three hearty ranch-style meals, and use of small boats and fishing gear. Tonquin Adventures offers a number of well-priced packages, including riding into the lodge on horses. Rates are reduced in winter. Getting there involves a 19-km (11.8-mile) journey from a trailhead opposite Mount Edith Cavell Hostel.

Nearby **Tonquin Valley Backcountry Lodge** (780/852-3909, www.tonquinvalley.com) offers a similar setup, with most guests arriving by horseback on a pre-arranged ride from the nearest road. In this case, the departure point is along Marmot Basin Road, from a parking lot at Portal Creek. Rates are $145 per person per night, with a five-night package—inclusive of horse rental—costing $850 per person.

Black Cat Guest Ranch

The ◼ **Black Cat Guest Ranch** mountain retreat (780/865-3084 or 800/859-6840, www.blackcatguestranch.ca) lies on the eastern edge of the park, surrounded by mountain wilderness. All 16 rooms have private baths and views of the mountains. Horseback riding is available during the day (June–Sept.), and in the evening guests relax in the large living room or hot tub. Meals are included in the rates of $145 s, $184 d. To get to the ranch, follow Highway 16 for 19 km (12 miles) beyond the east gate, head north along Highway 40 for six km (3.7 mikes), turn left to Brûlé and continue for 11 km (6.8 miles), and then turn right and follow the signs.

CAMPGROUNDS

Campgrounds in Jasper begin opening in mid-June, and all but Wapiti are closed by mid-October. All campsites have a picnic table and fire ring, with a fire permit costing $6 (includes firewood). A percentage of sites in the most popular campgrounds can be reserved through the Parks Canada Campground Reservation Service (877/737-3783, www.pccamping.ca) for a nominal fee. If you're traveling in July or August, know which dates you'll be in Jasper, and require electrical hookups, it is strongly advised to take advantage of this service. Whistlers and Wapiti are the only two campgrounds with powered sites, and therefore they're in great demand. A line usually forms well before the official check-out time of 11 A.M. If you don't have reservations, Parks Canada suggests planning to spend your first night without power, after which you'll receive priority for a powered site.

Unlike neighboring Banff National Park, Jasper's 10 campgrounds combine to handle all but the busiest summer nights. And on the rare occasion all campsites fill, campers are directed to overflow areas. These are glorified parking lots with no designated sites, but fees are reduced ($8 per vehicle).

Near the Town of Jasper

Whistlers Campground, at the base of Whistlers Road, three km (1.9 miles) south of town, has 781 sites, making it the largest campground in the Canadian Rockies. It is divided into four sections; prices vary with the services available—walk-in sites $19, unserviced sites $22, powered sites $26, full hookups $30. Each section has showers. Whistlers is open May to mid-October.

Two km (1.2 miles) farther south along the Icefields Parkway is **Wapiti Campground,** which offers 366 sites and has showers; unserviced sites $22, powered sites $26. This is the park's only campground open year-round, with serviced winter camping $17 per night.

Sites at **Wabasso Campground,** along Highway 93A approximately 16 km (10 miles) south of town, are set among stands of spruce and aspen; $17 per night.

East Along Highway 16

East of town, along Highway 16, are two smaller, more primitive campgrounds. **Snaring River Campground,** 17 km (11 miles) from Jasper on Celestine Lake Road, is $12; **Pocahontas Campground,** 45 km (28 miles) northeast, is $15. Both are open mid-May to early September.

FOOD

It's easy to get a good, or even great, meal in Jasper. Connaught Drive and Patricia Street are lined with cafés and restaurants. Considering this is a national park, menus are reasonably well priced. You should expect hearty fare, with lots of beef, game, and a surprisingly good selection of seafood.

Coffeehouses and Cafés

The **Soft Rock Cafe** (632 Connaught Dr., 780/852-5850; daily 7:30 A.M.–6:30 P.M.) occupies a sunny spot along Jasper's main thoroughfare. It is one of the most popular places in town to start the day. Seating is inside or out, and you order at the counter. Breakfast options include omelets and skillet dishes (all less than $10). If the cinnamon buns are still in the oven, you'll have to come back later in the day—they're gigantic! The variety of coffee concoctions here is mind-boggling, and all prices are reasonable. Back toward the heart of downtown, **Mountain Foods & Café** (606 Connaught Dr., 780/852-4050) offers a full cooked breakfast for $6 and healthy wraps, rolls, and sandwiches the rest of the day.

© ANDREW HEMPSTEAD

dining on the terrace at Jasper Park Lodge

One block back from Connaught Drive, **Truffles & Trout**, in Jasper Marketplace (corner of Patricia St. and Hazel St., 780/852-9676), is a popular local hangout, with all the usual coffees, as well as boxed picnic lunches on offer. Across the road, **Nutter's** (622 Patricia St., 780/852-5844) is another good prehiking stop, with a wide choice of goodies in bulk bins. **Coco's Café** (608 Patricia St., 780/852-4550) is another coffee-lover's meeting place.

You'll smell the wonderful aroma of freshly baked bread even before entering **Bear's Paw Bakery** (4 Cedar Ave., 780/852-3233; daily from 7 A.M.). The European-style breads are perfect for a picnic lunch, but not as tempting as the cakes and pastries.

Casual and Family-Style Dining

The ubiquitous family-style restaurant is alive and well in Jasper. One of the originals is the **L&W Restaurant** (corner of Patricia St. and Hazel Ave., 780/852-4114). It features a small outside patio and plenty of greenery that brings to life an otherwise ordinary restaurant—a good place to take the family for a basic but affordable meal.

Kontos Restaurant (622 Patricia St., 780/852-3444) is a newer addition to the Jasper dining scene. The menu is fairly standard, with especially hearty portions offered as lunch specials (ask, or you'll only be offered the regular menu) for $6–9. Dinner specials range $14–18, or choose from simple European dishes such as souvlaki for $15. (The bathrooms here are worthy of a special mention—they contain everything from sunscreen to hand cream.)

You won't be dazzled by the surroundings at **Palisades** (Cedar Ave., 780/852-5222; daily 4–9:30 P.M. and in summer 8:30–11:30 A.M. for breakfast), but the wide-ranging menu appeals to families: inexpensive vegetarian choices, pastas and pizza to $17, Greek specialties less than $20, a massive T-bone steak for $24, and a $5 kids' menu.

For pizza, you won't be able to miss **Jasper Pizza Place** (402 Connaught Dr., 780/852-3225). It's a large and noisy restaurant with bright furnishings, a concrete floor, exposed heating ducts, and walls lined with photos from Jasper's earliest days. Regular thick-crust pizzas are available from 11 A.M., but it's not until 5 P.M., when the wood-fired oven begins producing thin-crust pizzas with adventurous toppings, that this place really shines; expect to pay $13–16 for a 10-inch pizza.

On the same side of town as Jasper Pizza Place is one of Jasper's oldest restaurants, **Papa George's** (Astoria Hotel, 406 Connaught Dr., 780/852-3351; daily 7 A.M.–10 P.M.). Huge east-facing windows take in the panorama of distant mountain peaks. Breakfast is $4–8, a traditional English afternoon tea served 2:30–4:30 P.M. is $9, while lunch and dinner feature burgers, pasta, and steaks; daily specials are $12–19 and include soup and salad.

Steakhouses
Most restaurants feature Alberta beef prominently, but it's a specialty at these two places.

Tonquin Prime Rib Village (Tonquin Inn, 100 Juniper St., 780/852-4966; daily from 5 P.M.) has been a long-time Jasper favorite. Char-broiled steaks and hearty servings of prime rib cost $24–34, but the prime rib sandwich ($18), with a plate-load of extras, will fill any carnivorous cravings for a few dollars less. This restaurant also offers a surprisingly good selection of seafood.

Villa Caruso (640 Connaught Dr., 780/852-3920; daily 11 A.M.–midnight) is a steakhouse with a modern mountain vibe. The upstairs location—request a balcony table if the weather's warm—allows great views across the valley. The menu features a wide variety of Alberta beef dishes, including a massive 16-ounce T-bone for $32. But there's a lot more than steak on offer, including chicken, seafood, and pasta dishes from $15.

Seafood
Fiddle River Seafood Restaurant (upstairs at 620 Connaught Dr., 780/852-3032; daily 5–10 P.M.) is a long way from the ocean and not particularly coastal in feel, but it offers a wide variety of seafood. The striking decor matches dark polished wood with forest green furnishings, and large windows provide mountain views

(reservations are needed for window-side tables). Trout, arctic char, red snapper, ahi tuna, and halibut all make regular appearances on the blackboard menu. Expect to pay about $40 per person for a three-course meal.

European
Andy's Bistro (606 Patricia St., 780/852-4559; daily from 5–9:30 P.M.) is an elegantly casual eatery offering a wide range of uncomplicated dishes using Canadian game and produce prepared with Swiss-influenced cooking styles. Start with a plate piled high with Prince Edward Island steamed mussels ($12, but enough for two people), then choose between dishes such as pan-seared ostrich medallions ($24) or halibut cheeks with crystallized ginger sauce ($22). Andy's has an extensive cellar of wines but no official wine list. Instead, diners are encouraged to choose from red wines set along the bar and white wines from the fridge. At the unique *stammtisch*, a large table, up to 10 diners can be seated at once, free to come and go as they please. It's the perfect place to mingle with fellow travelers. Also notable at Andy's is the staff, who seem experienced and knowledgeable.

The best Greek meals in town are served at **Something Else Restaurant** (621 Patricia St., 780/852-3850; daily 11 A.M.–11 P.M.). Portions are generous, service is friendly, the prices are right, and you'll find plenty of alternatives if the Greek dishes don't appeal to you. Greek favorites are $14–18, pasta dishes $13–16, pizza from $13.

Miss Italia Ristorante (610 Patricia St., 780/852-4002), upstairs in the Patricia Centre Mall, features bright and breezy interior decor with tables also set on a narrow terrace bedecked in pots of colorful flowers. Cooked breakfasts (from 8 A.M.) are $6–9. The rest of the day, pastas made fresh daily average $15, a baked filet of Atlantic salmon is $16, and souvlaki with a side of salad and pita bread is just $16. Check out the daily specials before ordering—they are taken from the regular menu but discounted a couple of bucks and come with soup or salad.

Directly behind the park information center, **La Fiesta** (504 Patricia St., 780/852-0404;

daily 11:30 A.M.–11 P.M.) is a small eatery with a slightly Mediterranean feel. It offers a tapas menu as well as a full Canadian one. Tapas are $4.50–12 and include delights such as pork kebabs served with a fig and pine nut relish and mussels steamed in a tequila broth.

Asian

The **Cantonese Restaurant** (608 Connaught Dr., 780/852-3559; daily noon–10 P.M.) is the place to go for Chinese; combo specials are $9–13, and set five-course menus for two start at $28. **Denjiro** (410 Connaught Dr., 780/852-3780; daily 5–11:30 P.M.) features a traditional sushi bar and eight tatami booths for eating the Japanese cuisine; combination dinners average $19 per person.

Jasper Park Lodge

Jasper's premier accommodation, across the river from downtown, offers a choice of casual or elegant dining in a variety of restaurants and lounges. Across from the reception area is a dedicated dining reservation desk, staffed in summer daily 11 A.M.–8 P.M., or call 780/852-6052. Reservations are required for the Edith Cavell and Moose's Nook dining rooms.

The **Beauvert Dining Room** (6–9 A.M.) is a casual 500-seat eatery across the lobby from the Emerald Lounge. It features Jasper's most extensive buffet breakfast with a huge selection of hot and cold dishes for $22 per person.

The **Emerald Lounge** (daily 11:30 A.M.–9 P.M.) takes pride of place in the expansive lobby of the main building. Table settings of various configurations are spread throughout the room while also sprawling out and along the **Emerald Outdoor Patio,** from where views over picturesque Lac Beauvert to distant mountains are uninterrupted. Both lunch and dinner menus feature imaginative modern Canadian cuisine, but with dinner (from 5:30 P.M.) being decidedly more expensive. At lunch, salads ranging $8–13 can be made into a full meal by adding extras such as smoked salmon and slices of chicken breast, or stick to mains such as bison burger ($15). Generous dinner mains range $18–34—the Alberta ribeye roasted in red pepper butter is typical.

The elegantly rustic **M Moose's Nook Northern Grill** (daily 6–10 P.M.) is a good place to enjoy traditional Canadian fare, such as grilled wild boar chops, whiskey-flamed arctic char, or a chargrilled Albertan ribeye steak. Mains range $25–34. Be sure to leave room for dessert—the chestnut-crusted cheesecake smothered in maple syrup is incredible.

The **Edith Cavell Room** (daily 6–9 P.M.) is the finest fine-dining restaurant in Jasper. Its dark oak walls contrast with the white linens and large, bright windows overlooking Lac Beauvert and the mountains beyond. Even though the restaurant has changed little over time, its overly pretentious atmosphere has softened and service has become more comfortable. Still, this is seriously cultured dining, unequaled in Jasper. With an emphasis on local produce and Canadian game and seafood, the classic cuisine is served with a French flair. Prices for two-, three-, and four-course table d'hôte combos are a relatively reasonable $55, $70, and $80, respectively. Dress code is resort casual: no t-shirts or jeans; a jacket and tie are "recommended but not required." The Sunday brunch, served between 10 A.M. and 12:30 P.M., costs $30 and is especially popular.

The lodge also holds two casual eateries. From 7 A.M., light breakfasts, drinks, and snacks are served at the **1st Cup,** in the golf clubhouse opposite the first tee. Between 10 A.M. and 5 P.M., the smell of sizzling steaks served from a barbecue out front of the clubhouse wafts across the grounds. Expect to pay $7–11 for burgers, wraps, and the like. **Meadows Restaurant,** downstairs in the shopping arcade, is open for a breakfast buffet 7–11:30 A.M. and then in the evening for a dinner buffet 5:30–9 P.M. (summer only).

Other Hotel Dining

Most of the larger accommodations have restaurants. In general, they open for breakfast and dinner only, with a cold or cooked buffet complementing an à la carte menu.

Walter's Dining Room (Sawridge Hotel, 82 Connaught Dr., 780/852-5111; daily from 5 P.M.) is a cut above the rest and reasonably priced. Surrounded by the greenery of a four-story atrium, the setting is relaxed but elegant. The cooking is contemporary, but distinctly Canadian. You could start with the venison pâté, followed by maple-glazed salmon, spending a little more than $30 for the two courses. The adjacent lounge has the same pleasant setting and a smaller, less-expensive menu.

One block back from the Sawridge Hotel is the Jasper Inn and its **Inn Restaurant** (98 Geikie St., 780/852-3232), with a fine sheltered courtyard complete with an outdoor fireplace and heat lamps for those cooler evenings. As is usually the case in hotel restaurants, the menu is of wide appeal, presenting pastas from $14, beef dishes from $18 (including a creative buffalo and venison meatloaf), and seafood, such as baked halibut topped with a citrus vinaigrette ($24).

Restaurants Outside of Downtown

With so many dining choices in downtown Jasper, it's easy to ignore the many fine restaurants scattered elsewhere in the park.

One of Jasper's best restaurants, **M Becker's Gourmet Restaurant** (780/852-3535; May–mid-Oct. daily 8–11 A.M. and 5:30–9 P.M.) is six km (3.7 miles) out of town to the south along the Icefields Parkway, but well worth the short drive. From this cozy dining room where the atmosphere is intimate or the adjacent enclosed conservatory, the views of Mount Kerkeslin and the Athabasca River are inspiring. This restaurant is a throwback to days gone by, with an ever-changing menu of seasonal game and produce that includes a daily wild game special. A menu staple is the rack of lamb baked with Dijon mustard and fresh herbs then drizzled in a garlic butter sauce. Hot and cold starters range $9–13, while no main is more than $30. For dessert, the Saskatoon berry crisp is a delight. The breakfast buffet costs $12.

Back toward town from Becker's, on Highway 93A, is the dining room of historic **Tekarra Lodge** (780/852-4624; May–Sept. 7:30–11 A.M. and 5–11 P.M.). The setting may be mountain-style rustic, but the cooking appeals to modern preferences with combinations like banana-crusted chicken breast with sweet mango curry sauce ($19). All mains are less than $30, includ-

ing the fish-of-the-day, which is prepared in three different ways.

You'll probably want to eat at the **Treeline Restaurant** (780/852-3093) just for the view—it's high above town at the upper terminal of the Jasper Tramway. Daily breakfast and lunch buffets complement the à la carte menu, while the Sunset Dinner package costs $46, including the gondola ride.

INFORMATION
Park Information Center

The residence of Jasper's first superintendent, a beautiful old stone building dating to 1913, is now used by Parks Canada as the park information center. It's right downtown (Connaught Dr., 780/852-6176; summer daily 8 A.M.–7 P.M., the rest of the year daily 9 A.M.–5 P.M.). The staff provides general information on the park and can direct you to hikes in the immediate vicinity. Around the corner is the **Parks Canada Trail Office** (780/852-6177), which handles questions for those going into the backcountry and issues the relevant passes. **Jasper Tourism and Commerce** (780/852-3858, www.jaspercanadian rockies.com) also has a desk in the building, and the friendly staff never seem to tire of explaining that all the rooms in town are full. As well as providing general information on the town, they have a large collection of brochures on activities, shopping, and restaurants. Beside the main Parks Canada desk is the **Friends of Jasper National Park** outlet selling topographic maps, books, and local publications. Look for notices posted out front with the day's interpretive programs.

Other Sources of Information

Jasper's weekly newspaper, *The Booster,* is available throughout town on Wednesday. As well as newsworthy stories, it includes a list of upcoming events, trail reports, and a town map with funky little symbols highlighting the locations of various "crimes."

The official Town of Jasper website (www.jasper-alberta.com), with lists of current events, weather conditions, and loads of helpful links, is also worth checking out.

Jasper National Park Radio is on the AM band at 1490. For weather conditions in the park, call 780/852-6176.

Books and Bookstores

Housed in Jasper's original Royal Canadian Mounted Police detachment building, small **Jasper Municipal Library** (500 Robson St., 780/852-3652; Mon.–Thurs. 11 A.M.–9 P.M., Fri.–Sat. 11 A.M.–5 P.M.) holds just about everything ever written about the park.

Head to the **Friends of Jasper** store (780/852-4767) in the park information center or the **museum** for a good selection of books on the park's natural and human history. A larger selection of literature, including lots of western Canadiana, can be found at **Jasper Camera and Gift** (412 Connaught Dr., 780/852-3165; daily 9 A.M.–10 P.M.). **Counter Clockwise,** in the Jasper Marketplace (627 Patricia St., 780/852-3152) has a similar selection. **Maligne Lake Books** (Jasper Park Lodge, 780/852-4779) has a good selection of coffee-table books.

SERVICES

The **post office** (502 Patricia St.) is behind the park information center. Mail to be picked up here should be addressed General Delivery, Jasper, AB T0E 1E0. **More Than Mail** (620 Connaught Dr., 780/852-3151; daily 9 A.M.–10 P.M.) offers a wide range of communication services, including regular post, public Internet access, fax and copying facilities, a work area for laptops, international calling, and currency exchange.

The two **laundries** on Patricia Street are open 6 A.M.–11 P.M. and offer **showers** that cost $2 for 10 minutes (quarters).

The **hospital** is at 518 Robson St. (780/852-3344). For the **RCMP,** call 780/852-4848.

Internet Access

Send and receive email and surf the Internet at the following Jasper locations: **Digital Den** (upstairs at 610 Patricia St., 780/852-9765; daily 9 A.M.–10 P.M.); **Jasper Municipal Library** (Elm Ave., 780/852-3652; Mon.–Thurs. 11 A.M.–9 P.M., Fri.–Sat. 11 A.M.–5 P.M.); **More Than Mail** (620 Connaught Dr., 780/852-3151; daily 9 A.M.–10 P.M.); **Soft Rock Café** (632 Connaught Dr., 780/852-5850; daily 8 A.M.–10 P.M.).

GETTING THERE

Getting to Jasper by public transportation is easy, although the closest airport handling domestic and international flights is at Edmonton, 360 km (224 miles) to the east. The **VIA Rail station** and the **bus depot** (used by both Greyhound and Brewster) are in the same building, central to town at 607 Connaught Drive. The building is open 24 hours daily in summer (the rest of the year Mon.–Sat. 7:30 A.M.–10:30 P.M., Sun. 7:30–11 A.M. and 6:30–10:30 P.M.). Lockers are available for $1 per day. Car-rental agencies are here, too.

Rail

Jasper is on the Canadian route, the only remaining transcontinental passenger rail service in the country. Trains run either way three times weekly. To the west the line divides, going to both Prince Rupert and Vancouver; to the east it passes through Edmonton and all points beyond. For all rail information, contact **VIA Rail** (800/561-8630, www.viarail.ca). Another rail option is offered by **Rocky Mountaineer Railtours** (800/665-7245, www.rockymountaineer.com). This company operates a luxurious summer-only rail service between Vancouver and Jasper with an overnight in Kamloops (British Columbia).

Bus

Greyhound buses (780/852-332 or 800/661-8747, www.greyhound.ca) depart Jasper for all points in Canada (except Banff), including Vancouver (three times daily, 12–13 hours, $115 one-way), Edmonton (five times daily, 4.5 hours, $53 one-way) with connections to Calgary, and Prince Rupert (once daily, 18 hours, $154 one-way).

The main carrier up the Icefields Parkway from Calgary and Banff is Banff-based **Brewster** (780/852-3332 or 800/661-1152, www.brewster.ca). This company operates a shuttle between Calgary International Airport daily

May through October ($80 each way). It also offers a year-round tour (May–Oct. daily, Nov.–Apr. Sat. only) between Banff and Jasper. The trip takes 10 hours and costs $95 one-way. The round-trip fare is $124. The round-trip requires an overnight in Jasper. In winter, **Sun Dog Tours** (780/852-4056 or 888/786-3641, www.sundogtours.com) operates a skier shuttle between Calgary and Jasper. Sample fares to Jasper are: from Calgary, $100; from Banff, $55; and from Lake Louise, $44.

GETTING AROUND

The **Maligne Lake Shuttle** (780/852-3370) runs out to Maligne Lake May–September, four to six times daily ($28 round-trip) from its depot (627 Patricia St.). Stops are made at Maligne Canyon and Maligne Canyon Hostel ($9 one-way).

Rental cars start at $60 per day with 150 free kilometers. The following companies have agencies and their local numbers are: **Avis** (780/852-3970), **Budget** (780/852-3222), **Hertz** (780/852-3888), and **National** (780/852-1117).

Cabs in town are not cheap. Most drivers will take you on a private sightseeing tour or to trailheads if requested; try **Jasper Taxi** (780/852-3600 or 852-3146).

Tours

Brewster (780/852-3332) offers a four-hour Discover Jasper tour taking in Patricia and Pyramid Lakes, Maligne Canyon, and Jasper Tramway (ride not included in fare). It departs April–October daily at 8:30 A.M. from the railway station; $43. **Maligne Tours** (627 Patricia St., 780/852-3370, www.malignelake.com) schedules a variety of tours, including one to Maligne Lake ($65, includes cruise). **Jasper Adventure Centre,** in the Chaba Theatre (604 Connaught Dr., 780/852-5595, www.jasperadventurecentre .com) operates several well-priced tours, including the following: Mount Edith Cavell (departs 2 P.M., three hours; $50), Maligne Valley (departs 9:30 A.M., five hours; $85, including boat tour), and Miette Hot Springs (departs 6 P.M., four hours; $54). Similarly priced tours take in historical sites and local wildlife.

Waterton Lakes National Park

Everybody traveling to this small, rugged 526-square-km (203-square-mile) park does so by choice; tucked away in the extreme southwestern corner of Alberta, the park is not on a major highway or on the way to anywhere else. It's bounded to the north and east by the rolling prairies covering southern Alberta; to the south by the U.S. border and Glacier National Park in Montana; and to the west by the Continental Divide, which forms the Alberta–British Columbia border. The natural mountain splendor,

a chain of deep glacial lakes, large and diverse populations of wildlife, an unbelievable variety of day hikes, and a changing face each season make this park a gem that shouldn't be missed on any trip to the Canadian Rockies.

The route to Waterton is almost as scenic as the park itself. From whichever direction you arrive, the transition from prairie to mountains is abrupt, almost devoid of the foothills that characterize other areas along the eastern slopes of the Canadian Rockies. Between the park gate

Must-Sees

Look for **M** to find the sights and activities you
can't miss and **M** for the best dining and lodging.

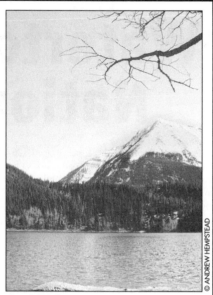

M Waterton Heritage Centre: This is a good
place to learn about the park's natural history
(page 237).

M Akamina Parkway: You'll want to take all the
scenic drives detailed in this chapter, but this one
gets the nod as a must-see attraction. Why? Because when you reach the end of the road you can
rent a canoe and paddle out onto magnificent
Cameron Lake (page 237).

M Crypt Lake: This hike is undoubtedly the most
spectacular trail in the park (page 240).

M Crandell Lake: If the Crypt Lake Trail is a little beyond you, or if you have a family in tow, plan
on hiking up the easy incline to this lake instead
(page 240).

M Cruising to Goat Haunt, Montana: Taking a
tour boat along Upper Waterton Lake and across
the border to Montana has been the most popular
activity in the park for over 50 years—and for
under $30 you can do it, too (page 242).

Crandell Lake

Waterton Lakes

WATERTON LAKES NATIONAL PARK

Waterton Lakes National Park

5 mi

5 km

To Cardston

Paine Lake

Belly River

Waterton River

To Pincher Creek

Dungarvan Creek

Newman Peak

Mt Glendowan

Goat Lake

Twin Lakes

Lost Lake

Lone Mtn

Anderson Peak

Mt Dungarvan

Mt Galwey

Galwey Brook

Bauerman Creek

Blakiston Falls

Mt Blakiston

RED ROCK CANYON PKWY

Red Rock Canyon

Lineham Creek

Lineham Lakes

Mt Lineham

Rowe Lakes

Akamina-Kishinena Provincial Park

Akamina Pass

Wall Lake

Forum Lake

Forum Peak

Akamina Creek

ALBERTA

BRITISH COLUMBIA

CRANDELL MOUNTAIN

CRANDELL LAKE

AKAMINA PARKWAY

Mt Carthew

Carthew Lakes

Mt Alderson

Bertha Lake

Cameron Creek

Cameron Lake

Mt Custer

Lake Wurderman

Boundary Creek

Campbell Mountain

Upper Waterton Lake

Hell Roaring Falls

Mt Boswell

MONTANA

UNITED STATES

CANADA

Glacier National Park

Lewis Range

Sofa Mountain

Vimy Peak

Middle Waterton Lake

CRYPT LAKE

CRUISING TO GOAT HAUNT, MONTANA

Waterton Townsite

SEE "WATERTON TOWNSITE" MAP

Mt Crandell

PASS CREEK

PARK GATE

Lower Waterton Lake

Blakiston Creek

Waterton Lakes National Park

Sofa Creek

CHIEF MOUNTAIN

Crooked Creek

Crooked Creek

WATERTON RIVERSIDE

WATERTON SPRINGS

INTERNATIONAL HWY

North Fork Belly River

BELLY RIVER

CUSTOMS

To US Hwy 89 and Saint Mary

5

6

6

5

17

N

© AVALON TRAVEL PUBLISHING, INC.

and the small township of Waterton, two roads penetrate the mountains to the west. One ends at a large glaciated lake, the other at a spectacular canyon. The town is a smaller version of those in Banff and Jasper. Like those towns, Waterton holds a grand hotel built by the railway, a golf course, and a wide range of services, but the atmosphere here is very different.

PLANNING YOUR TIME

Chances are, if you're planning on visiting Waterton Lakes, you're not the same type of traveler who thinks a trip to Banff entails staying at Best Western and eating at McDonald's.

The vast majority of visitors arrive in July and August. As with the other parks of the Canadian Rockies, June and September are fine times to visit, but as crowds are smaller here, avoiding high summer isn't as much of an issue. Many businesses, including accommodations, close between October and April, although basic services are still available. Cross-country enthusiasts will love winter in the park, but don't expect much else in the way of recreation.

Simply because of the out-of-the-way location, you'll want to spend at least one day in the park, but it's preferable to stay two or more. With two days and one night scheduled, plan on joining the boat cruise to **Goat Haunt** on one day and spending the second day exploring the two main roads, including the one to **Cameron Lake.** This still allows time to walk some shorter trails. If you're a keen hiker, add a third day to your itinerary and hike the trail to **Crypt Lake.**

If your tour of the Canadian Rockies originates south of the border and you're traveling by road, I highly recommend leaving Waterton Lakes until the end of your trip—the slower pace and solitude will create a pleasant ending for your travels.

THE LAND
Geology
Major upheavals under the earth's surface approximately 85 million years ago forced huge plates of rock upward and began folding them

over each other. One major sheet known as the Lewis Overthrust forms the backbone of Waterton's topography as we see it today. It slid up and over much younger bedrock along a 300-km (186-mile) length extending north to Bow Valley.

About 45 million years ago, this powerful uplift ceased and the forces of erosion took over. About 1.9 million years ago, glaciers from the sheet of ice that once covered most of Alberta crept through the mountains. As these thick sheets of ice advanced and retreated with climatic changes, they gouged out valleys such as the classically U-shaped Waterton Valley. The three Waterton Lakes are depressions left at the base of the steep-sided mountains after the ice had completely retreated 11,000 years ago. The deepest is 150 meters (500 feet). Cameron Lake, at the end of the Akamina Parkway, was formed when a moraine—the pile of rock that accumulates at the foot of a retreating glacier—dammed Cameron Creek. From the lake, Cameron Creek flows through a glaciated valley before dropping into the much deeper Waterton Valley at Cameron Falls, behind the town of Waterton. The town itself sits on an alluvial fan composed of silt and gravel picked up by mountain streams and deposited in Upper Waterton Lake.

Climate
Climate plays an active role in creating the park's natural landscape. This corner of the province tends to receive more rain, snow, and wind—much more wind—than other parts of Alberta. These factors, combined with the park's varied topography, create an environment where more than half the known species in Alberta have been recorded. Wind is the most powerful presence in the park. Prevailing winds from the south and west bring Pacific weather over the divide, creating a climate similar to that experienced farther west. These warm fronts endow the region with chinooks—dry winds that can raise temperatures in the park by up to 40°C (105°F) in 24 hours.

One of the nicest aspects of the park is that it can be enjoyed in all seasons. Summer is great for the sunny windless days, fall for the wildlife viewing, winter for the solitude, and spring for the long days of sunlight as the park seems to be waking up from its winter slumber. Be aware, however, that many of the park's best sights and hiking trails lie at high elevations; some areas may be snowed in until mid-June.

Flora

Botanists have recorded 1,200 species of plants growing within the park's several different vegetation zones. In the park's northeastern corner, near the park gate, a region of prairies is covered in semiarid vegetation such as **fescue grass.** As Highway 5 enters the park it passes Maskinonge Lake, a wetlands area of marshy ponds where aquatic plants flourish. Parkland habitat dominated by **aspen** is found along the north side of Blakiston Valley and near Belly River Campground, while montane forest covers most mountain valleys and lower slopes. This montane zone is dominated by a high canopy of **lodgepole pine** and **Douglas fir** shading a forest floor covered with wildflowers and berries. An easily accessible section of this habitat is along the lower half of Bertha Lake Trail; an interpretive brochure is available at the Waterton Visitor Centre.

Above the montane forest is the subalpine zone, which rises as far as the timberline. These distinct forests of **larch, fir, Engelmann spruce,** and **whitebark pine** can be seen along the Carthew Lakes Trail. On the west-facing slopes of Cameron Lakes are mature groves of subalpine trees up to 400 years old; this oldest growth in the park has managed to escape fire over the centuries. Blanketing the open mountain slopes in this zone is bear grass, which grows up to one meter in height and is topped by a bright blossom often likened to a lighted torch. Above the tree line is the alpine zone, where harsh winds and short summer seasons make trees a rarity. Only **lichens** and **alpine wildflowers** flourish at these high altitudes. Crypt Lake is a good place for viewing this zone.

Fauna

Wildlife viewing in the park requires patience and a little know-how, but the rewards are ample, as good as anywhere in the Canadian Rockies. **Elk** inhabit the park year-round. A large herd gathers by Entrance Road in late fall, wintering on the lowlands. By early fall, many **mule deer** are wandering around town. **Bighorn sheep** are often seen on the north side of Blakiston Valley or on the slopes above the Waterton Visitor Centre; occasionally they end up in town. **White-tailed deer** are best viewed along Red Rock Canyon Parkway. The park has a small population of moose, occasionally seen in low-lying wetlands. **Mountain goats** rarely leave the high peaks of the backcountry, but from Goat, Crypt, or Bertha Lake you might catch a glimpse of one high above you.

The most common predators in the park are the **coyotes,** which spend their summer days chasing ground squirrels around the prairie and parkland areas. For its size, Waterton has a healthy population of **cougars,** but these shy, solitary animals are rarely seen. About 50 **black bears** live in the park. They spend most of the summer in the heavily forested montane regions. During August and September, scan the slopes of Blakiston Valley, where the bears can often be seen feasting on saskatoon berries before going into winter hibernation. Much larger than black bears are **grizzlies,** which roam the entire backcountry but are rarely encountered. Larger even still are **bison.** Although these prairie dwellers never lived in the mountains, they would have grazed around the eastern outskirts of what is now the park. A small herd is contained in the **Bison Paddock,** just before the park gate.

Golden-mantled ground squirrels live on the Bear's Hump and around Cameron Falls. **Columbian ground squirrels** are just about everywhere. **Chipmunks** scamper about on Bertha Lake Trail. The best time for viewing **beavers** is at dawn and dusk along the Belly River. **Muskrats** can be seen on the edges of Maskinonge Lake eating bulrushes. **Mink** also live at the lake but are seen only by those with patience.

Two major flyways pass the park, and from September to November many thousands of waterfowl stop on Maskinonge and Lower Waterton Lakes. On a powerline pole beside the entrance to the park is an active **osprey** nest—ask staff to point it out for you. Waterton Heritage Centre has a great little free checklist for birders listing the 250 species recorded within park boundaries.

Waterton Lakes

HISTORY

Evidence found within the park suggests that the Kootenay people who lived west of the park made trips across the Continental Divide 8,000–10,000 years ago to hunt bison on the plains and fish in the lakes. They camped in the valleys during winter, taking shelter from the harsh weather. But by about 1,500 years ago, they were spending more time in the west and crossing the mountains only a few times a year to hunt bison. By the 1700s, the Blackfoot—with the help of horses—had expanded their territory from the Battle River throughout southwestern Alberta. They patrolled the mountains on horseback, making it difficult for the Kootenay hunting parties to cross. But their dominance was short-lived. With the arrival of guns and the encroaching homesteads of early settlers, Blackfoot tribes retreated to the east, leaving the Waterton Lakes Valley uninhabited.

Oil City

Kootenai Brown, the valley's first permanent settler, first noticed beads of oil floating on Cameron Creek. He and a business partner siphoned it from the water's surface, bottled it, and sold it in Fort Macleod and Cardston. This discovery created much interest among the oil-starved entrepreneurs of Alberta, who formed the Rocky Mountain Development Company to do some exploratory drilling. At this stage the park was still a Forest Reserve; the trees were protected, but prospecting and mining were still allowed. A rough road was constructed through the Cameron Creek Valley, and in September 1901 the company struck oil at a depth of 311 meters (1,020 feet). It was the first producing oil well in western Canada and only the second in the country. In the resulting euphoria, a townsite named Oil City was cleared and surveyed, a bunkhouse and dining hall were constructed, and the foundations for a hotel were laid. The boom was short-lived. Drilling rigs kept breaking down, and the flow of oil soon slowed to a trickle. A monument along the Akamina Parkway stands at the site of the well, and a little farther up the road at a roadside marker a trail leads through thick undergrowth to the townsite. All that remains are the ill-fated hotel's foundations and some depressions in the ground.

Waterton-Glacier International Peace Park

After becoming the valley's first permanent resident in 1869, Kootenai Brown began promoting the beauty of the area to the people of Fort Macleod. One of his friends, local rancher F.W. Godsal, began lobbying the federal government to establish a reserve. In 1895 an area was set aside as a Forest Reserve. Shortly after Montana's Glacier National Park was created in 1910, the Canadian government changed the name of the reserve to Waterton Lakes Dominion Park; it was later redesignated a national park. Many people followed in the footsteps of Kootenai Brown, and a small town named Waterton grew up on the Cameron Creek delta. The town had no rail link, so unlike Banff and Jasper—its famous mountain neighbors to the north—it didn't draw large crowds of tourists. Nevertheless, it soon became a popular summer retreat with a hotel, restaurant, and dance hall. The Great Northern Railway decided to operate a bus service from its Montana rail line to Jasper, with a stop at Waterton. This led to the construction of the **Prince of Wales Hotel.**

Boat cruises from the hotel across the international boundary were soon the park's most popular activity. This brought the two parks closer together, and in 1932, after much lobbying from Rotary International members on both sides of the border, the Canadian and U.S. governments agreed to establish Waterton-Glacier International Peace Park, the first of its kind in the world. The parks are administered separately but cooperate in preserving this pristine mountain wilderness through wildlife management, search-and-rescue operations, and interpretive programs. Peace Park celebrations take place each year, and the **Peace Park Pavilion** by the lake is dedicated to this unique bond. In 1979, UNESCO declared the park a **Biosphere Reserve,** only the second such reserve in Canada. In 1995 the park's importance was further recognized when UNESCO declared Waterton-Glacier International Peace Park a World Heritage Site.

Sights and Recreation

Hiking is definitely the reason most visitors are drawn to Waterton, but there are plenty of other activities to fit in between hikes or for all the family. The scenic drives described below are highly recommended activities, as is the boat cruise across the border to Goat Haunt in Glacier National Park.

Make your first stop the **Waterton Visitor Centre** (403/859-5133), on the slight rise before the road descends to the village.

⋈ Waterton Heritage Centre

The only official "sight" is the Waterton Heritage Centre (117 Waterton Ave., 403/859-2624; May–Sept. 10 A.M.–5 P.M., July and Aug. until 8 P.M.). This small museum contains exhibits telling the story of the park's natural and human history, including a section of aspen in which a trapper carved his initials over 100 years ago. It also holds a selection of paintings and woodcarvings created by local artists. The heritage center is operated by the Waterton Natural History Association, which runs a variety of educational programs. From the heritage center, wander south along the lakeshore to a large picnic area and the trailhead for the Waterton Lakeshore Trail (see *Hiking*) or north to the **International Peace Park Pavilion** and stunning views across Emerald Bay to the Prince of Wales Hotel.

SCENIC DRIVES

⋈ Akamina Parkway

This road starts in the townsite and switchbacks up into the Cameron Creek Valley, making an elevation gain of 400 meters (1,310 feet) before ending after 16 km (10 miles) at Cameron Lake. The viewpoint one km (.6 mile) from the junction of the park road is on a tight curve, so park off the road. From this lookout, views extend over the townsite and the **Bear's Hump,** which was originally part of a high ridge that extended across the lake to Vimy Peak (glacial action ultimately wore down the rest of the ridge). This

section of the road is also a good place to view bighorn sheep. Between here and Cameron Lake there are several picnic areas and stops of interest, including the site of Alberta's first producing oil well and, a little farther along the road, the site of **Oil City,** the town that never was.

Cameron Lake, at the end of the road, is a 2.5-km-long (1.5-mile-long) subalpine lake that reaches depths of more than 40 meters (130 feet). It lies in a large cirque carved out about 11,000 years ago by a receding glacier. Mount Custer at the southern end of the lake is in Montana. Waterton has no glaciers, but Herbst Glacier on Mount Custer can be seen from here. To the west (right) of Custer is **Forum Peak** (2,225 meters/7,300 feet), whose summit cairn marks the boundaries of Alberta, Montana, and British Columbia.

Beside the lakeshore are enclosed information boards and a concession stand (June–Aug. daily 10 A.M.–10 P.M.) selling light snacks and renting canoes, rowboats, and paddleboats ($18 for the first hour, $14 for additional hours). A narrow trail leads along the lake's west shoreline, ending after two km (1.2 miles); allow 40 minutes each way. Farther on, grizzlies frequent the avalanche slope at the southwestern end of the lake, so hike with someone you can outrun.

PARK ENTRY

Visitors to Waterton Lakes National Park are required to stop at the park gate and buy a permit. A **National Parks Day Pass** is adult $5, senior $4.25, child $2.50 to a maximum of $12.50 per vehicle and is valid until 4 P.M. the day following its purchase. An annual pass for entry to the park is adult $30, senior $22, child $15 to a maximum of $63 per vehicle.

If you're traveling to national parks beyond Waterton, a better deal is the annual **National Parks of Canada Pass,** good for entry into all of Canada's national parks; adult $45, senior $38, child $22, or $89 per vehicle. These passes can be purchased at any park gate; check www.pc.gc.ca for more information.

Waterton Lakes

Red Rock Canyon Parkway

The best roadside wildlife viewing within the park is along this 13-km (eight-mile) road that starts near the golf course and finishes at **Red Rock Canyon.** The transition between rolling prairies and mountains takes place abruptly as you travel up the Blakiston Valley. Black bears (and very occasionally grizzly bears) can be seen feeding on saskatoon berries along the open slopes to the north. **Mount Blakiston** (2,920 meters/9,580 feet), the park's highest summit, is visible from a viewpoint three km (1.9 miles) along the road. The road passes interpretive signs, picnic areas, and Crandell Mountain Campground. At the end of the road is Red Rock Canyon, a water-carved gorge where the bedrock, known as argillite, contains a high concentration of iron. The iron oxidizes and turns red when exposed to air—literally going rusty. A short interpretive trail leads along the canyon.

Chief Mountain International Highway

This 25-km (15.5-mile) highway, part of Highway 6, borders the eastern boundaries of the park and joins it to Glacier National Park in Montana. It starts east of the park gate at **Mask-inonge Lake** and climbs for seven km (4.3 miles) to a viewpoint where many jagged peaks and the entire Waterton Valley can be seen. The next stop, three km (1.9 miles) farther south, provides views of Chief Mountain, which has been separated from the main mountain range by erosion. The road then passes more spectacular viewpoints, Belly River Campground, and Chief Mountain.

Hours of operation at this port of entry are: mid-May to the end of May 9 A.M.–6 P.M., June to early September 7 A.M.–10 P.M., early September to the end of the month 9 A.M.–6 P.M. When the post is closed, you must use the Carway/Piegan port of entry (year-round daily 7 A.M.–11 P.M.). It's on Alberta Highway 2 south of Cardston (or on Montana Highway 89 north of St. Mary, depending on your direction of travel).

From the border it's 50 km (31 miles) to St. Mary and the spectacular Going-to-the-Sun Highway through **Glacier National Park.** Stop by the park's **St. Mary Visitor Center** (406/888-7800; mid-May–mid-Oct. 8 A.M.–5 P.M., until 9 P.M. in July and Aug.). A good source of pre-trip information is the official park website (www.nps.gov/glac).

HIKING

You can soak up the park's beauty along the scenic drives, but you'll be cheating yourself if you don't walk at least one trail. While the park does have its fair share of uphill slogs, don't be too daunted by the surrounding mountains—there are also some pleasant walks that everyone can enjoy, including the trail along Cameron Lake (see *Akamina Parkway*).

Although the park is relatively small, its trail system is extensive; 224 km (140 miles) of well-maintained trails lead to alpine lakes and lofty summits affording spectacular views. One of the most appealing aspects of hiking in Waterton is that with higher trailheads than other parks in the Canadian Rockies, the tree line is reached quickly. Most of the lakes can be reached in a few hours. Once you've finished hiking the trails in Waterton, you can cross the international border and start on the 1,200 km (746 miles) of trails in Glacier National Park.

The eight hikes detailed comprise only a small cross-section of Waterton's extensive trail system. Most of the hikes climb to alpine lakes or viewpoints. Topographic maps (one map covers the entire park) are available at various outlets in town. If you are planning to stay overnight in the backcountry, you must obtain a permit ($8 per person per night) from Waterton Visitor Centre or the park administration office.

Bear's Hump

- Length: 1.2 km/.7 mile (40 minutes) one-way
- Elevation gain: 215 meters/700 feet
- Rating: moderate
- Trailhead: Waterton Visitor Centre

This is one of the most popular short hikes in the park, and although steep, it affords panoramic views of the Waterton Valley. From the back of

KOOTENAI BROWN

John George Brown was born in England in the 1840s and reputedly educated at Oxford University. He joined the army and went to India, later continuing to San Francisco. Then, like thousands of others, he headed for the Cariboo goldfields of British Columbia, quickly spending any of the gold he found. After a while he moved on, heading east into Waterton Valley, where his party was attacked by a band of Blackfoot. He was shot in the back with an arrow and pulled it out himself. For a time he worked with the U.S. Army as a Pony Express rider. One day he was captured by Chief Sitting Bull, stripped, and tied to a stake until his fate could be decided, but he managed to escape during the night with his scalp intact. Brown acquired his nickname through his close association with the Kootenay (today's preferred spelling) people, hunting buffalo and wolves with them until the animals had all but disappeared.

Brown married in 1869 and built a cabin by Upper Waterton Lake, becoming the valley's first permanent resident. Even though he had been toughened by the times, he was a conservationist at heart. When a reserve was set aside in 1895, Brown was employed as its first warden. In 1911, the area was declared a national park and Brown, age 71, was appointed its superintendent. He continued to push for an expansion of park boundaries until his final retirement at age 75. He died a few years later. His final resting place is along the lakeshore—fitting for one of Canada's most celebrated mountain men. Look for the signed trail along the park access road; it's a five-minute walk from the road.

the visitor center parking lot, the trail switchbacks up the northern flanks of the Bear's Hump, finishing at a rocky ledge high above town. From this vantage point the sweeping view extends across the prairies and down Upper Waterton Lake to the northern reaches of Glacier National Park.

Bertha Lake

- Length: 5.8 km/3.6 miles (two hours) one-way
- Elevation gain: 460 meters/1,510 feet
- Rating: moderate
- Trailhead: south of the townsite at the end of Evergreen Avenue (near the far corner of Townsite Campground)

Bertha Lake is a popular destination with day hikers and campers alike. For the first 1.5 km (.9 mile), little elevation gain is made as the trail coincides with the Waterton Lakeshore Trail. Then the trail branches right and climbs steadily through a forest of lodgepole pine and Douglas fir along a well-maintained section to **Lower Bertha Falls.** Signs along this first, easier section correspond with the *Bertha Falls Self-Guiding Nature Trail* brochure available from the Visitor Centre. From here the trail passes **Upper Bertha Falls** and begins switchbacking steeply through a subalpine forest to its maximum elevation on a ridge above the hanging valley in which Bertha Lake lies. A trail encircles the lake.

The backcountry campground on the lake's edge is one of the park's busiest.

Waterton Lakeshore

- Length: 14 km/8.7 miles (four hours) one-way
- Elevation gain: minimal
- Rating: easy/moderate
- Trailhead: south of the townsite at the end of Evergreen Avenue

This trail follows the heavily forested western shores of Upper Waterton Lake across the international boundary to **Goat Haunt, Montana,** linking up with more than 1,200 km (746 miles) of trails in Glacier National Park. Many hikers take the Waterton Cruise Company's **MV International** (403/859-2362 June–Sept. only; $16;) one way and hike the other. The boat dock at Boundary Bay, six km (3.7 miles) from town, is a good place for lunch. Hikers heading south and planning to camp in Glacier National Park must register at the Waterton Visitor Centre.

Crypt Lake

- Length: 8.7 km/5.4 miles (3–4 hours) one-way
- Elevation gain: 680 meters/2,230 feet
- Rating: moderate/difficult
- Trailhead: Crypt Landing; access is by boat. The **Crypt Lake Shuttle** (403/859-2362; June–Sept.; $14 round-trip) leaves the marina daily at 9 A.M. and 10 A.M. for Crypt Landing; return trips depart at 4 P.M. and 5:30 P.M.

This is one of the most spectacular day hikes in Canada. Access to the trailhead on the eastern side of Upper Waterton Lake is by boat. The trail switchbacks for 2.5 km (1.6 miles) past a series of waterfalls and continues steeply up to a small green lake before reaching a campground. The final ascent to Crypt Lake from the campground causes the most problems, especially for those who suffer from claustrophobia or acrophobia. A ladder on the cliff face leads into a natural tunnel that you must crawl through on your hands and knees. The next part of the trail is along a narrow precipice with a cable for support. The lake at the end of the trail, nestled in a hanging valley, is no disappointment. Its dark green waters are rarely free of floating ice, and the steep walls of the cirque rise more than 500 meters (1,640 feet) above the lake on three sides. The international boundary is at the southern end of the lake. A good way to avoid the crowds on this trail is to camp at the dock and set out before the first boat arrives in the morning.

Crandell Lake

- Length: 2.4 km/1.5 miles (40 minutes) one-way
- Elevation gain: 120 meters/395 feet
- Rating: easy
- Trailhead: Crandell Campground, Red Rock Canyon Parkway

This easy hike to a subalpine lake is popular with campers staying at Crandell Campground. Alternatively, the trailhead can be reached by noncampers along the Canyon Church Camp access road. The lake can also be accessed from a trailhead seven km (4.3 miles) west of town along the Akamina Parkway. This trail is shorter (.8 km/.5 mile) and follows a wagon road that was cut through the valley to Oil City.

Goat Lake

- Length: 6.7 km/4.2 miles (two hours) one-way
- Elevation gain: 500 meters/1,640 feet
- Rating: moderate
- Trailhead: end of Red Rock Canyon Parkway, 18 km (11.2 miles) from Waterton townsite

The first hour of walking from the trailhead at Red Rock Canyon follows the Snowshoe Trail along **Bauerman Creek** before branching to the right and climbing switchbacks through a mixed forest. The steep gradient evens out as the trail enters the Goat Lake cirque. After the uphill slog, the lake is a welcome sight, its emerald-green waters reflecting the towering headwalls that surround it. Look for the lake's namesake on the open scree slopes west of the lake.

Carthew-Alderson

- Length: 20 km/12.4 miles (6–7 hours) one-way
- Elevation gain: 650 meters/2,130 feet

Waterton Lakes

Crandell Lake

- Rating: moderate/difficult
- Trailhead: end of Akamina Parkway, 16 km (10 miles) from Waterton townsite

This hike linking the end of the Akamina Parkway to Waterton townsite can be completed in one long strenuous day or done with an overnight stop at Alderson Lake, 13 km (eight miles) from the trailhead. It leads through most of the climatic zones of the park and offers some of the best scenery to be had on any one hike. Transportation to the trailhead can be arranged through **Waterton Visitor Services** (Tamarack Village Square, 403/859-2378; $10 one-way), which operates a hiker shuttle service to this and other trailheads in the park. From the Cameron Lake parking lot, the trail climbs four km (2.5 miles) to **Summit Lake,** a worthy destination

in itself. The trail then forks to the left and climbs steeply to Carthew Ridge. After rising above the tree line and crossing a scree slope, the trail reaches its highest elevation of 2,310 meters (7,580 feet) at **Carthew Summit.** The views from here are spectacular, even more so if you scramble up to one of Mount Carthew's lower peaks. To the north is a hint of prairie, to the southeast the magnificent bowl-shaped cirque around Cameron Lake. To the south, the Carthew Lakes lie directly below, while glaciated peaks in Montana line the horizon. From this summit, the trail descends steeply to the Carthew Lakes, reenters the subalpine forest, and emerges at **Alderson Lake,** which is nestled under the headwalls of Mount Alderson. The trail then descends through the Carthew Creek Valley and finishes at Cameron Falls in the townsite.

Vimy Peak

- Length: 12 km/7.5 miles (five hours) one-way
- Elevation gain: 825 meters/2,700 feet
- Rating: moderate
- Trailhead: Chief Mountain International Highway, a half km (.3 mile) from the Highway 5 junction

Vimy Peak overlooks the townsite from across Upper Waterton Lake. It was once part of a ridge that extended across the Waterton Valley and was worn down by the relentless forces of glacial action. The initial six-km (3.7-mile) stretch is along the eastern bank of Lower Waterton Lake through forest and grassland. The trail then continues along the lake to Bosporus Landing opposite the town or climbs steeply to Vimy Peak (2,379 meters/7,805 feet). The Vimy Peak Trail actually ends at a basin short of the summit, which is still a painfully steep 40-minute scramble away.

OTHER RECREATION

Cruising to Goat Haunt, Montana

This is the most popular activity in Waterton. From the marina in downtown Waterton townsite, **Waterton Inter-Nation Shoreline Cruise Company** (403/859-2362) runs scheduled cruises across the international boundary to Goat Haunt, Montana, at the southern end of Upper Waterton Lake. The 45-minute trip along the lakeshore passes spectacular mountain scenery and usually wildlife. A half-hour stopover is made at Goat Haunt, which lies in a remote part of Glacier National Park and consists of little more than a dock and interpretive displays. You can return on the same boat or go hiking and return later in the day. If you are planning an overnight hike from here, you are required to register at the Waterton Visitor Centre before heading out on the lake. Another popular option is to take an early boat trip and walk back to town on the **Waterton Lakeshore Trail,** which takes about four hours. Boats leave the Waterton marina five times daily (from 9 A.M.) during summer. Fewer trips are made during June and September. The cruises run until mid-October, but for the last

Scuba diving isn't usually associated with the Rockies, but Emerald Bay holds a sunken steamer attracting divers throughout summer.

two weeks of the season no stop is made at the end of the lake. Tickets cost $26 round-trip, $16 one-way (children are half price), and you'll need to book ahead in summer. The same company operates a regular shuttle service to the Crypt Lake trailhead for $14 round-trip.

Fishing

Fishing in the lakes is average, with most anglers chasing brook and rainbow trout, pike, and whitefish. A national park fishing license is required and can be obtained from the Waterton Visitor Centre or any of the administration offices. The license costs $7 for seven days or $20 for an annual permit.

Windsurfing

Winds of up to 70 kph (45 mph) attract hardcore windsurfers throughout summer and into fall. The winds are predominantly south to north, providing fast runs across Upper Waterton Lake from the beach at Cameron Bay. The lake is deep, keeping the water temperature low and making a wetsuit necessary. Read the warning signs at the beach before heading out.

Scuba Diving

On any given summer day, scuba divers can be seen slipping into the frigid waters of Emerald Bay. A steamer was scuttled in the bay in 1918. It had been used to haul logs and as a tearoom but now sits on the lake's floor, attracting divers who find it a novelty to explore a sunken ship so far from the ocean. No equipment rental is available in the park. The closest is at **Anderson Aquatics,** in Lethbridge (314 11th St. S, 403/328-5040), where you can also get your tanks filled. Full gear rental from Anderson is $50 per day, $75 for the weekend, including air fills. Through this shop, certification courses and field trips to Waterton Lakes are organized throughout the summer. Stop in on your way to the park for a rundown on all the dives, or ask at the Waterton Visitor Centre.

Golfing

The rolling fairways and spectacular mountain backdrop of **Waterton Lakes Golf Course** (403/859-2114) can distract even the keenest golfer's attention. The 18-hole course, designed by Stanley Thompson and dating to 1929, is not particularly long (6,103 yards) or difficult, but the surrounding mountains and unhurried pace of play make for a pleasant environment. The course is four km (2.5 miles) north of the townsite on the main access road and is open June to early October. A round of golf costs $38. Club rentals are $8, and a power cart is an additional $28 per round. At the end of your round, plan on relaxing at the clubhouse over a light meal and cold drink.

When the Sun Goes Down

Roasting marshmallows at your campsite, sitting around a roaring fire at your lodge, listening to a park's interpretive program, or going for a moonlit walk along the lakeshore—these are the best ways to spend your evenings, and they can all be yours at no charge.

Interpretive programs typically begin in late June and run through to the first weekend of September. The subject matter changes from year to year, but you can rely on interesting, interactive topics that mix learning with fun. Programs at Crandell Campground and at the **Falls Theatre,** opposite Cameron Falls, usually begin nightly at 8:30 P.M., with guest speakers appearing at the Falls Theatre Saturday night. Ask at the Waterton Visitor Centre (403/859-5133) for a schedule.

Waterton's few bars and lounges are all affiliated with lodgings. One of the nicest is the **Rams Head Lounge** in the Kilmorey Lodge (117 Evergreen Ave., 403/859-2334), which has a rustic mountain ambience centered around a wood-burning fireplace. On sunny afternoons and warmer nights, there is no finer place to spend an hour or two than this lounge's lakefront deck. Being the biggest and most central bar in town, the **Thirsty Bear Saloon** (Bayshore Inn, Waterton Ave., 403/859-2211; daily 11 A.M.–2 A.M.) gets crowded with young seasonal workers. It pours happy hour daily 3–6 P.M., and a band plays two or three nights a week. Another downtown bar is the **Wolf's Den Lounge** (Waterton Lakes Lodge, corner of Windflower Ave. and Cameron Falls Rd., 403/859-2151), which is quieter and more modern. In the Prince of Wales Hotel, the staid **Windsor Lounge** (403/859-2231) has panoramic views across the lake and live entertainment most summer nights.

Waterton Lakes Opera House (309 Windflower Ave., 403/859-2466) shows movies daily at 7:30 and 9:30 P.M.

Wintertime

Winter is a quiet time in the park. Traffic on the roads is light, the Prince of Wales Hotel sits empty, the snowcapped peaks and abundant big game provide plenty of photographic opportunities, and a few trails are maintained for cross-country skiing. The main access road is plowed regularly, and the Akamina Parkway is cleared to allow access to ski trails. Skiing in the park is usually possible from December to March, but conditions can change dramatically. Cold arctic fronts scream down from the north, and chinook winds from the west can raise temperatures by up to 20°C (37°F) in an hour. Ski trails are set on weekends, and the ski-touring opportunities are endless. Trails in the backcountry are not marked. Groups should carry avalanche beacons, be capable of self-rescue, and register with the warden before setting out.

Ice climbing, snowshoeing, and backcountry winter camping are also popular. Winter camping is possible at Pass Creek, where you'll find a kitchen shelter, woodstove, and pit toilets. Three accommodations stay open year-round and offer all-inclusive winter packages. Gas may or may not be available in winter. Obtain trail information and weather forecasts at the park administration office (Mount View Rd., 403/859-2224; year-round Mon.–Fri. 8 A.M.–4 P.M.). For information regarding backcountry skiing conditions and avalanche danger, contact the **Canadian Avalanche Association** (800/667-1105, www.avalanche.ca).

Accommodations and Camping

If you're camping, grab a campsite as early in the day as possible. If you're staying in an accommodation, you'll find them all within Waterton townsite and within walking distance of everywhere. If it's too early to check in, spend some time exploring the downtown core and lakefront on foot.

HOTELS, MOTELS, AND LODGES

Waterton has a limited number of accommodations. Most start opening in May and by mid-October are closed, with only the hostel, Kilmorey Lodge, Crandell Mountain Lodge, and Waterton Glacier Suites open year-round. All accommodations are within the townsite, so walking to the marina and shops isn't a problem.

Finding a room on short notice shouldn't be too difficult in May, June, and September, but for July and August call as early as possible.

Under $50

N HI–Waterton Alpine Centre (101 Clematis Dr., 403/859-2150 or 888/985-6343, www.watertonlakeslodge.com) is in a wing of Waterton Lakes Lodge, one of the village's premier accommodations. Just 21 beds are spread through six rooms, with a maximum of four beds in any one room. Guests have use of all lodge facilities, including the Waterton Spa and Recreation Centre (for a small fee), as well as a common lounge area, shared kitchen, and bathrooms. Beds are $31 for members of Hostelling International, $35 for nonmembers, respectively—a great deal for those travelers who are willing to share living facilities. Family rooms are $93 and $105. Check-in is after 4 P.M.

$50–100

One block from the main street, the **El Cortez Motel** (208 Mount View Rd., 403/859-2366; mid-May–Sept.) is an older park-at-your-door motel with basic furnishings and no phones. Standard rooms are $80 s, $85 d, with some kitchenettes from $110.

Also in this price bracket is **Northland Lodge** (Evergreen Ave., 403/859-2353, www.northlandlodgecanada.com; mid-May–mid-Oct.), a converted house backing onto wilderness built in 1929 by Louis Hill, who also built the Prince of Wales Hotel. Cameron Falls and downtown Waterton are both just a short walk away. It features nine guest rooms, a large lounge with a TV and fireplace, and a large balcony. The two rooms that share a bathroom are $85 s or d, while the remainder are $110–155 s or d; rates include tea, coffee, and muffins in the morning.

$100–150

N Kilmorey Lodge (117 Evergreen Ave., 403/859-2334 or 888/859-8669, www.kilmoreylodge.com), a historic 1920s inn on the shores of Emerald Bay, provides an excellent value for the money. Victorian furnishings, lots of exposed timber, squeaking floorboards, and historic

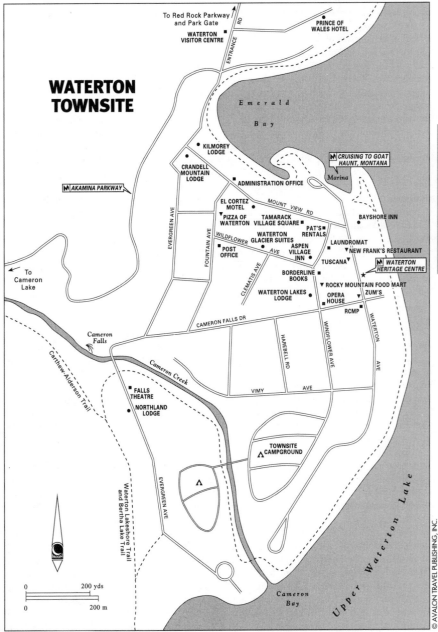

WATERTON TOWNSITE

To Red Rock Parkway and Park Gate

ENTRANCE RD

WATERTON VISITOR CENTRE

PRINCE OF WALES HOTEL

Emerald Bay

KILMOREY LODGE

CRANDELL MOUNTAIN LODGE

ADMINISTRATION OFFICE

CRUISING TO GOAT HAUNT, MONTANA

Marina

AKAMINA PARKWAY

MOUNT VIEW RD

EL CORTEZ MOTEL

EVERGREEN AVE

PIZZA OF WATERTON

TAMARACK VILLAGE SQUARE

BAYSHORE INN

WILDFLOWER AVE

WATERTON GLACIER SUITES

PAT'S RENTALS

LAUNDROMAT

FOUNTAIN AVE

POST OFFICE

ASPEN VILLAGE INN

NEW FRANK'S RESTAURANT

TUSCANA

CLEMATIS AVE

BORDERLINE BOOKS

ROCKY MOUNTAIN FOOD MART

WATERTON HERITAGE CENTRE

To Cameron Lake

WATERTON LAKES LODGE

OPERA HOUSE

ZUM'S

RCMP

CAMERON FALLS DR

Cameron Falls

HAREBELL RD

WINDFLOWER AVE

WATERTON AVE

Carthew-Alderson Trail

Cameron Creek

VIMY AVE

FALLS THEATRE

NORTHLAND LODGE

EVERGREEN AVE

Waterton Lakeshore Trail and Bertha Lake Trail

TOWNSITE CAMPGROUND

Upper Waterton Lake

Cameron Bay

| 0 | 200 yds |
| 0 | 200 m |

© AVALON TRAVEL PUBLISHING, INC.

Waterton Lakes

photographs add to the charm. From the lobby a narrow stairway leads up to 23 rooms tucked under the eaves, many of which have spectacular lake views. Each is furnished with antiques, and the beds have down comforters to ensure a good night's sleep. Downstairs is one of the town's finest restaurants and the library, where guests congregate to chat about their adventures around a roaring log fire. Outside is a gazebo for enjoying a quiet drink on those warm summer nights. Standard rooms during summer start at $120 s or d, rising to $230 for the spacious Deluxe King. Some rooms have lake views, but book in advance for these. Inexpensive packages are offered in winter.

Across the road from the Kilmorey Lodge is **Crandell Mountain Lodge** (Mount View Rd., 403/859-2288 or 866/859-2288, www.crandell mountainlodge.com), a centrally located country-style inn. The lodge has seen many changes since it first opened in 1940 with shared bathrooms and wood-heated water. Today each of the 17 rooms has a private bath and is beautifully finished with country-style furnishings (no phones), and out back is a private garden area. Two rooms are wheelchair-accessible. The smallest rooms are $129 s or d, most—with a choice of fireplace or kitchenette—are $159, and the largest suites are $199. Rates are reduced around 30 percent between mid-September and May.

For families, the **Aspen Village Inn** (111 Windflower Ave., 403/859-2255 or 888/859-8669, www.aspenvillageinn.com; May–mid-Oct.) is an excellent choice. For starters, the rooms are super-spacious, but there's also a playground and a picnic area. Grownups aren't forgotten—the outdoor hot tub is the perfect place to soak weary bones. Accommodations are in two wings and freestanding cottages. The latter range from one bedroom, no kitchen ($159 s or d) to three bedrooms and a kitchen ($198). Lodge rooms range $139–245 s or d, with, for example, a two-bedroom kitchen equipped unit selling for $210.

At the **Bayshore Inn** (Waterton Ave., 403/859-2211 or 888/527-9555, www.bayshore inn.com; mid-Apr.–mid-Oct.) you're paying for a prime waterfront location rather than a memorable room. On-site amenities include a hot tub, restaurant, and lounge. Rooms are $145 s or d, $155 lake view. For the first two months of the season, the Bayshore offers excellent meal-inclusive packages for the same price as their summertime, room-only rates.

$150–200

Waterton Glacier Suites (Windflower Ave., 403/859-2004 or 866/621-3330, www.waterton suites.com) is open year-round and provides excellent value. Each of 26 units features stylish, modern decor that hints at Western, is air-conditioned, and offers a fridge and microwave. Two-bedroom suites are $169 s or d, units with a jetted tub and fireplace are $225, and spacious loft units are $259. Off-season rates range $125–175.

Over $200

Modern **Waterton Lakes Lodge** (corner of Windflower Ave. and Cameron Falls Rd., 403/859-2151 or 866/985-6343, www.waterton lakeslodge.com; Feb.–Nov.) is on a 1.5-hectare (3.7-acre) site in the heart of town. All 80 rooms are large and modern, and each has mountain-themed decor and mountain views. Amenities include air-conditioning, a TV/VCR combination, Internet access, and a coffeemaker. The lodge complex also holds the Waterton Spa and Recreation Centre (free entry for guests), a restaurant, a small café, and a lounge. Lodge rooms are $205 s, $215 d, while those with kitchenettes are $265 s, $285 d. Check the website for steeply discounted off-season rates.

Waterton's best-known landmark is the **Prince of Wales Hotel** (403/859-2231 or 406/892-2525, www.glacierparkinc.com; mid-May–mid-Sept.), a seven-story gabled structure built in 1927 on a hill overlooking Upper Waterton Lake. It was another grand mountain resort financed by the railway, except, unlike those in Banff and Jasper, it had no rail link and has always been U.S.-owned. It was built as part of a chain of first-class hotels in Glacier National Park and is still owned by the company that controls those south of the border. Early guests were transported to the hotel by bus from the Great Northern Railway in Montana. After extensive restoration

The Prince of Wales Hotel is the grandest of Waterton's accommodations.

inside and out, the hotel has been returned to its former splendor. Rates for the smallest (and they're small) Value Rooms are $265–275 s or d, depending on the view. Standard rooms start at $290, rising to $340 for those with a lake view. The opulence and history of this hotel are unequaled in Waterton, but don't expect the facilities of a similarly priced city hostelry: rooms have no television, and some have no elevator access.

CAMPGROUNDS

If you want to enjoy the warm summer nights of southern Alberta, you will find several options for camping within and around the park.

Park Campgrounds

Waterton Lakes National Park has three campgrounds holding 391 campsites. No reservations are taken, so to ensure a site, try to time your arrival with check-out time, which is 11 A.M. The three campgrounds detailed are open only in summer. The rest of the year, camping is allowed at the Pass Creek day-use area, along the park access road.

The most popular camping spot—thanks to a central location and top-notch amenities—is the **Townsite Campground** (mid-Apr.–mid-Oct.), within walking distance of many trailheads, restaurants, and shops. Many of its more than 238 sites have power, water, and sewer hookups. The campground also offers showers and kitchen shelters. Sites are available on a first-come, first-served basis and fill up by early afternoon most summer days. Walk-in tent sites are $19, unserviced sites $22, hookups $30.

The 129 sites at **Crandell Campground** (mid-May–early Sept.), 10 km (6.2 miles) from the townsite on Red Rock Canyon Parkway, are sprinkled through a lightly forested area of the valley bottom. Fees are $14 per site per night. This campground has flush toilets and kitchen shelters but no hookups. Pleasant Crandell Lake is an easy 2.4-km (1.5-mile) walk from the southwest corner of the campground.

Belly River Campground (mid-May–early Sept.), 26 km (16 miles) from the townsite on Chief Mountain International Highway, is the smallest (24 sites) and most primitive of the park's developed campgrounds. It has pit toilets and kitchen shelters; sites are $12 per night.

Campfires are not allowed at the Townsite Campground, but at the other two facilities, a $6 fire permit includes unlimited wood.

Waterton also holds 12 backcountry campgrounds. Each has pit toilets, a cook shelter, and a water supply. Open fires are discouraged and are prohibited during periods of high fire danger; check with a warden. If you are planning to camp in the backcountry, you must obtain a Wilderness Use Permit from the Waterton Visitor Centre or the administration office. Permits are $6 per person per night. Half of all sites can be reserved in advance ($10 per booking). Call 403/859-5133 for reservations. If your planned backcountry itinerary takes you over the border, ask at the information center about border-crossing regulations.

Commercial Campgrounds

You're a little way from the action at the commercial campgrounds outside the park, but the wider range of facilities (especially if you have a young family) and the peace of mind in being able to reserve a site with hookups make them a viable alternative.

Waterton Springs Campground (three km/1.9 miles north of the park gate on Hwy. 6, 403/859-2247 or 866/859-2247, www.waterton springs.com; late May–Sept.) centers around a large facility building holding modern bathrooms, a lounge, a general store, and a laundry room. Also on site is a fishing pond stocked with rainbow trout. Some sites are a fair walk from the main bathrooms. Tent sites are $16; trailers and RVs pay $20–24.

On Highway 5, six km (3.7 miles) east of the park gate, is **Crooked Creek Campground** (403/653-1100; mid-May–Sept.), operated by the not-for-profit Waterton Natural History Association. The sites are close together, so it's best suited to RVs, but the price is right—$18 for full hookups. Back along the road a little is the turn for **Waterton Riverside Campground** (403/653-2888; mid-May–Sept.), with a mix of tent sites ($17) and powered sites ($20).

Other Practicalities

FOOD

When it's time to eat, the park offers everything from meals to fit the most austere budget to fine dining. Unless you're planning a meal at the Prince of Wales, dress code in park restaurants is casual.

If you plan on cooking your own food, stock up before you get to the park. Groceries are available at the **Rocky Mountain Food Mart** (Windflower Ave.; daily 8 A.M.–10 P.M.) and in the Tamarack Village Square on Mount View Road. The Food Mart sells hot chickens—an easy and inexpensive camping or picnicking meal.

Cafés and Cheap Eats

Waterton has a smattering of coffee shops and small cafés. **Waterton Bagel & Coffee Co.** (in the theater building on the corner of Windflower Ave. and Cameron Falls Dr.) brews up the best coffee in town. **Borderline Books** (305 Windflower Ave., 403/859-2284; Sat.–Thurs. 9 A.M.–5 P.M.) also has decent coffee. Next door is the **Country Bakery & Hacienda Cafe** (303 Windflower Ave., 403/859-2181; daily from 6 A.M.) has a menu of short-order grills and waffles for breakfast, then goes south of the border for Mexican made from scratch.

Pizza of Waterton (103 Fountain Ave., 403/859-2660; Wed.–Sun. midday–midnight) dishes up the best—okay, the only—pizza in town. It's actually pretty good, piled high with toppings of your choice. A 12-inch (good for two) costs $20. Eat inside or out, or take your order back to your campsite.

High Tea

High tea is a tradition at the landmark **Prince of Wales Hotel** (403/859-2231; daily 2–5 P.M.; $36), but it's an overpriced one. Still, it's popular, especially with the tour bus crowd that stays at the hotel as an extension of a tour through adjacent

Glacier National Park. Sure, it's tasty and memorable—think finger sandwiches, pastries and cakes, tea, coffee, and other beverages served up on white linen at tables with the best view in town—but as any self-respecting Brit will tell you, it's more of an *afternoon* tea rather than the more substantial *high* tea.

Restaurants

One of the park's most popular restaurants is the ℕ **Lamp Post Dining Room** (Kilmorey Lodge, 403/859-2334; daily 7:30 A.M.–10 P.M.). It has all the charm of the Prince of Wales Hotel but with a more casual atmosphere and reasonable prices to match. The game-oriented menu offers mouthwatering mains ranging from curried couscous ($18) to medallions of elk broiled in a red wine demi-glaze ($35). Leave room to finish with a delicious piece of Saskatoon berry pie ($5). An impressive wine list is dominated by Canadian offerings. Breakfast is good also. Choose hot oatmeal and a warmed bagel ($6), an egg-white omelet ($8.50), or the best eggs Benedict ($9.25) in southern Alberta.

Along the main street, the selection of places to eat is varied, but none are outstanding. If you're looking for a decent family restaurant, **Zum's** (116 Waterton Ave., 403/859-2388; daily 8 A.M.–9 P.M.) is a good choice. The burgers are tasty and come in all forms (including with buffalo patties) for $6–9, with fries extra. The dinner menu includes varied preparations of chicken, seafood, and beef for $16–33. Wash it all down with a milk shake ($5). **Tuscana** (113 Waterton Ave., 403/859-0003; daily for lunch and dinner) offers satisfying build-your-own pastas ($14–18) with as many tables outside as in.

The **Kootenai Brown Dining Room** (Bayshore Inn, 403/859-2211; daily 7 A.M.–10 P.M.) has predictable hotel dining, with a menu to suit all tastes. The lake views through the dining room windows make this place that much more enjoyable. In July and August a breakfast buffet costs $15.

The big windows at the **Royal Stewart Dining Room** (403/859-2231), a formal restaurant in the Prince of Wales Hotel, allow you to gaze down along Upper Waterton Lake while soaking up an Old World elegance unequaled in the park. The menu is old-fashioned, but with choices like rainbow trout sautéed in a mix of lemony garlic butter and almonds ($25), no one complains. Prices are similar to any big-city restaurant of the same standard—expect to pay around $100 for two without alcoholic drinks. If you are going to splurge, do it here. A large breakfast buffet every morning (6:30–9:30 A.M.; $24 per person) is worth trying if you won't be coming for dinner. Lunch is served 11:30 A.M.–2 P.M.; dinner is 5–9:30 P.M.

INFORMATION

On the main access road opposite the Prince of Wales Hotel, the **Waterton Visitor Centre** (403/859-5133; June–Aug. 9 A.M.–8 P.M., May and early Sept. 9 A.M.–5 P.M., closed the rest of the year) provides general information on the park, sells fishing licenses, and issues Wilderness Use Permits. The park's administration office on Mount View Road (403/859-2224; year-round weekdays 8 A.M.–4 P.M.) offers the same services as the visitor center. For more information on the park, write to Superintendent, Waterton Lakes National Park, Waterton Park, AB T0K 2M0. The Parks Canada website is www.pc.gc.ca. For general tourist information, the local chamber of commerce website, www.watertonchamber.com, provides plenty current information and links to accommodations.

Books and Maps

For everything from local interest to trashy bestsellers, you'll find what you're looking for in **Tamarack Village Square** (Mount View Rd., 403/859-2378; daily 8 A.M.–8 P.M.). For everything from natural history to new age, wander over to **Borderline Books** (305 Windflower Ave., 403/859-2284; Sat.–Thurs. 9 A.M.–5 P.M.). The **Waterton Natural History Association,** based in the Waterton Heritage Centre (117 Waterton Ave., 403/859-2624; May–Sept. 10 A.M.–5 P.M., July and August until 8 P.M.), stocks every book ever written about the park (except this one), as well as many titles pertaining to western Canada in general.

Although the free park maps handed out at the Waterton Visitor Centre suffice for hiking any of the trails detailed in this book, I highly recommend picking up the Gem Trek map (available at any of the park bookstores; $8), which puts the varied topography in perspective and helps identify natural features of note.

SHOPPING AND SERVICES

The numerous tourist-oriented gift shops along Waterton Avenue are worth browsing through when the weather isn't cooperating. **Tamarack Village Square** (Mount View Rd., 403/859-2378; daily 8 A.M.–8 P.M.) is a five-generation family business that stocks a little of everything. Here you'll find a good bookshop, a currency exchange, and a sports store selling camping gear and fishing tackle. Waterton has no banks, but traveler's checks are accepted at most businesses, and **ATMs** are scattered throughout town.

The **post office** is beside the fire station on Fountain Avenue. **Itussiststukiopi Coin-Op Launderette** (301 Windflower Ave.) is open daily 8 A.M.–10 P.M.

Emergency Services

The closest **hospitals** are in Cardston (403/653-4411) and Pincher Creek (403/627-3333). The park's 24-hour emergency number is 403/859-2636. For the **RCMP**, call 403/859-2244.

TRANSPORTATION
Getting There

The nearest commercial airport is at Lethbridge, 140 km (87 miles) away. The closest **Greyhound** buses come to the park is Pincher Creek, 50 km (31 miles) away. From the depot (1015 Hewetson St., 403/627-2716), a cab to the park (call **Crystal Taxi,** 403/627-4262) will run around $60 each way. **Westcastle Car & Truck Rentals** (403/627-4266 or 888/209-3648) has vehicles from $55 per day with 200 free kilometers, but if you're going to drive at all you should consider picking up a vehicle in Calgary (240 km/150 miles north).

Getting Around

Waterton Visitor Services (Tamarack Village Square, Mount View Rd., 403/859-2378, www.watertonvisitorservices.com) operates hiker shuttle services to various trailheads within the park. Cameron Lake, the starting point for the Carthew-Alderson Trail (which ends back in town), is a popular drop-off point; $8 one-way. You could take one of these shuttles, then return on the bus later in the day if driving the steep mountain roads doesn't appeal to you. The company also offers two-hour tours ($30 per person) through the park and runs a local taxi service.

Pat's (Mount View Rd., 403/859-2266) rents mountain bikes for $7 for the first hour then $5 per hour thereafter to a maximum of $34 per day. Motorized scooters are $22 per hour or $70 per day.

Other Parks of the Canadian Rockies

Note: Please see color map of **Canadian Rockies** *on pages ii-iii.*

The previous chapters have covered the better-known parks of the Canadian Rockies, but many other areas of special appeal are protected as provincial and wilderness parks. These parks give visitors the chance to enjoy the natural beauty and wildlife of the mountains away from the crowds associated with the national parks. They have no fancy hotels, golf courses, or shopping malls, and in some cases not even roads.

Seven provincial parks lie on the British Columbia side of the mountains. **Mount Robson Provincial Park,** west of Jasper National Park, protects the highest peak in the Canadian Rockies. The Berg Lake Trail, which climbs to a high alpine lake at the base of Mount Robson, is the

MOUNT ROBSON

most popular overnight hike in all of the mountains. **Mount Assiniboine Provincial Park** has no roads—access is on foot or by flying in by helicopter. The other provincial parks—**Akamina–Kishinena, Elk Lakes, Height of the Rockies, Top of the World,** and **Whiteswan Lake**—all have their own appeal and are well worth the effort required to reach them. On the Alberta side of the mountains, three designated wilderness areas—**White Goat, Siffleur,** and **Willmore**—offer even more solitude.

PLANNING YOUR TIME

Unlike the other chapters that cover individual parks, this section of the book brings together lesser-known parks scattered the length of the Canadian Rockies. Therefore, plan on visiting the ones that sound interesting to you in conjunction with those covered in previous chapters. For example, if you are based in the town of Jasper, you could visit **Mount Robson Provincial Park** in a day, with time to go rafting on the Fraser River, enjoy a picnic lunch in the shadow of the famous peak, do a afternoon hike, then be back in Jasper for dinner. At the other end of the mountain range, it's a three-hour drive to **Akamina–Kishinena Provincial Park** from the nearest town, but you can reach the park on foot in less than an hour from Waterton Lakes National Park.

Mount Assiniboine Provincial Park, in the geographical heart of the Canadian Rockies, is both the easiest and hardest park to reach. You'll need to read more to see why, but if you take the easy route, you'll need reservations well in advance.

British Columbia Parks

Provincial parks are—as you may have guessed—managed by the provincial government. Those covered in this chapter all lie on the west side of the Continental Divide, in British Columbia. Facilities vary dramatically, and a discussion of what you can expect is included below. Only one of the parks (Mount Robson) has a visitor center, so your best source of information is the website of the government's Ministry of Water, Land, and Air Protection (www.bcparks.ca or http://wlapwww.gov.bc.ca/bcparks). The provincial parks covered in this chapter fall within the Kootenay and Okanagan Regions boundary. You can contact this office at 250/354-6333; the exception is Mount Robson Provincial Park (250/566-9174).

AKAMINA–KISHINENA PROVINCIAL PARK

Bordering Glacier National Park (Montana, U.S.) and Waterton Lakes National Park (Alberta), this remote tract of 10,922 hectares (27,000 acres) protects the extreme southeastern corner of British Columbia. The park is named for its two main waterways, which flow southward into Montana from the Flathead Basin. This was the main reason for the park's creation, because now, alongside Waterton Lakes National Park, entire watersheds of Glacier National Park are protected.

The landscape has changed little in thousands of years, since the Kootenay rested in the open meadows beside Kishinena Creek before crossing the Continental Divide to hunt bison on the prairies. The park supports a healthy population of grizzly bears, along with other endangered species such as wolverines, wolves, and lynx.

The only access is on foot from one of two trailheads. The longer option is from the end of an unsealed road that leaves Highway 3 at 16 km (10 miles) south of Fernie, British Columbia. The road leads 110 km (68 miles) into the Flathead River Valley, where trails climb along Kishinena then Akamina Creek into the park.

Access from Waterton Lakes National Park

The most popular and easiest access to the park is by hiking trail from the Akamina Parkway in Waterton Lakes National Park (Alberta). The signposted trailhead is 15 km (9.3 miles) along this road from Waterton townsite. From the parkway, the trail gains 110 meters (360 feet) of elevation in 1.5 km (.9 mile) before reaching the boundary of the park high atop the Continental Divide. After a further 700 meters (.4 mile), the trail divides. The closest of two subalpine bodies of water, **Forum Lake,** is 2.2 km (1.4 miles) to the left up a tedious ascent of Forum Creek. Colorful meadows surround the lake's outlet, while a layered headwall provides a stunning backdrop. Allow 1.5 hours for this 4.4-km (2.7-mile) hike. Nestled below Akamina Ridge, **Wall Lake** is straight ahead from the junction, 2.7 km (1.7 miles). This trail gains only minimal elevation and passes Akamina Creek Campground.

Campgrounds

The park's only facility is **Akamina Creek Campground,** 2.4 km (1.5 miles) from the Akamina Parkway along the trail to Wall Lake. In a forest of Engelmann spruce, each site has a picnic table and fire pit; $5 per night.

Fernie

The nearest town to the Flathead River Valley access point is Fernie (pop. 5,200), out on Highway 3 and a worthwhile destination in itself. It's traditionally been a coal-mining and forestry center, but the town has great skiing and boarding at **Fernie Alpine Resort** (250/423-4655, www.skifernie.com), generally regarded as one of North America's undiscovered gems. Beside the highway, through town to the north, is **Fernie Visitor Info Centre** (250/423-6868, www.ferniechamber.com), a good source of information for those traveling to Akamina–Kishinena Provincial Park.

Fernie's range of inexpensive accommodations makes the town a great base for budget-conscious travelers. Best of the bunch is **Samesun International Lodge** (Hwy. 3, 250/861-3001 or 877/562-2783, www.samesun.com). This converted motel has a game room, communal kitchen, loads of parking, a laundry, Internet access, and even an outdoor pool. Accommodations are in dorms ($21.40 per bed) and private rooms ($59–119 s or d). In between the high summer and winter seasons, regular motel rooms

go for as low as $40—a great deal. Up at the alpine resort, **Griz Inn** (250/423-9221 or 800/661-0118, www.grizinn.com) offers 45 kitchen-equipped suites, an indoor pool, hot tub, and restaurant. Through summer, room rates start at a reasonable $85 s or d, while a condo unit is $130 for up to four people.

The best bet for campers is **Mount Fernie Provincial Park** (mid-May–Sept.), 12 km (7.5 miles) south of town and four km (2.5 miles) north of the Akamina-Kishinena Provincial Park access road. Facilities are basic, but it's a pleasant setting, and a short trail leads along Lizard Creek to a waterfall. Sites are $14 per night.

You can find a good selection of restaurants scattered through the downtown core, but my best picks are along the highway. **Jamochas Coffee House** (851 7th Ave., 250/423-6977) is the pick of many local caffeine joints (and it serves up some delicious homemade soups). Opposite the Samesun lodge, the **Ⓜ Curry Bowl** (932 7th Ave., 250/423-2695; Tues.–Sun. 5–10 P.M.) won't win any design awards, but with delicious dishes like mango shrimp curry ($14) and a Vietnamese chicken stir-fry ($11), it really doesn't matter. **Ⓜ Yamagoya** (741 7th Ave., 250/430-0080) is a stylish dining room that offers top-notch Japanese cuisine at reasonable prices.

ELK LAKES PROVINCIAL PARK

This park encompasses more than 17,000 hectares (42,000 acres) of rugged wilderness along the British Columbia side of the Canadian Rockies. The park lies adjacent to the southern border of Peter Lougheed Provincial Park in Alberta (see the *Kananaskis Country* chapter), but the only road access is from Highway 3, more than 120 km (75 miles) to the south. Head north for 35 km (22 miles) from Sparwood, between Cranbrook and the Alberta border, on a paved road to **Elkford,** then take an unpaved forestry road 67 km (42 miles) farther north into the park.

The end of the road, where you'll find a kiosk with a park map and up-to-date trail conditions, is the park's main trailhead. From this point it's an easy one km (.6 mile) to **Lower Elk Lake** and then another kilometer beyond the end of the lake to **Upper Elk Lake.** At the lower lake, a narrow trail climbs to a lookout. Aside from the long drive in, the ratio of effort to reward in reaching these lakes is unmatched in the Canadian Rockies. The stunningly beautiful upper lake is surrounded by steep snowcapped peaks, and several avalanche paths end right at water's edge. Fishing in the lower lake is productive for Dolly Varden and cutthroat trout.

Practicalities

The park has no facilities. The nearest town is Elkford (pop. 2,500), a small coal-mining community 67 km (42 miles) south. The community has few services, but there's a small **municipal campground** within walking distance of downtown ($16 with hookups). The **Elkford Visitor Info Centre** (Front St., 250/865-4614 or 877/355-9453, www.tourismelkford.ca) is a good source of park information.

HEIGHT OF THE ROCKIES PROVINCIAL PARK

This long and narrow, 68,000-hectare (134,000-acre) park protects a 50-km-long (31-mile-long) section of the Canadian Rockies, including a 25-km-long (15.5-mile-long) stretch bordering the Continental Divide. The park lies entirely in British Columbia, bordered by Elk Lakes and Peter Lougheed Provincial Parks to the east and Banff National Park at its narrow northern reaches. It is accessible only on foot and is not a destination for the casual day-tripper. Mountains dominate the landscape, with 26 peaks—some of which remained unnamed until recently—rising over the magical 10,000-foot (3,050-meter) mark. They lie in two distinct ranges: the **Royal Group** in the north and the **Italian Group** in the south. The dominant peak is 3,460-meter (11,350-foot) **Mount King George,** in the Royal Group, which is flanked by massive hanging glaciers on its north- and east-facing slopes. Mountain goats thrive on all massifs, while the remote valleys are home to high concentrations of elk and grizzly bears.

The park can be reached from two directions. Neither is signposted, so before setting out for the park, pick up a good map of the area at a local information center or Forest Service office. The following directions are intended only as a guide.

Connor Lake is the most popular destination in the south of the park. It is reached by passing through Whiteswan Lake Provincial Park (see *Whiteswan Lake Provincial Park*), then continuing along a rough logging road that parallels the White River to its upper reaches. (The most important intersection to watch for is 11 km/6.8 miles from Whiteswan Lake; stay right, immediately crossing the river.) At the end of the road, a tortuous 72 km (45 miles) from Highway 93/95, is a small area set aside for tents and horse corrals. From this trailhead, it's an easy walk up Maiyuk Creek and over a low ridge to Connor Lake, where you'll enjoy great views of the Italian Group to the north and Mount Forsyth to the southwest.

Small **Queen Mary Lake** lies in the western shadow of the impressive Royal Group. It is generally the destination only of those on horseback or mountaineers continuing into the Royal Group. To get there, turn off Highway 93/95 at Canal Flats and follow a logging road up the Kootenay River watershed. For the first 48 km (30 miles), the road follows the Kootenay itself. Then it turns westward and climbs along the south side of the Palliser River 35 km (21.7 miles) farther to road's end. From this point, it's a 12-km (7.5-mile) hike up a forested valley, with numerous creek crossings, to the lake.

Campgrounds

Primitive campgrounds lie on the shores of **Connor** and **Queen Mary Lakes** ($5 per person). An eight-person cabin sits at the north end of Connor Lake. Beds are offered on a first-come, first-served basis for $15 per person per night.

MOUNT ASSINIBOINE PROVINCIAL PARK

Named for one of the Canadian Rockies' most spectacular peaks, this 39,050-hectare (96,500-acre), roughly triangular park lies northeast of

Radium Hot Springs, sandwiched between Kootenay National Park to the west and Banff National Park to the east. It's inaccessible by road; access is on foot or by helicopter. A haven for experienced hikers, the park offers alpine meadows, lakes, glaciers, and many peaks higher than 3,050 meters (10,000 feet) to explore. The park's highest peak, 3,618-meter (11,870-foot) Mount Assiniboine (seventh-highest in the Canadian Rockies), is known as the Matterhorn of the Rockies for its resemblance to that famous Swiss landmark. The striking peak can be seen from many points well outside the boundaries of the park, including Buller Pond in Kananaskis Country and Sunshine Village winter resort in Banff National Park.

The peak is named for the Assiniboine people, who ventured into this section of the Canadian Rockies many thousands of years before European exploration. The name Assiniboine means "stone boilers"—a reference to these people's preferred cooking method. The mountain was sighted and named by a geological survey team in 1885, but the first ascent wasn't made until 1901.

Lake Magog is the destination of most park visitors. Here you'll find the park's only facilities and the trailheads for several interesting and varied day hikes. One of the most popular walks is along the Sunburst Valley/Nub Ridge trail. From Lake Magog, small Sunburst Lake is reached in about 20 minutes, then the trail continues northwest a short distance to Cerulean Lake. From this lake's outlet, the trail descends slowly along the Mitchell River to a junction four km (2.5 miles) from Lake Magog. Take the right fork, which climbs through a dense subalpine forest to Elizabeth Lake, nestled in the southern shadow of Nub Peak. From this point, instead of descending back to Cerulean Lake, take the Nub Ridge trail, which climbs steadily for one km (.6 mile) to a magnificent viewpoint high above Lake Magog. From the viewpoint, it's just less than four km (2.5 miles), downhill all the way, to the valley floor. The total length of this outing is 11 km (6.8 miles), and as elevation gained is only just over 400 meters (1,310 feet), the trail can comfortably be completed in four hours.

Approaching the Park on Foot

Three trails provide access to Lake Magog, the park's largest body of water. The most popular comes in from the northeast, starting at Sunshine Village winter resort in Banff National Park and leading 29 km (18 miles) via Citadel Pass to the lake. Not only is this trail spectacular, but the high elevation of the trailhead (2,100 meters/6,890 feet) makes for a relatively easy approach. Another approach is from the east, in Spray Valley Provincial Park (Kananaskis Country). The trailhead is at the southern end of Spray Lake; take the Mount Shark staging area turnoff 40 km (25 miles) south of Canmore. By the time the trail has climbed the Bryant Creek drainage to 2,165-meter (7,100-foot) Assiniboine Pass, all elevation gain (450 meters/1,480 feet) has been made. At 27 km (16.8 miles), this is the shortest approach, but its elevation gain is greater than the other two trails. The longest and least-used access is from Highway 93 at Simpson River in Kootenay National Park. This trail climbs the Simpson River and Surprise Creek drainages and crosses 2,270-meter (7,450-foot) Ferro Pass to the lake for a total length of 32 km (20 miles).

The Easy Way In

If these long approaches put visiting the park out of your reach, there's one more option: you can fly in by helicopter from the Mount Shark Helipad, at the southern end of Spray Valley Provincial Park, 40 km (25 miles) southwest of Canmore. Flights depart at 11:30 A.M. Wednesday, Friday, and Sunday and cost $128.40 per person each way, including an 18-kilogram (40-pound) per-person baggage limit. Although Alpine Helicopters operates the flights, all bookings must be made through the Mount Assiniboine Lodge (call 403/678-2883 Mon.–Fri. 8 A.M.–2 P.M.; www.assiniboinelodge.com).

If you're planning on hiking into the park, Alpine Helicopters will fly your gear in for $1.50 per pound. This same company, which also operates from a base in Canmore, charges $185 per person for a 30-minute flightseeing trip over the park. For more information, call Alpine Helicopters (403/678-4802, www.alpine helicopter.com).

Other Parks

Mount Assiniboine Lodge

Getting to and staying at ⓜ **Mount Assiniboine Lodge** isn't cheap, but the number of repeat guests is testament to an experience that you will never forget. The mountain scenery may take most of the kudos, but the lodge's congenial atmosphere, overseen by longtime hosts the Renners, makes the stay equally memorable. Built in 1928 by the CPR, the delightfully rustic lodge is set in a lakeside meadow below the distinctive peak. The main building holds six double rooms that share bathroom facilities and a dining area where hearty meals (included in the rates) are served up communal-style. Scattered in the surrounding trees are six one-room cabins that sleep two to five people. Each has running water and uses propane to heat and light the space. Outhouses and showers are shared. The rate for lodge rooms is $190 per person, while cabin accommodations range $190–240. Children 12 and under are $120. You can reach the lodge on foot or fly in with Alpine Helicopters from a helipad in Kananaskis Country. The fare and departure days are the same as for campers; the only difference is that guests depart at 1 P.M. Visitors flying in may bring 18 kilograms (40 pounds) of gear plus one pair of skis. If you decide to hike in (or out), the charge for luggage transfers is $1.50 per pound (0.45 kilogram).

The operating season is mid-June to the first weekend of October and then mid-February to mid-April for cross-country skiing. There is a minimum stay of two nights. The lodge has no landline phone; for reservations or information call 403/678-2883 (Mon.–Fri. 8 A.M.–2 P.M.) or check the website www.assiniboinelodge.com.

Between 4 and 5 P.M. each afternoon, the lodge opens its doors to campers for a simple afternoon tea of lemonade, fresh pastries, and tea ($7).

Campgrounds

Lake Magog is the park's main facility area, such as it is. A designated camping area on a low ridge above the lake's west shore provides a source of drinking water, pit toilets, and bear-proof food caches. Open fires are prohibited. Sites are $5 per person per night. No reservations are taken, but

even those who visit frequently have told me they've never seen it full. Also at the lake are the **Naiset Huts,** where bunk beds cost $20 per person per night (book through Mount Assiniboine Lodge at 403/678-2883 Mon.–Fri. 8 A.M.–2 P.M., www.mountassiniboine.com). The cabins contain nothing more than bunk beds with mattresses, so you'll need a stove, food, a sleeping bag, and your own source of light.

Information

In addition to the government agency responsible for the park (Ministry of Water, Land, and Air Protection, www.bcparks.ca or http://wlapwww.gov.bc.ca/bcparks), park information centers in Radium Hot Springs, Lake Louise, and Banff provide information and up-to-date trail conditions.

MOUNT ROBSON PROVINCIAL PARK

At the northern end of the Canadian Rockies, spectacular 224,866-hectare (555,650-acre) Mount Robson Provincial Park was created in 1913 to protect a vast wilderness of steep canyons and wide forested valleys; icy lakes, rivers, and streams; and rugged mountain peaks permanently blanketed in snow and ice. The park lies along the Continental Divide in British Columbia, adjacent to Jasper National Park, and shelters the headwaters of the Fraser River, one of British Columbia's most important waterways. Towering over the park's western entrance is magnificent 3,954-meter (12,970-foot) **Mount Robson,** the highest peak in the Canadian Rockies.

Highway 16 splits the park in two, and many sights of interest are visible from the highway. But you'll have to leave the car behind to experience one of the park's biggest draws; the famous Berg Lake Trail is strictly for hikers.

Flora and Fauna

The elevation differences within the park are as great as anywhere else in the Canadian Rockies, making for a great variety of flora and fauna. The main service center lies in a forested valley at an elevation of just 840 meters (2,750 feet), right in the heart of the montane. The oft-pho-

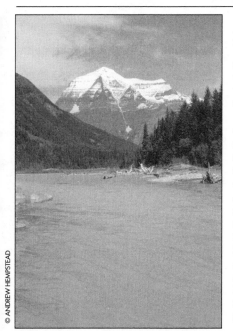

© ANDREW HEMPSTEAD

Mount Robson (3,954 meters/12,970 feet) is the highest peak in the Canadian Rockies.

tographed view of Mount Robson from the visitor center is framed by a stand of trembling aspen across a cleared meadow, but the most common tree at this elevation is **Douglas fir,** which covers the valley floor. **Western red cedar** and **hemlock** thrive in damp sections of the park. As in the rest of the Canadian Rockies, the subalpine zone is dominated by **Engelmann spruce** and, at higher elevations, **subalpine fir.** The alpine zone in the park begins at around 2,300 meters (7,550 feet).

In spring, **black bears** are often seen feasting on dandelions by the roadside, but their larger relative, the **grizzly,** rarely makes an appearance in the busy valley through which Highway 16 winds. **Elk, moose,** and **mountain goats** are also present, as are many smaller critters. More than 170 bird species have been identified, with the rare **harlequin duck** a special joy to watch as it passes though the park each spring.

History

Local Shuswap natives called Mount Robson Yuh-hai-has-hun (Mountain of the Spiral Road) for its layered appearance. Historians guess that the peak's European name honors a member of the Hudson's Bay Company, although details of the christening have been lost to history.

Mountaineers were attracted to the challenge of climbing Mount Robson in the early 1900s; the first official ascent took place in 1913 (the same year the park as we know it today was created). Led by Swiss guide Conrad Kain, the first ascent party was made up of members of the Alpine Club of Canada. Although this was the first official summit climb, the summit had been attempted four years earlier by the Reverend George Kinney and friends. Kinney thought he'd made the summit, but he was climbing the summit ridge in a heavy fog; a cairn and a message recording the names of the members of Kinney's climbing team were later found on the ridge about 100 vertical meters (320 vertical feet) from the top.

Roadside Sights

Highway 16 enters the park from the east at 1,066-meter (3,500-foot) **Yellowhead Pass,** on the British Columbia–Alberta border. It's the lowest highway pass over the Continental Divide. From the divide, it's 60 km (37.2 miles) to the park's western boundary and the visitor center. Just west of the divide, a rest area beside picturesque **Portal Lake** is a good introduction to the park.

Continuing westward, the highway passes long, narrow **Yellowhead Lake** at the foot of 2,458-meter (8,060-foot) **Yellowhead Mountain,** then crosses the upper reaches of the Fraser River. The Moose River drains into the Fraser River at **Moose Marsh,** a good spot for watching wildlife at the southeast end of **Moose Lake.** Moose often feed here at dawn and dusk, and waterfowl are present throughout the day.

Continuing west, the highway parallels Moose Lake; waterfalls on the lake's far side create a photogenic backdrop. As the road descends steeply to a wide, open section of the valley, it passes the main facility area, where you'll find a

Other Parks

MOUNT ROBSON PROVINCIAL PARK

Mt Stornoway

De Smet Range

Mt Sassenach

Mt Strange

Jasper

National

Park

Harvey Lake

Snaring

Mt McCord

Mt Mahood

Mt McNaughton

Victoria Cross Ranges

BRITISH COLUMBIA

ALBERTA

Mt Bridgland

Deer Creek

Miette

Portal Lake

16

To Jasper

Yellowhead Mtn

Yellowhead Lake

LUCERNE

Yellowhead Pass

Fitzwilliam Basin

Mt Fitzwilliam

Ghita Creek

Fraser

Waddington Peak

Clairvaux Creek

River

The Ramparts

visitor center, campgrounds, a gas station, and a restaurant. On a clear day the panorama from this lump of commercialism is equal to any sight in British Columbia. The sheer west face of Mount Robson slices skyward just seven km (4.3 miles) away across a flower-filled meadow. This is as close as you can get to the peak in your car.

If you're approaching the park from the west, you'll see Mount Robson long before you reach the park boundary (provided the weather is cooperating). It's impossible to confuse this distinctive peak with those that surround it—no wonder it's known as the "Monarch of the Canadian Rockies."

Berg Lake Trail
- Length: 19.5 km/12 miles (eight hours) one-way
- Elevation gain: 725 meters/2,380 feet
- Rating: moderate/difficult
- Trailhead: two km (1.2 miles) north of Mount Robson Visitor Centre

This is the most popular overnight hike in the Canadian Rockies, but don't let the crowds put you off—the hike is well worth it. Beautiful aqua-colored Berg Lake lies below the north face of Mount Robson, which rises 2,400 meters (7,880 feet) directly behind the lake. Glaciers on the mountain's shoulder regularly calve off into the lake, resulting in the icebergs that give the lake its name.

The trail begins by following the Robson River 4.5 km (2.8 miles) through dense sub-alpine forest to glacially fed **Kinney Lake.** There the trail narrows, crossing the fast-flowing river at the eight-km (five-mile) mark and climbing alongside it. The next four km (2.5 miles), through the steep-sided Valley of a Thousand Falls, are the most demanding, but views of four spectacular waterfalls ease the pain of the 500-vertical-meter (1,640-vertical-foot) climb. The first glimpses of Mount Robson come soon after reaching the head of the valley, from where it's one km (.6 mile) farther to the outlet of Berg Lake, 17.5 km (10.9

Other Parks

miles) from the trailhead. The first of three lake-side campgrounds is two km (1.2 miles) from this point.

While the panorama from the lake is stunning, most hikers who have come this far will want to spend some time exploring the area. From the north end of the lake, trails lead to Toboggan Falls and more mountain views, to the head of Robson Glacier, and to Robson Pass, which opens up the remote northern reaches of Jasper National Park.

Berg Lake Trail Practicalities

It's possible to traverse the trail's first section and return the same day; to get all the way to Berg Lake and back you'll need to stay in the backcountry overnight. Along the route seven primitive campgrounds hold 75 campsites, including three campgrounds along the lakeshore. Bookings for these sites can be made up to three months in advance by calling the BC Parks' Discover Camping hotline (604/689-9025 or 800/689-9025); the reservation fee is $6.42 per night to a maximum of $19.26. Book early because the quota fills quickly. Upon arrival in the park, all overnight hikers must then register at the visitor center and pay a camping fee of $6 per person per night.

If the uphill walk in seems too ambitious, contact **Robson Helimagic** (250/566-4700 or 877/454-4700, www.robsonhelimagic.com), which makes helicopter drop-offs at Robson Pass from Valemount every Monday and Friday; $185 per person (minimum four).

Other Hikes in the Park

Aside from the popular trail to Berg Lake, the park holds only two other established trails. The shortest ascends the slopes of 2,458-meter (8,060-foot) **Yellowhead Mountain.** From the trailhead across the rail line at Yellowhead Lake, it's a steady climb through subalpine forest to the first viewpoint at the one-km (.6-mile) mark. Another three km (1.9 miles) and an elevation gain of 720 meters (2060 feet) bring you to flower-filled meadows and panoramic views extending east to the Continental Divide and west to the Selwyn Range. Allow two hours each way for this hike.

The other option is the 13-km (eight-mile) **Fitzwilliam Basin Trail,** which requires an overnight stay in the backcountry. Elevation gain is 950 meters (3,120 feet), so it's a demanding trail. From the trailhead on the south side of Highway 16, three km (1.9 miles) east of Lucerne Campground, the trail climbs steadily for six km (3.7 miles) to the confluence of Rockingham and Fitzwilliam Creeks. Although easy to follow, the remaining seven km (4.3 miles) along the northern slopes of 2,911-meter (9,550-foot) Mount Fitzwilliam are rough going. After ascending a steep ridge, the trail all but dissipates, but many camping spots can be found in the wide lake-filled basin.

Accommodations

The park has no indoor accommodations, but two lodges lie just outside the park's western boundary, and motel accommodations are available 42 km (26 miles) to the southwest in Valemount.

Mountain River Lodge (four km/2.5 miles west of the visitor center, 250/566-9899 or 888/566-9899, www.mtrobson.com) is in a delightful setting right alongside the Fraser River. The main lodge holds four guest rooms, each with a different character, a balcony, and private bathroom. The smallest of the rooms (with twin beds and a private bathroom down the hall) is $85 s or d, while the other three are $105; rates include a cooked breakfast. Self-contained cabins costs $125 per night, with breakfast available at an extra charge.

One km (.6 mile) west of Mountain River Lodge is **Mount Robson Lodge** (250/566-4821 or 888/566-4821, www.mountrobsonlodge.com; May–Oct.), with 18 freestanding cabins ($70–125 s or d); the more expensive ones have kitchens, or eat at the small coffee shop.

Campgrounds

Within the park four auto-accessible campgrounds are open May to mid-September, with another just outside the park boundary. Three of these are park-operated. Closest to the visitor center (and my favorite) is **Robson River Campground,** where numerous trails lead down to the river for the classic upstream view of Mt. Robson. It's also only a short walk to the visitor center and a café. Across the highway is the larger **Robson Meadows Campground,** with 125 sites on a spiral road system that centers on an outdoor theater that hosts evening interpretive programs through summer. A number of sites at Robson Meadows can be reserved through www.discover camping.ca. Both campgrounds have flush toilets and showers but no hookups; $17 per site.

Beside the east end of Yellowhead Lake (swimming for the brave), 50 km (31 miles) from the visitor center, is the more rustic **Lucerne Campground,** where sites are $14. Facilities include drinking water, pit toilets, and picnic tables.

Emperor Ridge Campground (250/566-8438; mid-May–late Sept.) is a small commercial facility right behind the visitor center; $14.50 per site including hot showers but no hookups.

Robson Shadows Campground is part of Mount Robson Lodge (250/566-4821 or 888/566-4821, www.mountrobsonlodge.com; May–Oct.), outside of the park and five km west of the visitor center. It also has showers but no hookups. Sites are $15 per night.

Information

At the park's western entrance, **Mount Robson Visitor Centre** (250/566-9174, www.bcparks.ca; mid-June–mid-Sept. daily 8 A.M.–8 P.M., mid-May–mid-June and mid-Sept.–mid-Oct. daily 8 A.M.–5 P.M.) features informative natural-history slide shows, an evening interpretive program, and trail reports updated daily. The center stocks the brochure *Mount Robson Provincial Park,* which provides sufficient information if you're only driving through the park. Hikers and climbers can pick up more detailed trail descriptions and topographical maps ($11) at the center.

TOP OF THE WORLD PROVINCIAL PARK

This wild and remote 8,790-hectare (21,720-acre) park lies beyond Whiteswan Lake Provincial Park (see *Whiteswan Lake Provincial Park*), a rough 52 km (32 miles) from Highway 93/95 (turn off the Whiteswan Lake access road at Alces

Whiteswan Lake

Lake). You can't drive into the park, but it's a fairly easy six-km (3.7-mile) walk from the end of the road to picturesque **Fish Lake,** the park's largest body of water. The trail climbs alongside the pretty Lussier River to the lake, which is encircled with Engelmann spruce and surrounded by peaks up to 2,500 meters (8,200 feet) high. The hike to the lake gains just over 200 vertical meters (660 vertical feet) and makes a good day trip. Trails from the lake lead to other alpine lakes and to a viewpoint that allows a good overall perspective on the high plateau for which the park is named. Fish Lake is productive for cutthroat trout and Dolly Varden.

Practicalities

Bring everything you'll need because there are no services within the park. Camping is possible at one of four designated areas for $5 per person, or you can stay in the large cabin nestled in trees beside Fish Lake ($15 per person). For park information and trail conditions, contact **BC Parks** (250/354-6333, http://wlapwww.gov.bc.ca /bcparks).

WHITESWAN LAKE PROVINCIAL PARK

Access to this popular British Columbia park is from Highway 93/95, 50 km (31 miles) south of Radium Hot Springs and 28 km (17.4 miles) north of Skookumchuck. From a signed turnoff, an unpaved logging road takes off east into the mountains, leading first to 1,994-hectare (4.930-acre) Whiteswan Lake Provincial Park, then to Top of the World Provincial Park. The road climbs steadily from the highway, entering Lussier Gorge after 11 km (6.8 miles). Within the gorge, a steep trail leads down to **Lussier Hot Springs.** Two small pools have been constructed to contain the odorless hot (43°C/110°F) water as it bubbles out of the ground and flows into the Lussier River. Within the park itself, the road closely follows the southern shorelines of first **Alces Lake** then the larger **Whiteswan Lake.** The two lakes attract abundant birdlife; loons, grebes, and herons are all common. They also attract anglers, who come for great rainbow trout fishing. Both lakes are stocked and have a daily quota of two fish per person.

Campgrounds

The main road skirts the lakes and passes four popular campgrounds. The sites are $14 per night and fill on a first-come, first-served basis. All sites come with a picnic table and fire grate. There are no hookups or showers.

Alberta Parks

Abutting the famous national parks of Banff and Jasper are three vast tracts of land protected by the Alberta government as "wilderness areas." No motorized vehicles are allowed within their boundaries, and hunting and fishing are prohibited, as is all construction. This, ironically, gives these lightly traveled regions more protection than national parks. The drawback, and the reason so few people explore these areas, is that wilderness really means *wilderness,* sans roads, bridges, or campsites. With one exception at Willmore, no roads even lead to the areas' boundaries; the only access is on foot.

For more information, call **Alberta Community Development** (780/427-9383 or 866/427-3582) or click on the "Preserving Alberta" link at www.cd.gov.ab.ca. If you happen to be in Edmonton, stop by the department's excellent information center (9945 108th St., 780/944-0313).

SIFFLEUR WILDERNESS AREA

This remote region on the Alberta side of the Canadian Rockies lies south of Highway 11, which crosses west-central Alberta between Rocky Mountain House and Saskatchewan River Crossing, in Banff National Park. It is completely protected from any activities that could have an impact on the area's fragile ecosystems. That includes road and trail development; no bridges have been built over the area's many fast-flowing streams, and the few old trails that do exist are not maintained. Elk, deer, moose, cougars, wolverines, wolves, coyotes, black bears, and grizzly bears roam the area's four main valleys, while higher, alpine elevations harbor mountain goats and bighorn sheep.

The main trail into the 41,200-hectare (101,800-acre) wilderness begins from a parking area two km (1.2 miles) south of the Two O'Clock Creek Campground at Kootenay Plains. The area's northeastern boundary is a seven-km (4.3 miles) hike from here. Even if you're not heading right into Siffleur, the first section of this trail, to **Siffleur Falls,** is worth walking. Along the first section, the trail crosses the North Saskatchewan River via a swinging bridge, then at the two-km (1.2-mile) mark crosses the Siffleur River, reaching the falls after four km (2.5 miles); allow 70 minutes one-way. These are the official Siffleur Falls, but others lie farther upstream at the 6.2-km (3.9-mile) and 6.9-km (4.3-mile) marks.

Once inside the wilderness area, the trail climbs steadily alongside the Siffleur River and into the heart of the wilderness. Ambitious hikers can continue through to the Dolomite Creek Area of Banff National Park, finishing at the Icefields Parkway, seven km (4.3 miles) south of Bow Summit. Total length of this trail is 68 km (42 miles), a strenuous five-day backcountry expedition. Another access point for the area is opposite Waterfowl Lake Campground in Banff National Park. From here it is six km (3.7 miles) up Noyes Creek to the wilderness area boundary; the trail peters out after 4.5 km (2.8 miles) and requires some serious scrambling before descending into Siffleur. This trail—as with all others in the wilderness area—is for experienced hikers only.

Practicalities

Two O'Clock Creek Campground lies two km (1.2 miles) from the park's main trailhead in Kootenay Plains Provincial Recreation Area. It is a primitive facility with a picnic shelter, firewood, and drinking water; the 24 sites each have a picnic table and fire pit. Sites are $12 per night.

WHITE GOAT WILDERNESS AREA

White Goat comprises 44,500 hectares (110,000 acres) of high mountain ranges, wide valleys, hanging glaciers, waterfalls, and high alpine lakes. It lies north and west of Highway 11, abutting the north end of Banff National Park and the south end of Jasper National Park. The area's vegetation zones are easily recognizable: subalpine forests of Engelmann spruce, subalpine fir, and lodgepole pine; alpine tundra higher up. Large mammals here include a large population of bighorn sheep, as well as mountain goats, deer, elk, woodland caribou, moose, cougars, wolves, coyotes, black bears, and grizzly bears.

The most popular hike is the **McDonald Creek Trail,** which first follows the Cline River, then McDonald Creek to the creek's source in the heart of the wilderness area. McDonald Creek is approximately 12 km (7.5 miles) from the parking area on Highway 11, but a full day should be allowed for this section because the trail crosses many streams. From where McDonald Creek flows into the Cline River, it is 19 km (11.8 miles) to the McDonald Lakes, but

allow another two full days; the total elevation gain for the hike is a challenging 1,222 meters (4,000 feet). Other hiking possibilities include following the Cline River to its source and crossing Sunset Pass into Banff National Park, 17 km (10.6 miles) north of Saskatchewan River Crossing, or heading up Cataract Creek and linking up with the trails in the Brazeau River area of Jasper National Park.

WILLMORE WILDERNESS PARK

Willmore Wilderness Park is a northern extension of Jasper National Park. It lies south and west of Grande Cache, a small town on Highway 40 between Hinton and Grande Prairie. The 460,000-hectare (1,137,000-acre) wilderness area is divided roughly in half by the Smoky River. The area west of the river is reached from Sulphur Gates. The east side is far less traveled—the terrain is rougher and wetter. The park is accessible only on foot, horseback, or, in winter, on skis. It is totally undeveloped; the trails that do exist are not maintained and in most cases are those once used by trappers.

The park is made up of long, green ridges above the tree line and, farther west, wide passes and expansive basins along the Continental Divide. Lower elevations are covered in lodgepole pine and spruce, while at higher elevations the cover changes to fir. The diverse wildlife is one of the park's main attractions; white-tailed and mule deer, mountain goats, bighorn sheep, moose, elk, caribou, and black bears are all common. The park is also home to wolves, cougars, and grizzly bears.

Park Access and Travel

The easiest way to access the park is from Sulphur Gates Provincial Recreation Area, six km (3.7 miles) north of Grande Cache on Highway 40 and then a similar distance along a gravel road to the west. Those not planning a trip into the park can still enjoy the cliffs at **Sulphur Gates** (formerly known as Hell's Gate), which is only a short walk from the end of the road. These 70-meter (230-foot) cliffs are at the confluence of the Sulphur and Smoky Rivers. The color difference between the glacial-fed Smoky River and spring-fed Sulphur River is apparent as they merge.

One of the most popular overnight trips from Sulphur Gates is to **Clarke's Cache,** an easy 16-km (10-mile) hike to the remains of a cabin where trappers once stored furs before taking them to trading posts farther afield. A good option for a day trip for fit hikers is to the 2,013-meter (6,600-foot) summit of **Mount Stearn** from a trailhead 3.5 km (2.2 miles) along the access road to Sulphur Gates. The trail begins by climbing alongside a stream through montane, then subalpine forest, and then through open meadows before reentering the forest and forking and rejoining. The official trail then climbs steeply and continuously to Lightning Ridge (10 km/6.2 miles one-way), but an easier summit is reached by heading up through the grassed slopes to a summit knob, 6.5 km (four miles) and 1,000 vertical meters (3,280 vertical feet) from the road; allow 6–6.5 hours for the round-trip.

Practicalities

Anyone planning an extended trip into the park should be aware that no services are available, most trails are unmarked, and certain areas are heavily used by horse-packers. Led by Dave Manzer, a 20-year veteran of leading trips into Willmore, **Wildrose Outfitting** (780/693-2296, www.wildroseoutfitting.com) offers pack trips into the park; expect to pay around $225 per person per day, all-inclusive.

More information is available by contacting the department of Community Development in Edmonton (780/427-9383 or 866/427-3582, www.cd.gov.ab.ca).

GRANDE CACHE

This town of 4,400, the most remote in the Canadian Rockies, is at the gateway to Willmore Wilderness Park and is surrounded by total wilderness, offering endless opportunities for hiking, canoeing, kayaking, fishing, and horseback riding. It perches on the side of Grande Mountain above the Smoky River, which flows from its source in Jasper National Park through Willmore Wilderness Park, eventually joining the Peace River and draining into the Arctic Ocean.

The first Europeans to explore the area were fur trappers and traders, who cached furs near the site of the present town before taking them to major trading posts. At one point there was a small trading post on a lake south of

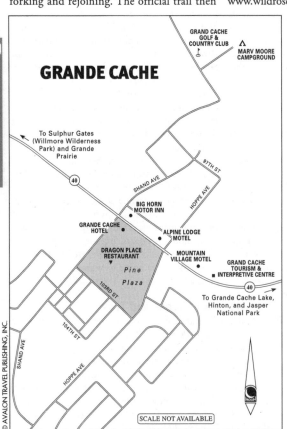

Other Parks (sidebar)

town on Pierre Gray Lakes; its remains are still visible. Grande Cache is a planned town. Construction started in 1969 in response to a need for services and housing for miners and their families working at the McIntyre Porcupine Coal Mine. The town was developed 20 km (12.4 miles) south of the mine to maintain a scenic environment. The mine closed in 2000, but the population level remains stable, with many residents employed at a nearby federal penitentiary.

Sights and Recreation

For great views of the surrounding area, consider climbing **Grande Mountain.** It's a steep trail, gaining 730 meters (2,400 feet) of elevation in 3.5 km (2.1 miles), but from the summit, the view across the Smoky River Valley to the Rocky Mountains is spectacular. The trail follows a power line the entire way to the peak and is easy to follow. To get to the trailhead, head northwest of town one km (.6 mile) and turn right at the cemetery gate. Park, walk along the road to the power line, veer right, and start the long slog to the summit. **Grande Cache Lake,** five km (3.1 miles) south of town, has good swimming, canoeing, and fishing; rainbow and brook trout, whitefish, and arctic grayling are commonly caught. Many of the forestry roads are suitable for mountain biking; **Grande Cache Adventure Sports** (780/827-3764) rents bikes.

In recent years, Grande Cache has placed itself on the calendar of extreme, ultra-marathoners the world over as host of the **Canadian Death Race** series (www.canadiandeathrace.com). Races take place three times annually along the same demanding 125-km (78-mile) course, which summits three peaks: on snowshoes the third weekend of January, on foot the first weekend of August, and on mountain bikes the first weekend of September.

Accommodations and Camping

Room rates in this mountain hideaway are surprisingly inexpensive, but because fewer than 250 rooms are available in the whole town, reservations should be made in advance. On the highway through town, the **Big Horn Motor Inn**

(780/827-3744 or 888/880-2444, www.bighorn inn.com; $55 s, $65 d) is the best value. Each room has a small fridge, some have kitchenettes, and a laundry room and a restaurant are on the premises. Also along the highway are the similarly priced **Alpine Lodge Motel** (780/827-2450) and **Mountain Village Motel** (780/827-2453).

The only camping right in town is at **Marv Moore Campground** (780/827-2404, May–mid-Sept.), which has semiprivate, well-shaded sites and showers, kitchen shelters, a laundry, and firewood. Sites in the tenting area are $20; powered sites are $22. It's at the north end of town on Shand Avenue beside the golf course. Four forestry campgrounds at regular intervals along Highway 40 are managed by North of 40 Campgrounds (780/827-6521). Of special note is the one at **Sulphur Gates Provincial Recreation Area** (west off Hwy. 40 north of town; May–Oct.; $14), which makes a good base for exploring Willmore Wilderness Park. It has just 10 sites.

Food

On a clear day, the view from the **Family Restaurant** (Grande Cache Hotel, 780/827-3377) is worth at least the price of a coffee. Soup and sandwich lunch specials are approximately $6, and pizza and pasta dishes start at $8. At the back of the hotel is **Rockies Bar and Grill,** with a regular bar menu and occasional live music. Across the plaza is **Dragon Place Restaurant** (780/827-3898, daily 11 A.M.–10 P.M.). This is your quintessential small-town Chinese restaurant, with big portions of all the usual westernized Chinese favorites. All mains except the seafood dishes are under $10. Up on the highway, the **Big Horn Motor Inn** (780/827-3744) has a restaurant that opens daily at 5:30 A.M.

Information and Services

The excellent **Grande Cache Tourism and Interpretive Centre** (780/827-3300 or 888/827-3790, www.visitgrandecache.com; summer daily 9 A.M.–7 P.M., the rest of the year Mon.–Fri. 9 A.M.–5 P.M.) is a great source of park information.

The **post office** is in the plaza, as is a **laundry** (beside IGA). **Home Hardware,** in the Pine Plaza, stocks camping and fishing gear.

Know the Canadian Rockies

The Land

The Rocky Mountains rise from the dense forests of central Mexico and run north through the U.S. states of New Mexico, Colorado, Wyoming, and Montana. Continuing north across the 49th parallel (the U.S.–Canada border), the range forms a natural border between the Canadian provinces of British Columbia and Alberta. Mountainous British Columbia is Canada's westernmost province, extending to the Pacific Ocean, while Alberta, to the east, is mostly prairie. The provincial boundary is the Continental Divide, an imaginary line that runs along the Rockies' highest peaks. Although it is a subjective matter, perhaps most would agree that this particular stretch of the Rocky Mountains—the Canadian Rockies—is the most spectacular segment. North of British Columbia and Alberta, the Rockies descend to their northern terminus in the boreal forests of northern Canada.

The Canadian Rockies are relatively low compared to other mountain ranges of the world; the highest peak, Mount Robson, tops out at 3,954 meters (12,970 feet). Running parallel to the mountains along their eastern edge is a series of long, rolling ridges known as the foothills. To the west is the Rocky Mountain Trench, a long, wide valley that in turn is bordered to the west by various subranges of the Columbia Mountains.

GEOLOGY

The Rocky Mountains began rising 75 million years ago, making them relatively young compared to the world's major mountain ranges. But to fully appreciate the geology of the Rockies, you must look back many hundreds of millions of years, to the Precambrian era. At this time, about 700 million years ago, the Pacific Ocean covered most of the western provinces and states. The ocean advanced, then receded, several times over the next half billion years. Each time the ocean flooded eastward it deposited layers of silt and sand on its bed—layers that built up with each successive inundation. Starting approxi-

mately 550 million years ago, the oceans began to come alive with marine invertebrates and the first crustaceans. As these creatures died and sank to the ocean floor, they added to the layers of sediment. Over time, the ever-increasing sediment load compressed the underlying layers into sandstone, shale, and quartzite.

Birth of the Rockies

Some 200 million years ago, the stability of the ocean floor began wavering along the West Coast of North America, culminating 75 million years ago as two plates of the earth's crust collided. According to plate tectonics theory, the earth's crust is broken into several massive chunks (plates) that are always moving and occasionally bump into each other. This isn't something that happens overnight; a plate may move only a few centimeters over thousands of years. In the case of the Rockies, the Pacific Plate butted into the North American Plate and was forced beneath it. The land at this subduction zone was crumpled and thrust upward, creating the Rocky Mountains. Layers of sediment laid down on the ocean floor over the course of hundreds of millions of years were folded, twisted, and squeezed; great slabs of rock broke away, and in places older strata were pushed on top of younger. By the beginning of the Tertiary period, around 65 million years ago, the present form of mountain contours was established and the geological framework of the mountains was in place.

The Ice Ages

No one knows why, but around one million years ago the world's climate cooled a few degrees. Ice caps formed in Arctic regions and slowly moved south over North America and Eurasia. These advances, followed by retreats, occurred four times.

The final major glaciation began moving south 35,000 years ago. A sheet of ice up to 2,000 meters (6,560 feet) deep covered all but the highest peaks of the Rocky Mountains. The ice scoured

FOOTHILLS ERRATICS TRAIN

During the last ice age, a sheet of ice up to 1,000 meters (3,280 feet) thick crept southward across the area that is now Jasper National Park. A landslide deposited hundreds of large quartzite boulders atop the ice, which continued moving south, carrying the boulders with it. Many thousands of years later, as temperatures warmed and the ice melted, the boulders were deposited far from their source, creating what geologists call an "erratics train"—a string of glacially-deposited rocks that in this case extends 650 km (400 miles) south through Alberta. The largest of these boulders—the world's largest erratic, weighing an estimated 18,000 tons—lies just beyond the foothills, seven km (4.3 miles) west of Okotoks. The name is difficult to forget; it's called the **Big Rock.**

© ANDREW HEMPSTEAD

the terrain, destroying all vegetation as it crept slowly forward. In the mountains, these rivers of ice carved hollows, known as *cirques,* into the slopes of the higher peaks. They rounded off lower peaks and reamed out valleys from their preglacier V shape to a trademark, postglacial U shape. The retreat of this ice sheet, beginning around 12,000 years ago, also radically altered the landscape. Rock and debris that had been picked up by the ice on its march forward melted out during the retreat, creating high ridges known as lateral and terminal *moraines.* Many of these moraines blocked natural drainages, resulting in the formation of lakes. Meltwater drained into rivers and streams, incising deep channels into the sedimentary rock of the plains. Today, the only remnants of this ice age are the scattered icefields along the Continental Divide, including the 325-square-km (125-square-mile) **Columbia Icefield.**

Waterways

Water in its various forms has had a profound effect on the appearance of the Canadian Rockies. In addition to the scouring action of the glaciers, flowing water in rivers and streams has, over the millennia, deeply etched the landscape. The process continues today.

The flow of water is directly related to *divides,* or high points of land that dictate the direction of water flow. The dominant divide in the Canadian Rockies, and indeed North America, is the Continental Divide. The natural boundary created by this divide forms the Alberta–British Columbia border, while other, less obvious divides form borders of many parks of the Canadian Rockies.

The five national parks are classic examples of this scenario. The divides forming the boundaries of Banff National Park encompass the entire upper watershed of the **Bow River.** The Bow flows southward through the park then heads east out of the mountains and into the Saskatchewan River system, whose waters continue east to Hudson Bay and the Atlantic Ocean. The Bow River is fed by many lakes famed for their beauty, including the **Bow, Louise,** and **Moraine.** To the south, the rivers of Kananaskis Country and Waterton Lakes National Park also drain into the Saskatchewan River system.

The boundary between Jasper and Banff National Parks is an important north–south divide. The **Columbia Icefield,** a remnant of the last ice age, lies on either side of this divide. Runoff from the south side of the icefield flows south into the Saskatchewan River system, while runoff from the north side forms the upper headwaters of the **Athabasca River** system. The Athabasca flows north through Jasper National Park and into the Mackenzie River system, which continues north to the Arctic Ocean. All water draining off the western slopes of the Continental Divide ends up in the Pacific Ocean via two major river systems: the **Columbia** and the **Fraser.** The mighty Columbia makes a wide northern loop before heading south into the U.S. state of Washington and draining into the Pacific Ocean. Along the way it picks up the waters of the **Kootenay River,** which begins high in Kootenay National Park and makes a lazy loop south through Montana and Idaho before joining the Columbia at Castlegar, British Columbia, and the **Kicking Horse River,** which flows down from the divides that form the borders of Yoho National Park. The **Fraser River,** the longest river entirely within British Columbia, begins in the high reaches of Mount Robson Provincial Park.

CLIMATE

More than any other factor, prevailing moisture-laden westerlies blowing across British Columbia from the Pacific Ocean dictate the climate of the Canadian Rockies. The cold heights of the mountain peaks wring the winds dry, making for clear, sunny skies in southern Alberta; Calgary gets up to 350 hours of sunshine in June alone—good news, unless you're a farmer. In winter, the dry winds blasting down the eastern slopes of the Rockies can raise temperatures on the prairies by up to 40°C (72°F) in 24 hours. Called *chinooks,* these desiccating blows are a phenomenon unique to Alberta.

Elevation and, to a lesser degree, latitude are two other factors affecting the climate within the mountain ecosystem. Elevations vary from 800 meters (2,600 feet) above sea level at Radium Hot Springs to 1,500 meters (4,920 feet) at Lake Louise to 3,954 meters (12,970 feet) at the summit of Mount Robson. As a general rule, temperatures fall 5°C (9°F) for every 1,000 meters (3,280 feet) of elevation gained. Another interesting phenomenon occurring in the Canadian Rockies is the *temperature inversion,* in which a layer of warm air sits on top of a cold air mass. During these inversions, high- and low-country roles are reversed; prairie residents can be shivering and bundling up, while their mountain fellows are sunning themselves in short sleeves.

The Seasons

Summer in the mountains is short, but the days are long. With up to 17 hours of daylight around the summer solstice of June 21, this is an ideal time for travel and camping out. The months on either side of summer are ideal for touring, especially September when rainfall is minimal. Winter is cold, but the skiing and snowboarding are fantastic.

January is usually the coldest month, when Banff's average temperature is –10°C (14°F). In winter, extended spells of –30°C (–22°F) are not uncommon anywhere in the mountains, and temperatures occasionally drop below –40°C (–40°F). The coldest temperature recorded was –52°C (–62°F), in Lake Louise on January 25, 1950. Severe cold weather is often accompanied by sunshine; the cold is a dry cold, unlike the damp cold experienced in coastal regions. Cold temperatures and snow can be expected through mid-March.

CHINOOK WINDS

On many days in the dead of winter, a distinctive arch of clouds forms in the sky over the southwestern corner of Alberta as a wind peculiar to the Rockies swoops down over the mountains. The warm wind, known as a *chinook* (snow eater), can raise temperatures by up to 20°C (36°F) in an hour and up to 40°C (72°F) in a 24-hour period. The wind's effect on the snowpack is legendary. One story tells of a backcountry skier who spent the better part of a day traversing to the summit of a snow-clad peak on the front range of the Canadian Rockies. As he rested and contemplated skiing down, he realized that the slope had become completely bare!

Chinooks originate over the Pacific Ocean when warm, moist air is pushed eastward by prevailing westerlies. The air pressure of these winds is less than at lower elevations, and, therefore, as the air moves down the front ranges of the Canadian Rockies, it is subjected to increased pressure. This increasing of the air pressure warms the winds, which then fan out across the foothills and prairies. The "chinook arch" is formed as the clear air clashes with the warmer cloud-laden winds. The phenomenon is most common in southern Alberta but occurs to a lesser degree as far north as the Peace River Valley. Pincher Creek, the gateway to Waterton Lakes National Park, experiences about 35 chinooks each winter.

Although March, April, and May are, more or less, the official months of spring, snow often falls in May, many lakes may remain frozen until June, and snow cover on higher mountain hiking trails remains until early July. During this period of the year the mountains are often affected by low-pressure weather patterns from the southeast, creating continuous days of rain, especially in the south.

Things warm up in summer. July is the hottest month, with Banff, Jasper, and Canmore's average daytime temperature topping out above 23°C (73°F) and Radium Hot Springs and Golden enjoying average daytime highs of 29°C (84°F)

and 27°C (81°F), respectively. On hot days, the temperature can hit 30°C (86°F) along lower elevation valleys. Again, because of the dryness of the air, these temperatures are more bearable here than in coastal regions experiencing the same temperatures.

By late September the mountain air begins to have a distinct chill. October brings the highest temperature variations of the year; the thermometer can hit 30°C (86°F) but also dip as low as –20°C (–4°F). Mild weather can continue until early December, but generally the first snow falls in October, and by mid-November winter has set in.

Flora

Botanists divide the Canadian Rockies into three distinct vegetation zones (also called *biomes*): montane, subalpine, and alpine. The boundaries of these zones are determined by several factors, the most important being altitude. Latitude and exposure are also factors, but less so. Typically, within any 1,500 meters (4,920 feet) of elevation change, you'll pass through each of the three zones. These changes can be seen occurring most abruptly in Waterton Lakes National Park. Conifers (evergreens) predominate in the montane and subalpine, whereas above the tree line, in the alpine, only low-growing hardy species survive.

MONTANE

The foothills, along with most major valleys below an elevation of about 1,500 meters (4,920 feet), are primarily cloaked in montane forest. **Aspen, balsam poplar,** and **white spruce** thrive here. Lodgepole pine is the first species to emerge

after fire. Its hard seed cones are sealed by a resin that is melted only at high temperatures. When fire races through the forest, the resin melts and the cones release their seeds. The lodgepole is named for its straight, slender trunk, which natives used as a center pole for tepees. On dry, south-facing slopes, **Douglas fir** is the climax species. Where sunlight penetrates the forest, such as along riverbanks, flowers like **lady's slipper, Indian paintbrush,** and **saxifrage** are common. Large tracts of **fescue grassland** are common at lower elevations. The montane forest holds the greatest diversity of life of any vegetation zone and is prime winter habitat for larger mammals. But this is the habitat where most development occurs and therefore is often much changed from its natural state.

SUBALPINE

Subalpine forests occur where temperatures are lower and precipitation higher than in the mon-

Fireweed is easily recognized by a long spike of bright pink flowers.

tane. In the Canadian Rockies, this is generally 1,500–2,200 meters (4,920 –7,220 feet) above sea level. The upper limit of the subalpine zone is the tree line. Approximately half the flora of the mountains falls within this zone. The climax species are **Engelmann spruce** and **subalpine fir** (recognized by its spirelike crown), although extensive forests of **lodgepole pine** occur in areas that have been scorched by fire in the last 100 years. At higher elevations, stands of **larch** are seen. Larches are deciduous conifers—unlike those of other evergreens, their needles turn a burnt-orange color each fall, producing a magnificent display for photographers.

ALPINE

The alpine zone extends from the tree line to mountain summits. The upper limit of tree growth in the Canadian Rockies varies between 1,800 and 2,400 meters (5,900–7,900 feet) above sea level, dropping progressively to the north until it meets the treeless tundra of the Arctic. Vegetation at these high altitudes occurs only where soil has been deposited. Large areas of alpine meadows burst with color for a short period each summer as **lupines, mountain avens, alpine forget-me-nots, avalanche lily, moss campion,** and a variety of **heathers** bloom.

Fauna

One of the biggest attractions of the Canadian Rockies is the abundance of wildlife, especially large mammals such as elk, moose, bighorn sheep, and bears, which are widespread and easily viewed throughout the mountains.

THE DEER FAMILY
Mule Deer and White-Tailed Deer
Mule deer and white-tailed deer are similar in size and appearance. Their color varies with the season but is generally light brown in summer, turning dirty-gray in winter. While both species are considerably smaller than elk, the mule deer is a little stockier than the white-tailed deer. The mule deer has a white rump, a white tail with a dark tip, and large mulelike ears. It inhabits open forests along valley floors. Waterton townsite has a healthy population of mule deer. The white-tailed deer's tail is dark on top, but when the animal runs, it holds its tail erect, revealing an all-white underside. White-tails frequent thickets along the rivers and lakes of the foothills. They are most common on the British Columbia side of the Continental Divide.

Elk
The elk, or *wapiti,* is the most widespread and common of the larger mammals living in the Canadian Rockies. It has a tan body with a dark-brown neck, dark-brown legs, and a white rump. This second-largest member of the deer family weighs 250–450 kg (550–1,000 lb.) and stands 1.5 meters (five feet) at the shoulder. Beginning each spring, stags grow an impressive set of antlers, covered in what is known as velvet. The velvet contains nutrients that stimulate antler growth. By fall, the antlers have reached their full size and the velvet is shed. Rutting season takes place between August and October; listen for the shrill bugles of the stags serenading the females. During the rut, randy males will challenge anything with their antlers and can be dangerous. The stags shed their antlers each spring, but don't relax too much because also in spring, females protecting their young can be equally dangerous. Large herds of elk live in around the towns of Banff and Jasper, often nonchalantly wandering along streets and feeding on tasty plants in residential gardens, and always safe from predators.

Moose
The giant of the deer family is the moose, an awkward-looking mammal that appears to have been designed by a cartoonist. It has the largest antlers of any animal in the world, stands up to 1.8 meters (six feet) at the shoulder, and weighs

WILDLIFE AND YOU

An abundance of wildlife is one of the biggest drawing cards of the Canadian Rockies. To help preserve this precious resource, obey fishing and hunting regulations and use common sense.

Do not feed the animals. Many animals may seem tame, but feeding them endangers yourself, the animal, and other visitors, as animals become aggressive when looking for handouts.

Store food safely. When camping, keep food in your vehicle or out of reach of animals. Just leaving it in a cooler isn't good enough.

Keep your distance. Although it's tempting to get close to animals for a better look or photograph, it disturbs the animal and, in many cases, can be dangerous.

Drive carefully. The most common cause of premature death for larger mammals is being hit by cars.

© ANDREW HEMPSTEAD

Grizzlies are identified by a distinctive hump behind their necks.

up to 500 kg (1,100 lb.). Its body is dark brown, and it has a prominent nose, long spindly legs, small eyes, big ears, and an odd flap of skin called a bell dangling beneath its chin. Apart from all that, it's good-looking. Each spring the bull begins to grow palm-shaped antlers that by August will be fully grown. Moose are solitary animals preferring marshy areas and weedy lakes, but they are known to wander to higher elevations searching out open spaces in summer. They forage in and around ponds on willows, aspen, birch, grasses, and all aquatic vegetation. They are not particularly common in the Canadian Rockies, numbering around 350. Although they may appear docile, moose will attack humans if they feel threatened.

Caribou

Small populations of caribou inhabit the backcountry of Banff and Jasper National Parks. Native people named the animal *caribou* (hoof scraper) for the way in which they feed in winter, scraping away snow with their hooves. Caribou are smaller than elk and have a dark-brown coat

with creamy patches on the neck and rump. Both sexes grow antlers, but those of the females are shorter and have fewer points. On average males weigh 180 kg (400 lb.), females 115 kg (250 lb.). Like the elk, they breed in fall, with the males gathering a harem.

BEARS

The two species of bears present in the mountains—black bears and grizzlies—can be differentiated by size and shape. Grizzlies are larger than black bears and have a flatter, dish-shaped face and a distinctive hump of muscle behind their neck. Color is not a reliable way to tell them apart. Black bears are not always black. They can be brown or cinnamon, causing them to be confused with the brown-colored grizzly.

Black Bears

If you spot a bear feeding beside the road, chances are it's a black bear. These mammals are widespread throughout all forested areas of the Canadian Rockies and are good swimmers and

black bear

climbers. Their weight varies considerably, but males average 150 kg (330 lb.) and females 100 kg (220 lb.). Their diet is omnivorous, consisting primarily of grasses and berries but supplemented by small mammals. They are not true hibernators, but in winter they can sleep for up to a month at a time before changing position. During this time, their heartbeat drops to 10 beats per minute, body temperature drops, and they lose up to 30 percent of their body weight. Females reach reproductive maturity after five years; cubs, usually two, are born in late winter, while the mother is still asleep.

Grizzly Bears

Grizzlies, second largest of eight recognized species of bears (only polar bears are larger), have disappeared from most of North America but are widespread throughout the Canadian Rockies, numbering around 300 in the region. Grizzlies are only occasionally seen by casual observers; most sightings occur in alpine and subalpine zones, although sightings at lower elevations are not unusual, especially when snow falls early or late. The bears' color ranges from light brown to almost black, with dark tan being the most common. On average, males weigh 200–350 kg (440–770 lb.). The bears eat small and medium-sized mammals, and berries in fall. Like black bears, they sleep through most of the winter. When they emerge in early spring, the bears scavenge carcasses of animals that succumbed to the winter, until the new spring vegetation becomes sufficiently plentiful. Females first give birth at four years old, and then every three years, with cubs remaining with their mother for two to three years.

WILD DOGS AND CATS

Coyotes

The coyote is often mistaken for a wolf when in fact it is much smaller, weighing up to only 15 kg (33 lb.). It has a pointed nose and long bushy tail. Its coloring is a mottled mix of brown and gray, with lighter-colored legs and belly. The coyote is a skillful and crafty hunter, preying mainly on rodents. Coyotes have the remarkable ability to hear the movement of small mammals under the snow, allowing them to hunt these animals without actually seeing them. They are often seen patrolling the edges of highways and crossing open meadows in low-lying valleys.

Wolves

Wolves that inhabit the Canadian Rockies are larger than coyotes and larger than the wolves of eastern Canada. They weigh up to 60 kg (132 lb.), stand up to one meter (3.2 feet) high at the shoulder, and resemble large huskies or German shepherds. Their color ranges from snow white to brown or black; those in the Canadian Rockies are, most often, shades of gray. They usually hunt in packs of up to eight members, traveling, hunting, and resting together, and adhering to a hierarchical social order. As individuals, they are complex and intriguing, capable of expressing happiness, humor, and loneliness.

Once the target of a relentless campaign to exterminate the species, the wolf has made an incredible comeback in the Canadian Rockies; today about 120 wolves roam the region.

Cougars

Rarely encountered by casual hikers, cougars (known in other parts of North America as mountain lions, pumas, or catamounts) measure up to 1.5 meters (five feet) long. The average male weighs 75 kg (165 lb.) and the female 40–55 kg (90–120 lb.). Cougars are versatile hunters whose acute vision takes in a peripheral span in excess of 200 degrees. They typically kill a large mammal such as an elk or deer every 12–14 days, eating part of it and caching the rest. Their diet also includes chipmunks, ground

WILDLIFE VIEWING: THE BEST SPOTS

Where's the best place to view animals? This is probably the most common question posed by visitors to the Canadian Rockies. While a precise answer is impossible—this isn't a zoo, after all—noting a couple rules of thumb can make your chances of observation more likely. Spring is the best time for viewing wildlife from the roadside; larger mammals come down into the valleys in winter and stay through spring, moving back up to higher elevations as the snow melts. Mammals are most active at dawn and dusk, which are great times of day for scanning the landscape for movement.

In most cases, all species listed below are widespread in their particular habitat throughout the Canadian Rockies. The single location listed below for each species is simply the one that will give you the best chance of seeing that species.

Beaver: Athabasca River wetlands, Jasper National Park

Bighorn sheep: Mount Norquay Road, Banff National Park

Bison: Buffalo Paddock, Waterton Lakes National Park

Black bear: Icefields Parkway, Banff and Jasper National Parks

Caribou: Bald Hills, Jasper National Park

Cougar: forested valleys around Canmore

Coyote: along Highway 16, east of the town of Jasper, Jasper National Park

Elk: around the outskirts of Banff and Jasper towns

Grizzly bear (stuffed): Lake Louise Visitor Centre, Banff National Park

Human beings: Banff Avenue, Banff National Park

Lynx: Vermilion Pass, Kootenay National Park

Marmot: end of Stanley Glacier Trail, Kootenay National Park

Moose: Peter Lougheed Provincial Park, Kananaskis Country

Mountain goat: Disaster Point, Jasper National Park

Mule deer: Waterton townsite, Waterton Lakes National Park

Porcupine: Yoho Valley Road, Yoho National Park

White-tailed deer: Sheep River Valley, Kananaskis Country

Wolf: Bow Valley (winter only), Banff National Park

squirrels, snowshoe hares, and occasionally porcupines. Their athletic prowess puts Olympians to shame. They can spring forward more than eight meters from a standstill, leap four meters into the air, and safely jump from a height of 20 meters (65 feet).

The cougar is a solitary animal with distinct territorial boundaries. This limits its population density, which in turn means that its overall numbers are low. They are most common in the foothills along the eastern slopes of the Canadian Rockies.

Lynx

The elusive lynx is identifiable by its pointy black ear tufts and an oversized tabby cat appearance. The animal has broad, padded paws that distribute its weight, allowing it to float on the surface of snow. It weighs up to 10 kg (22 lb.) but appears much larger because of its coat of long, thick fur. The lynx, uncommon but widespread throughout the region, is a solitary creature that prefers the cover of subalpine forests, feeding mostly at night on snowshoe hares and other small mammals.

OTHER LARGE MAMMALS

Mountain Goats

The remarkable rock-climbing ability of these nimble-footed creatures allows them to live on rocky ledges or near-vertical slopes, safe from predators. They also frequent the alpine meadows and open forests of the Canadian Rockies, where they congregate around natural licks of salt. The goats stand one meter at the shoulder and weigh 65–130 kg (140–290 lb.). Both sexes possess a peculiar beard, or rather, goatee. Both sexes have horns. It is possible to determine the sex by the shape of the horns; those of the female grow straight up before curling slightly backward, whereas those of the male curl back in a single arch. The goats shed their thick coats each summer, making them look ragged, but by fall they've regrown a fine, new white woolen coat.

Bighorn Sheep

Bighorn sheep are some of the most distinctive mammals of the Canadian Rockies. Easily recognized by their impressive horns, they are often seen grazing on grassy mountain slopes or at salt

© ANDREW HEMPSTEAD

Bighorn sheep are easily recognized by their long, curled horns.

licks beside the road. The color of their coat varies with the season; in summer it's a brownish gray with a cream-colored belly and rump, turning lighter in winter. Fully grown males can weigh up to 120 kg (270 lb.), while females generally weigh around 80 kg (180 lb.). Both sexes possess horns, rather than antlers like members of the deer family. Unlike antlers, horns are not shed each year and can grow to astounding sizes. The horns of rams are larger than those of ewes and curve up to 360 degrees. The spiraled horns of an older ram can measure longer than one meter (3.2 feet) and weigh as much as 15 kg (33 lb.). During the fall mating season, a hierarchy is established among the rams for the right to breed ewes. As the males face off against each other to establish dominance, their horns act as both a weapon and a buffer against the head butting of other rams. The skull structure of the bighorn, rams in particular, has become adapted to these head-butting clashes, keeping the animals from being knocked unconscious.

Bighorn sheep are particularly tolerant of humans and often approach parked vehicles; although they are not especially dangerous, as with all mammals, you should not approach or feed them.

Bison

Before the arrival of Europeans, millions of bison roamed the North American plains, with some entering the valleys of the Canadian Rockies to escape harsh winters. Several factors contributed to their decline, including the combined presence of explorers, settlers, and natives. By the 1800s they were wiped out, and since then a couple of attempts at reintroduction have taken place, including the release of a small herd in Jasper National Park. (No one has sighted them for many years.) Today, your best chance of viewing these shaggy beasts is in Waterton Lakes National Park, where a small herd is contained in the buffalo paddock.

SMALL MAMMALS
Beavers

One of the animal kingdom's most industrious mammals is the beaver. Growing to a length of 50 cm (20 in.) and tipping the scales at around 20 kg (44 lb.), it has a flat, rudderlike tail and webbed back feet that enable it to swim at speeds up to 10 kph (6 mph). The exploration of western Canada

© ANDREW HEMPSTEAD

Beavers are common in lakes and rivers throughout the Canadian Rockies.

can be directly attributed to the beaver, whose pelt was in high demand in fashion-conscious Europe in the early 1800s. The beaver was never entirely wiped out from the mountains, and today the animals can be found in almost any forested valley with flowing water. Beavers build their dam walls and lodges of twigs, branches, sticks of felled trees, and mud. They eat the bark and smaller twigs of deciduous plants and store branches under water, near the lodge, as a winter food supply.

Squirrels

Several species of squirrel are common in the Canadian Rockies. The **golden-mantled ground squirrel,** found in rocky outcrops of subalpine and alpine regions, has black stripes along its sides and looks like an oversized chipmunk. Most common is the **Columbian ground squirrel,** which lives in burrows, often in open grassland. It is recognizable by its reddish legs, face, and underside, and a flecked, grayish back. The bushy-tailed **red squirrel,** the bold chatterbox of the forest, leaves telltale shelled cones at the base of conifers. Another member of the species, the nocturnal **northern flying fox,** glides through the montane forests of mountain valleys but is rarely seen.

Hoary Marmots

High in the mountains, above the tree line, hoary marmots are often seen sunning themselves on boulders in rocky areas or meadows. They are stocky creatures, weighing 4–9 kg (9–19 lb.). When danger approaches, these large rodents emit a shrill whistle to warn their colony. Marmots are active only for a few months each summer, spending up to nine months a year in hibernation.

Porcupines

This small, squat animal is easily recognized by its thick coat of quills. It eats roots and leaves but is also known as being destructive around wooden buildings and vehicle tires. Porcupines are common and widespread throughout all forested areas, but they're hard to spy because they feed most often at night.

Other Rodents

Widespread throughout western Canada, **muskrats** make their mountain home in the waterways and wetlands of all low-lying valleys. They are agile swimmers, able to stay submerged for up to 12 minutes. They grow to a length of 35 cm (18 in.), but the best form of identification is the tail, which is black, flat, and scaly. Closely related to muskrats are **voles,** which are often mistaken for mice. They inhabit grassed areas of most valley floors.

Shrews

A member of the insectivore family, the **furry shrew** has a sharp-pointed snout and is closely related to the mole. It must eat almost constantly because it is susceptible to starvation within only a few hours of its last meal. Another variety present throughout the region, the **pygmy shrew,** is the world's smallest mammal; it weighs just four grams (.1 oz.).

Pikas

Pikas, like rabbits, are lagomorphs, which are distinguished from rodents by a double set of incisors in the upper jaw. The small, grayish pika is a neighbor to the marmot, living among the rubble and boulders of scree slopes above timberline.

Weasels

The weasel family, comprising 70 species worldwide, is large and diverse, but in general, all members have long, slim bodies and short legs, and all are carnivorous and voracious eaters, consuming up to one-third of their body weight each day. Many species can be found in the Canadian Rockies, including the **wolverine,** largest of the weasels worldwide, weighing up to 20 kg (44 lb.). Known to natives as *carcajou* (evil one), the wolverine is extremely powerful, cunning, and cautious. This solitary creature inhabits forests of the subalpine and lower alpine regions, feeding on any available meat, from small rodents to the carcasses of larger mammals. Rarely sighted by humans, the wolverine is a true symbol of the wilderness.

The **fisher** has the same habitat as the wolverine but is much smaller, reaching just five kg (11 lb.) in weight and growing up to 60 cm (24 in.) in length. This nocturnal hunter preys on small birds and rodents, but reports of fishers bringing down small deer have been made. Smaller still is the **marten,** which lives most of its life in the trees of the subalpine forest, preying on birds, squirrels, mice, and voles. Weighing just one kg (2.2 lb.) is the **mink,** once highly prized for its fur. At home in or out of water, it feeds on muskrats, mice, voles, and fish. Mink numbers in the Canadian Rockies are low.

As well as being home to the largest member of weasel family, the region also holds the smallest—the **least weasel** (the world's smallest carnivore), which grows to a length of just 20 cm (8 in.) and weighs a maximum of 60 grams (2 oz.). Chiefly nocturnal, it feeds mostly on mice and lives throughout open wooded areas, but it is not particularly common.

REPTILES AND AMPHIBIANS

Two species of snake, the **wandering garter snake** and the **red-sided garter snake** (North America's northernmost reptile), are found at lower elevations in the Canadian Rockies. **Frogs** are also present; biologists have noted two different species, which are also present at the lower elevations in the Canadian Rockies.

FISH

The lakes and rivers of the Canadian Rockies hold a variety of fish, most of which belong to the trout and salmon family and are classed as coldwater species—that is, they inhabit waters where the temperature ranges 4–18°C (39–64°F). The predominant species, the **rainbow trout,** is not native to the mountains; it was introduced from more northern Canadian watersheds as a sport fish and is now common throughout lower elevation lakes and rivers. It has an olive-green back and a red strip running along the center of its body. Only three species of trout are native to the mountains. One of these, the **bull trout,** is

Alberta's provincial fish. Throughout the mid-1900s, this truly native Canadian trout was perceived as a predator of more favored introduced species, and was mostly removed. Today, what was once the most widespread trout east of the Continental Divide is confined to the headwaters of Canadian Rockies' river systems and is classed as a threatened species. While the bull trout has adapted to the harsh conditions of its reduced habitat, its continuing struggle for survival can be attributed to many factors, including a scarcity of food and a slow reproductive cycle. Bull trout grow to 70 cm (27 in.) in length and weigh up to 10 kilograms (22 lb.).

The **lake trout,** which grows to 20 kg (44 lb.), is native to large, deep lakes throughout the mountains. Identified by a silvery-gray body and irregular white splotches along its back, this species grows slowly, taking up to eight years to reach maturity and living up to 25 years. Named for a bright red dash of color that runs from below the mouth almost to the gills, the **cutthroat trout** is native to southern Alberta's mountain streams, but it has been introduced to high-elevation lakes and streams on both sides of the Canadian Rockies. The **brown trout,** introduced from Europe in 1924, is found in the Bow and Red Deer Rivers and some slower streams in the eastern zones of Kananaskis Country. Its body is a golden brown color, and it is the only trout with both black and red spots. The **brook trout** is a colorful fish identified by a dark green back with pale-colored splotches and purple-sheened sides. It is native to eastern Canada but was introduced to the mountains as early as 1903 and is now widespread throughout lakes and streams on the Alberta side of the Continental Divide. **Golden trout** were introduced to a few mountain lakes around 1960 as a sport fish. They are a smallish fish, similar in color to rainbow trout.

The **mountain whitefish** (commonly but incorrectly called arctic grayling by Albertan anglers) is a light gray fish native to most lower-elevation lakes and rivers of the Canadian Rockies. Also inhabiting the region's waters are **arctic grayling** and **Dolly Varden** (named for a colorful character in a Charles Dickens story).

BIRDS

Bird-watching is popular in the mountains, thanks to the approximately 300 resident bird species and the millions of migratory birds that pass through each year. All it takes is a pair of binoculars, a good book detailing species, and patience. Dense forests hide many species, making them seem less common than they actually are. The Columbia River wetland, between Radium Hot Springs and Golden, lies on the Pacific Flyway and is a major bird-watching area.

Raptors

A wide variety of raptors are present in the Canadian Rockies—some call the mountains home year-round, while others pass through during annual spring and fall migrations. **Golden eagles** migrate across the Canadian Rockies, heading north in spring to Alaska and crossing back

© ANDREW HEMPSTEAD

Clark's nutcracker

over in fall en route to Midwest wintering grounds. Golden eagles—more than 10,000 of them annually—soar high above the mountains on thermal drafts. **Bald eagles** also soar over the Canadian Rockies during annual migrations; mature birds can be distinguished from below by their white head and tail (immature birds resemble the dark brown–colored golden eagle). **Ospreys** spend summers in the region, nesting high up in large dead trees, on telephone poles, or on rocky outcrops, but always overlooking water. They feed on fish, hovering up to 50 meters (160 feet) above water, watching for movement, then diving into the water, thrusting their legs forward and collecting prey in their talons.

Distinct from all previously listed species is a group of raptors that hunt at night. Best known as owls, these birds are rarely seen because of their nocturnal habits but are widespread throughout forested areas of the mountains. Most common is the **great horned owl,** identified by its prominent "horns," which are actually tufts of feathers. Also present are the **snowy owl** and, in the north of the region, the **great gray owl,** the largest of the owls, which grows to a height of 70 cm (2.4 feet).

Other Birds

Bird-watchers will be enthralled by the diversity of eastern and western bird species in the Canadian Rockies. Widespread are **magpies, sparrows, starlings, grouse, ravens,** and **crows. Blackbirds, finches, thrushes, hummingbirds, woodpeckers, flycatchers,** and 28 species of **warblers** are common in forested areas. **Ptarmigan** are common in open meadows above the tree line. A popular campground visitor, the cheeky **gray jay,** is similar in appearance to the curious **Clark's nutcracker.**

History

THE EARLIEST INHABITANTS

Human habitation of the Canadian Rockies began at the end of the last ice age, approximately 11,000 years ago. The descendants of the people who migrated from northeast Asia across a land bridge spanning the Bering Strait had fanned out across North America, and as the receding ice cap began to uncover the land north of the 49th parallel, groups of people moved northward with it, in pursuit of large mammals at the edge of the melting ice mass. The mountain landscape then was far different than it is today. Forests were nonexistent; the retreating ice had scoured the land, and most of the lower valleys were carpeted in tundra.

The Kootenay

The Kootenay (other common spellings include Kootenai, Kootenae, and Kutenai) were the first human beings to enter the Canadian Rockies.

Once hunters of buffalo on the great American plains, they were pushed westward by fierce enemies. As the ice cap melted, they moved north, up the western edge of the Rocky Mountains. This migration was by no means fast—perhaps only 40 km (25 miles) in each generation—but about 10,000 years ago the first Kootenay arrived in the Columbia River Valley. They were hunters and gatherers, wintering along the Columbia and Kootenay River Valleys, then moving to higher elevations during the warmer months. Over time they developed new skills, learning to fish the salmon-rich rivers using spears, nets, and simple fish weirs. The Kootenay were a serious people with few enemies. They mixed freely with the Shuswap and treated the earliest explorers, such as David Thompson, with respect. They regularly traveled east over the Rockies to hunt—to the wildlife-rich Kootenay Plains or farther south to the Great Plains in search of bison. But as the fearsome Blackfoot extended

This trestle bridge, which once linked Canmore coal mines to the main rail line, is one of the more visible signs of the Bow Valley's history.

their territory westward to the foothills of present-day Alberta, the Kootenay made fewer trips onto the plains. By the early 1700s, they had been driven permanently back to the west side of the Continental Divide.

The Shuswap

The Shuswap make up only a small chapter in the human history of the Canadian Rockies, although they traveled into the mountains on and off for many thousands of years. They were a tribe of Salish people, who, as the Kootenay did farther east, moved north then east with the receding ice cap. By the time the Kootenay had moved into the Kootenay River Valley, the Salish had fanned out across most of southwestern and interior British Columbia, following the salmon upstream as the glacial ice receded. Those who settled along the upper reaches of the Columbia River became known as the Shuswap. They spent summers in the mountains hunting caribou and sheep, put their fishing skills to the test each fall, then wintered in pit houses along the Columbia River Valley. The descendants of these people live on the Kinbasket Shuswap Reserve, just south of Radium Hot Springs.

The Stoney

The movement of humans into the mountains from the east was much more recent. Around 1650, the mighty Sioux nation began splintering, with many thousands moving north into present-day Canada. Although these immigrants called themselves *Nakoda* (people), other tribes called them *Assiniboine* (people who cook with stones) because their traditional cooking method was to heat stones in a fire, place the hot stones in a rawhide or birchbark basket with water, and cook meat and vegetables in the hot water. The white people translated Assiniboine as Stone People, or Stoney for short.

Slowly, generation after generation, smaller groups of the Stoney moved westward along the Saskatchewan River system, allying themselves with the Cree but keeping their own identity. They pushed through the Blackfoot territory of the plains and reached the Rockies' foothills

about 200 years ago. There they split into bands, moving north and south along the foothills and penetrating the wide valleys where hunting was productive. They lived in small familylike groups and developed a lifestyle different from that of the Plains Indians, diversifying their skills and becoming less dependent on buffalo. Moving with the seasons, they gathered berries in fall and became excellent hunters of mountain animals. They traveled over the mountains to trade with the Shuswap, but rarely ventured onto the plains, home of the warlike Peigan, Blackfoot, and Blood bands of the Blackfoot Confederacy. The Stoney were a steadfast yet friendly people. Alexander Henry the Younger reported in 1811 that the Stoney, "although the most arrant horse thieves in the world . . . are at the same time the most hospitable to strangers who arrive in their camps."

As the great buffalo herds were decimated, the Stoney were affected less than the Plains Indians, but the effect of white settlers' intrusion on their lifestyle was still apparent. The missionaries of the day found their teachings had more effect on the mountain people than on those of the plains, so they intensified their efforts on the Stoney. Reverend John McDougall gained their trust and in 1873 built a small mission church by the Bow River at Morleyville. When the Stoney were presented with Treaty 7 in 1877, they chose to locate their reserve around the Morleyville church. Abandoning their nomadic lifestyle, they quickly became adept at farming; unlike the Plains Indians, who relied for their survival on government rations, the Stoney were almost self-sufficient on the reserve.

EUROPEAN EXPLORATION AND SETTLEMENT

In 1670, the British government granted the Hudson's Bay Company the right to govern Rupert's Land, roughly defined by all the land that drained into Hudson Bay. A vast area of western Canada, including present-day Manitoba, Saskatchewan, Alberta, Northwest Territories, and Nunavut, fell under that definition. The land was rich in fur-bearing mammals, which both the British and the French sought to exploit for profit. The Hudson's Bay Company first built forts around Hudson Bay and encouraged Indians to bring furs to the posts. But soon, French fur traders based in Montreal began traveling west to secure furs, forcing their British rivals to do the same. On one such trip, Anthony Henday became the first white man to view the Canadian Rockies when, on September 11, 1754, he climbed a ridge above the Red Deer River near present-day Innisfail. Henday returned to the east the following spring, bringing canoes loaded with furs and providing reports of snow-capped peaks.

In 1792, Peter Fidler became the first in a long succession of Europeans to actually enter the mountains. The following year Alexander Mackenzie became the first man to cross the continent, traveling the Peace and Fraser river watersheds to reach the Pacific Ocean. Mackenzie's traverse was long and difficult, so subsequent explorers continued to seek an easier route farther south. In 1807, David Thompson set out from Rocky Mountain House, traveling up the North Saskatchewan River to Howse Pass, where he descended to the Columbia River. He established a small trading post near Windermere Lake, but warring Peigan and Kootenay natives forced him to search out an alternate pass to the north. In 1811, he discovered Athabasca Pass, which was used as the main route west for the next 50 years.

In 1857, with the fur trade in decline, the British government sent Captain John Palliser to investigate the agricultural potential of western Rupert's Land. During his three-year journey he explored many of the watersheds leading into the mountains, including one trip up the Bow River and over Vermilion Pass into the area now encompassed by Kootenay and Yoho National Parks.

The Dominion of Canada

By the 1860s, some of the eastern provinces were tiring of British rule, and a movement was abuzz to push for Canadian independence. The British government, wary of losing Canada as it had lost the United States, passed legislation establishing the Dominion of Canada. At that time, the North-West Territories, as Rupert's Land had become known, was a foreign land to those in eastern Canada; life out west was primitive with

---

DAVID THOMPSON

One of Canada's greatest explorers, David Thompson was a quiet, courageous, and energetic man who drafted the first comprehensive and accurate map of western Canada. He arrived in Canada from England as a 14-year-old apprentice clerk for the Hudson's Bay Company. With an inquisitive nature and a talent for wilderness navigation, he quickly acquired the skills of surveying and mapmaking. Natives called him Koo-koo-sint, which translates as "the man who looks at stars."

Between 1786 and 1812, Thompson led four major expeditions into western Canada—the first for the Hudson's Bay Company and the last three for its rival, the North West Company. The longest and most important one was the last, during which he traveled up and crossed the Continental Divide at **Howse Pass.** After descending into the Columbia River Valley, he established Kootenae House on Lake Windermere, using this outpost for a five-year odyssey of exploration of the entire Columbia River system. In the process, he discovered the **Athabasca Pass,** which for the next 50 years was the main route across the Canadian Rockies to the Pacific Ocean.

In 1813, Thompson began work on a master map covering the entire territory controlled by the North West Company. The map was four meters long and two meters wide, detailing more than 1.5 million square miles. On completion it was hung out of public view in the council hall of a company fort in the east. Years later, after his death in 1857, the map was discovered and Thompson became recognized as one of the world's greatest land geographers.

no laws, and no outpost held more than a couple of dozen residents. But in an effort to solidify the Dominion, the government bought the North-West Territories back from the Hudson's Bay Company in 1867. In 1871, British Columbia agreed to join the Dominion as well, but only on the condition that the federal government build a railway to link the fledgling province with the rest of the country.

The Coming of the Railway

The idea of a rail line across the continent, replacing canoe and cart routes, was met with scorn by those in the east, who saw it as unnecessary and uneconomical. But the line pushed westward, reaching Winnipeg in 1879 and what was then Fort Calgary in 1883.

Many routes across the Continental Divide were considered by the Canadian Pacific Railway, but Kicking Horse Pass, surveyed by Major A. B. Rogers in 1881, got the final nod. The line and its construction camps pushed into the mountains, reaching Siding 29 (known today as Banff) early in the fall of 1883, Laggan (Lake Louise) a couple of months later, then crossing the divide and reaching the Field construction camp in the summer of 1884. The following year, on November 7, 1885, the final spike was laid, opening up the lanes of commerce between British Columbia and the rest of the Canada. In 1914, rival company Grand Trunk Pacific Railway completed a second rail line across the Rockies, at Yellowhead Pass to the north.

PARKS AND TOURISM
The Parks of Today Take Shape

In 1883, three Canadian Pacific Railway (CPR) workers stumbled on hot springs at the base of Sulphur Mountain, near where the town of Banff now lies. This was the height of the Victorian era, when the great spa resorts of Europe were attracting hordes of wealthy clients. With the thought of developing a similar-style resort, the government designated a 2,600-hectare (6,425-acre) reserve around the hot springs, surveyed a townsite, and encouraged the CPR to build a

world-class hotel there. In 1887, Rocky Mountains Park was officially created, setting aside 67,300 hectares (166,300 acres) as a "public park and pleasure ground for the benefit, advantage, and enjoyment of the people of Canada." The park was later renamed Banff. It was Canada's first national park and only the third national park in the world.

Across the Continental Divide, the railway passed by a small reserve that had been created around the base of Mount Stephen. This was the core of what would become Yoho National Park, officially dedicated in 1901. In anticipation of a flood of visitors to the mountains along the more northerly Grand Trunk Pacific Railway, Jasper National Park was established in 1907. Kootenay National Park was created to protect an eight-km-wide strip of land on either side of the Banff–Windermere Road, which was completed in 1922. Of the five national parks in the Canadian Rockies, Waterton Lakes National Park was the only one created purely for its aesthetic value. It was established after tireless public campaigning by local resident John George "Kootenai" Brown, who also became the park's first superintendent.

The First Tourists Arrive

In the era the parks were created, the Canadian Rockies region was a vast wilderness accessible only by rail. The parks and the landscape they encompassed were seen as economic resources to be exploited rather than as national treasures to be preserved. Logging, hunting, and mining were permitted inside park boundaries; all but Kootenay National Park had mines operating within them for many years (the last mine, in Yoho National Park, closed in 1952). To help finance the rail line, the CPR began encouraging visitors to the mountains by building grand mountain resorts: Mount Stephen House in 1886, the Banff Springs Hotel in 1888, a lodge at Lake Louise in 1890, and Emerald Lake Lodge in 1902. Knowledgeable locals, some of whom had been used as guides and outfitters during railway construction, offered their services to the tourists the railway brought. Tom Wilson, Bill Peyto, Jim and

Bill Brewster, the Otto Brothers, and Donald "Curly" Phillips are synonymous with this era, and their names grace everything from pubs to mountain peaks.

Early Mountaineering

Recreational mountaineering has been popular in the Canadian Rockies for more than 100 years. Reports of early climbs on peaks around Lake Louise spread, and by the late 1880s the area had drawn the attention of both European and American alpinists. Many climbers were inexperienced and ill-equipped, but first ascents were nevertheless made on peaks that today are still considered difficult. In 1893, Walter Wilcox and Samuel Allen, two Yale schoolmates, spent the summer climbing in the Lake Louise area, making two unsuccessful attempts to reach the north peak of Mount Victoria. The following summer they made first ascents of Mount Temple and Mount Aberdeen, extraordinary achievements considering their lack of experience and proper equipment. Accidents were sure to happen, and they did. During the summer of 1896, P. S. Abbot slipped and plunged to his death attempting to climb Mount Lefroy. In doing so, he became North America's first mountaineering fatality. Following this incident, Swiss mountain guides were employed by the CPR to satisfy the climbing needs of wealthy patrons of the railway and make the sport safer. During the period of their employment, successful climbs were made of Mount Victoria, Mount Lefroy, and Mount Balfour.

In 1906, Arthur O. Wheeler organized the Alpine Club of Canada, which was instrumental in the construction of many trails and backcountry huts still in use today. In 1913, Swiss guide Conrad Kain led a group of the club's members on the successful first ascent of Mount Robson, the highest peak in the Canadian Rockies. By 1915, most of the other major peaks in the range had been climbed as well.

Changing Times

One major change that occurred early on was the shift from railroad-based to automobile-based tourism. Until 1913, motorized vehicles were banned from the mountain parks, allowing the CPR a monopoly on tourists. Wealthy visitors to the mountains came in on the train and generally stayed in the CPR's own hotels for weeks on end and often for the entire summer. The burgeoning popularity of the automobile changed all this; the motor-vehicle ban was lifted, and road building went ahead full steam. Many of the trails that had been built for horseback travel were widened to accommodate autos, and new roads were built: from Banff to Lake Louise in 1920, to Radium Hot Springs in 1923, and to Golden in 1930. The Icefields Parkway was finally completed in 1940. Visitor numbers increased, and facilities expanded to keep pace. Dozens of bungalow camps were built specially for those arriving by automobile. Many were built by the CPR, far from their rail line, including in Kootenay National Park and at Radium Hot Springs. The company also built lodges deep in the backcountry, including at Mount Assiniboine and Lake O'Hara.

Another major change that has occurred over the last 90 years is in the way the complex human-wildlife relationship in the parks has been managed. Should the relationship be managed to provide the visiting public the best viewing experience, or rather to provide the wildlife with the most wild and natural environment possible? Today the trend favors the wildlife, but early in the history of the Canadian Rockies' parks, the operating strategy clearly favored the visitor. The Victorian concept of wildlife was that it was either good or evil. Although an early park directive instructed superintendents to leave nature alone, it also told them to "endeavor to exterminate all those animals which prey upon others." A dusty century-old philosophy, perhaps, but as recently as the 1960s, a predator-control program led to the slaughter of nearly every wolf in the park. Seventy years ago, you could view a polar bear on display behind the Banff Park Museum. Only 40 years ago, hotels were taking guests to local dumps to watch bears feeding on garbage. Creating a balance between growth and its impact on wildlife is today's critical issue in the Canadian Rockies. Many high-traffic areas are fenced, with passes built over and under the highway for animal movement. Development in the national park towns of Banff and Jasper is strictly regulated, unlike areas outside the parks, such as Canmore and the Columbia River Valley, where development continues unabated.

Amazingly enough, throughout unsavory sagas of the 20th century and ever-increasing human usage, the Canadian Rockies have remained a prime area for wildlife viewing and will hopefully continue to be so for a long time to come.

Recreation

The Canadian Rockies are a four-season playground, their great outdoors offering something for everyone. Hiking grabs first place in the popularity stakes; many thousands of kilometers of trails crisscross the entire region. But you can also enjoy canoeing and kayaking, mountain climbing, golfing, horseback riding, photography, skiing and snowboarding, scuba diving, and everything in between. An overview of available outdoor-recreation opportunities is provided in the following sections, and you'll find more detail in the individual travel chapters.

National Park Passes

Unless you're passing directly through, passes are required for entry into all five national parks covered in this book. Profits raised from these passes go directly to Parks Canada for park maintenance and improvements.

A **National Parks Day Pass** is adult $7, senior $6, child $3.50 up to a maximum of $14 ($12 for two or more seniors) per vehicle. It is interchangeable among parks and is valid until 4 P.M. the day following its purchase. An annual **National Parks of Canada Pass,** good for entry into all of Canada's national parks for one year from the date of purchase, is adult $45, senior $38, child $22 up to a maximum of $89. This pass comes with a booklet of discount coupons. Both types of pass can be purchased at park gates (at the entrance to Banff, Kootenay, and Waterton Lakes National Parks), at the tollbooths at either end of the Icefields Parkway, at all park information centers, and at campground fee stations. For more information, check the Parks Canada website (www.pc.gc.ca).

HIKING

The Canadian Rockies are a hiker's paradise. Hiking is free, and the mountains offer some of the world's most spectacular scenery. **Banff National Park** holds the greatest variety of trails. Here you can find anything from short interpretive trails with little elevation gain to strenuous slogs up high alpine passes. Trailheads for some of the best hikes are accessible on foot from the town of Banff. Those farther north begin at higher elevations, from which access to the tree line is less arduous. The trails in **Jasper National Park** are oriented more toward the experienced backpacker, offering plentiful routes for long backcountry trips.

Waterton Lakes National Park is small but has a complex trail system geared especially for the day hiker. Many of the hikes in **Yoho National Park** entail significant elevation gain, but they reward your extra effort with spectacular mountain panoramas rivaling those of the more famous parks across the divide. Many less-visited parts of the mountains hold unexpected gems. Examples include Grassi Lakes, near Canmore; Rawson Lake, Kananaskis Country; Fish Lake, Top of the World Provincial Park; and Grande Mountain, near Grande Cache.

With exceptions made for the most popular overnight hikes, all trails detailed in this book are day hikes. Anyone of moderate fitness could complete them in the time allotted. Strong hikers will need less time, and if you stop for lunch it will take you a little longer. Remember, all distances and times are one-way, so allow yourself time at the objective and time to return to the trailhead.

Know the Canadian Rockies

SAFE HIKING

When venturing out on the trails of the Canadian Rockies, using a little common sense will help keep you from getting into trouble. First, don't underestimate the forces of nature; weather can change dramatically anywhere in the mountains at any time. That clear, sunny sky that looked so inviting during breakfast can turn into a driving snowstorm within hours. Go prepared for all climatic conditions (always carry food, a sweater, a waterproof jacket, and matches), and take plenty of water—open slopes can get very hot on sunny days.

All national park visitor centers, as well as those in Kananaskis Country, post daily trail reports and weather forecasts. Check trail conditions before heading out; lingering snow, wildlife closures, or a washed-out trail could ruin your best-laid plans. Also, hikers must register at park information centers for all overnight hikes in national parks.

Topographic maps aren't required for the hikes detailed in this book, but they provide an interesting way to identify natural features. For extended hiking in the backcountry, topo maps are vital. For most hikes, the maps produced by **Gem Trek Publishing** (www.gemtrek.com) are sufficient. You can purchase them from park information centers, bookstores, gas stations, and other outlets through the region.

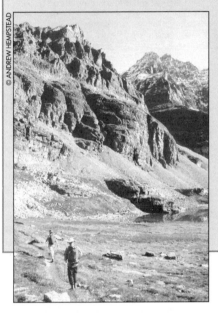
© ANDREW HEMPSTEAD

Scrambling

The Canadian Rockies hold many peaks that can be reached without ropes or climbing skills, provided you have a good level of fitness and, more important, common sense. Obviously, this type of activity has more inherent dangers than hiking, but these can be minimized by planning ahead. Check weather forecasts; take food, water, and warm clothing; and be aware of the terrain. Routes to the top of the most popular peaks are flagged with tape or marked with rock cairns showing the way, but you should always check with information centers or locals before attempting any ascent. The Bow Valley offers a good selection of well-traveled scrambles. These include Mount Rundle, Cascade Mountain, and Chinaman's Peak.

Backpacking

Most hikers are just out for the day or a few hours, but staying overnight in the backcountry offers many rewards. Some effort is involved in a backcountry trip—you'll need a backpack, lightweight stove, and tent, among other things—but you'll be traveling through country inaccessible to the casual day hiker, well away from the crowds and far from any road. **Lake O'Hara,** in Yoho National Park, is the trailhead for what is generally considered to be Canada's finest backcountry hiking area. The lake is easily accessible; a shuttle bus runs from the highway up an old fire road to this alpine gem. Unlike at other backcountry destinations, visitors to Lake O'Hara not equipped for camping have the option of visiting for just a day. **Mount Assiniboine Provincial Park** is another popular spot far from civilization. Like Lake O'Hara, there's a lodge for hikers not equipped to camp out. Banff and Jasper National Parks also have backcountry lodges. Another option for backcountry accommodations is offered by the **Alpine Club of Canada** (403/678-3200, www.alpineclubof canada.ca). The club maintains a series of huts, each generally a full-day hike from the nearest road, throughout the Canadian Rockies.

Heli-Hiking

Heli-hiking is an easy way to appreciate high alpine areas without having to gain the elevation on foot. The day starts with a helicopter ride into the alpine, where short, guided hikes are offered and a picnic lunch is served. For details, contact **Alpine Helicopters** (Canmore, 403/678-4802, www.alpinehelicopter.com) or **Robson Helimagic** (250/566-4700 or 877/454-4700, www.robsonhelimagic.com), near Mount Robson Provincial Park. Expect to pay from $280 for 30 minutes of flight time, a guided hike, and a mountaintop lunch. Primarily known for its heli-skiing operations, **Canadian Mountain Holidays** (403/762-7100 or 800/661-0252, www .cmhhike.com) has a summer program of heli-hiking trips, with overnights spent in luxurious backcountry lodges; expect to pay about $600 per person per night, all-inclusive.

CLIMBING AND MOUNTAINEERING

The Canadian Rockies are a mecca for those experienced in climbing and mountaineering, but for those who aren't, instruction is available. **Canmore,** in the Bow Valley, is the self-proclaimed capital of mountain sports. Surrounded by towering peaks of limestone, routes to challenge all levels of ability can be found on the immediate outskirts of town and along narrow canyons that open to the valley. The distinctive south face of Yamnuska, easily recognized to the north of the TransCanada Highway as you enter the Bow Valley from the east, is the most popular climbing spot in the mountains, with dozens of routes up its sheer 350-meter-high (1,150-foot-high) walls. *Bow Valley Rock* (Rocky Mountain Books, 2002) is an indispensable book for Yamnuska-bound climbers. Experienced climbers should also gather as much information as possible before attempting any unfamiliar routes; quiz locals, hang out at climbing stores, and contact park information centers.

Learning the Ropes

For the inexperienced, the Canadian Rockies are the perfect place to learn to climb. Climbers and mountaineers can't live on past accomplishments alone, so to finance their lifestyle some turn to teaching others the skills of their sport. Canmore is home to many qualified mountain guides who operate both in and out of Banff National Park. One of these—and one of North America's most respected climbing schools—is **Yamnuska** (403/678-4164, www .yamnuska.com). Learn basic climbing skills over an Outdoor Rock Intro weekend ($215 per person), with the option to make a full climb (an extra $190) the following Monday. The school also offers guided climbs of peaks throughout the Canadian Rockies, wilderness first-aid classes, and ice-climbing instruction.

ROAD CYCLING AND MOUNTAIN BIKING

The Canadian Rockies are perfect for both road biking and mountain biking. On-road cyclists will appreciate the wide shoulders on all main highways, while those on mountain bikes will enjoy the many designated trails. The most challenging and scenic on-road route is the 290-km (180-mile) **Icefields Parkway** between Lake Louise and Jasper (*Outside* magazine rates it as one of North America's 10 best). Most cyclists allow 4–5 days, but it's easy to spend a lot longer on the parkway. With 11 campgrounds, four hostels, and four lodges along the way, you'll have plenty of accommodation options. An extension of the Icefields Parkway is the **Bow Valley Parkway,** the original route between Banff and Lake Louise, which can easily be cycled in one day.

Backroads (510/527-1555 or 800/462-2848, www.backroads.com) offers a wide variety of trips through the Canadian Rockies. These trips are designed to suit all levels of fitness and all budgets. An average of six hours is spent cycling each day, but there's also always the option of riding in the support van. You can choose to camp each night (US$1,400 for six days) or stay in grand mountain lodges (US$2,400 for six days). **VBT** (800/245-3868, www.vbt.com) offers a seven-day ride through the four contiguous national parks with midrange lodging and all meals included in the price of US$1,700.

Mountain biking is allowed on designated trails throughout the national parks. Park information centers hand out brochures detailing these trails and giving them ratings. The **Canmore Nordic Centre** is home to 70 km (43.5 miles) of biking trails, some steep enough to hold international downhill competitions each summer. Doug Eastcott's *Backcountry Biking in the Canadian Rockies* (Rocky Mountain Books) covers more than 200 routes through the mountains; pick up a copy from local bookstores. Bikes can be rented throughout the national parks and Kananaskis Country. Road and town bikes rent for $5–7 per hour and $22–28 per day. All shops rent front- and full-suspension bikes; expect to pay up to $15 per hour and $45 per day for these.

HORSEBACK RIDING

Horses were used for transportation in the mountains by the earliest explorers. Even after the completion of the railway, horses remained as the most practical way to get deep into the backcountry because crossing unbridged rivers and carrying large amounts of supplies was impossible on foot. The names of early outfitters—Tom Wilson, Jim and Bill Brewster, Bill Peyto, Jimmy Simpson, and Curly Phillips were the best known—crop up again and again through the mountains. Another legacy of their trade is that many of the main hiking trails began as horse trails.

The tradition of travel by horseback continues today in the Canadian Rockies; some companies have been operating since before the parks were established. Trail riding is available in Banff, Jasper, Waterton Lakes, and Yoho National Parks as well as in Canmore, Kananaskis Country, Ra-

dium Hot Springs, and Grande Cache. Expect to pay around $30 for a one-hour ride (usually covering around three km/1.9 miles), $50 for a two-hour ride, and $70–85 for a ride that includes a meal. If you're an experienced rider, consider heading out of the mountains 40 minutes east of Canmore to **Griffin Valley Ranch** (north of Hwy. 1A, 403/932-7433). This sprawling property is one of the few places in western Canada that allows unguided riding. Horse rentals are similarly priced to trail riding; the only additional cost is an annual membership (simply sign a waiver and pay a $50 fee). Trails lead through the valley and to high viewpoints where the panorama extends back to the Canadian Rockies.

Pack Trips and Guest Ranches

Overnight pack trips consist of up to six hours of riding per day, with nights spent at a remote mountain lodge or a tent camp, usually in a scenic location where you can hike, fish, or ride farther.

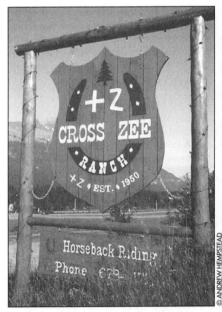

Cross Zee, overlooking Canmore, is one of many local horseback riding operations.

Rates range $150–210 per person per day, which includes the riding, accommodations, and food. These trips are offered by the **Brewster Guest Ranch,** east of Canmore (403/762-5454 or 800/691-5085, www.brewsteradventures.com); **Boundary Ranch,** in Kananaskis Valley (403/591-7171 or 877/591-7177, www.boundaryranch .com); through the south end of Banff National Park by **Warner Guiding and Outfitting** (403/762-4551 or 800/661-8352, www.horse back.com); and in Jasper National Park by **Skyline Trail Rides** (780/852-4215 or 888/852-7787, www.skylinetrail.com) and **Tonquin Valley Adventures** (780/852-1188, www.tonquinadventures .com). The remote location of Willmore Wilderness Park makes it a popular destination for those on horseback; contact **Wild Rose Outfitting** (780/693-2296, www.wildroseoutfitting.com).

Guest ranches, where accommodations and meals are included in nightly packages, include **Brewster Kananaskis Ranch,** east of Canmore (403/673-3737 or 800/691-5085, www.brewster adventures.com), and **Black Cat Guest Ranch,** on the northeastern outskirts of Jasper National Park (780/865-3084 or 800/859-6840, www .blackcatguestranch.ca). Expect to pay $130–170 per person per day for accommodations, meals, and trail riding.

GOLFING

The Canadian Rockies hold special appeal for golfers because some of the world's most scenic courses lie in their midst. All of the best courses are public, lying in national parks or on provincial land, so anyone can play at any time. The scenery alone stands the courses of the Canadian Rockies apart from others, but there are many other reasons that the region is a golf destination in itself. Stanley Thompson, generally regarded as one of the preeminent golf course architects of the early 1900s, designed three courses in the Canadian Rockies, typified by holes aligned with distant mountains, elevated tee boxes, and fairways following natural contours of the land. (As most of Thompson's work was in Canada, he is still little known in the United States.)

The golfing season is fairly short, from mid-May to early October, depending on snow cover. (The golf courses at Radium Hot Springs and Golden are the first to open each spring.) But with the long days of summer, there's plenty of time for golfing. Greens fees range from $28 at the nine-hole layout at Brewster's Kananaskis Guest Ranch to $195 for 18 holes at the Banff course. The greens fee at Kananaskis Country Golf Course ($70) is also worth noting: it is regularly featured in *Golf Digest* as North America's best-value course. At the resort courses, greens fees usually include the use of practice facilities and a cart (complete with global positioning system at SilverTip). The sport's popularity in the mountains is such that tee times need to booked well in advance—up to a month for preferred times at some courses.

The Courses

The jewel in the golfing crown is the **Stanley Thompson 18,** part of a 27-hole layout that graces the grounds of the Fairmont Banff Springs and is rated one of the world's most scenic courses. The **Jasper Park Lodge Golf Course,** a challenging par-73 course surrounded by spectacular mountain scenery, is of the same high standard. The **Kananaskis Country Golf Course,** a 36-hole, Robert Trent Jones–designed course built in the 1980s at a cost of $1 million per hole, was the first of the resort-style courses built in the Canadian Rockies. At Canmore, **SilverTip** set a new standard in golf course difficulty in Canada when it opened in 1998. It promotes itself as an extreme experience, and it is: 7,300 yards long, with elevation changes up to 40 meters (130 feet) on any one hole, and a slope rating of 153—the highest of any Canadian course. Across the valley from SilverTip, **Stewart Creek** opened in the summer of 2000, bringing the total number of courses in Canmore to three. Other resort courses are **Radium Resort** (36 holes), at Radium Hot Springs; **Greywolf** at Panorama Mountain Village; and **Wintergreen** at Bragg Creek, while the towns of Canmore and Golden offer excellent 18-hole public layouts, as does Waterton Lakes National Park.

ON THE WATER

Canoeing

This traditional form of Canadian transportation is a great way to explore the waterways of the mountains that are otherwise inaccessible—places such as **Vermilion Lakes** in Banff National Park, where beavers, elk, and a great variety of birds can be appreciated from water level. Canoes can be rented on the **Bow River** in the town of Banff, **Lake Louise,** and **Moraine Lake** in Banff National Park; **Pyramid** and **Maligne Lakes** in Jasper National Park; **Cameron Lake** in Waterton Lakes National Park; and **Emerald Lake** in Yoho National Park. Expect to pay around $10–25 per hour, and up to $40 per hour on Lake Louise. The more adventurous visitor can rent a canoe and paddle down the Bow River from Lake Louise to downtown Banff.

White-Water Rafting

The rafting season is relatively short, but the thrill of careening down a river laced with rapids is not easily forgotten. Qualified guides operate on many rivers flowing out of the mountains. The **Kicking Horse River,** which flows through Yoho National Park to Golden, is run by companies based in Golden, Lake Louise, and Banff. This is the most popular river for rafting trips. The **Sunwapta River** in Jasper National Park and the the upper reaches of the **Fraser River** through Mount Robson Provincial Park are others offering big thrills. For a more sedate river trip, try the **Bow River** in Banff National Park or the **Athabasca River** in Jasper National Park. Both are run commercially. All companies offer half- and full-day trips, including transportation, wetsuits, and often light snacks.

Scuba Diving

Being landlocked, the Canadian Rockies are not renowned for scuba diving. A few interesting opportunities do exist, however, and rentals are available in Lethbridge, Calgary, and Edmonton. The old townsite of **Minnewanka Landing,** in Banff National Park, has been flooded, and although a relatively deep dive, the site is interesting. **Patricia Lake,** in Jasper National

The thrills and spills of white-water rafting can be enjoyed on many local rivers.

Park, conceals a sunken barge that Winston Churchill had built as an aircraft carrier that was also capable of functioning as an icebreaker, and due to the high altitude and clear water, visibility is exceptional. Another sunken boat lies at the bottom of **Emerald Bay** in Waterton Lakes National Park, not far from some wagons that fell through the ice many winters ago. For a list of dive shops and sites, contact the Alberta Underwater Council (780/427-9125 or 888/307-8566, www.albertaunderwatercouncil.com).

FISHING

The Canadian Rockies are an angler's delight. Fish are abundant in many lakes and rivers (the exceptions to good fishing are the lakes and rivers fed by glacial runoff, such as Lake Louise), and outfitters provide guiding services throughout the mountains. Many lakes are stocked annually with a variety of trout—most often rainbows—and although stocking was discontinued in the national parks in 1988, populations have been maintained. In Banff National Park, **Lake Minnewanka** is home to the mountains' largest fish—lake trout—as well a variety of other trout and whitefish. This lake, along with **Maligne Lake** in Jasper National Park, are major fishing centers, with boats and tackle for rent and guides offering their services.

Fish Species

Rainbow trout are the fighting fish of the Canadian Rockies; they are to western Canada what bass are to the United States. Although not native, through stocking they are found in lakes and streams throughout the mountains. The Bow River is considered one of the world's great trout rivers, but most of the action happens downstream of Calgary. Wet flies and small spinners are preferred methods of catching these fish. The largest fish found in the region is the **lake trout,** which grows to 18 kg (40 lb.). It feeds near the surface after breakup and then moves to deeper, colder water in summer. Long lines and heavy lures are needed to hook onto these giants. **Brown trout,** introduced from Europe, are found

in the Upper Bow River (downstream from Banff) and slow-flowing streams in the foothills of Kananaskis Country. They are most often caught on dry flies, but are finicky feeders, and therefore difficult to hook. **Brook trout** are widespread throughout lower elevation lakes and streams. **Cutthroat trout** inhabit the cold and clear waters of the highest lakes, which generally require a hike to access. Fishing for cutthroat requires using the lightest of tackle because the water is generally very clear; fly-casting is most productive on the still water of lakes, while spinning is the preferred river-fishing method.

Arctic grayling, easily identified by their large dorsal fins, are common in cool, clear streams throughout the far north, but they are not native to the Canadian Rockies; Wedge Pond (Kananaskis Country) is stocked with these delicious fish. **Dolly Varden** can be caught in many high-elevation lakes on the British Columbia side of the mountains; Whiteswan Lake is a local favorite. **Whitefish** are a commonly caught fish in lower-elevation lakes and rivers (many anglers in Alberta call whitefish "arctic grayling," but they are in fact two distinct species—and grayling aren't native to the mountains). Hydroelectric dams, such as those east of Canmore and in the Spray Valley Provincial Park, are popular with anglers chasing whitefish.

Note: The **bull trout** is an endangered species and is a catch-and-release fish. Possession of bull trout—a dark-colored fish with light spots—is illegal. The defining difference between the bull trout and the brook trout, with which it is often confused, is that the bull trout has *no black spots on its dorsal fin;* due to its status, correct identification of this species is especially important.

Regulations and Licenses

Three different licenses are in effect in the Canadian Rockies—one license covers all the national parks, another Albertan waters, and a third the freshwater of British Columbia.

National parks: Licenses are available from park offices and some sport shops; $7 for a seven-day license, $20 for an annual license. The brochure *Fishing Regulations Summary,* available from all park information centers, details limits and closures.

Alberta: Alberta has an automated licensing system, with licenses sold from sporting stores, hardware stores, and gas stations. To use the machines, the vendor needs you to supply a Wildlife Identification Number (WIN) card. These numbers are sold by all license vendors and cost $8 (valid for five years). Once you have your card, it is swiped through a vending machine to purchase a license. An annual license for Canadian residents older than age 16 is $21 (no license required for those 16 years or younger or Albertans older than 64); for nonresidents age 16 and older, it is $60, or pay $22 for a one-day license or $40 for five days.

The *Alberta Guide to Sportfishing Regulations,* which outlines all the open seasons and bag limits, is available from outlets selling licenses and online at the Fish & Wildlife section of the Department of Sustainable Resource Development website (780/944-0313, www3.gov .ab.ca/srd). In addition to having the entire regulations online, the site also holds statistics for the provincial stocking program (which lakes, when, and how many fish) and details of Alberta's barbless hook rules.

British Columbia: In British Columbia, the cost of a license varies according to your age and place of residence. Canadian residents pay $36 for a freshwater adult license, good for one year. All other Canadians pay $20 for a one-day license, $36 for an eight-day license, or $55 for a one-year license. Nonresidents pay $20, $50, and $80, respectively. For more information contact the Ministry of Water, Land, and Air Protection (250/387-4573, www.gov.bc.ca/wlap) and request the *British Columbia Freshwater Fishing Regulations Synopsis.*

WINTERTIME
Downhill Skiing and Snowboarding

Six world-class winter resorts are perched among the high peaks of the Canadian Rockies. The largest, and Canada's second-largest (only Whistler/Blackcomb is larger), is **Lake Louise,** overlooking the lake of the same name in Banff National Park. The resort boasts 1,700 hectares (4,200 acres) of skiing and boarding on four distinct faces, with wide-open bowls and runs for all abilities. Banff's other two resorts are **Sunshine Village,** sitting on the Continental Divide and accessible only by gondola, and **Ski Banff @ Norquay,** a resort with heart-pounding runs overlooking the town of Banff.

Kananaskis Country is home to **Nakiska,** a resort developed especially for the downhill events of the 1988 Winter Olympic Games in Calgary, and nearby **Fortress Mountain,** in a spectacular location and with runs for all abilities. **Marmot Basin,** in Jasper National Park, has minimal crowds and a maximum variety of terrain. Across the border in British Columbia, near Golden, **Kicking Horse Mountain Resort** is a big hill that has gained an even bigger reputation for its challenging terrain since opening for the 2001–2002 season.

Winter is low season in the mountains, so many accommodations reduce their rates drastically. Lift and lodging package deals at many resorts start around $80 per person per night. Sunshine Village and Fortress Mountain have on-slope lodging, while the other resorts are served by shuttle buses from the nearest towns. Most major resorts open in early December and close in May.

Heli-Skiing

Helicopters are banned in the national parks of the Canadian Rockies, but two surrounding heli-ski operators provide transfers from Banff and Jasper. One such company is **R.K. Heli-Ski** (250/342-3889 or 800/661-6060, www .rkheliski.com), which is based on the west side of the mountains at Panorama but provides daily transfers from Banff and Lake Louise for a day's heli-skiing or boarding high in the Purcell Mountains. The cost is $612–712 per person. The only other company that offers day trips is **Robson Helimagic,** based west of Jasper at Valemont (250/566-4700), which charges $500 for a day's skiing on the northern boundary of Mount Robson Provincial Park.

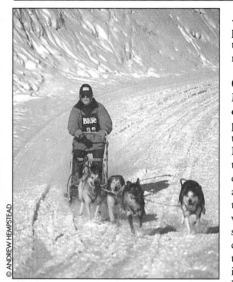

Visitors are encouraged to try dogsledding, a traditional form of transportation.

Banff is also headquarters for the world's largest heli-skiing operation, **CMH Heli-Skiing** (403/762-7100 or 800/661-0252, www.cmhski

.com), founded by Hans Gmoser. Seven-day packages in British Columbia's interior mountain ranges begin at around $5,100 per person, rising to more than $8,900 in the high season.

Other Winter Activities

Many hiking trails provide ideal routes for **cross-country skiing,** and many are groomed for that purpose. The largest concentration of groomed trails is in Kananaskis Country. Other areas are Banff, Jasper, Kootenay, Waterton, and Yoho National Parks. The Canmore Nordic Centre was developed for the 1988 Winter Olympic Games and is now a public facility. The townsite in Waterton Lakes National Park all but closes down for winter, but this park is one of the most enjoyable spots for a skiing sojourn. Anywhere you can cross-country ski you can **snowshoe,** a traditional form of winter transportation that is making a comeback. **Sleigh rides** are offered in Banff, Lake Louise, and Jasper.

Winter travel brings its own set of potential hazards, such as hypothermia, avalanche, frostbite, and sunburn. Necessary precautions should be taken. All park information centers can provide information on hazards and advice on current weather conditions.

Getting There

For international travelers, Vancouver and Calgary are the main gateways to the Canadian Rockies. From these two cities, as well as points across Canada, scheduled train and bus services pass through the region year-round.

AIR

The closest city to the Canadian Rockies is **Calgary,** Alberta, 128 km (80 miles) east of Banff. **Vancouver,** British Columbia's largest city, is also a major gateway to the mountains. It lies on Canada's West Coast, 830 km (515 miles) west of Banff. **Edmonton,** 360 km (224 miles) east of Jasper, also has an international airport. Even though Vancouver is a lot farther from the Cana-

dian Rockies than Calgary, it is a popular starting point, as the trip across British Columbia by rail, bus, or car is spectacular.

Air Canada

Canada's national airline, Air Canada (604/688-5515 or 888/247-2262, www.aircanada.ca or aircanada.com in the U.S.) is one of the world's largest airlines. It offers direct flights to Calgary and Vancouver from all major Canadian cities, as well as from Seattle, Los Angeles, San Francisco, Reno, Las Vegas, Phoenix, Chicago, Boston, Washington, D.C., Dallas/Fort Worth, New York, Atlanta, and St. Louis.

From Europe, Air Canada flies directly from London to Vancouver and Calgary, and from other major European cities via Toronto. From the South Pacific, Air Canada operates flights via Honolulu from Sydney and in alliance with Air New Zealand from Auckland and other South Pacific islands to Honolulu and Los Angeles, where passengers change to an Air Canada plane for the flight to Vancouver. Asian cities served by direct Air Canada flights from Vancouver include Beijing, Hong Kong, Nagoya, Osaka, Seoul, Shanghai, Taipei, and Tokyo. Air Canada's flights originating in the South American cities of Buenos Aires and Sao Paulo are routed through Toronto, where you'll need to change planes for either Calgary or Vancouver.

Other Canadian Airlines

WestJet (604/606-5525 or 800/538-5696, www.westjet.com) is a budget-priced airline, with specials advertised year-round. It has daily flights to its Calgary hub, as well as to Vancouver and Edmonton from the following Canadian cities: Hamilton, Ottawa, Regina, Saskatoon, Thunder Bay, and as far east as St. John's, Newfoundland.

Air Canada operates several smaller affiliated airlines. **Tango** (800/315-1390, www.flytango.com) is a no-frills carrier with routes across

---

AIR TAXES

The federal government imposes a tax of 7 percent of the ticket price plus $6 to a maximum of $55 on all flights departing Canada for the United States. For all other international destinations, the departure tax is set at $55. These taxes are generally included in the ticket purchase price, but it pays to ask when booking. Also built into the ticket price is Canada's **Air Travellers Security Charge;** $12 each sector for domestic flights, $20 for international flights.

Additionally, both Vancouver and Calgary International Airports charge an **Airport Improvement Fee** to all departing passengers, ranging $5–15 depending on the final destination. This fee is also included in your ticket price.

Canada. **Air Canada Jazz** (888/247-2262, www.flyjazz.com) links regional centers throughout western Canada and flies between Calgary and Spokane (Washington).

From the United States

Air Canada offers the most flights into Calgary and Vancouver from the United States, but one or both of the cities are also served by the following U.S. carriers: **Alaska Airlines** (800/252-7522, www.alaksaair.com) from Anchorage, Las Vegas, Los Angeles, Palm Springs, Phoenix, San Francisco, and Seattle; **American Airlines** (800/433-7300, www.aa.com) from Chicago and Dallas; **Continental Airlines** (800/231-0856, www.continental.com) from its Houston hub and New York (Newark); **Delta** (800/221-1212, www.delta.com) with summer-only flights from Atlanta; **Harmony Airways** (866/868-6789, www.harmonyairways.com) from Honolulu, Kahului, and Los Angeles; **Horizon Air** (800/547-9308, www.horizonair.com) from nearby Portland and Seattle; **Northwest Airlines** (800/225-2525, www.nwa.com) from Detroit, Memphis, and Minneapolis; **Skywest** (800/221-1212, www.skywest.com) from Salt Lake City; and finally **United Airlines** (800/241-6522, www.ual.com) from Chicago, Denver, San Francisco, and Seattle.

From Europe

In addition to Air Canada's flights to Calgary and Vancouver, **British Airlines** (800/247-9297, www.britishairlines.com) also flies this route daily. Air Canada flights between Vancouver and Continental Europe are routed through Toronto, but **KLM** (800/447-4747, www.klm.nl) has a daily nonstop flight to Vancouver from Amsterdam, and **Lufthansa** (800/563-5954, www.lufthansa.de) flies from Frankfurt and Munich.

From Australia and New Zealand

Qantas (604/279-6611, www.qantas.com.au) flies to Vancouver via Honolulu from Sydney, Melbourne, and Brisbane. **Air New Zealand** (800/663-5494, www.airnewzealand.com) operates in alliance with Air Canada to either Calgary or Vancouver, with a variety of interesting options including stops in South Pacific destinations like Nandi (Fiji). **Air Pacific** (800/227-4446, www.airpacific.com) offers flights from points throughout the Pacific to Honolulu and then on to Vancouver.

From Asia

Vancouver is the closest West Coast gateway to Asia, being more than 1,200 kilometers closer to Tokyo than Los Angeles. This and the city's large Asian population mean that it is well served by carriers from across the Pacific. In addition to

Air Canada's eight Asian destinations, Vancouver is served by: **Air China** (800/685-0921, www.airchina.com) from Beijing; **All Nippon Airways** (888/422-7533, www.ana.co.jp) from Osaka and Tokyo in affiliation with Air Canada; **Cathay Pacific** (604/606-8888, www.cathaypacific.com) twice daily from Hong Kong; **Eva Air** (800/695-1188, www.evaair.com.tw) from Taipei; **Japan Airlines** (800/525-3663, www.jal.co.jp) from Tokyo; **Korean Air**, 800/438-5000, www.koreanair.com, from Seoul; **Philippine Airlines** (800/435-9725, www.philippineair.com) from Manila; and **Singapore Airlines**

CUTTING FLIGHT COSTS

Ticket structuring for international air travel is so complex that finding the best deal requires some time and patience (or a good travel agent). The first step when planning your trip to the Canadian Rockies is to contact the airlines that fly to Vancouver or Calgary and ask for the best price they have for the time of year you wish to travel. Then shop around the travel agencies—you should be able to save 30–50 percent of the price you were quoted by the airline. The Internet has changed the way many people shop for tickets, but even if you use this invaluable tool for preliminary research, having a travel agent that you are comfortable dealing with—who takes the time to call around, does some research to get you the best fare, and helps you take advantage of any available special offers or promotional deals—is an invaluable asset in starting your travels off on the right foot.

In the first place, though, to get an idea of what your agent should be able to come up with, call the airlines or check their websites and compare fares. Also look in the travel sections of major newspapers—particularly in weekend editions—where budget fares and package deals are frequently advertised.

Within Canada, **Travel Cuts** (888/359-2887, www.travelcuts.com) and **Flight Centre** (888/967-5355, www.flightcentre.ca), both with offices in all major cities, consistently offer the lowest airfares available, with the latter guaranteeing the lowest. Flight Centre offers a similar guarantee

from its U.S. offices (877/967-5351, www.flightcentre.us), as well as those in Great Britain (tel. 0870/499-0040, www.flightcentre.co.uk), Australia (tel. 13-31-33, www.flightcentre.com.au), and New Zealand (tel. 0800/24-35-44, www.flightcentre.co.nz). All Flight Centre toll-free numbers will put you through to the closest office from where you are calling. In London, **Trailfinders** (215 Kensington High St., Kensington, tel. 020/7937-5400, www.trailfinders.com) always has good deals to Canada and other North American destinations. Reservations can be made directly through airline or travel agency websites, or use the services of an Internet-only company such as **Travelocity** (www.travelocity.com) or **Expedia** (www.expedia.com).

Many cheaper tickets have strict restrictions regarding changes of flight dates, lengths of stay, and cancellations. A general rule: The cheaper the ticket, the more restrictions. Most travelers today fly on APEX (advance-purchase excursion) fares. These are usually the best value, though some (and, occasionally, many) restrictions apply. These might include minimum and maximum stays, and nonchangeable itineraries (or hefty penalties for changes); tickets may also be nonrefundable once purchased.

When you have found the best fare, open a **frequent flyer** membership with the airline—**Air Canada** (www.aeroplan.com) has a very popular reward program that makes rewards easily obtainable.

(604/689-1223, www.singaporeair.com) from Singapore via Seoul. For the short hop between Vancouver and Calgary on Air Canada, expect to pay around $100 extra.

RAIL

The original transcontinental line passed through Banff, crossing the Continental Divide at Kicking Horse Pass and continuing to Vancouver via Rogers Pass. But this form of transportation, which opened up the Canadian Rockies to tourists, began to fade with the advent of efficient air services, and the last scheduled services on this line ended in 1991. Government-run VIA Rail provides coast-to-coast rail service using a more northerly route that passes through Jasper National Park. At Jasper, the westbound transcontinental line divides, with one set of tracks continuing west to Prince Rupert via Prince George and the other heading southwest to Vancouver. Another, more luxurious option, is the privately run Rocky Mountaineer, with summer service to Banff and Jasper from Vancouver.

VIA Rail

Government-run VIA Rail (416/366-8411 or 888/842-7245, www.viarail.ca) provides passenger-train service right across Canada. The *Canadian* is a thrice-weekly service between Toronto and Vancouver via Winnipeg, Saskatoon, Edmonton, Jasper, and Kamloops. Service is provided in two classes of travel: Economy features lots of leg room, reading lights, pillows and blankets, and a Skyline Car complete with bar service, while Silver and Blue is more luxurious, featuring sleeping rooms, daytime seating, all meals, a lounge and dining car, and shower kits for all passengers. At Jasper the westbound transcontinental line divides, with one set of tracks continuing slightly north to Prince Rupert. Along this route, the *Skeena* makes three trips per week. It is a daytime-only service, with passengers transferred to Prince George accommodations for an overnight stay. It also offers first-class travel, in Totem Class.

If you're traveling anywhere in western Canada from the eastern provinces, the least expensive way to travel is on a **Canrailpass,** which allows unlimited travel anywhere on the VIA Rail system for 12 days within any given 30-day period. During high season (June 1–Oct. 15) the pass is adult $741, senior (over 60) and child $667, with extra days (up to three are allowed) $63 and $57, respectively. The rest of the year the fare is adults $461, seniors and students $405, with extra days $40 and $36, respectively. VIA Rail has cooperated with Amtrak (800/872-7245) to offer a North American Rail Pass, with all the same seasonal dates and discounts as the Canrailpass. The cost for unlimited travel over 30 days is adult $1,004, senior and child $904; $711 and $640 respectively through the low season.

On regular fares, discounts of 25–40 percent apply to travel in all classes Oct.–June. Those over 60 and under 25 receive a 10 percent dis-

Rail travel opened up the Canadian Rockies to tourism and today continues as a popular form of transportation in the mountains.

count that can be combined with other seasonal fares. Check for advance-purchase restrictions on all discount tickets.

Rocky Mountaineer

Rocky Mountaineer Vacations (604/606-7245 or 800/665-7245, www.rockymountaineer.com) runs a luxurious rail trip between Vancouver and Banff or Jasper, through the spectacular interior mountain ranges of British Columbia. Travel is during daylight hours only so you don't miss anything. Trains depart in either direction in the morning (every second or third day), overnighting at Kamloops. One-way travel in RedLeaf Service, which includes light meals, nonalcoholic drinks, and Kamloops accommodations costs $699 per person d, $779 s from either Banff or Jasper and $769 and $849 respectively from Calgary. GoldLeaf Service is the ultimate in luxury. Passengers ride in a two-story glass-domed car, eat in a separate dining area, and stay in Kamloops's most luxurious accommodations. GoldLeaf costs $1,379 per person d, $1,459 s from Banff or Jasper to Vancouver and $1,499 and $1,579 respectively from Calgary. Outside of high season (mid-April to May and the first two weeks of October), fares are reduced around $150 per person in RedLeaf and $200 per person in GoldLeaf. Trains terminate in Vancouver off Terminal Avenue at 1755 Cottrell Street (behind Pacific Central Station).

BUS

Greyhound

Greyhound (403/762-1092 or 800/661-8747, www.greyhound.ca) serves areas throughout Canada and the United States. Travel by Greyhound is simple—just roll up at the depot and buy a ticket. No reservations are necessary. Greyhound bus depots are always close to downtown and generally link up with local public transportation. Always check for any promotional fares that might be available at the time of your travel. Regular-fare tickets are valid for one year and allow unlimited stopovers between paid destinations.

From Calgary: Greyhound runs five times daily from its depot (850 16th St. NW, 403/265-9111) to Canmore and Banff, with most services continuing through Lake Louise to Golden and beyond.

From Edmonton: Buses run year-round between Edmonton's depot (10324 103rd St., 780/420-2400) and Jasper along a much longer route through western Canada that runs as far west as Prince Rupert and Vancouver.

From Vancouver: The main Greyhound routes from Vancouver include the TransCanada Highway to Golden, Field, and Banff; a northern route along Highway 5 through Jasper to Edmonton and beyond; and a southern route on Highway 3, through Cranbrook to Radium Hot Springs and on to Banff. The fare between Vancouver and Banff is around $130 one-way. The bus depot in Vancouver is at 1150 Station Street (604/482-8747).

From the United States: If you're traveling from the United States, get yourself to Great Falls, Montana, from which regular services continue north to the Coutts/Sweetgrass port of entry. There you change to a Canadian Greyhound bus for Calgary, where you can make connections to Banff.

When calling for ticket information, ask about any special deals—including the **Go Anywhere Fare,** on which you can travel between any two points in North America for one low fare; $129 one way and $199 round-trip if bought 14 days in advance. Other discounts apply to regular-fare tickets bought seven and 14 days in advance, travelers 65 and over, and two people traveling together. Greyhound's **Discovery Pass** comes in many forms, including passes valid only in Canada, in the western states and provinces, and in all of North America. The **Canada Pass** is sold in periods of seven days ($309), 10 days ($389), 15 days ($459), 21 days ($499), 30 days ($579), 45 days ($639), and 60 days ($719) and allows unlimited travel west of Montreal. Passes can be bought 14 or more days in advance online, seven or more days in advance from any Canadian bus depot, or up to the day of departure from U.S. depots. The **Domestic North America**

CanAm Pass, valid for Greyhound travel through North America, ranges from US$439 for a 15-day pass to US$719 for a 60-day pass. Outside of North America, the passes are the same, but they're sold as **International Discovery Passes,** with significant discounts; purchase them online.

From Calgary International Airport

This airport, 128 km (80 miles) west of Banff, is the main gateway to the Canadian Rockies. In addition to car rental desks, many shuttles are represented opposite the baggage carousels. Companies that offer service out to the Canadian Rockies are **Brewster** (403/762-6767 or 800/661-1152, www.brewster.ca), **Banff Airporter** (403/762-3396 or 888/449-2901, www.banff airporter.com), and **Rocky Mountain Sky Shuttle** (403/762-5200 or 888/762-8754, www .rockymountainskyshuttle.com). Brewster is the only one of these services that continues beyond Lake Louise to Jasper.

The advantage of traveling with either of the latter two companies is that they offer door-to-door-service for around the same price. Reserve a seat by booking over the phone or online in advance. Expect to pay $46 each way to Canmore or Banff and around $50 to Lake Louise. Brewster charges $80 for the Calgary–Jasper run.

Backpacker Bus

For young travelers on a budget, the **Moose Travel Network** (604/777-9905 or 888/244-6673, www.moosenetwork.com) is an excellent way to travel to and around the Canadian Rockies. It runs along a number of different routes, including a 10-day loop originating in Vancouver and traveling to Jasper and Banff via Whistler ($449 per person), a six-day trip between Vancouver and Banff via Jasper ($309), a two-day Banff–Jasper–Banff trip ($95), and a Banff–Vancouver shuttle that overnights in Kamloops ($107). On any of these trips, you can get on and off wherever you please (and jump aboard the next bus as it passes through) or bond with the crowd and stay on the fixed itinerary. Nights are spent at hostels en route. This cost isn't in-

cluded in the tour, but your reservation is (so you don't need to worry about trying to find an empty bed at each stop). Food is also extra, but often all travelers pitch in a token amount to purchase dinner at a grocery store along the way. Buses run 3–7 times a week through a May to mid-October season.

CAR

Driving to the Canadian Rockies is possible from anywhere in North America but is most convenient if you live in western Canada or the Pacific Northwest. Driving saves money on transportation costs and allows you to bring along camping equipment and sporting gear such as mountain bikes and canoes.

Routes in Canada

The TransCanada Highway (Highway 1) stretches from one end of Canada to the other and is the world's longest national highway (7,821 km/4,860 miles from end to end). It passes through the Canadian Rockies' towns of Canmore, Banff, and Golden. The first major city east of the mountains is Calgary, 128 km (80 miles) from Banff along the TransCanada. The northern route across western Canada is the Yellowhead Highway, which passes through the town of Jasper, in Jasper National Park, 364 km (226 miles) east of Edmonton. From Vancouver, on the west coast of British Columbia and the major air gateway from Asia, it's 836 km (519 miles) west to Banff along the TransCanada Highway and 781 km (486 miles) northwest to Jasper along Highway 5. The TransCanada and Yellowhead Highways are linked within the Canadian Rockies by the Icefields Parkway, which runs parallel to the Continental Divide between Lake Louise and Jasper, a distance of 230 km (143 miles).

Routes from the United States

Reaching the Canadian Rockies from the United States is possible via a number of routes. From Seattle, the shortest approach is to follow I-5 north to Vancouver and jump on the TransCanada Highway. If you're traveling north from the Rocky Mountain states, Highway 93 will provide a warm-up for the mountain scenery north of the border. This route crosses into Canada north of Kalispell, merging with Highway 95 from Spokane, Washington, at Cranbrook, then continuing up the west side of the Canadian Rockies to Radium Hot Springs, where you can cut through Kootenay National Park to Banff. Much quicker is I-15, which begins in Los Angeles, looping through Las Vegas and Salt Lake City on its way north to Montana. I-15 enters Canada at the 24-hour Coutts/Sweetgrass border crossing south of Lethbridge, Alberta. From Lethbridge, it's a three-hour drive to Banff, or you can choose to head west to Waterton Lakes National Park. Total distance from Los Angeles to Banff via Interstate 15 is 2,600 km (1,617 miles). From the Midwest and eastern states, there are innumerable options, including I-94 through Minneapolis or crossing into Canada east of the Great Lakes and driving the entire way within Canada.

Getting Around

BUS

Getting around the Canadian Rockies is easiest with your own vehicle because public transportation is limited. **Brewster** (403/762-6767, www.brewster.ca) is primarily a tour company but also runs a scheduled bus service linking Calgary International Airport, Canmore, Banff, and Lake Louise, with a summer-only service between Lake Louise and Jasper. **Greyhound** (403/762-1092) serves the TransCanada Highway, providing a link between Canmore, Banff, Lake Louise, and Golden three times daily. Once daily, buses run through Kootenay National Park, between Banff and Radium Hot Springs. You can also take **Moose Travel Network** buses (see *Getting There*) between Banff and Jasper.

CAR

Driving in Canada

United States and International Driver's Licenses are valid in Canada. All highway signs give distances in kilometers and speeds in kilometers per hour. Unless otherwise posted, the maximum speed limit on the highways is 100 kph (62 mph).

Use of safety belts is mandatory, and motorcyclists must wear helmets. Infants and toddlers weighing up to nine kilograms (20 pounds) must be strapped into an appropriate children's car seat. Use of a child car seat for larger children weighing 9–18 kilograms (20–40 pounds) is required of British Columbia residents and recommended to nonresidents. Before venturing north of the 49th parallel, U.S. residents should ask their vehicle insurance company for a Canadian Non-resident Inter-provincial Motor Vehicle Liability Insurance Card. You may also be asked to prove vehicle ownership, so carry your vehicle registration form.

If you're a member in good standing of an automobile association, take your membership card—the Canadian AA provides members of related associations full services, including free maps, itineraries, excellent tour books, road- and weather-condition information, accommodations reservations, travel agency services, and emergency road services. For more information contact the **Alberta Motor Association** (780/430-6800 or 800/222-6578, www.ama.ab.ca) or the **British Columbia Automobile Association** (604/268-5600 or 877/325-8888, www.bcaa.com).

Note: Drinking and driving (with a blood-alcohol level of .08 percent or higher) in Canada can get you imprisoned for up to five years on a first offense and will cost you your license for at least 12 months.

Car and RV Rental

All major car rental agencies have outlets at Calgary and Vancouver International Airports. Car rentals are also available in Banff, Canmore, and Jasper, but it is strongly recommended to rent a vehicle *before* arriving in the Canadian Rockies for two reasons: cost and mileage charges (the now-standard unlimited mileage with major car rentals doesn't apply in Banff, Canmore, or Jasper). Generally, vehicles can be booked through parent companies in the United States. Rates start at $60 per day for a small economy car, $75 for a midsize car, and $85 for a full-size car.

Major rental companies with outlets in Calgary, Edmonton, and Vancouver are: **Alamo** (800/462-5266, www.alamo.com), **Avis** (800/974-0808, www.avis.ca), **Budget** (800/268-8900, www.budget.com), **Discount** (800/263-2355, www.discountcar.com), **Dollar** (800/800-4000, www.dollar.com), **Enterprise** (800/325-8007, www.enterprise.com), **Hertz** (800/263-0600, www.hertz.ca), **National** (800/227-7368, www.nationalcar.com), **Rent-a-wreck** (800/327-0116, www.rentawreck.ca), and **Thrifty** (800/847-4389, www.thrifty.com).

Camper vans, recreational vehicles, and travel trailers are a great way to get around the Canadian Rockies without having to worry about accommodations each night. The downside is cost. The smallest vans, capable of sleeping two people, start at $150 per day with 100 free kilometers (62 miles) per day. Standard extra charges include insurance, a preparation fee (usually around $50 per rental), a linen/cutlery charge (around $60 per person per trip), and taxes. Major agencies, with rental outlets in both Calgary and Vancouver, include **Cruise Canada** (403/291-4963 or 800/327-7799, or, in the U.S., 800/327-7778, www.cruisecanada.com), **Canadream** (403/291-1000 or 800/461-7368, www.canadream.com), and **Go West** (604/987-5288 or 800/661-8813, www.go-west.com). In most cases, a drop-off fee of $400 applies to drop-offs made in Vancouver from rentals originating in Calgary, or vice versa. At the end of the summer season (early September), look for some great online bargains.

TOURS

For those with limited time, an organized tour is the best way to see the Canadian Rockies. **Brewster** (403/762-6767 or 800/661-1152, www.brewster.ca) offers day tours and overnight tours throughout the mountains, as well as car rental and accommodation packages. Rocky Mountaineer Rail Tours (see *Getting There*) offers a wide variety of longer tours in conjunction with rail travel between Vancouver and Banff or Jasper. At the opposite end of the price spectrum, by joining a **Moose Travel Network** (604/777-9905 or 888/244-6673, www.moosenetwork.com) tour you get to see the Canadian Rockies with like-minded budget travelers.

On a smaller scale, **Good Earth Travel Adventures** (403/678-9358 or 888/979-9797, www.goodearthtravel.com) provides one-on-one consultations for all aspects of travel through the Canadian Rockies—from day tours to accommodation reservations.

Accommodations and Camping

Following is a summary of the types of accommodations you can expect to find throughout the Canadian Rockies. Individual properties are detailed in each travel chapter, along with prices and contact information. Nearly all accommodations now have toll-free numbers and websites, through which you can find out more information about each property and make bookings.

Accommodation Taxes

Except for campgrounds and bed-and-breakfasts with fewer than four guest rooms, accommodations collect tax on behalf of various levels of government. In British Columbia, an 8 percent provincial hotel room tax is administered, while in Alberta, a 4 percent tourism tax is added. This is in addition to the Canada-wide 7 percent goods-and-services tax, refundable to visitors from outside the country. As a general rule, quoted rates don't include any of these taxes.

HOTELS AND MOTELS

Hotels and motels throughout the Canadian Rockies range from substandard road motels to sublime resorts such as the famous Fairmont Banff Springs. Bookings throughout the mountains, but especially in Banff, Lake Louise, and Jasper, should be made as far in advance as possible. Finding inexpensive lodging in the mountain national parks is difficult in summer. By late afternoon, the only rooms left will be in the more expensive categories, and by nightfall all of these will go.

Hotel rooms in Banff begin around $150; those in Jasper and Waterton Lakes are a little less. Accommodation prices are slashed by as much as 70 percent outside summer. Always ask for the best rate available and check local tourist literature for discount coupons. All rates quoted in this handbook are for the cheapest

Staying in a self-contained log cabin, like this one at the Post Hotel in Lake Louise, is a typical mountain experience.

Know the Canadian Rockies

GETTING THE BEST LODGING DEAL

It can't be stressed enough: the Internet is an invaluable tool for searching out the best accommodation deals.

Rates quoted in this book are for a standard double room throughout the high season, which generally extends from late June to mid-September. Almost all accommodations are less expensive outside of these busy months. As a general rule of thumb, the more expensive the property, the steeper the discount. For example, and at different ends of the spectrum, the cost of a dorm bed at the Banff Alpine Centre drops $4 per night on September 15, while in downtown Banff, already reasonably priced Brewster's Mountain Lodge halves its rates to $120 in winter, with graduated discounts in spring and fall. Plan on traveling a few weeks on either side of the peak season, then use hotel websites to check when individual properties are offering discounts. Most accommodations post seasonal specials on their websites well in advance.

While you have no influence over seasonal pricing fluctuations, *how* you reserve a room *can* make a difference in how much you pay. Book through a central reservations agency or travel agent, or pay for accommodations as part of a tour package, and you'll pay the full published price.

In some years, getting a room in July and August without advance reservations is almost impossible. In others, hotels will be selling rooms well into the night for a fraction of the published rate. Leaving reservations until the last minute is a risky proposition if you're not prepared to be flexible, but it's a good way to save a lot of money.

Don't be afraid to negotiate during slower times. Even if the desk clerk has no control over rates, there's no harm in asking for a bigger room or one with a better view. Just look for a Vacancy sign hanging out front.

Most hotels offer auto association members an automatic 10 percent discount, and whereas senior discounts apply only to those 60 or 65 and older on public transportation and at attractions, most hotels offer discounts to those over 50. Some chains, such as Best Western, also allow senior travelers a late checkout. "Corporate Rates" are a lot more flexible than in years past; some hotels require nothing more than the flash of a business card for a 10–20 percent discount. Finally, when it comes to frequent flyer programs, you really do need to be a frequent flyer to achieve free flights, but the various loyalty programs offered by hotel chains often provide benefits simply for signing up.

---

category of rooms during the most expensive time period (summer).

Park-at-your-door, single-story road motels are mostly a thing of the past in the mountains, although Radium Hot Springs, just outside Kootenay National Park, still has many of these motels (one of which proudly boasts "Electric Heat"). In most cases rooms are fine, but check before paying, just to make sure. Most have a few rooms with kitchenettes, but these fill fast. Expect to pay $50–70 s, $50–85 d. You will also find this style of accommodation in Canmore, Waterton townsite, and Golden.

Information and Reservations

For a list of all hotels, motels, lodges, and bed-and-breakfasts in Alberta, pick up a copy of *Alberta Accommodation Guide*, produced by the

Alberta Hotel & Lodging Association (www.explorealberta.com). The guide is available online or order a free copy through **Travel Alberta** (780/427-4321 or 800/252-3782, www.travelalberta.com). The same association produces the *Alberta Campground Guide* (also online at www.explorealberta.com). **Tourism British Columbia** (250/387-1642 or 800/435-5622, www.hellobc.com) produces the free *British Columbia Approved Accommodation* brochure, which lists all accommodations and campgrounds in the province.

BED-AND-BREAKFASTS

The bed-and-breakfast phenomenon is well entrenched in Canada. This type of accommodation is a good option if you don't mind sacrificing some privacy to meet locals and to mingle with like-minded travelers. Bed-and-breakfasts are usually private residences, with up to four guest rooms, although bylaws are different throughout the region. Amenities can vary greatly—the "bed-and-breakfast" may be a single spare room in an otherwise regular family home or a full-time business in a beautifully restored heritage home. This uncertainty as to what to expect upon arrival can be off-putting for many people, especially with the possibility of sharing a bathroom with other guests—which is both a common and accepted practice in European bed-and-breakfasts. If having a bathroom to yourself is important to you, clarify with the bed-and-breakfast operator when reserving. Also, as bed-and-breakfasts also function as private residences, book in advance—don't just turn up. Finally, check payment methods when booking; not all establishments take credit or debit cards.

Rates fluctuate greatly, with the least expensive rooms costing $50 s, $60 d and the most expensive well over $100. Bed-and-breakfasts are located in Banff, Canmore, Bragg Creek, and Jasper. In Jasper National Park, a park bylaw that prevented such establishments from serving breakfast was recently lifted; some have started serving meals, but those that don't are still known as private home accommodations. The best way to find out about individual lodging is from local tourist information centers or from listings in the *Alberta Accommodation Guide* or *British Columbia Approved Accommodation* brochure.

Bed-and-Breakfast Associations and Agencies

The **Western Canada Bed and Breakfast Innkeepers Association** (www.wcbbia.com) represents bed-and-breakfasts across the region. The association produces an informative brochure with simple descriptions and a color photo of each property, but it doesn't take bookings. Without the color photos, **Jasper Home Accommodation Association** (www.stayinjasper.com) offers the same kind of literature and online links.

Canada-West Accommodations (604/990-6730 or 800/561-3223, www.b-b.com) does take bookings, along with providing recommendations based on your likes and dislikes.

OTHER LODGING OPTIONS
Seasonal Accommodations

As roads through the mountains were improved in the 1920s, the number of tourists arriving by automobile increased greatly. To cater to this new breed of traveler, many bungalow camps were constructed along the highways. Many remain today, offering a high standard of accommodation away from the hustle and bustle of the towns. Generally they consist of freestanding, self-contained units and are open for the summer only.

Backcountry Huts and Lodges

Throughout the backcountry of the Canadian Rockies is an extensive system of 18 rustic huts managed by the **Alpine Club of Canada** (403/678-3200, www.alpineclubofcanada.ca). Due to their locations around favorite climbing areas, they are most often used by mountaineers as an overnight stop before assaulting some of the park's highest peaks, but they are available to anyone who wishes to take advantage of their remote location. Their accessibility ranges from the Elizabeth Parker Hut (Yoho National Park), which can be reached by bus, to the Neil Colgan Hut, Canada's highest habitable structure, 2,960 meters (9,700 feet) from sea level on a windswept ledge above Moraine Lake. Often of historical significance, each of the huts has a stove, lantern, kitchen utensils, and foam mattresses. Rates range $15–24 per person per night.

Privately operated backcountry lodges are found in Banff, Jasper, and Yoho National Parks, as well as Mount Assiniboine Provincial Park. The most luxurious is **Lake O'Hara Lodge** in Yoho National Park. It lies 11 km (6.8 miles) from the nearest public road—access is on foot or shuttle bus—and is surrounded by some of the finest hiking in all the Canadian Rockies. Banff National Park has two backcountry lodges: **Shadow Lake Lodge,** northwest of Banff, and **Skoki Lodge,** east of Lake Louise. Jasper

National Park is home to **Tonquin Amethyst Lake Lodge** and **Tonquin Valley Backcountry Lodge.** All require some degree of effort to reach—either on foot or on horseback in summer, or on cross-country skis or snowshoes in winter. **Mount Assiniboine Lodge** is farthest from the road system but can be reached by helicopter. Rates at these lodges begin at $150 per person, including three meals. None have television, but all have running water and a congenial atmosphere.

BACKPACKER ACCOMMODATIONS

Throughout the Canadian Rockies, traditional hostels operated by Hostelling International are still the most common form of accommodation for budget travelers, but other options do exist. Banff and Radium Hot Springs have privately run backpacker lodges, and Banff has a YWCA with dormitory accommodations for men and women. Generally, you need to supply your own sleeping bag or linen, but most places supply extra bedding at a minimal cost.

Hostelling International

Hostelling International–Alberta operates 13 hostels in the Canadian Rockies. Five of these are in Banff National Park, five in Jasper National Park, and one each in Canmore, Yoho National Park (British Columbia), and Waterton Lakes National Park. Whenever you can, make reservations in advance, especially in summer. Make bookings by contacting Central Reservations (403/521-8421 or 866/762-4122, www.hihostels.ca).

All of the hostels are equipped with a kitchen and lounge room, and some have laundries and private rooms. Those in Banff and Lake Louise are world-class, with hundreds of beds as well as libraries and cafés. The five rustic hostels along the Icefields Parkway are evenly spaced, perfect for a bike trip along one of the world's great mountain highways. A sheet or sleeping bag is required at more remote locations, although these can usually be rented. Rates for members are $13–31 per night, nonmembers $27–35. Staying in hostels is an especially good bargain for skiers and snowboarders; packages including accommodation and a day pass at a local resort start at $65.

You don't *have* to be a member to stay in an affiliated hostel of Hostelling International, but membership pays for itself after only a few nights of discounted lodging. Aside from lower rates, benefits of membership vary from country to country but often include discounted air, rail, and bus travel; discounts on car rental; and discounts on some attractions and commercial activities. For Canadians, the membership charge is $35 annually, or $175 for a lifetime membership. For more information contact **HI–Canada** (604/684-7111, www.hihostels.ca). Joining the Hostelling International affiliate of your home country entitles you to reciprocal rights in Canada, as well as around the world. In the United States the contact information is **Hostelling International USA** (301/495-1240, www.hiusa.org); annual membership is adult US$28 and senior US$18, or become a lifetime member for US$250. International chapters include: **YHA England and Wales** (0870/770-8868, www.yha.org.uk); **YHA Australia,** based in all capital cities (including at 422 Kent St., Sydney, 02/9261-1111, www.yha.com.au); and **YHA New Zealand** (03/379-9970, www.yha.org.nz). Otherwise, click through the links on the Hostelling International website (www.hihostels.com) to your country of choice.

CAMPING

Camping is the way to stay cheaply in the Canadian Rockies. Each of the five national parks has excellent campgrounds, which have a combined total of 6,000 sites plus large areas set aside for overflow camping. Many of the campgrounds consist of nothing more than picnic tables, drinking water, pit toilets, and firewood ($6 per site per night), but at least one campground in each park has hot showers and full hookups. Each park also has an area set aside for winter camping.

Beginning in 2005, a percentage of sites in the most popular campgrounds can be reserved through the **Parks Canada Campground Reser-**

vation Service (877/737-3783, www.pccamping .ca) for a nominal fee. If you're traveling in the height of summer and require electrical hookups, this booking system is highly recommended. Most campsites in the national parks operate on a first-come, first-served basis and often fill by midday in July and August.

Each of the road-accessible provincial parks covered in this book provides camping facilities, usually only with drinking water, picnic tables, and pit toilets. The exceptions are Peter Lougheed and Bow Valley Provincial Parks in Kananaskis Country, where hookups and showers are provided. Campground operations in Kananaskis Country are contracted to private operators but ultimately come under the auspices of the Alberta Community Development (www.cd.gov.ab.ca). This department is also in charge of other campgrounds on public lands, including those in provincial recreation areas along the eastern slopes of the Canadian Rockies. BC Parks (www.bcparks.ca) manages similar facilities along the other side of the divide; camp fees range $14–21 per night.

Commercial campgrounds operate in Canmore, Radium Hot Springs, at the entrance to Waterton Lakes National Park, in Golden, in Mount Robson Provincial Park, and in Grande Cache. They provide full hookups and have showers but generally lack the natural surroundings found in national and provincial parks. In Kananaskis Country, the privately operated Mount Kidd RV Park boasts a tennis court, recreation room, spa, and sauna.

Backcountry Camping

Backcountry camping in all national parks is $8 per person per night, or purchase an annual pass ($56), valid for unlimited backcountry travel and camping for 12 months from its purchase date. Before heading out, you must register at the respective park information center (regardless of whether you have an annual pass) and pick up a Wilderness Pass (for those without an annual pass, the nightly camping fee multiplied by the number of nights you'll be in the backcountry). Many popular backcountry campgrounds have quotas, with reservations taken up to three months in advance. The reservation fee is $12 per party per trip. Most campgrounds in the backcountry have pit toilets, and some have bear bins for secure food storage. Fires are discouraged, so bring a stove.

Visas and Officialdom

ENTERING CANADA

U.S. Citizens

United States citizens and permanent residents need only present some form of identification that proves citizenship and/or residency, such as a birth certificate, voter-registration card, driver's license with photo, or alien card (essential for nonresident aliens to reenter the United States). It never hurts to carry your passport as well.

Other Foreign Visitors

All other foreign visitors entering Canada must have a valid passport and may need a visa or visitor permit depending on their country of residence and the vagaries of international politics. At present, visas are not required for citizens of the United States, British Commonwealth, or Western Europe. The standard entry permit is for six months, and you may be asked to show onward tickets or proof of sufficient funds to last you through your intended stay. Extensions are available from Citizenship and Immigration Canada offices in Vancouver and Victoria. This department's website (www.cic.gc.ca) is the best source of the latest entry requirements.

CUSTOMS

You can take the following into Canada dutyfree: reasonable quantities of clothes and personal effects, 50 cigars and 200 cigarettes, 200 grams of tobacco, 1.14 liters of spirits or wine, food for personal use, and gas (normal tank capacity). Pets from the United States can generally be brought into Canada, with certain caveats. Dogs and cats must be more than three months old and have a rabies certificate showing date of vaccination. Birds can be brought in only if they have not been mixing with other birds, and parrots need an export permit because they're on the endangered species list.

Handguns, automatic and semiautomatic weapons, and sawn-off rifles and shotguns are not allowed into Canada. Visitors with firearms must declare them at the border; restricted weapons will be held by Customs and can be picked up on exit from the country. Those not declared will be seized and charges may be laid. It is illegal to possess any firearm in a national park unless it is dismantled or carried in an enclosed case. Up to 5,000 rounds of ammunition may be imported but should be declared on entry.

On reentering the United States, if you've been in Canada more than 48 hours you can bring back up to US$400 worth of household and personal items, excluding alcohol and tobacco, duty-free. If you've been in Canada fewer than 48 hours, you may bring in only up to US$200 worth of such items duty-free.

For further information on all customs regulations contact **Canada Border Services Agency** (204/983-3500 or 800/461-9799, www.cbsa-asfc.gc.ca).

Tips for Travelers

EMPLOYMENT AND STUDY

Banff is especially popular with young workers from across Canada and beyond. Aside from Help Wanted ads in local papers, a good place to start looking for work is the **Job Resource Centre** (314 Marten St., Banff, 403/7620-3311).

International visitors wishing to work or study in Canada must obtain authorization *before* entering the country. Authorization to work will only be granted if no qualified Canadians are available for the work in question. Applications for work and study are available from all Canadian embassies and must be submitted with a nonrefundable processing fee. The Canadian government has a reciprocal agreement with Australia for a limited number of **holiday work visas** to be issued each year. Australian citizens aged 30 and under are eligible; contact your nearest Canadian embassy or consulate. For general information on immigrating to Canada contact **Citizenship and Immigration Canada** (604/666-2171, www.cic.gc.ca).

VISITORS WITH DISABILITIES

A lack of mobility should not deter you from traveling to the Canadian Rockies, but you should definitely do some research before leaving home.

If you haven't traveled extensively, start by doing some research at the website of the **Access-Able Travel Source** (www.access-able.com), where you will find databases of specialist travel agencies and lodgings in western Canada that cater to travelers with disabilities. **Flying Wheels Travel** (507/451-5005, www.flyingwheelstravel .com) caters solely to the needs of travelers with disabilities. The **Society for Accessible Travel and Hospitality** (212/447-7284, www.sath.org) supplies information on tour operators, vehicle rentals, specific destinations, and companion services. For frequent travelers, the membership fee (US$45 per year) is well worthwhile. **Emerging Horizons** (www.emerginghorizons.com) is a U.S. quarterly magazine dedicated to travelers with special needs.

Access to Travel (800/465-7735, www.access totravel.gc.ca) is an initiative of the Canadian government that includes information on travel within and between Canadian cities. The website also has a lot of general travel information for those with disabilities. The **Canadian National Institute for the Blind** (www.cnib.ca) offers a wide range of services from offices in Calgary (403/266-8831) and Vancouver (604/431-2121).

Finally, the **Canadian Paraplegic Association** (877/324-3611, www.canparaplegic.org), with chapter offices in Calgary (403/228-3001) and Vancouver (604/324-3611), is another good source of information.

TRAVELING WITH CHILDREN

The natural wonders of the Canadian Rockies are a marvelous place to bring children on a vacation, and luckily for you many of the best things to do—walking, watching wildlife, and more—don't cost a cent.

Admission and tour prices for children are included throughout the Explore chapters of this book. As a general rule, these reduced prices are for children aged 6–16 years. For two adults and two or more children, always ask about family tickets. Children under 6 nearly always get in free. Most hotels and motels will happily accommodate children, but always try to reserve your room in advance and let the reservations desk know the ages of your kids. Often, children stay free in major hotels, and in the case of some major chains—such as Holiday Inn—eat free also. Generally, bed-and-breakfasts aren't suitable for children and in some cases don't accept kids at all. Ask ahead.

As a general rule when it comes to traveling with children, let them help you plan the trip, looking at websites and reading up on the Canadian Rockies together. To make your vacation more enjoyable if you'll be spending a lot of time on the road, rent a minivan (all major rental agencies have a supply). Don't forget to bring along favorite toys and games from home—whatever you think will keep will keep your kids entertained when the joys of sightseeing wear off.

The websites of **Travel Alberta** (www.travel alberta.com) and **Tourism British Columbia** (www.hellobc.com) have sections devoted to children's activities within the two provinces. Another handy source of information is **Kid Friendly!** (604/541-6192, www.kidfriendly.org), a nonprofit organization that has compiled an online database of, you guessed it, kid-friendly attractions, lodgings, and restaurants throughout British Columbia. The website even has room for your children to write about their vacation. Another useful online tool is the website **Traveling Internationally with Your Kids** (www.travel withyourkids.com).

Health and Safety

Compared to other parts of the world, Canada is a relatively safe place to visit. That said, wherever you are traveling, carry a medical kit that includes bandages, insect repellent, sunscreen, antiseptic, antibiotics, and water-purification tablets. Good first-aid kits are available through most outdoor shops.

Giardia

Giardiasis, also known as beaver fever, is a real concern for those who drink water from backcountry water sources. It's caused by an intestinal parasite, *Giardia lamblia,* that lives in lakes, rivers, and streams. Once ingested, its effects, although not instantaneous, can be dramatic; severe diarrhea, cramps, and nausea are the most common. Preventive measures should always be taken and include boiling all water for at least 10 minutes, treating all water with iodine, or filtering all water using a filter with a small enough pore size to block the *Giardia* cysts.

Winter Travel

Travel through the Canadian Rockies during winter months should not be undertaken lightly. Before setting out in a vehicle, check antifreeze levels and always carry a spare tire and blankets or sleeping bags. **Frostbite** is a potential hazard, especially when cold temperatures are combined with high winds (a combination known as *windchill*). Most often it leaves a numbing, bruised sensation, and the skin turns white. Exposed areas of skin, especially the nose and ears, are most susceptible.

Hypothermia occurs when the body fails to produce heat as fast as it loses it. It can strike at any time of year but is more common during cooler months. Cold weather, combined with hunger, fatigue, and dampness, creates a recipe for disaster. Symptoms are not always apparent to the victim. The early signs are numbness, shivering, slurring of words, dizzy spells, and, in extreme cases, violent behavior, unconsciousness, and even death. The best way to dress for the cold is in layers, including a waterproof outer layer. Most important, wear headgear. The best treatment is to get the patient out of the cold, replace wet clothing with dry, slowly give hot liquids and sugary foods, and place the victim in a sleeping bag. Warming too quickly can lead to heart attacks.

Other Considerations

Believe it or not, AIDS and other venereal and needle-communicated diseases are as much of a concern in the Canadian Rockies as anywhere in the world today. Take exactly the same precautions you would at home—use condoms, and don't share needles.

It's a good idea to get health insurance or some form of coverage before heading to Canada if you're going to be there for a while, but check that your plan covers foreign services. Hospital charges vary from place to place but can start at around $1,000 a day, and some facilities impose a surcharge for nonresidents. Some Canadian companies offer coverage specifically aimed at visitors.

If you're on medication, take adequate supplies with you, and get a prescription from your doctor to cover the time you will be away. You may not be able to get a prescription filled at Canadian pharmacies without visiting a Canadian doctor, so don't wait till you've almost run out. If you wear glasses or contact lenses, ask your optometrist for a spare prescription in case you break or lose your lenses, and stock up on your usual cleaning supplies.

Information and Services

MONEY

All prices quoted in this guidebook are in Canadian dollars and cents unless otherwise noted.

Canadian currency is based on dollars and cents, with 100 cents equal to one dollar. Coins come in denominations of one, five, 10, and 25 cents, and one and two dollars. The 11-sided, gold-colored, one-dollar coin is known as a "loonie" for the bird featured on it. The unique two-dollar coin is silver with a gold-colored insert. The most common notes are $5, $10, $20, and $50. A $100 bill does exist but is uncommon.

The safest way to carry money is in the form of traveler's checks from a reputable and well-known U.S. company such as American Express, Visa, or Bank of America; those are also the easiest checks to cash. Cash only the amount you need when you need it. Banks offer the best exchange rates, but other foreign-currency exchange outlets are available. It's also a good idea to start off with a couple of traveler's checks in Canadian dollars so you're never caught without *some* money if you don't make it to a bank on time.

Visa and MasterCard credit and debit cards are also readily accepted in the Canadian Rockies. By using these cards you eliminate the necessity of thinking about the exchange rate—the transaction and rate of exchange on the day of the transaction will automatically be reflected in the bill from your credit-card company. On the downside, you'll always get a better exchange rate when dealing directly with a bank.

Costs

The cost of living in the Canadian Rockies is generally higher than in other parts of Canada, especially when it comes to accommodations. Provincially, the cost of living is lower in Alberta than in British Columbia but higher than in the United States. By planning ahead, having a tent or joining Hostelling International, and being prepared to cook your own meals, it is possible to get by on $60 per person per day.

CURRENCY EXCHANGE

The Canadian dollar lost value against the greenback through most of the last decade, dipping to record lows in 2002, when it was trading at US$1 per CDN$1.65.

At press time, exchange rates (into CDN$) for major currencies are:

US$1 = $1.22
AUS$1 = $.96
EUR€ = $1.60
HK$10 = $1.60
NZ$1 = $.85
UK£1 = $2.30
¥100 = $1.20

On the Internet, check current exchange rates at www.xe.com/ucc.

All major currency can be exchanged at banks in Canmore, Banff, and Jasper, or in the gateway cities of Calgary and Edmonton. Many Canadian businesses will accept U.S. currency, but you will get a better exchange rate from the banks.

Gasoline is sold in liters (3.78 liters equals one U.S. gallon) and is generally 80–90 cents per liter for regular unleaded.

Tipping charges are not usually added to your bill. You are expected to add a tip of 15 percent to the total amount for waiters and waitresses, barbers and hairdressers, taxi drivers, and other such service providers. Bellhops, doormen, and porters generally receive $1 per item of baggage.

Taxes
Canada imposes a 7 percent **goods and services tax (GST)** on most consumer purchases. The British Columbia government imposes its own 7.5 percent tax (PST) onto everything except groceries and books. Alberta has no provincial tax. So when you are looking at the price of anything, remember that the final cost you pay will include an additional 7–14.5 percent in taxes.

Visitor Rebate Program
Nonresident visitors can get a rebate for the GST they pay on short-term accommodations and on most consumer goods bought in the country and taken home. Items not included in the Visitor Rebate Program include: gifts left in Canada, meals and restaurant charges, campground fees, services such as dry cleaning and shoe repair, alcoholic beverages, tobacco, automotive fuels, groceries, agricultural and fish products, prescription drugs and medical devices, and used goods that tend to increase in value, such as paintings, jewelry, rare books, and coins.

The rebate is available on services and retail purchases of at least $50 each, that total at least $200, or that were purchased within 60 days prior to your exit from the country. Rebates can be claimed any time within one year from the date of purchase. You'll need to include with your claim all receipts or vouchers that prove the GST was paid. Most visitors apply for the rebate at duty-free shops (also called Visitor Rebate Centres) when exiting the country. The duty-free shops can rebate up to $500 on the spot. For rebates over $500, you'll need to mail your completed GST rebate form directly to Visitor Rebate Program, Summerside Tax Centre, Canada Revenue Agency, 275 Pope Rd., Suite 104, Summerside, PE C1N 6C6, Canada. You can also submit rebate forms for amounts less than $500 directly to the Canada Revenue Agency. If you've claimed by mail before, be aware that the rules have changed. Claims for goods (not accommodations) must be accompanied by a Proof of Export stamp, which you'll get at the border upon presentation of both the goods and corresponding receipts. Rebate checks from the government are issued in Canadian funds. For more info, contact the program directly (902/432-5608 or 800/668-4748, www.cra.arc.gc.ca/visitors).

MAPS AND TOURIST INFORMATION
Maps
The best maps of the Canadian Rockies are produced by **Gem Trek Publishing,** a local company based between Calgary and Banff (403/932-4208 or 877/688-6277, www.gemtrek.com). Gem Trek maps of varying scales cover all of

HEADING FARTHER AFIELD

I f your travels take you beyond the Canadian Rockies, you may find the following resources helpful for pre-trip planning:

Travel Alberta: 780/427-4321 or 800/252-3782, www.travelalberta.com
Tourism British Columbia: 250/387-1642 or 800/435-5622, www.hellobc.com
Yukon Department of Tourism: 867/667-5036 or 800/661-0494, www.touryukon.com
Alaska Division of Tourism: 907/465-2010, www.travelalaska.com
NWT Arctic Tourism: 867/873-7200 or 800/661-0788, www.nwttravel.nt.ca
Nunavut Tourism: 867/979-6551 or 866/686-2888, www.nunavuttourism.com
Tourism Saskatchewan: 306/787-9600 or 800/667-7191, www.sasktourism.com
Travel Manitoba: 204/945-3777 or 800/665-0040, www.travelmanitoba.com

the Canadian Rockies, using computer-generated "3D Imagery" to clearly define changes in elevation and GPS to plot hiking trails. The backs of maps are filled with trail information as well as tidbits of history. Waterproofing is an added bonus.

Maps are available at bookstores, gas stations, and gift shops throughout the Canadian Rockies. In Calgary, **Map Town** (400 5th Ave. SW, 403/266-2241) is a specialist map shop worth stopping at as you pass through. In Vancouver, pick up maps at these specialty bookstores: **International Travel Maps and Books** (530 W. Broadway, 604/879-3621, www.itmb.com), **The Travel Bug** (3065 W. Broadway, 604/737-1122, www.travelbugbooks.ca), or **Wanderlust** (1929 W. 4th Ave., Kitsilano, 604/739-2182).

Park Information

Each of the five national parks has at least one **park information center.** These are the places to head for interpretive displays, all park-related information, trail reports, weather forecasts, and Wilderness Passes. Individual addresses and websites are listed in the relevant travel chapters. The national parks are managed by **Parks Canada** (www.pc.gc.ca). On the Alberta side of the Canadian Rockies, all other parks are managed by **Alberta Community Development** (780/944-0313, www.cd.ab.ca). British Columbia's provincial parks are managed by **BC Parks** (www.bcparks.ca).

Tourism Information

Begin planning your trip by contacting the government tourist offices of Alberta and British Columbia: **Travel Alberta** (780/427-4321 or 800/252-3782, www.travelalberta.com) and **Tourism British Columbia** (250/387-1642 or 800/435-5622, www.hellobc.com). Both will fill your mailbox with useful literature and maps, which can be ordered by phone or through their respective websites.

In Calgary, you'll find an information booth on the arrivals level of the airport. The **Vancouver Visitor Info Centre** is at 200 Burrard Street (604/683-2000). For general tourism information, the towns of Banff, Canmore, Jasper, Radium Hot Springs, and Golden have information centers that provide advice on local attractions, accommodations, and restaurants.

COMMUNICATIONS
Postal Services

Canada Post (www.canadapost.ca) issues postage stamps that must be used on all mail posted in Canada. First-class letters and postcards sent within Canada are $.49, to the United States $.80, to foreign destinations $1.40. Prices increase along with the weight of the mailing. You can buy stamps at post offices, automatic vending machines, most hotel lobbies, the airports, many retail outlets, and some newsstands.

Telephones

Alberta and British Columbia have two area codes each. The **area code** for southern Alberta, including Banff and Canmore, is **403.** The area code for northern Alberta, including Jasper National Park, is **780.** The area code for all of British Columbia except Vancouver and environs is **250.** The area code for Vancouver is **604.** Unless otherwise noted, all numbers must be dialed with this prefix, including long-distance calls made within the province that you are calling from. The country code for Canada is 1, the same as the United States.

Public phones accept five-, 10-, and 25-cent coins. Local calls cost 35 cents, and most long-distance calls from public phones cost at least $2 for the first minute. Phone cards, available from drug and grocery stores, provide considerable savings for those using public phones.

Internet Access

If your Internet provider doesn't allow you to access your email away from your home computer, open an email account with **Hotmail** (www.hot mail.com) or **Yahoo** (www.yahoo.com). Although there are restrictions to the size and number of emails you can store and junk mail can be a problem, these services are handy and, best of all, free.

Public Internet access is available throughout the Canadian Rockies. Many larger hotels have high-speed access from guest rooms. Those that don't—usually mid- and lower-priced properties—often have an Internet booth in the lobby. Except for wilderness hostels, backpacker lodges provide inexpensive Internet access. You'll also find Internet booths in many cafés, in McDonald's restaurants, and in public areas, such as Cascade Plaza (Banff), where a credit card will get you as long as you need on the Net. Aside from a lack of privacy, the downside to these public access points is the lack of a mouse at most terminals—instead you must move around the screen using a touch pad.

WEIGHTS AND MEASURES
The Metric System

Canada officially adopted the metric system back in 1975, though you still hear grocers talking in ounces and pounds, golfers talking in yards, and seamen talking in nautical miles. Metric is the primary unit used in this book, but we've added imperial conversions for readers from the United States, Liberia, and Myanmar, the only three countries that have not adopted the metric system. You can also refer to the metric conversion chart in the back of this book.

Time Zones

Alberta is in the **mountain time zone,** one hour later than Pacific time, two hours earlier than eastern standard time. The mountain time zone extends west into southern British Columbia, which includes Yoho and Kootenay National Parks as well as the towns of Golden and Radium Hot Springs. The rest of British Columbia, including Mount Robson Provincial Park, is in the **Pacific time zone.**

Suggested Reading

NATURAL HISTORY

The Atlas of Breeding Birds of Alberta. Edmonton: Federation of Alberta Naturalists, 1992. Comprehensive study of all birds that breed in Alberta with easy-to-read distribution maps, details on nesting and other behavioral patterns, and color plates.

Busch, Robert H. *The Wolf Almanac.* New York: Lyons & Burford, 1995. A detailed analysis of the wolf, from its evolution as a distinct species to the issues surrounding breeding wolves as pets. Includes 12 pages of color plates.

Gadd, Ben. *Handbook of the Canadian Rockies.* Jasper: Corax Press, 1999. The latest edition of this classic guide is in color, and although bulky for backpackers, it's a must-read for anyone interested in the natural history of the Canadian Rockies.

Gray, D. M., and D. H. Male. *Handbook of Snow.* Toronto: Pergamon Press, 1991. Comprehensive guide on everything you ever wanted to know about snow but didn't ask because no one else would have known either.

Hallworth, Beryl, and C. C. Chinnappa. *Plants of Kananaskis Country.* Calgary: University of Calgary Press, 1997. An incredibly detailed book, encompassing more than 400 species of flora, complete with color plates and illustrations. It could be used in the field anywhere in the Canadian Rockies.

Hare, F. K., and M. K. Thomas. *Climate Canada.* Toronto: John Wiley & Sons, 1974. One of the most extensive works on Canada's climate ever written. Includes a chapter on how the climate is changing.

Herrero, Stephen. *Bear Attacks: Their Causes and Avoidances.* New York: Nick Lyons Books, 1995. Through a series of gruesome stories, this book catalogs the stormy relationship between people and bruins, provides hints on avoiding attacks, and tells what to do in case you're attacked.

Jones, Karen. *Wolf Mountains.* Calgary: University of Calgary Press, 2002. Explores the history of wolves in the Canadian Rockies, with emphasis on the often-controversial relationship between man and wolf.

Lauriault, Jean. *Identification Guide to the Trees of Canada.* Markham, Ontario: Fitzhenry & Whiteside, 1989. Makes tree identification easy through drawings of leaves. Maps detail distribution of species.

Patterson, W. S. *The Physics of Glaciers.* Toronto: Pergamon Press, 1969. A highly technical look at all aspects of glaciation, why glaciers form, how they flow, and their effect on the environment.

Rezendes, Paul. *Tracking and the Art of Seeing.* Charlottesville, Virginia: Camden House Publishing, 1992. This is one of the best of many books dedicated to tracking North American mammals. It begins with a short essay on the relationship of humans with nature.

Sharp, Robert P. *Living Ice: Understanding Glaciers and Glaciation.* Cambridge, England: Cambridge University Press, 1988. A detailed but highly readable book on the formation, types, and results of glaciers.

Slinger, Joey. *Down & Dirty Birding.* Toronto: Key Porter Books, 1996. A hilarious but practical look at the art of bird-watching, with sections of text such as "How to steer clear of people who think bird-watching is better than sex."

Vacher, André. *Summer of the Grizzly.* Saskatoon: Western Producer Prairie Books, 1985. True story of a grizzly bear that went on a terrifying rampage near the town of Banff.

Whitaker, John. *National Audubon Society Field Guide to North American Mammals.* New York: Random House, 1997. One of a series of field guides produced by the National Audubon Society, this one details mammals through color plates and detailed descriptions of characteristics, habitat, and range.

Wilkinson, Kathleen. *Wildflowers of Alberta.* Edmonton: University of Alberta Press, 1999. Color plates of all flowers found in the mountain national parks and beyond. Color plates and line drawings are indispensable for identification.

Wright, William H. *The Grizzly Bear.* Originally produced by the University of Nebraska Press in 1909 and reprinted many times since, this book was authored by a hunter turned naturalist whose change of attitude throughout a lifetime of association with bears is poignant.

HUMAN HISTORY

Barnes, Christine. *Great Lodges of the Canadian Rockies.* Seattle: Sasquatch Books, 1999. This book delves into the history of the many famous mountain lodges—such as the Fairmont properties and Emerald Lake Lodge—and lesser known but equally interestingly historic accommodations like Num-Ti-Jah and Skoki. Includes many historic photos.

Engler, Bruno. *Bruno Engler Photography.* Calgary: Rocky Mountain Books, 2002. Swiss-born Engler spent 60 years exploring and photographing the Canadian Rockies. This impressive hardcover book showcases more than 150 of his most timeless images.

Hart, E. J. *Jimmy Simpson: Legend of the Rockies.* Banff: Altitude Publishing, 1991. Details the life of one of the most colorful of the pioneer outfitters in the Canadian Rockies.

Jenness, Diamond. *The Indians of Canada.* Toronto: University of Toronto Press, 1977. Originally published in 1932, this is the classic study of natives in Canada, although Jenness's conclusion, that they were facing certain extinction by "the end of this century," is obviously outdated.

Lavallee, Omer. *Van Horne's Road.* Montreal: Railfare Enterprises, 1974. William Van Horne was instrumental in the construction of Canada's first transcontinental railway. This is the story of his dream and the boomtowns that sprang up along the route. Lavallee devotes an entire chapter to telling the story of the railway's push over the Canadian Rockies.

Marty, Sid. *Men for the Mountains.* New York: Vanguard Press, 1979. Written by a park warden, this book tells the story of those who lived in the Canadian Rockies and the risks and adventures involved.

Marty, Sid. *Switchbacks: True Stories from the Canadian Rockies.* Toronto: McClelland & Stewart, 1999. This book tells of Marty's experiences in the mountains and of people he came in contact with in his role as a park warden. Along the way he describes the way his experiences with both nature and fellow humans have shaped his views on conservation today.

McMillan, Alan D. *Native Peoples and Cultures of Canada.* Vancouver: Douglas & McIntyre, 1995. A comprehensive look at the archaeology, anthropology, and ethnography of the native peoples of Canada. The last chapters delve into the problems facing these people today.

Sandford, R. W. *The Canadian Alps: The History of Mountaineering in Canada.* Canmore: Altitude Publishing, 1990. Complete human history of the Canadian Rockies from the earliest explorers to first ascents of major peaks.

Schäffer, Mary T. S. *A Hunter of Peace.* Banff: Whyte Museum of the Canadian Rockies, 1980. This book was first published in 1911 by

G.P. Putnam & Sons, New York, under the name *Old Indian Trails of the Canadian Rockies.* Tales recount the exploration of the Rockies during the turn of the 20th century. Many of the author's photographs appear throughout.

Scott, Chic. *Pushing the Limits.* Calgary: Rocky Mountain Books, 2000. A chronological history of mountaineering in Canada, with special emphasis on many largely unknown climbers and their feats, as well as the story of Swiss guides in Canada and a short section on ice climbing.

Smith, Cyndi. *Off the Beaten Track.* Jasper: Coyote Books, 1989. Accounts of women adventurers and mountaineers and their impact on the early history of western Canada.

Touche, Rodney. *Brown Cows, Sacred Cows.* Calgary: Johnson Gorman Publishers, 1990. The story of the development of Lake Louise ski area as told by a former general manager.

Whyte, Jon. *Indians in the Rockies.* Banff: Altitude Publishing, 1985. Written from firsthand experiences, this is an excellent insight into the first humans to live in the Canadian Rockies.

RECREATION

Copeland, Cathy, and Craig Copeland. *Don't Waste Your Time in the Canadian Rockies.* Canmore: hikingcamping.com, 2004. In case you hadn't guessed, the title is a play on words—the Copelands really do want you enjoy the region. To help, they've put together this book, which details hiking trails in parks throughout the region.

Corbett, Bill. *Day Trips from Calgary.* Vancouver: Whitecap Books, 2002. Multiple books have been written about the things to do and see in Banff, which this book covers, along with dozens of ideas for day-tripping south and north of the famous park.

Daffern, Gillean. *Kananaskis Country Trail Guide.* Calgary: Rocky Mountain Books, 1997. Two volumes cover all the official and unofficial trails in Kananaskis Country.

Eastcott, Doug. *Backcountry Biking in the Canadian Rockies.* Calgary: Rocky Mountain Books, 1999. Details more than 220 bicycling routes using simple maps, road logs, and black-and-white photography.

Kane, Alan. *Scrambles in the Canadian Rockies.* Calgary: Rocky Mountain Books, 1999. Routes detailed in this guide lead to summits, without the use of ropes or mountaineering equipment.

Kariel, Herbert G. *Alpine Huts in the Canadian Rockies, Selkirks, and Purcells.* Canmore: Alpine Club of Canada, 1986. Covers the history of all huts in the Rockies, with access routes and status and descriptions of nearby peaks to climb.

Martin, John, and Jon Jones. *Sport Climbs in the Canadian Rockies.* Calgary: Rocky Mountain Books, 2002. Details 1,400 climbs through the Bow Valley and Banff National Park.

Mitchell, Barry. *Alberta's Trout Highway.* Red Deer: Nomad Creek Books, 2001. "Alberta's Trout Highway" is the Forestry Trunk Road (Highway 40), which runs the length of the Canadian Rockies, including through the heart of Kananaskis Country. Entertaining and useful descriptions of Mitchell's favorite fishing holes are accompanied by maps and plenty of background information.

Patton, Brian, and Bart Robinson. *The Canadian Rockies Trail Guide.* Banff: Summerthought, 2000. This regularly updated guide, first published in 1971, covers 230 hiking trails and 3,400 km (2,100 miles) in the mountain national parks as well as in surrounding provincial parks. A full page is devoted to each trail, making it the most comprehensive hiking book available.

Potter, Mike. *Backcountry Banff.* Banff: Luminous Compositions, 2001. This book's title is a little misleading, for included are many shorter trails that can be enjoyed by everyone. Includes logged distances and readable trail descriptions of over 100 hikes in Banff National Park.

Potter, Mike. *Fire Lookouts in the Canadian Rockies*. Banff: Luminous Compositions, 1998. This book specializes in hikes to fire lookouts. Trail descriptions are detailed, and each is accompanied by the history of the lookout.

Spring, Vicky and Tom Kirkendall. *Glacier–Waterton International Peace Park*. Seattle: Mountaineer Books, 2003. This book concentrates on hiking in the adjacent national parks of Waterton Lakes and Glacier.

Townsend, Chris. *The Backpacker's Handbook*. Camden, Maine: Ragged Mountain Press, 1998. Although some of the specifics on gear recommendations need updating, this is the best book for reading up on your backcountry and hiking skills.

GUIDEBOOKS AND MAPS

Gem Trek Publishing. Cochrane, Alberta. This company produces tearproof and waterproof maps for all regions of the Canadian Rockies. Relief shading clearly and concisely shows elevation, and all hiking trails have been plotted using a global positioning system. On the back of each map are descriptions of attractions and hikes, along with general, practical, and educational information. Highly recommended. Website: www.gemtrek.com.

Hempstead, Andrew. *Moon Handbooks Alberta* and *Moon Handbooks British Columbia*. Emeryville, CA: Avalon Travel Publishing. Regularly updated guides that comprehensively cover Canada's westernmost provinces.

MapArt. Driving maps for all of Canada, including provinces and cities. Maps are published as old-fashioned foldout versions, as well as laminated and in atlas form. Website: www.mapart.com.

The Milepost. Bellevue, WA: Vernon Publications. This annual publication is a must-have for those traveling through western Canada. The maps and logged highway descriptions are incredibly detailed. Most northern bookstores stock *The Milepost*, or call 800/726-4707 or go to www.milepost.com.

PERIODICALS

The Canadian Alpine Journal. Canmore, Alberta. The annual magazine of the Alpine Club of Canada, with mountaineering articles from its members and climbers from around the world. Website: www.alpineclubofcanada.ca.

Canadian Geographic. Ottawa: Royal Canadian Geographical Society. Bimonthly publication pertaining to Canada's natural and human histories and resources. Website: www.canadiangeographic.ca.

Explore. Toronto. Bimonthly publication of adventure travel throughout Canada. Website: www.explore-mag.com.

Nature Canada. Ottawa, Ontario. Quarterly magazine of the Canadian Nature Federation. Website: www.cnf.ca.

Western Living. Vancouver, British Columbia. Lifestyle magazine for western Canada. Includes travel, history, homes, and cooking. Website: www.westernliving.ca.

FREE CATALOGS

Alberta Accommodation Guide. Alberta Hotel & Lodging Association. Lists all hotels, motels, and other lodging in the province. Available at all Tourist Information Centres or by calling 780/427-7321 or 800/252-3782, www.explorealberta.com.

Alberta Campground Guide. Alberta Hotel Association. Lists all campgrounds in the province. Available at all Tourist Information

Centres or by calling 780/427-7321 or 800/252-3782, www.explorealberta.com.

British Columbia Approved Accommodation Guide. Tourism British Columbia. Lists all accommodations, including commercial and provincial campgrounds in the province. Available at all Visitor Information Centres or by calling 250/387-1642 or 800/435-5622, www.hellobc.com.

REFERENCE

Daffern, Tony. *Avalanche Safety for Skiers & Climbers.* Calgary: Rocky Mountain Books, 1992. Covers all aspects of avalanches, including their causes, practical information on how to avoid them, and a section on rescue techniques and first aid.

Guide to Manuscripts: The Fonds and Collections of the Archives, Whyte Museum of the Canadian Rockies. Banff: Whyte Museum of the Canadian Rockies, 1988. This book makes finding items in the museum easy by providing alphabetical lists of all parts of the collection.

Johnson, Leslie. *Basic Mountain Safety from A to Z.* Canmore: Altitude Books, 2000. All you need to know about safety in the mountains, including a large section on camping.

Karamitsanis, Aphrodite. *Place Names of Alberta.* Calgary: University of Alberta Press, 1991. Volume 1 alphabetically lists all geographic features of the mountains and foothills with explanations of each name's origin. Volume 2 does the same for southern Alberta.

Internet Resources

Travel Planning
Canadian Tourism Commission
www.canadatourism.com
Official tourism website for all of Canada.

Tourism British Columbia
www.hellobc.com
Learn more about the province, plan your travels, and order tourism literature.

Travel Alberta
www.travelalberta.com
Similar to the British Columbia tourism website, but includes information on Banff and Jasper national parks.

Travel to Canada
www.westerncanadatravel.com
Website of the author, Andrew Hempstead. Includes general and up-to-date tips on travel to Canada.

Parks
BC Parks
http://wlapwww.gov.bc.ca/bcparks

This department oversees management of provincial parks in British Columbia.

Parks Canada
www.pc.gc.ca
Official website of the agency that manages Canada's national parks. Website has information on each park, including fees, camping, and wildlife.

Parks Canada Campground Reservation Service
www.pccamping.ca
Online reservation service for national park campgrounds.

Government
Citizenship and Immigration Canada
www.cic.gc.ca
Check this government website for anything related to entry into Canada.

Government of Canada
www.gc.ca
The official website of the Canadian government.

Accommodations

Alberta Hotel & Lodging Association
www.explorealberta.com

Publishes Alberta's official accommodation and camping guides. You can use the website to check for accommodations or order a free hard copy.

Canadian Rocky Mountain Resorts
www.crmr.com

Small chain of four upscale resorts.

Discover Camping
www.discovercamping.ca

Online reservation service for booking provincial campgrounds in British Columbia.

Fairmont Hotels and Resorts
www.fairmont.com

Lodging chain that owns famous mountain resorts such as the Banff Springs, Chateau Lake Louise, and Jasper Park Lodge.

Hostelling International–Canada
www.hihostels.ca

Canadian arm of the worldwide organization.

Conservation

Biosphere Institute of the Bow Valley
www.biosphereinstitute.org

Canmore-based organization mandated to gather and circulate information on management of the Bow River watershed.

Canadian Parks and Wilderness Society
www.cpaws.org

Non-profit organization that is instrumental in highlighting conservation issues throughout Canada.

Yellowstone to Yukon Conservation Initiative
www.y2y.net

Network of 800 groups working on conservation issues in the Canadian Rockies and beyond.

Tours

Brewster
www.brewster.ca

Banff-based operator offering day trips, airport shuttles, and package tours.

Canadian Mountain Holidays
www.cmhski.com

The world's largest heli-ski operation, with lodges scattered through western Canada.

Transportation

Air Canada
www.aircanada.ca

Canada's national airline.

Rocky Mountaineer Vacations
www.rockymountaineer.com

Luxurious rail service to Banff and Jasper.

VIA Rail
www.viarail.ca

Passenger rail service across Canada.

Regional Information

Banff/Lake Louise Tourism Bureau
www.bannflakelouise.com

Golden Tourism Association
www.tourismgolden.com

Jasper Tourism and Commerce
www.jaspercanadianrockies.com

Radium Hot Springs Visitor Information Centre
www.rhs.bc.ca

Tourism Canmore
www.tourismcanmore.com

Town of Jasper
www.jasper-alberta.com

Waterton Chamber of Commerce
www.watertonchamber.com

Index

Camping

Glaciers

Hiking

U.S. ~ Metric Conversion

1 inch = 2.54 centimeters (cm)
1 foot = .304 meters (m)
1 yard = 0.914 meters
1 mile = 1.6093 kilometers (km)
1 km = .6214 miles
1 fathom = 1.8288 m
1 chain = 20.1168 m
1 furlong = 201.168 m
1 acre = .4047 hectares
1 sq km = 100 hectares
1 sq mile = 2.59 square km
1 ounce = 28.35 grams
1 pound = .4536 kilograms
1 short ton = .90718 metric ton
1 short ton = 2000 pounds
1 long ton = 1.016 metric tons
1 long ton = 2240 pounds
1 metric ton = 1000 kilograms
1 quart = .94635 liters
1 US gallon = 3.7854 liters
1 Imperial gallon = 4.5459 liters
1 nautical mile = 1.852 km

To compute Celsius temperatures, subtract 32 from Fahrenheit and divide by 1.8. To go the other way, multiply Celsius by 1.8 and add 32.

Keeping Current

Although we strive to produce the most up-to-date guidebook humanly possible, change is unavoidable. Between the time this book goes to print and the moment you read it, a handful of the businesses noted in these pages will undoubtedly change prices, move, or even close their doors forever. Other worthy attractions will open for the first time. If you have a favorite gem you'd like to see included in the next edition, or see anything that needs updating, clarification, or correction, please drop us a line. Send your comments via email to atpfeedback@avalonpub.com, or use the address below.

Moon Handbooks Canadian Rockies
Avalon Travel Publishing
1400 65th Street, Suite 250
Emeryville, CA 94608, USA
www.moon.com

Editor: Ellie Behrstock
Series Manager: Kevin McLain
Acquisitions Manager: Rebecca K. Browning
Copy Editor: Deana Shields
Graphics Coordinator: Tabitha Lahr
Production Coordinators: Jacob Goolkasian, Domini Dragoone
Cover Designer: Kari Gim
Interior Designer: Amber Pirker
Map Editor: Kat Smith
Cartographers: Kat Kalamaras, Mike Morgenfeld
Indexer: Deana Shields

ISBN: 1-56691-699-2
ISSN: 1546-2129

Printing History
1st Edition—1999
4th Edition—May 2005
5 4 3 2 1

Text © 2005 by Andrew Hempstead.
Maps © 2005 by Avalon Travel Publishing, Inc.
All rights reserved.

AVALON
publishing group incorporated

Avalon Travel Publishing is an Imprint of Avalon Publishing Group, Inc.

Some photos and illustrations are used by permission and are the property of the original copyright owners.

Front cover photo: © Andrew Hempstead

Printed in USA by Malloy